The American Epic

Cambridge Studies in American Literature and Culture

THE AMERICAN EPIC

Transforming a Genre, 1770–1860

JOHN P. MCWILLIAMS, JR.

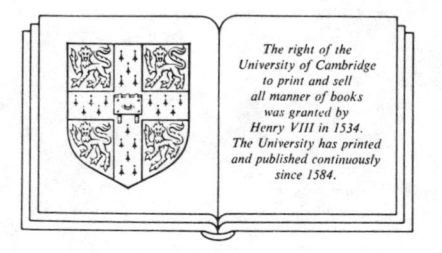

The right of the
University of Cambridge
to print and sell
all manner of books
was granted by
Henry VIII in 1534.
The University has printed
and published continuously
since 1584.

CAMBRIDGE UNIVERSITY PRESS

CAMBRIDGE

NEW YORK   PORT CHESTER   MELBOURNE   SYDNEY

Published by the Press Syndicate of the University of Cambridge
The Pitt Building, Trumpington Street, Cambridge CB2 1RP
40 West 20th Street, New York, NY 10011, USA
10 Stamford Road, Oakleigh, Melbourne 3166, Australia

First published 1989

Printed in the United States of America

Library of Congress Cataloging-in-Publication Data
McWilliams, John P.
The American epic.
(Cambridge Studies in American literature and cul-
ture)
Bibliography: p.
1. Epic literature, American – History and criticism.
2. American literature – Revolutionary period, 1775–
1783 – History and criticism.   3. American literature
– 1783–1850 – History and criticism.   I. Title.
II. Series.
PS169.E63M38   1989   811'.03209   89–9839

British Library Cataloguing in Publication applied for

ISBN 0–521–37322–0 hard covers

For Mireille

CONTENTS

ACKNOWLEDGMENTS

The breadth of this book's concerns has created debts both wide and deep. My conception of "primary" oral epic poetry, and of the heroic culture with which it deals, has been formed by H. M. Chadwick's *The Heroic Age*, C. M. Bowra's *Heroic Poetry*, and A. B. Lord's *The Singer of Tales*. Bowra's *From Virgil to Milton*, E. M. W. Tillyard's *The English Epic and Its Background*, and Maurice McNamee's *Homer and the Epic Hero* have shaped my understanding of the evolution of "secondary" literary epic. Four surveys of eighteenth- and nineteenth-century attitudes toward the epic poem have been invaluable: Stuart Curran's *Poetic Form and British Romanticism*, Norman Foerster's *The Fortunes of Epic Poetry*, H. T. Swedenberg's *The Theory of the Epic in England 1650–1800*, and Brian Wilkie's *Romantic Poets and Epic Tradition*. Among studies of American literature that treat the early national period, I am especially indebted to Leon Howard's *The Connecticut Wits*, Benjamin Spencer's *The Quest for Nationality*, and Lawrence Buell's *New England Literary Culture*. My point of departure has been the cumulative findings of Roy Harvey Pearce's "The Long View: An American Epic" (in *The Continuity of American Poetry*), James E. Miller's *The American Quest for a Supreme Fiction*, and Michael Bernstein's *The Tale of the Tribe*. Although I dispute their confining of epic to poetry, this book could not exist without their remarkable abilities to formulate and to explore a very real tradition of its own. I wish I could have benefited more fully from George Dekker's *The American Historical Romance*, published while this book was in press.

The following libraries generously provided access to their holdings: the Abernethy Library at Middlebury College, the American Antiquarian Society, the Boston Athenaeum, the Boston Public Library, the Houghton Library, the Newberry Library, the New York Public Library, the Swem Library at the College of William and Mary, the University of California at Berkeley, and especially the Widener Library. Barnes and Noble granted permission to revise my essay "Red Achilles,

ix

Red Satan: Cooper and the American Indian Epic" for inclusion in the fifth chapter. Farrar, Straus, and Giroux granted permission to quote a passage from Tom Wolfe's *The Bonfire of the Vanities*. For the time needed to complete research and writing, I am grateful to the National Endowment for the Humanities and to Middlebury College. Cynthia Ketcham, Karen Benfield, and the editors of Cambridge University Press have helped immeasurably in preparing and checking the final manuscript.

I should like to thank colleagues, correspondents, and friends who have provided particular points of information, qualified my oversimplifications, and given me the great gift of their reading time: Eve Adler, Alicia Andreu, Barbara Bellows, Lawrence Buell, Stuart Curran, George Dekker, Stepehn Donadio, Albert Gelpi, Dustin Griffin, Albert Lord, John McCardell, Elizabeth Napier, Joel Porte, Kenneth Silverman, Lewis Simpson, John Wilders, and Joseph Wittreich.

The joy that Mireille, Christopher, and Isabel have brought into my life is beyond my power to express.

Middlebury, Vermont   John McWilliams

INTRODUCTION

The epic and the novel, these two major forms of great epic literature, differ from one another not by their authors' fundamental intentions but by the given historico-philosophical realities with which the authors were confronted. The novel is the epic of an age in which the extensive totality of life is no longer directly given, in which the immanence of meaning in life has become a problem, yet which still thinks in terms of totality. It would be superficial – a matter of mere artistic technicality – to look for the only and decisive genre-defining criterion in the question of whether a work is written in verse or prose.

George Lukacs, *The Theory of the Novel* (1914)

I

To create some kind of heroic song for the New World remained a pressing cultural need from the time the Republic was formed until the time it was severed, yet the history of this initially embarrassing quest has not yet been written. This neglect is not justified, but it has surely been understandable. Readers with New Critical assumptions about literary art have scarcely been able to endure the poems of Timothy Dwight and Joel Barlow. No one, to my knowledge, has yet even considered the many later attempts to wrench a "Homeric" verse epic out of American experience.[1] Dogged patience is sometimes needed to read them; to write about them depletes one's resources of humor. Moreover, much of the debate over the substance and style of the American epic was carried on in literary periodicals that appeared, and usually foundered, between the Revolution and the Civil War. As long as the American epic is seen as a closed couplet cul-de-sac, a cemetery for long patriotic poems, the debate cannot seem worth the exhumation.

I shall contend that the American epic did not expire in the first quarter of the nineteenth century only to be revived, in troublingly imagistic

1

form, by such dissimilar poets as Pound, Crane, and Williams a century later. The disgrace of the imitative verse epic led authors to portray American heroic subjects in new literary forms more engaging to contemporary readers. If we mercifully except *Hiawatha,* Whitman's *Leaves of Grass* is still the one work commonly believed to have fulfilled this end. Perhaps now, however, America's heroic leaves might be looked for under someone else's bootsoles. Long before 1855, Cooper, Simms, and Melville had deliberately assimilated the spirit and conventions of the epic poem within the prose romance. Prescott and Parkman, who were admiring readers and reviewers of Scott and Cooper, had adapted epic techniques of the historical romance into heroic history. If we view Barlow's and Dwight's imitative poems as the beginning of a generic transformation into newer, more open forms, the effaced inscriptions upon the older verse-epic tombstones become decipherable, important, even interesting.

Authors of longstanding reputation need to be seen in a new generic context. The chasm of scholarly interest and literary quality separating Whitman from Barlow, Fenimore Cooper from Daniel Bryan, Prescott from James Ralph, suggests a liberating contradiction. When American writers attempted to shape their prospect of American glory into traditional epic form, they created grave, elephantine poems crammed with the husks of epic convention but lacking the pressure of a significant credible heroic action associated with the epic since Aristotle. As early as 1810, however, the breakdown of generic categories was allowing for the rise of what Charles Olson would later call "open field" forms.[2] Romance, novel, history, and epic became overlapping rather than discrete literary types; their infinite possibilities for blending produced exhilarating possibilities as well as pathless confusion. The historical romancer, the romantic historian, and the free-verse poet (to use our century's terminology) were able to capture epic qualities – and plausibly adopt epic conventions – not only because the authors who used them were better artists, but because the new forms subverted the epic as it was traditionally defined. Just as Virgil and Milton had contributed to epic tradition only by transforming it, so an epic for the New World had to be something other than a Homeric, Virgilian, or Miltonic poem. The New World epic somehow had to supplant what Whitman called "feudal chants" while still seeming to be their recognizable outgrowth. Humor and new literary forms would thus prove to be as essential to the American epic as democratic values.

Writing a literary history is a sometimes dusty but always risky pilgrimage. Before arriving at the heavenly gate inscribed "New Reordering," literary histories must trudge past – and may fall into – beckoning pits of scholarly falsity. There is the seeming inevitability of periodiza-

tion, of dividing literary history up as if it conformed to political and social history (for "Americanists," 1776, 1865, 1914, 1945 come to mind). There is the easy resort to all the familiar categories of genre, stylistics, and intellectual history that can so readily assimilate new information to old ways of seeing – and thereby box that information into unmemorable obscurity. There is the imposing of an a priori pattern upon all the anarchies of life, with the concomitant slighting of all those texts, or parts thereof, that do not fit one's thesis. There is the danger of nationalism, of ignoring the possibility that "American" should mean "of the New World" rather than "of the United States." And now in the 1980s there is the prospect that literary history's connections to cultural history, once assumed, seem to many scholar-critics not to matter in a world where words are regarded as interreferential signs. So why bother to try? In this instance, because I believe I have discovered a neglected, consequential truth about a segment of literary history, and that I can prove it.

At times this book may stray into all these pitfalls, but I hope it is never mired in them. Some degree of muddying may even be both desirable and necessary. The failing of Hawthorne's Mr. Smooth-It-Away, after all, was to believe that the Celestial City could readily be reached by filling in all the pitfalls with abstractions. But this literary history, dealing as it does with the epic, requires more than these expectable caveats. All literary histories have a suspect facticity in their impartial surfaces, but the history of epic criticism from Aristotle to Bowra and beyond has thrived on the act of subjective judgment. Not only have critics wished to reserve the word "epic" for the best, the highest, and the most comprehensive of literary artifacts; "epic" immediately suggests an affirmation of essential cultural values through particularly stylized conventions.

Although so loaded a term demands definition, securing a workable definition that is not idiosyncratic proves exasperating. A genre commonly considered to include *Gilgamesh,* Homer, Virgil, Lucan, *Beowulf,* Tasso, Milton, *The Prelude, Leaves of Grass, Ulysses,* and *Paterson* is not a genre easily defined with precision. When one contemplates such titles as James B. Walker's *The Epic of American Industry,* H. R. Hamilton's *The Epic of Chicago,* D. B. Parke's *The Epic of Unitarian Boston,* and Herbert Hoover's four-volume *An American Epic* (on the relief mission), one may well conclude that the word "epic" is only a substanceless advertisement for size and length, as it has long since become for jacket blurbs and film promotion. Even if one attempts to be safely traditional, however, the problem of definition remains. Because *The Odyssey* is in many ways unlike *The Iliad,* because Virgil sang of both Arms and the Man, yet made them serve a new interest in historical forces, and because Mil-

ton was convinced that the Fall was an "argument / Not less but more Heroic Than the / Wrath of stern *Achilles*,"[3] we must acknowledge that the word "epic" describes a tradition founded, not only upon change, but upon conscious reshaping of its own defining qualities. Although oral heroic poetry can and has been studied as a distinct separate genre, no precise meaning of "epic" can be found that will suit even those few texts that centuries of readers have agreed to call epics. To confront the essential disagreement in the definitions of epic literature proposed by Aristotle, Vida, Le Bossu, Voltaire, Lord Kames, and Jones Very – to mention only a few epic theorists – makes one aware that all such definitions are largely determined by the critical assumptions of their age and by the particular models the theorist had in mind.

In an ill-concealed defense of *The Conquest of Canaan*, Timothy Dwight reminds us that the word *"epos"* originally signified only "narration" or "discourse" and that further specification is likely to end in haggling over terms or in the barren and indefensible conclusion that *Paradise Lost* is not an epic because it is not *The Iliad*.[4] Dwight was not contending that all comparisons are idle, nor that any long ambitious work should be called an epic; he simply recognized that the tradition of epic literature had to evolve if it were to survive. I should like to claim a similar latitude toward the problem of definition. I propose that an epic must be a heroic narrative, but that heroic narrative may assume many forms. To determine whether *Moby-Dick* is a tragedy, an epic, or a romance, whether the *History of the Conquest of Mexico* is history, romance, or epic, or whether "Song of Myself" is a prophetic, lyric, or heroic poem, are ultimately barren exercises. All three works cross over once-accepted boundaries of genre; inclusiveness of form is essential to their achievement. To apply any proscriptive definition of "epic" to American writing after 1815 would only deny to an era the opportunity gained through a new flexibility in the conception of literary genre. When the need for "the American Epic" shifted to various possibilities for "American Epic," longstanding models of hierarchy, societal as well as generic, were being successfully challenged, although many writers and reviewers could not recognize it.

II

My title phrase also engages a more particular issue of academic scholarship. The words "American Epic" are presently associated with soporific poems of the early Republic, with the modern verse epic originating in Whitman and/or Pound, and with nothing in between. The reason for the absent center, two ends without a middle, is that in the three commanding studies of American epic literature, Roy Harvey Pearce, James E. Miller, and Michael Bernstein assume, in spite of particular differences, that an epic is a poem, and that ambitious cultural poems,

mostly of the twentieth century, are the texts to be studied. I have assumed that, once histories and novels became the dominant literary forms
in the 1820s and 1830s, "the American Epic" was far more likely to be
written in prose, and probably would not be valued by a wide reading
public unless it were written in prose. This assumption has led me to
seek continuities rather than discontinuities between the poets of the early
Republic and writers of the next two generations. I sought confirmation
of a liberating generic flexibility in the literary journals of the antebellum
era, and I have found it. Thus it now seems to me a touching anachronism that Robert Lowell, in his essay titled "Epics," should have asserted
that *Moby-Dick* is "our best book," our one epic in prose," but then, in
his very next sentence, worried "Are there epics in prose?"[5] Cooper,
Simms, Prescott, and Parkman, to say nothing of Melville, had written
as if Lowell's question were already rhetorical. To them, it was no longer
fruitful to consider "epic" and "prose" as possibly separate entities. Because of the attention paid to the modern American verse epic, we have
overlooked the possibility that twentieth-century writers and scholars have been more categorical in their thinking about genre than their
nineteenth-century predecessors, not less so.

My assumptions about prose epic, in turn, have been shaped by the
speculative conclusions of Lukacs's *The Theory of the Novel* (1914) and
Bakhtin's rejoinder, "Epic and Novel" (1940), neither of which mentions one American text. Both Lukacs and Bakhtin believed that the essence of epic was the literary conveying of cultural values in a heroic and
empirical mode that presents those values as "immanent" in the physical
world. Both tried to predict whether the demise of the long poem and
the dominance of the novel would allow the epic to survive. Although
they foresaw that only the novel could continue to reach a wide readership, they also associated the novel with a godless world, a subjectivity
of authorial vision, an openness of form, and a mixing of linguistic levels, all of which worked against the unifying affirmations of traditional
epic literature.

At this point their views sharply diverged. Lukacs, who clearly hoped
that the unifying force of epic would reemerge in a new form, argued
that the modern fictional hero who attains a glimpse of immanent meaning in a world abandoned by God is a worthy successor to his prototype
in heroic poetry. The achievements of Cervantes, Fielding, Balzac, Goethe,
and especially Tolstoy led Lukacs to conclude that empirical renderings
of a culture's immanent values are still possible. Not only do "the really
great novels have a tendency to overlap into the epic," but "the novel is
the necessary epic form of our time."[6] To Bakhtin, however, the great
epic poems constitute a completed, closed genre, dealing with an utterly
past world of "fathers, beginnings and peak times." The twentieth-

century novel, which thrives on present-day ironies, on improvisation in open forms, and on a stylistic *polyglossia* that parodies its own heroic language, is so different from epic that assimilation must totally efface the older genre. Accordingly, Bakhtin argues that "the novel took shape precisely at the point when epic distance was disintegrating" (the eighteenth century) and that the succeeding "novelization of all genres" has meant that the closed unitary world of epic poetry has no vestige.[7]

This book accepts the premise of both Lukacs and Bakhtin that, once prose became the dominant literary medium, no poem could any longer do the cultural work (to use Jane Tompkins's term) required of the epic.[8] I also share the premise that the novel is a comparatively open, subjective, ironic, and willfully diverse literary form. In pursuing my inquiry into American heroic literature, however, I follow Lukacs in believing that epic fiction and epic prose had been probabilities at least in Balzac's era and perhaps as early as Cervantes's. Bakhtin's brilliant argument for closing the epic out of post-Renaissance literature rests upon an assumption that is fundamentally misleading. Bakhtin's view of epic as a static genre elegizing past heroism does not allow for the rebellion and transformations that have occurred within the epic tradition itself. Virgil, Dante, Milton, Wordsworth, and Whitman all felt that they possessed their own "higher argument" that would transform the tradition begun by Homer and modified by intervening poets. As ideas of heroic behavior changed, so did the form of the epic poem; its admittedly special conventions have been a way of measuring change as well as enforcing conformity. As long as the heroic narrative poem retained power over its audience, the cultural prestige of the familiar form of epic was assured. Why then is it not possible for still higher – or simply different – models of heroism to be convincingly represented in the genre that enjoys contemporary power and prestige? If the essence of *epos* is heroic narrative, even its oldest poetic conventions may convincingly survive if properly altered for an appropriate new medium.

To Bakhtin, the epic is antithetical to modern man's suspicion of absolutes and to our belief that heroism, if it exists, lies in a momentary act rather than fixed character traits. Once life is perceived as flux, everything becomes potentially absurd. "Laughter destroyed epic distance," Bakhtin claims; "the first and essential step [in the destruction of epic] was the comic familiarization of the image of man."[9] Perhaps we might recall that the need to prove one's heroism repeatedly was scarcely unknown to Achilles, nor was ironic doubt toward absolutes incompatible with Virgil's imperial theme. Even if, however, we accept Bakhtin's contrasted terms, we need not conclude that laughter and epic are necessarily antithetical in nineteenth- or twentieth-century texts. The prevailing claim of this book is that American heroic literature succeeded

only after many attempts to write *either* serious imitative epics *or* burlesque mock epics had severally failed. It was the eventual combining of laughter with sublimity, familiarity with awe, folly with heroism, neoclassic knowledge with the provincial's scorn for it, that enabled Melville and Whitman to achieve splendid seriocomic works of prose and poetry. In *Moby-Dick* and the first edition of *Leaves of Grass,* truly New World models of heroic behavior and of the epic genre finally emerged because their authors were able to laugh at the portentous gravity of their own creations.

A close reading of the battle between the red and black ants in the "Brute Neighbors" chapter of *Walden* may suggest the ways in which epic and mock-epic, heroism and mock heroism, finally became one in the 1850s.[10] After characterizing three of the most unbrutish neighbors imaginable (mouse, partridge, and otter), Thoreau discovers absolute ferocity and courage in tiny unnoticed insects. The single combat he witnesses between one red and one black ant is in reality a race war covering all the hills and vales in his woodyard, "not a *duellum,* but a *bellum,"* an "internecine war" between "the red republicans" and "the black imperialists" (229). The overmatched red republican ant who engages Thoreau's particular attention is soon joined by a fellow republican who had withdrawn from battle, "some Achilles, who had nourished his wrath apart, and had now come to avenge or rescue his Patroclus" (229). "Locked in each other's embraces," "prepared to fight till the sun went down," the three ants gnaw away each other's feelers and forelegs, acting out their heroic defiance of death in ways that seem the more admirable because no human has noticed them (229). The red ant (Patroclus) is the first to die, his breast ripped open to his vitals, but still attacking so that "the dark carbuncles of the sufferer's eyes shone with a ferocity such as war only could excite" (231). But the inevitable victor is the Brobdignagian black imperialist, who displays the two severed heads of his red enemies as trophies, then limps away so crippled that he "would not be worth much thereafter" (231).

In his journal version of this battle, Thoreau had rendered the ant war as a sparse factual narrative, almost without comparisons, references or judgment.[11] For inclusion in *Walden,* however, he embellished the narrative so as to force comparisons between the ant war, the Trojan War, and the American Revolution. All the ants in his yard collectively become "the legions of these Myrmidons" (229). The two attacking red ants are now identified with Achilles rescuing Patroclus. Ten lines are added likening the ant war to "Concord Fight," in which "Two [were] killed on the patriot's side and Luther Blanchard wounded" (230). After the black ant's victory, Thoreau adds an entirely new paragraph to show how "battles of ants have long been celebrated," beginning in the era of

Aeneas Silvius, progressing through the pontificate of Eugenius the Fourth and the tyranny of Christiern the Second, down to the modern entomologist François Huber, and finally to Thoreau himself (232). The revised version then ends with a new sentence that fixes the historical battle by a politically purposeful misdating: "The battle which I witnessed took place in the Presidency of Polk, five years before the passage of Webster's Fugitive Slave Bill."[12]

If we choose to interpret the *Walden* version as evidence of the persistence of the Homeric world in American nature and Revolutionary Man, Thoreau provides us plenty of supporting evidence. He summarizes his own response by declaring "I felt for the rest of that day as if I had had my feelings excited and harrowed by witnessing the struggle, the ferocity and carnage, of a human battle before my door" (231). His admiration for the courage displayed by the red republicans is reinforced by his invoking the names of Concord "patriots" in 1775. Among the Minutemen as among the ants, "there was not one hireling there" (230). The red ants are even granted noble motivation: "I have no doubt that it was a principle they fought for, as much as our ancestors" (230). On one level, the passage thus shows Thoreau's desire to keep the heroism of the Revolution alive by seeing it reenacted in contemporary life.

Ever since "The Battle of the Frogs and Mice," however, the ascribing of heroic postures to inappropriately tiny creatures has been a staple of the mock-heroic. Do Thoreau's comparisons elevate heroic ants to the stature of Homeric warriors and Concord patriots? Or do they deflate Homeric warriors and Concord patriots by reducing them to totally instinctual and almost imperceptible insects? After his close view of the ants' dismemberings, Thoreau suddenly shifts perspective, trivializing the combat by a technique adopted from Alexander Pope: "I should not have wondered by this time to find that they [the ants] had their respective musical bands stationed on some eminent chip, and playing their national airs the while, to excite the slow and cheer the dying combatants."[13] As the black victor crawls away to some formic "Hotel des Invalides," Thoreau quietly remarks, in devastating throw-away phrases, "I never learned which party was victorious, nor the cause of the war" (231). If the collective bloodshed of Troy, Concord Fight, and Walden woodpile is all so truly inconclusive, so without ultimate meaning, the ants' courage can be no more than the instinct of a "Brute Neighbor." Thoreau's praise of his literary predecessors suddenly seems satiric. His catalogue of poetic entomologists becomes an exercise in mock pedantry very like Ishmael's mockery of Scoresby and all literary cetologists, including himself.

There is yet a third possibility. The tiny ants may be more heroic than Trojans or Americans, because they fight to an unknown, hapless out-

come. One sentence elevates the ants above all Revolutionary heroics: "Certainly there is not the fight recorded in Concord History, at least, if not in the history of America, that will bear a moment's comparison with this, whether for the numbers engaged in it, or for the patriotism and heroism displayed" (230). After insisting that ants and Minutemen both fought for a "principle," Thoreau undermines his own assertion by insisting that the ants would never have fought merely "to avoid a three penny tax on their tea" (230). The courage of the red ants seems more noble than Homer's Greeks, because the ants are never told that their sacrifice will secure an eventual victory. The black imperialist conqueror is surely meant to represent Daniel Webster, whose pyrrhic victory in 1850 may have left the Republic even more crippled in integrity than Webster was in person.

The wonder of the passage is that all these diverse possibilities are co-present, held in suspension without an attempt to resolve them. Heroic and mock-heroic, epic and burlesque, do not cancel one another out; they flow together as we read, leaving us finally delighted at the shifting meanings Thoreau provides for us. Thoreau presents himself simply as the "witness to events" (228), a surprised observer who becomes so transfixed by his Trojan–Concordian–ant war that he makes a microscope out of a glass tumbler in order to continue his gazing. As a non-participating observer, Thoreau seems less important than any of the combatants. But as the writer, he becomes a kind of virtuoso who relishes his self-contained tour de force about creatures so outsized as these tiny ants.

Extreme self-consciousness must pervade such a literary entertainment because of Thoreau's position in American cultural history. Six decades of rhetoric about the epic heroism of Revolutionary forefathers lay deep in the bone of his generation. Like Melville and Whitman, Thoreau can neither discard such rhetoric nor refrain from parodying it. Such an inseparable mixing of epic with mock-epic, heroic with burlesque, becomes a distinctive trait of the literature of the 1850s. As in this passage, tone and language levels shift frequently, heightening our sense of the writer's joy in his own artifice. Insofar as New World heroism serves as the subject of the literature of "the American Renaissance," any "rebirth" of the old epic tradition is actually its seriocomic transformation.

III

At the present moment, when the needed recovery of women's literature absorbs much attention, while studies of genre are unfashionable, the seeming exclusion of women writers from this study deserves an accounting. The easy explanation that the epic has always been a male literary tradition founded upon warrior cultures is not wholly adequate.

During the period under study here, Robert Southey published *Joan of Arc* (1796) and at least two British women attempted epic poetry.[14] Nor is this book's middle-aged male author so wholly resistant to change that he would have excluded American epic literature by or about women had he found it. Nonetheless, its absence presents difficulties of logic. To claim, as I do, that by 1830 the future of epic lay in prose, then to make claims for Whitman's early poetry as well as for Melville's fiction, and yet to recognize that the most widely read novelists in America between 1850 and 1860 were all women, seems an untenable contradiction.[15]

Perhaps it is so. But it would have been equally contradictory to try to approach *Uncle Tom's Cabin* as an American *Odyssey,* or *The Wide, Wide World* as an American *Paradise Lost.* However powerful the cultural impact of these two novels may have been, however comprehensive they were in rendering the totality of their culture, their authors did not re-gard them as an outgrowth of epic tradition. Unlike Cooper's or Simm's frontier romances, the domestic novel was not conceived in epic terms. "Hero" was a word still habitually applied to males. For male authors like Cooper and Simms, the word "heroine" connoted the sprightly but finally submissive young woman (Elizabeth Temple, Bess Matthews) who married the white hero. To the women who wrote domestic nov-els, the word "heroine" connoted something entirely different, but the heroine's virtues of womanly fortitude and Christian piety under trial were not thought of in terms of epic precedent. Perhaps sex roles were even more sharply divided in antebellum America than in nineteenth-century Britain. Whatever the cause, I have found no American instances of women writing epic poems, of men writing epic poems about women heros, or of women writing novels that are meant to recall the heroic tradition we think of as epic. *Uncle Tom's Cabin* may provide us with a deeper total sense of a culture's immanent values than any other Ameri-can text of the century. But to force a comparison between Mrs. Stowe and Homer would tell us more of our age than of the nineteenth century, and would violate the obligation of recovering a literary climate that is so essential to writing a literary history.

A final mention of assumptions. I believe that the opinions of periodical writers and reviewers, however stridently authors may claim to be above them, are a crucial agent of literary change. Americanist scholars and critics, intent on analyzing the individual literary text, have slighted their presumably ephemeral contributions to literary history long enough. But I also believe that, although all persons may be created equal, all literary texts are not. The power of words is not separable from clarity, vigor, and grace of style any more than a writer's depth of vision is separable

from confronting life's complexities. Not all discriminations among authors are based upon political considerations. Academics alone will never have the power to determine what is now self-reflexively called "the canon."

PART I

IMITATIONS: HOMER'S
TYRANNOUS EYE

1

INVOCATIONS

There shall be sung another golden age,
    The rise of empire and of arts,
The good and great inspiring epic rage,
    The wisest heads and noblest hearts.

Not such as Europe breeds in her decay;
    Such as she bred when fresh and young,
When heav'nly flame did animate her clay,
    By future poets shall be sung.

Westward the course of empire takes its way;
    The four first acts already past,
The fifth shall close the drama with the day;
    Time's noblest offspring is the last.

> George Berkeley, "Verses on the Prospect of Planting Arts and Learning in America" (1752)

I. THE NEED

The last act of epic poetry, Americans have long suspected, must create the future, not memorialize the past. Among the rising glories that Brackenridge and Freneau envisioned, even before the Revolution, was the presence of a great indigenous poet:

I see a Homer and a Milton rise,
In all the pomp and majesty of song,
Which gives immortal vigour to the deeds
Atchieved by Heroes in the fields of fame.[1]

Shortly after the Peace of Paris, John Adams urged John Trumbull to raise his literary ambitions beyond the Hudibrastic mock epic: "I should hope to live to see our young America in Possession of an Heroic Poem, equal to those the most esteemed in any Country."[2] In the 1840s, after

15

at least twelve American epic poems had been published, Emerson regretted that "We have yet had no genius in America, with tyrannous eye, which knew the value of our incomparable materials, and saw, in the barbarism and materialism of the times, another carnival of the same gods whose picture he so much admires in Homer."[3] As late as 1957, Robert Frost ventured to suggest, with the examples of Virgil's success and American failures in mind, that "a good epic would grace our history."[4]

These four statements attest to the recurrence of Berkeley's hopes for a golden age and an epic rage. To the generation that won the Revolution, and then glorified the prospects for a New World republicanism, Berkeley's rendering of the *Translatio Studii* posed a crucial literary challenge. Like Berkeley, contemporaries of Dwight and Barlow were convinced that the forces of history were transferring a heroic culture and its epic poet progressively westward, from Homer's Greece, to Virgil's Latium, to Milton's England, and finally to an America whose epic genius was yet to appear. Because the *Translatio Imperii* seemed as irreversible as the *Translatio Studii*,[5] the great American Epic was conceived as an eventual certainty. The sooner it appeared however, the sooner would the Western consummation of art and empire be proven. No matter if there was no agreement on the exact subject, form, or date of the great work; the need for it was paramount and primary. By its mere existence, an American epic would refute Buffon's galling claim that humanity and all its arts must degenerate in the western wilds. An American epic would be incontestable proof of cultural maturity; it would justify the sons' rebellion against the fathers, clarify the superiority of the New World to the Old, and show the autonomy of a formerly colonial literature. Its primary purpose, however, was not so defensive. The genius of the American bard was to be his ability to perceive in the Republic's recent past the seeds of future glory.

Although the reign of the goddess Freedom was to make the New World epic the culmination of all heroic poems, Freedom was habitually seen arriving in borrowed robes. Samuel Low's "Peace" (1784) predicts that America's heaven-taught bards "shall chant the memorable tale / How Freedom fought, and did at last prevail." Low's account of the poems which the Muse of Freedom will inspire, however, suggests merely an anxiety to transplant: "Then Homer's genius here sublime shall soar. / And a new Virgil grace this western shore."[6] St. John Honeywood's first published poem calls forth an American example of Rome's stateliest measure: "A Virgil in heroic strains shall please / With Roman grandeur and unequalled ease."[7] Equivalent literary worth was often an underlying anxiety. A 1784 commencement orator at the University of Pennsylvania claimed to be sure that Helicon and Parnassus had recently

removed to the New World and that Americans would soon see "poets that will equal the daring sublimity of Homer, the correct majesty of Virgil."[8] Throughout *The Powers of Genius,* John Blair Linn looks forward to a native bard, the Genius of Columbia, who will "give to Glory the Columbian name" by expressing still undescribed glories.[9] In a commencement ode of 1798, Linn wonders "Who shall awake the sleeping lyre, / Once smote by Grecian hand? / What bard with awful Homer's fire / Shall bless our infant land?"[10]

Because the imminence of America's Homer must first be declared, the particular quality of his greatness could be decided later. Warren Dutton's Yale commencement poem, "The Present State of Literature" (1800), vaguely anticipates "some native bard, / Whose bosom, kindling with the living fire / That blazed in Grecian song . . . Darts her exploring glance, and quick surveys / The various shades that Character displays."[11] To David Humphreys, the existence of Barlow's *The Vision of Columbus* was more crucial than its content: "Another bard in conscious genius bold, / Sings the new world happier than the old."[12] In spite of his concern for a national language, Noah Webster treasured the expectation, at once regional and international, that gentlemanly epic poets of Yale were creating an Augustan age in Connecticut:

> Soon o'er the land these glorious arts shall reign
> And blest Yalensia lead the splendid train.
> In future years unnumber'd Bards shall rise
> Catch the bold flame and tower above the skies;
> Their brightening splendor gild the epic page
> And unborn Dwights adorn th' Augustan Age.

Webster's concern is not to specify the particular epic qualities of Dwight's verse; he wishes to praise Dwight as a Christian gentleman of "extensive views," "exalted mind," and "zeal reformed" who has written a poem that will "nourish science and adorn the land."[13]

The urgency of these kinds of summonses exactly reverses pre-Revolutionary attitudes toward the possibilities of American heroic verse. Phillis Wheatley opened her *Poems on Various Subjects, Religious and Moral* (1773) with "To Maecenas," in which, addressing Homer, she exclaims:

> O could I rival thine and Virgil's page,
> Or claim the Muses with the Mantuan sage;
>
> . . . .
>
> Then should my song in bolder notes arise,
> And all my numbers pleasingly surprise.
> But here I sit and mourn a groveling mind,
> That fain would mount, and ride upon the wind.[14]

Wheatley laments that her muse lacks not only the poetic fire, but an appropriately heroic subject. Similarly, Jane Turell, daughter of Benja-

min Colman, had concluded "On the Poems of Sir Richard Blackmore" by acknowledging her futile longing to be part of a parent British culture sufficiently rich to sustain three contemporary epics.[15] Such self-denigration is not merely an eighteenth-century woman poet's expected deference to an overwhelmingly male tradition. It reflects a void of subject and audience. Readers of Franklin's *Autobiography* will recall his mockery of James Ralph's attempt to write "large specimens of an epic poem" and then to arouse a British audience for it.[16] Among American pre-Revolutionary writings, only Cotton Mather's *Magnalia* could assert any plausible claim to epic dimensions. Mather begins his "General Introduction" with a Proposition ("I WRITE the WONDERS of the CHRISTIAN RELIGION flying from depradations of Europe to the American Strand,"), then slightly revises the invocation of the *Aeneid* to make Virgil's lines apply to all Puritan forefathers:

> The reader will doubtless desire to know what it was that "tot volvere casus / Insignes pietate viros, tot adire labores / Impulerit."[17]

By pluralizing Virgil's phrase "Insignem pietate virum" Mather begins a long American tradition of trying to elevate the entire cultural enterprise, rather than a single individual, to heroic stature. His embracing of a representative totality would, however, become the tradition of American epic poetry rather than American epic prose. As a Christian writing a prose filiopietistic history, Mather is finally content to allow his Virgilian references to establish an analogy, rather than to place the *Magnalia* directly within the epic tradition recently renewed by Milton.

Some fifty years after the Revolution, the burden of creating the still undelivered national epic was forcefully promoted by Edward Everett. For his 1824 Harvard Phi Beta Kappa oration, Everett chose "The Peculiar Motives To Intellectual Exertion In America" as his subject. As a professor of Greek, Everett is willing to relax his claim for the primacy of Homeric models only slightly. Having admitted "it is impossible to anticipate what garments our native muses will weave for themselves,"[18] Everett nonetheless promptly claims that the libertarian polity of republican Greece spurred Homer to write *The Iliad*. Everett's purpose is to release the literary energies of the young gentlemen before him by convincing them of two constants in cultural history: (1) The greatest literary works of a nation are always choric expressions of its people's character; and (2) because such works have always been written during presumably libertarian eras (Mycenaean Greece, republican Rome, the English Interregnum), the heroic muse can henceforth arise only in another libertarian republic.

After quoting Berkeley's stanza on the westward course of empire,

Everett directly challenges his audience with the duties their privileges entail:

> In that high romance, if romance it be, in which the great minds of antiquity sketched the fortunes of the ages to come, they pictured to themselves a favored region beyond the ocean, a land of equal laws and happy men. The primitive poets beheld it in the islands of the blest; the Doric bards surveyed it in the Hyperborean regions; the sage of the academy placed it in the lost Atlantis; and even the sterner spirit of Seneca could discern a fairer abode of humanity in distant regions then unknown. We look back upon these uninspired predictions and almost recoil from the obligation they imply. By us must these fair visions be realized, by us must be fulfilled these high auspices which burst in trying hours from the longing hearts of the champions of truth. There are no more continents or worlds to be revealed; Atlantis hath arisen from the Ocean, the farthest Thule is reached. There are no more retreats beyond the sea, no more discoveries, no more hopes. Here then a mighty work is to be fulfilled, or never by the race of mortals.[19]

Everett's vocabulary is somewhat updated ("romance," "primitive") but the crux of his appeal is unchanged from the 1780s. America's "peculiar motive to intellectual exertion" is a cultural obligation dependent upon a symbiotic relationship between politics and literature. For Everett, as for his eighteenth-century predecessors, literature remains a branch of rhetoric, not an art form. By celebrating the wonders of Freedom, the sons can sustain the commitments necessary to expand the new republican empire inaugurated by their fathers. If they do so, an epic worthy of Homer and Virgil will surely emerge because our new Atlantis, earth's farthest "Thule," offers the political conditions needed for contemporary heroism. In Everett's version of the Jeremiad, only the appearance of a New World Homer can prove that Western culture's last, best hope has not failed.

Such cherished yet inchoate literary prospects suggest that Revolutionary and post-Revolutionary generations must have had an unusually acute interest in epic tradition. Evidence of such interest is everywhere. Washington, Jefferson, John Adams, and even Benjamin Franklin owned copies of Pope's *Iliad*.[20] Jefferson quoted Homer many times in his *Commonplace Book,* considered *The Iliad* a guide for farming practices, inscribed two lines from *The Iliad* on his wife's tomb, and proclaimed his literary priorities with the sentence "I suspect we are left at last only with Homer and Virgil, perhaps with Homer alone."[21] Pope's version of Hector's farewell to Andromache became a common piece of school declamation; until the Civil War, *Paradise Lost* was used as a school text throughout New England.[22] For decades, Yale freshmen devoted their major efforts to parsing *The Aeneid*. As a supplemental means of self-

preparation, Timothy Dwight says he rose sufficiently early to read his hundred lines of Homer, in Greek, before 5:30 prayers.[23] Because mock epic is an apposite, not opposite, form of epic, it is not surprising that the author of *M'Fingal* not only began a thirty-year rage for short mock epics, but gravely drew up a numbered list of sixteen names and then titled it "Trumbull's Rank Epic Poets" ("1. Homer, 2. Milton, 3. Virgil," on down to Silius Italicus).[24] Harvard's two eminent professors of Greek, Edward Everett and Cornelius Conway Felton, praised Homer to generations of students including Emerson (who proclaimed "Homer's is the only epic")[25] and Thoreau (who kept *The Iliad* on his table at Walden). William Munford and William Cullen Bryant translated *The Iliad*, Bryant translated *The Odyssey*, and Christopher Pearse Cranch translated *The Aeneid*.

Literary periodicals of the day reflect similar interests. *Port Folio* printed cantos of Voltaire's *Henriade*, commented guardedly about John Blair Linn's dismissal of epic rules, and published articles on Virgil and Camoens, as well as appraisals of such now-forgotten British epic poets as Richard Glover and William Wilkie. The *Monthly Anthology and Boston Review*, a magazine conducted by Federalist gentlemen who did not believe an American epic was possible, printed six articles on Virgil between 1807 and 1809, as well as articles on Homer, Cowper's translations, and *Paradise Lost*. When the startling theory of Wolf's *Prolegomena* (1795) became widely known in America (Wolf had argued that the Homeric poems were gatherings of separate oral lays), it inspired lengthy articles in the *American Quarterly Review* (1827) and the *North American Review* (1833). Such interest surely stimulated still more heroic poetry. From the outset, projectors of the new republic's literature had not greeted the epic with the same acute suspicion of amoral fabrication meted out to drama and fiction. John Adams called for an American epic, but he was no friend of plays and romances.

A civilization steeped in Homer, Virgil, and Milton, which reverenced the epic and had won a civil war for political independence, inevitably began to define itself in epic terms. Newspapers urged young men to fight the British by printing verses with such first-line titles as "Let's look to Greece and Athens," "When Satan First From Heaven's Bright Region Fell," "Two Parties Slay Whole Hecatombs to Jove," and "Aid Me Ye Nine, My Muse Assist."[26] Among the names given to raw villages in upper New York were Troy, Rome, and Ithaca. The favored figure of American poets and orators, Columbia, combines a guardian goddess of place with an Olympian who, in flowing robes, presides over a war to enthrone Freedom. Speaking to the troops at Morristown, Hugh Henry Brackenridge justified his noncombatant status by the following comparison:

> What could old Nestor do in battle, with a feeble arm and failing foot? but as the *chaplain* of Agamemnon's army, great was the service he rendered in counseling obedience and exhorting to combat.[27]

Even apolitical citizens victimized by the war saw themselves in the heroic texts. Ann Eliza Bleecker's fine bitter poem "On Reading Dryden's Virgil" likens her sorrow for losing her daughter during Burgoyne's invasion of New York to Aeneas' lament for losing Creusa during the burning of Troy. Why, Bleecker protests, do contemporaries still reserve more tears for Virgil's imagined heroes than for contemporary flesh and blood?

The successful outcome of the war allowed Americans to pass by complicating details and to elevate patriots to full heroic stature. In the course of one "Eulogy on Washington" (1800), Fisher Ames compared Washington to Fabius, Cincinnatus, Leonidas, and Epaminondas.[28] Robert Treat Paine, with no apparent recognition that his similes might be contradictory, likened Washington to Mars, Jove, Christ, Julius Caesar, Cincinnatus, Leonidas, and Aeneas.[29] Because an informed citizenry electing persuasive s' :smen was considered essential to maintaining the Republic's strength, ιamiliarity with the council scenes of epic poetry became an educational imperative. Never conceiving that literature and politics might become separable, the *Boston Magazine* declared in 1785:

> The greatest modern statesmen have caught the flame of their inspiration from the altars which ancient Greece erected to honour and to virtue. And for these altars, built by solid science, Greece was indebted to Homer, who stands first in the class of polite literature. From Homer Greece derived that spirit which made her the wonder of other nations. Immortal bard! Thou alone didst sound the charge of Thermopylae! Thou alone didst conquer at Salamis and at Marathon![30]

John Quincy Adams's influential *Lectures on Rhetoric* (1810) advised that the training of republican orators should include study of the most sublime speeches in *The Iliad:* "Innumerable passages in the *Iliad* and *Odyssey,"* Adams says, "leave no doubt that rhetoric was taught, and oratory practiced, in high refinement, during and before the war of Troy."[31] The ease with which some Americans could reshape Homer to fit their own national image reveals how readily new subjects and old models were conflated. A writer for *Port Folio* declared in 1822: "He [Homer] beheld the spirit of liberty in the very bosom of monarchy; he saw the rising arts cultivated and soon brought to perfection by a people who were enthusiasts in every thing that affected the senses or the imagination."[32] George Bancroft urged that Homer be "studied, and understood, and valued by our young countrymen," because Homer honored bravery and perseverance, esteemed the ties of family and friendship, and defended liberty against tyrannous commanders.[33]

Bancroft's view that Homer's poems could have a wholesome moral effect upon American citizens was, among his contemporaries, almost unique. One of the most revealing of American literary responses is the consistency and vehemence with which Homer's world and Homer's morality were damned by those who simultaneously asserted that Homer was the first and greatest of poets. To a people convinced that Divine Providence was creating a regenerative civilization founded upon republican politics, freeholding farmers, and Christian ethics, the conduct of Achilles and Odysseus seemed to embody everything from which they wished to escape. The world of Homeric poems, they commonly concluded, had been a barbarous feudal chaos, ruled by nearly omnipotent but amoral gods who casually rewarded plunder and murder. Achilles's slaughter of Trojans after the death of Patroclus, Odysseus's trickery during the night raid on the Trojan camp, and the brutality with which Odysseus reordered his Ithakan household were not patterns of heroic behavior that a New World republican should be willing to excuse. Worse yet, Homer seemed to have accepted the barbarity of his world. The father of poetry had declined to portray a just or harmonious universe, had dwelt upon the technique of slaughter, and had not questioned the duty of revenge.

Trained as neoclassicists, Americans of the early Republic grew up despising the contents of the epic poems they revered. Among widely read authors the tone of outrage is especially marked. Charles Brockden Brown believed he was stating an accepted fact when he wrote "Homer was a man of a barbarous age, and a rude nation. Superstition was vigorous; science was unknown; war and depradation made up the business and delight of mankind."[34] A less guarded response appears in a journal letter Brown wrote during the 1790s: "Can the harmony and energy of Homer shroud from our view the horrid forms of revenge and cruelty that stalk with rapid and gigantic steps through every page of the *Iliad?*"[35] Once readers are shown that the Homeric deities are "as foolish and freakish as they are wicked," they will understand "the meanness and grossness and worthlessness of Homer's supernatural machinery."[36]

Because Virgil was commonly regarded as the epic poet of judgment, decorum, and empire, his intimations of the tears in things and of war's inevitable melancholy went practically unnoticed. His admiration for commanding rulers of nominal republics did not. Brockden Brown merely followed a current misperception when he judged *The Aeneid* to be "a remarkable instance of servile adulation to tyrants and superstitious reverence for antiquity."[37]

For those who could not reconceive Homer as a humane libertarian, his value for an American's moral education had to be abandoned. Unlike George Bancroft, Benjamin Rush had vehemently attacked the teaching

of Latin and Greek classics in American schools because such works were full of "indelicate amours" and "the vices both of gods and men." Homer and Virgil, Rush asserted, had described "little else but the histories of murders, perpetrated by kings."[38] Joel Barlow wrote *The Columbiad* under the conviction that "the works of Homer . . . have caused more mischief to mankind than those of any other."[39] Homer could have advanced and not impeded progress had he written an epic designed "to celebrate the useful arts of agriculture and navigation," rather than *The Iliad*.[40] John Quincy Adams, much as he admired Virgil's metric, was revolted by the death of Turnus; no reader, Adams wrote, should be forced "to see the hero of Virgil, the pious Aeneas, steeling his bosom against mercy, and plunging his pitiless sword into the bosom of a fallen and imploring enemy, to avenge the slaughter of his friend."[41]

Such remarks attest to the cultural power literature was thought to exert. Long after Poe's era, art for the sake of art would continue to be an unacceptable notion, especially as applied to the epic. Whittier protested that "the brawny butcher work of men whose wits, like those of Ajax, lie in their sinews, and who are 'yoked like draught oxen and made to plough up the wars,' is no realization of my ideal of true courage."[42] By the time Bryant had finished his Homeric translations, he was convinced that Achilles was "a ferocious barbarian at best," and that the Greek Gods were "debauched, mercenary, rapacious and cruel." Bryant even confided in a letter that the Gods' "conduct is so detestable that I am sometimes half tempted to give up them and Homer together."[43] In the context of these judgments, Whitman's familiar condemnations of the feudalism of Old World bards must be seen as comparatively temperate wordings of a widely held response.[44]

The Iliad and *The Aeneid* were stridently denounced because they were not regarded as historical artifacts but as affective models for a heroic culture. To Bryant, judging *The Iliad* as literary art or as a document of Greek history would have reduced its significance immeasurably. By rejecting the heroic world of Homer and Virgil, but not the epic genre, Americans could dismiss Old World barbarity while holding high the heritage that had yielded the revered figure of John Milton. As one might expect, post-Revolutionary Americans perceived Milton as a principled Puritan rebelling against a tyrannical monarch, as well as the sublime singer of the word of God. For prospective writers of epic, the example of Milton was especially awesome because *Paradise Lost* had proven that the classical epic could be successfully adapted to a Christian cosmology.[45] Slighting Milton's sixth book, Americans regarded *Paradise Lost* as the work that brought the epic beyond Old World nationalism and the glorification of war. During his 1770 commencement oration at Yale, John Trumbull called for an American epic poet of the spirit, a sacred

bard who would sing of the resurrection or of the last judgment, and whose lays would "with lofty Milton vie."[46] Charles Brockden Brown's short article, "A Comparison Between the Poems of Homer and Milton" condemns Homer as a heathen fatalist in order to praise Milton for insisting upon free will and Christian Right Reason.[47] The author of "Remarks on the Epopoea" for *Port Folio* claimed *Paradise Lost* to be "the greatest effort of human genius and the most sublime of all sacred poems."[48] John Blair Linn, in spite of his love for Homer and Ossian, declared that "Milton is only inferior to the voice of inspiration."[49] It was to Milton, then, that Americans would look, not for the form of epic, but for the master spirit who had combined heroic grandeur with Christian ethics.

II. THE SUBJECT

Berkeley's rendering of the *Translatio Studii* had implied that the American epic was to affirm history's culminating act of mortal heroism. Mere imitation of epic predecessors, even of Milton, would not suit "Time's noblest offspring." The phrases "Annuit Coeptis" and "Novus Ordo Saeclorum" on the Great Seal of the United States also promised glorious new beginnings for American civilization. And yet the one quality C. M. Bowra has claimed to be essential to all heroic poetry or primary epic – a warrior's willingness to confront death for the sake of honor and renown – was obviously not the epic subject with the greatest appeal for progressive republicans in a new world. Berkeley's fifth act of heroic literature must rather be some further development of Milton that would combine, as in Berkeley's rhyme, epic rage with the golden age. Precisely which era the second golden age was, however, depended upon one's regional and religious perspective. The possibilities were at least fivefold: New England's founding, the achieving of a nation during the Revolution, cultural independence emerging from the War of 1812, the winning of the west from the heroic-age Indian, and the growth of progressive republicanism in the entire western hemisphere.

A separable minority of writers, wary of connecting heroism with politics, were sure that Milton had shown the way to an inexhaustible source of workable epic subjects. In "A Dissertation on the History, Eloquence, and Poetry of the Bible" (1772), Timothy Dwight justified his choice of a biblical subject for his own recently begun epic on grounds both literary and moral. In his view, the prose of the Old Testament was heroic poetry as well as inspired scripture: "Shall we be blind . . . to Poetry more correct and tender than Virgil, and infinitely more sublime than him who has long been honoured, not unjustly, with that magnificent appellation 'the Father of Poetry.' "[50] Dwight evidently believed that an American who wrote an epic on a nonnational subject could still

create the great national poem, so long as he successfully captured the heroic and sublime qualities of scripture. His idea has some importance because it underlies the writing, not only of *The Conquest of Canaan,* which we shall discuss, but also of later biblical verse epics, which we shall mercifully ignore. Such poems as Thomas Brockway's *The Gospel Tragedy: An Epic Poem* (1795), Elhanahan Winchester's *Process and Empire of Christ* (1805), Jacob Dixon's *Divination Overruled* (1833), Johnson Pierson's *The Judiad* (1844), and Phineas Robinson's *Immortality: A Poem in Ten Cantos* (1846) are clumsy Miltonic imitations devised under the assumption that a Christian America's epic poem could be created by transferring the diction, sonority, and didacticism of *Paradise Lost* to other biblical subjects.[51]

Because New Englanders like Dwight and Barlow were known to have written epics of supranational themes, the era of Puritan plantation came to seem too regional for a national epic. Not until Rhode Island's Judge Job Durfee wrote *Whatcheer* (1832) about Roger Williams's exodus to Rhode Island ("I sing of trials stern and sufferings great, / Which Father Williams in his exile bore") did a verse epic on the matter of Puritanism appear.[52] In spite of Durfee's occasional attempts to nationalize Williams's supposed commitment to an eighteenth-century liberty of conscience, Durfee's passions for local facts and exact closed rhymes served him ill. By Durfee's time the increasingly questionable heroism of the Puritan forefathers was becoming a widespread concern of historical novelists, for whom any likening of Graeco-Roman heroes to the pilgrims would have seemed ludicrous.

The geographical determinism current in the late eighteenth century led more nationalistic and less devout Americans to believe that their country's epic must combine the sublimities of American nature with the heroic acts of the Revolution. As early as Freneau's and Brackenridge's "The Rising Glory of America," readers were assured that the values of "Ajax and great Achilles" would be superseded by an American "New Jerusalem" in which "Freedom's established reign" would be based upon "agriculture's toil" and "great Commerce," themselves dependent upon an immensity of land blessedly free of the curse of gold.[53] Forty years later, C. J. Ingersoll, author of the popular, if turgid, *Inchiquin, The Jesuit's Letters* (1810), was still sure that "the conquest of America, its magnificent rivers, stupendous mountains, immense wealth, and the avulsion of these states from their mother country, afford as fruitful and fine an argument as could be imagined for epic operation."[54]

Unfortunately, this argument was often reduced to the absurdities of defensive comparisons. The author of the first book-length critique of American letters, Samuel Lorenzo Knapp, was certain that a great national poet must emerge because the Tiber and the Scamander were no

match for the Missouri and the Amazon.[55] Forgetting that natural description had entered classical epic almost solely through the simile, a critic for the *Monthly Anthology* assured his readers "Our green fields are as pleasant, our cataracts roar as loudly, and our mountains project the same grandeur of shade as those which the pages of Homer or Virgil describe."[56] America's fertile vastness was at least as suited to Longinus's sublimity as Homer's Greece, though the rhetoric would need updating. Italicizing the crucial terms lest the reference be missed, the *Columbian Magazine* asked that Burkean aesthetics be applied to American ground: "The face of nature, throughout the United States, exhibits the *sublime* and *beautiful,* in the most exalted degree."[57]

An early attempt to portray the American landscape in a long narrative poem, Alexander Wilson's "The Foresters" (1805) begins by regretting that no American bard had adequately praised the sublime grandeur of American scenery. Recounting his journey into the wilderness, Wilson compares himself to Odysseus and ends with an extended description of the paradigm of New World sublimity, Niagara Falls. By the time Joel Barlow decided to revise *The Vision of Columbus* into *The Columbiad,* the expectation that the American epic would incorporate descriptions of the natural sublime had been firmly established.

Shortly after the Revolutionary War began, writers discovered the narrative action upon which the fifth act of epic literature could be founded. In a speech of 1779, Brackenridge claimed that slain American soldiers were true epic heroes because they had died both for political principle and for country, rather than for feudal loyalty, blind attachment to family, or personal revenge. Providing catalogues of place names that future bards could memorialize, along with footnotes from Job, Virgil, Revelations, Milton, and Ossian, Brackenridge predicted that at Bunker Hill "the muses shall observe the night, and hymn heroic acts, and trim their lightful lamps to the dawn of morning."[58] In 1789 a Harvard graduate who called himself "Cantabrigiensis," evidently convinced that the lamps were still trimmed too low, wrote a poem titled "Anticipation of the Literary Fame of America," in which he predicted that "Some future Virgil shall our wars rehearse / In all the dignity of epic verse."[59]

The imaginative and challenging prospectus for an epic on the Revolutionary War was advanced by a poet now better known for turning against the epic – Philip Freneau. While embracing the Revolution as a worthy subject, Freneau also redefined it:

> It has been for some time announced to the public, that an Epick Poem, on the subject of the American revolution, was in preparation, by a gentleman from Europe, now resident in this country.[60] Perhaps no other event in the history of man, as a subject for epic poetry, has an equal claim on the exertion and animation of genius, with the emanci-

pation of the western world. Poems of the epic strain that have been handed down from the remote periods of antiquity, are founded on a comparatively narrow basis. The Rape of Helen, the Return of Ulysses to Ithaca, from the siege of Troy; or the transferring an insignificant colony in a few barques from the Lesser Asia to the western coast of Italy, have been the subjects of these great masterpieces of poetry, penned by Homer and Virgil, which stand at the head of all poetic excellence, and have commanded the attention of mankind for hundreds of years back, and have been preserved as the most precious of all reliques, when in danger from the devastation of war, vandalism, and conflagration. If the genius of such authors as Homer and Virgil, could aggrandize events, even in those limited times, of no great moment in the eyes of the historian, so as to render them immortal in the memory of mankind, by the "magic of song," how much the more should this sublime incident of our own times, the AMERICAN REVOLUTION, awaken genius, and enable it to transmit to posterity, in all the solidity of philosophy, and the beautiful colorings of poetry, this STORY OF FAME, this *real revolution,* which, in its consequences, includes no less in the general condition of man, than a transfer from tyranny, slavery, and subjugation, to the benignity of rational government, equal liberty, and the advancement of that temporal felicity designed for man by Nature.[61]

Following the convention of claiming the higher argument, Freneau here contends that the truly heroic subject, the "real revolution," is not the battlefield heroics of Bunker Hill, but the change in human nature made possible through political republicanism. The glory of a hero's death is to be supplanted by the glory of mankind's future. The higher heroism lies in cultural progress, not in the martial courage that admittedly must bring it about. Freneau longingly imagines an epic with no particular hero and no climactic heroic deed. If the poet can persuade the reader that the "real revolution" is mental and political, his epic will have achieved its end. "Solidity of philosophy" and "the beautiful colorings of poetry" are complementary, not discrete, because both are subsidiary to a religion of Freedom. Were it not that Freneau still conceives this epic as a "Story of Fame," one might almost suspect him of sharing Whitman's notion that the true epic is the heroism created in the reader.

III.   THE FORM

However "real" his revolutionary subject, any well-read poet maturing in the 1770s, English or American, inherited a stiflingly rigid conception of epic tradition and epic form. Although a few Americans like Trumbull and Barlow had read Tasso and Camoens, the word "epic" basically meant a tradition made up of Homer, Virgil, and Milton. *The Divine Comedy* and *Beowulf* were virtually unknown in America until the

North American Review introduced them in articles by John Chipman Gray in 1819 and Longfellow in 1838. Familiarity with the Latin *Aeneid* was common, but few Americans read Homeric Greek easily. To illustrate epic qualities, examples were chosen from *The Iliad* or *The Aeneid,* but rarely from *The Odyssey,* partly because Americans were more interested in creating a nation than in reordering a homeland. Americans gained their conception of an epic poem, not directly from Aristotle, but from the prefaces of Dryden and Pope. These prefaces were influenced by, and led Americans to, Le Bossu's *Treatise of the Epick Poem.* Dwight and Barlow cited Andrew Ramsay's "A Discourse on Epic Poetry" and Voltaire's *Essay On Epick Poetry;* they were encouraged by the eighteen *Spectator* papers in which Addison had argued that *Paradise Lost* fulfilled the standards for epic proposed by Aristotle and Le Bossu. The most recent influences were the rhetorics of Lord Kames and Hugh Blair, both commonly used as school textbooks between 1780 and 1830.

Before 1815 the debate over the subject of the American epic was not accompanied by any thoughtful debate over its form. The kind of poem that seventeenth- and eighteenth-century critics had associated with the epic was fundamentally different in origin, language, and purpose from our idea of Homer, shaped as it had been by A. B. Lord, C. M. Bowra, and Cedric Whitman. The distinction now made between "primary" oral poetry, in which a singer recites traditional verses concerning the battles of a past heroic age, and "secondary" literary epic, in which a poet writes verse connecting heroic acts to a national spirit or world force, was utterly unknown in late-eighteenth-century America. Homer was considered to be a penman and a moralist who strove through exalted language to arouse the epic emotion, variously defined as Admiration or Awe, in his readers. Having settled upon a dominant moral, the epic poet should select a suitable fable by which to exemplify it. Nearly all critics, deferring ultimately to Aristotle, insisted that the fable be an imitation of one heroic action which must be probable, great, and complete in itself. Episodes such as the 10th *Iliad,* the 11th *Odyssey,* or the 4th *Aeneid* should be integrated to the central action. The language should be as distinct as possible from ordinary speech, and to this end should avail itself of the inversions, compound epithets, and exalted diction of the sublime, as practiced preeminently by John Milton.

So formidable a consensus about major matters permitted disagreement about lesser ones. Traditionalist critics contended that the epic poet must observe in medias res, had best obey the unities of time and place, and should devise a fable that ended triumphantly. Following Le Bossu, traditionalists approvingly observed that the great epic models all contained certain conventions: a proposition, invocation of the Muse, epic similes, catalogues, prophecies, and intervening deities. Some critics went

so far as to prescribe what are now called "type scenes" or "themes": any true epic must contain councils of chieftains, epic games, feasts, a visit to the underworld, preparation of an epic weapon, and a climactic single combat. Only a few critics considered whether an epic might be written in prose (e.g., Fénelon and Ossian) or might concern a contemporary historical event. Instead of questioning the viability of received epic form, both British and American critics questioned the pertinence of divine machinery within it. Challenging the authority of Dryden and Pope, Kames and Blair had argued that the intervention of a god, even a Christian god, would deprive a modern epic of all credibility. The absurdity of the word "machinery" should not blind us to the importance of the issue. To rid the epic of gods would deprive the poet of any suprahuman sanction for heroic behavior.

Until at least 1800, influential critics did not directly challenge the premise that an epic was a long, ambitious poem, morally instructive, concerned to some degree with martial heroism, and written in sublime language.[62] Neither Kames nor Blair nor Cowper would have considered *The Prelude* for inclusion within the genre of epic poetry. Lest this summary of eighteenth-century epic theory seems a caricature of a neoclassic rules critic, let us recall a few crucial statements, all often reprinted throughout the century. The first words of Dryden's "Dedication of the Aeneis" are a neat compression of Le Bossu, Horace, and Aristotle, in that order:

> A HEROIC POEM, truly such, is undoubtedly the greatest work which the soul of man is capable to perform. The design of it is to form the mind to heroic virtue by example; 'tis conveyed in verse, that it may delight, while it instructs. The action of it is always one, entire, and great.[63]

Pope's translations of Homer were far more innovative than his theory of epic; following Le Bossu almost verbatim, Pope argued that the greatest epic poet had conceived of characters as moral exempla chosen to affirm a certain teleology: "He [Homer] resolv'd to sing the Consequences of Anger; he consider'd what Virtues and Vices would conduce most to bring his Moral out of the Fable; and artfully disposed them in his chief persons after the manner in which we generally find them."[64] In *Spectator* No. 285, Addison insisted "it is requisite that the Language of an Heroic Poem should be both Perspicuous and Sublime. . . . To this end, it ought to deviate from the common Forms and ordinary Phrases of Speech."[65] Ramsay, in a sentence that Dwight and Barlow heeded, stated that "The Epopoea may take in the actions of several years; but according to the critics, the time of the principal action, from the place where the poet begins his narration, cannot exceed a year."[66]

After 1750 the deference paid to Le Bossu often changed to resent-

ment, but the tone of epic theorists continued to be peremptory. Voltaire may have written of Homer and Virgil "we should be their admirers, not their slaves," but he also insisted that any epic must imitate an action that is *"great* to strike us with Awe, *interesting* because we delight in being mov'd, *entire,* that our minds may be wholly satisfy'd."[67] The grandiose similes of Dwight and Barlow indicate their respect for Lord Kames's most un-Homeric fiat "It is a rule, that a grand object ought never to be resembled to one that is diminutive."[68] Perhaps the constant striving for elevation in late-eighteenth-century epic poems should partially be traced to Hugh Blair's insistence that nothing disgusting, gross, or savage should ever enter a modern epic, the style of which must reflect "every thing that is sublime in description, tender in sentiment, and bold and lively in expression."[69]

Deference to the critical history of literature's highest genre rendered such authoritative pronouncements all the more imposing, however much Americans might protest against them. Brockden Brown's disgust with the barbarity of the Homeric world did not deter him from gravely setting forth a wholly derivative definition of the epic genre:

> An Epic Poem is the narrative, in verse, of some momentous and solemn event, generally connected with the fate of nations or large bodies of men. The earliest performance of this kind with which we are acquainted is the *Iliad* of Homer. The reverence for what is ancient, and the influence of education, have combined to make this poem the object of our praise and our imitation. It is, in considerable degree, the model by which every thing that is called an epic poem is to be fashioned. The metrical form, the distribution into books, the artificial arrangement of incidents, the influence of preternatural agents, the scenes of war and battle, the embellishment of similes and allegories, accompany most works of this kind, chiefly because these constitute the pattern which the Grecian bard has exhibited.[70]

Brown's definition, written in 1799, is far closer to Le Bossu, Dryden, and Pope than to such comparative moderns as Kames and Blair. Brown's insistence on *The Iliad* as the definitive model for the genre, by which he means Pope's *Iliad,* suggests an important complication in tracing literary influence. The epic poems written by Dwight, Barlow, McGill, and Emmons are all written in heroic couplets and incorporate the conventions Brown deems essential to the epic kind. If Pope's *Iliad* remains the model of epic, however, one must beware of assuming an identity between Pope's poem and Homer's. Pope had often moralized Homer's song by developing the abstract political or cultural issues of Homer's narrative, by attributing poetic justice to Homer's gods, and by describing Homer's world in language appropriate to Pope's own culture.[71] When Americans brought up on Pope's Homer set out to write their own epics, they were likely to believe they could imitate Homer by imitating Pope.

IV. DIFFICULTIES OF ADAPTATION

The poet who would make an epic of American materials thus confronted two interrelated problems. Did America provide a heroic fable truly worthy of epic stature? Even if it did, how could America's heroic subjects be plausibly adapted to the epic genre? To begin with, the subjects themselves posed inherent difficulties. The American Revolution, no matter how heroic, had not transpired in a sufficiently remote past to have become a series of legends that an entire people accepted as myth. The poet faced the alternatives of adhering to historical fact or of creating, rather than transmitting, an epic legend. If he were to describe Revolutionary fathers as spotless Christian warriors, he would satisfy his culture's need for a heroic ultimate, but his heroes might seem incredible paragons to those whose memories of recent history were clear. But if he adhered rigidly to historical fact, his poetic effort might devolve into a chronicle rather than an epic; he would be limited to the role Voltaire had ascribed to Lucan: "a declamatory gazeteer."[72] American writers wished to prove that their Revolutionary fathers were truly heroic by comparing them to epic heroes, even if the comparison seemed absurdly incongruous. But they also wished to assert that the Christian gentleman farmer was the greatest of all heroes, even though he was unlike the hero of any epic known to them.

Although the higher heroism seemed to demand a new set of poetic conventions, epics had long been identified by their use of older ones. Epic games, visits to the underworld, and climactic single combats had admittedly not been common experiences either for Washington or his recruits, but how could one abandon these type scenes and still compose a recognizably epic poem? Another vexingly apparent problem was the portrayal of divine agents. To assert that God's Providence had willed republican victories was not quite the same as claiming that Moloch had physically walked the battlefield at Saratoga. Picturing intervening deities was historically false, but machinery heightened heroic action while giving it absolute approval. What was an enlightened modern to do? A near agnostic like Joel Barlow might agree with Voltaire that "it is *almost* impossible for us to venture on any Machinery. The ancient Gods are exploded out of the World"[73] (italics mine). A cautious classicist like Hugh Swinton Legaré might foreclose the contemporary epic because the gods are gone.[74] Or a reviewer of the *Henriade* might delight that poets are beginning to abandon such improbable, therefore ridiculous, creatures.[75] Whatever one's attitude toward machinery might be, however, no one was convinced that a successful epic poem could be written without it.

The problem of imitating inappropriate machinery became insolubly real to the first poet who attempted an epic directly concerned with the

American Revolution. In 1782 and 1783, thirty-two-year-old Nathaniel Tucker, author of the respected topographical poem *The Bermudian,* and older brother of St. George Tucker of Williamsburg, began to write "America Delivered: An Heroic Poem" while living as a physician in the remote village of Malton, Yorkshire. Convinced that the spirit of Liberty evident in the Revolution provided him "a more bold and sublime subject and scene for the interference of the turbulent spirits of the dark abyss . . . than the capricious determination of our first mother to rob the orchard of Paradise," Tucker anticipated a three-part, twelve-book, subscription-supported poem that would comprise "nothing less than an epic poem on a modern subject, the American Revolution."[76] After proposing to sing "FREEDOM triumphant, and her sacred cause / With renovated might on western plains / Asserted and assailed," Tucker began his epic action following Burgoyne's defeat at Saratoga. He clearly intended to trace the deliverance of a newer Jerusalem than Tasso's through the "final overthrow of proud Cornwallis."[77] While writing the first canto of his poem, however, Tucker became aware of problems. In a letter to his sister, Tucker insisted that, though he had no single hero, he did have a single, united epic action that would eventually emerge. He sought her advice "particularly as to the language and stile of composition, the machinery and allegory it comprehends, and the effect of these applied to a modern subject."[78]

Tucker believed he had the higher argument, but he used all the conventions of Milton's now lower argument to unfold it. His problem was how to render a meeting between Milton's angels and America's men. In book one, after the British fleet arrives to recoup Burgoyne's disaster, archangel Michael praises God's providence and prepares to exhort the Continental Congress to be ever vigilant in pursuing peace with liberty. But Tucker then switches the scene to Pandemonium, where Satan, Beelzebub, Belial, Mammon, and Moloch, after long debate, conclude that the best means of regaining heaven is to corrupt English rulers so thoroughly that they will oppress the Americans, thereby ending a Berkeleyan "Golden age of happiness" in the New World. When Mammon approaches Philadelphia, the heavenly and human levels of the poem's action finally have to intersect:

> Stagnant in air now sat upon his cloud
> The Mammon of unrighteousness accurst
> And overlook'd the City, far and wide,
> Whose noble structures and extended streets
> Stretch o'er that insulated ground that lies
> Between the forks of Schulykil and of Delaware
> Great confluent rivers:

With these words, Tucker's manuscript abruptly and without explanation ends.

Even if Tucker had been able to find the subscribers, he probably could not have completed his manuscript. His imagination was filled with the vastness of heaven and hell, but he could have had no sure sense of the events or settings of the American Revolution. Neither his poem nor his comments upon it indicate that he ever fastened upon a cohesive narrative. His invocation to Liberty demonstrates the syntactic obscurities that resulted from imitating Milton's inversions and Milton's run-on line:

> And Thou, O daring Spirit,
> That didst the souls of heroes unsubdued
> In that contention warm with patriot ardour
> Fearless to brave in council and the field
> Dismay on all sides, and the clamorous tongues
> Of calumny and reproach, with all that power
> And pride offended of a mighty nation,
> Haughty in arms, by warfare could inflict
> Upon her sons in firm rebellion leagued
> Against her sway, with dangerous revolt,
> Themselves endanger'd.

Despite all these difficulties, Tucker abandoned his poem only when Mammon's appearance in Philadelphia posed a double-edged impossibility. To apply the machinery of Milton's cosmos to the Continental Congress would result in laughable incongruity, but to attempt an epic poem without machinery was to write no epic at all.

To his credit, Tucker knew where his failings lay. He worriedly wrote his sister "The language is an attempt to imitate the Miltonic. Tell me how far you think I have succeeded if at all." The very grandeur of the attempt became an increasing burden: "It [the poem's composition] was attended with a force and constraint that confined my imagination and made me look forward to its completion like a school boy to the end of his labour." Shortly after he stopped writing, he reluctantly agreed with his sister that his poem could have no contemporary audience because "we could not reconcile ourselves to the interference of that machinery in a revolution which has been effected under our own eyes." Writing to St. George Tucker a year later, Nathaniel was able to judge "America Delivered" with rueful acuity: "Upon a late perusal of what I did in it, I perceive I had fallen into too close an imitation of Milton, and I believe if I were to undertake the thing again I should execute it in a different way."[79] Although Tucker could not specify what the "different way" might have been, he had recognized the constraints and absurdities of writing an imitative epic on an American subject, and he had yielded to his recognition.

Tucker stopped before he had to select a language suitable to describing American nature. Nouns like "Vale," "Pile," "Deep," or "Flood,"

verbs like "glister," "heave," or "round," adjectives like "vasty," "re-dounding," or "darksome" comprised the accepted diction for the sub-lime. Could such words, so effective in describing Milton's cosmos, be successfully applied to American settings, especially when the American language, as Noah Webster stated, was developing toward colloquial simplicity? Moreover, an epic had to remain a heroic narrative. If the poet relied frequently upon pictorial description, his epic might sacrifice narrative intensity.

The most acute problem of fitting the old form to the new muse was not formalistic but cultural: Americans' vision of their civilization did not suit the traditional substance of heroic narrative. For Americans, courage in battle was at best a barbarous means to the heroic end of creating an empire based upon rural virtues, profitable commerce, and libertarian politics. The nation's epic must portray the fields of valor on which the British father had been killed while somehow subsuming such scenes within an antimartial heroic code. The problem, to be sure, was one that both Virgil and Milton had faced but that neither had resolved. The weary doubt and melancholy that define Aeneas throughout Virgil's first six books largely disappear when Aeneas becomes a warrior in La-tium. Although Milton condemns the barbarity of Achilles, his Christ displays Homeric valor while expelling the Satanic host from heaven. For many Americans, the problem was aggravated because the Revolu-tion seemed in retrospect to have been a war fought to end all wars, at least in the New World. Repulsed by the rage of Achilles, the wiles of Odysseus, and the truckling of Aeneas, American poets needed to find a way of praising physical courage without the will to conquer. But an epic lacking martial heroism seemed no less problematic to them than reclothing Jesus as a warrior; some kind of accommodation with the matter of Troy clearly needed to be struck.

Seeking to place themselves through epic analogies, Americans were likely to agree with Edward Everett that "the war of 1776 is the Trojan War of America."[80] Americans were not likely, however, to identify their recent victory with the successful invasion of the Greeks, whose moral superiority to the Trojans had been of no concern to Homer. In-stead, they preferred to see themselves as the Trojans of the second *Aeneid* – patriots defending homeland and family against wily, haughty invad-ers from across the sea. "Cantabrigiensis" had specified that an American Virgil was needed to sing the American war, and Mrs. Bleecker's "On Reading Dryden's Virgil" had drawn the parallels between Greeks and Englishmen, Trojans and Americans. The fact that Troy had fallen and America survived did not prevent Americans from reading *The Aeneid* as typological literature linking the foundings of the Roman and Ameri-can republics. The same commencement orator at the University of

Pennsylvania who had predicted American Homers and Virgils began "The Former, Present and Future Prospects of America" with an epigraph selected from Aeneas' speech to his shipwrecked Trojans in Virgil's first book. The words *"Per varios casus, per tot discrimina rerum, / Tendimus in Latium"* thus establish a parallel between Aeneas' difficulties in founding a second Troy in Latium and the equally protracted struggle to found the American republic.[81]

In the next generation, Virgilian analogies would become a staple of commemorative rhetoric. Delivering perhaps his most famous oration, "The Bunker Hill Monument" (1825), before a large crowd in Charlestown, Daniel Webster likened Anchises' discourse on the soul to the revolutionary impulse of 1775. After picturing the embattled American militia, Webster quoted, apparently without translation, Anchises' words *"totamque infusa per artus / Mens agitat molem, et magno se corpore miscet."*[82] Webster evidently expected his listeners to recognize that Virgil's "immanent mind, filling matter with divine spirit" had finally manifested itself in the groundswell of indignation filling all American breasts after the battles of Lexington and Concord. And yet, the forcing of so awkward a parallel reveals that *The Aeneid* also posed problems of epic precedent. The defense of Troy might have been a defense of *pietas* in all its familial and political senses, but it had not been a defense of man's natural rights nor even of longstanding civil liberties. Latium and America might both have been providentially favored rural republics, which were to display remarkable powers of commerce and civilization building, but Americans did not wish to imagine a future for their Latium that culminated in the rule of an Augustus Caesar.

A new model of epic heroism was clearly needed. Although the physical valor of Achilles and Odysseus seemed almost precivilized, the spiritual virtues of Adam or Christ had not linked republicanism to cultural progress. Aeneas provided the closest model, but his politics were vague and his military posture, once he arrived in Italy, seemed perilously close to that of Achilles. Americans sought a hero who would have the physical courage of Homer's warriors without their drive for personal honor, the piety and decency of Aeneas without his subservience to the imperial forces of history, and Christian Right Reason dedicated primarily to the New World rather than to God. The concept of heroism that resulted was a blending of Roman historical models, responses to heroic poetry, and recent national history. The new hero was to be a Christian gentleman who treasured *otium cum dignitate* on his rural estate. Because of his faith in republican political principle, he had resigned himself to those acts of military heroism necessary to create the American republic. His basic commitment was to the spread of Christian agrarian civilization in the New World, but his selflessness

was apparent in his willingness to leave the farm to defend liberty's cause.

The eulogies of Washington by Robert Treat Paine, Joseph Story, and Fisher Ames reflect this model, as do David Humphreys's "An Essay on the Life of General Putnam" and Daniel Webster's "Adams and Jefferson." Even as wide-ranging a poem as Humphreys's "On the Happiness of America" pauses to define the soldier-farmer's heroism through the supplanting of Old World models:

> Swords turned to shares, and war to rural toil,
> The men who sav'd, now cultivate the soil.
> In no heroic age, since time began,
> Appear'd so great the majesty of man.[83]

A particularly clear formulation of this heroic type is advanced by Edward Everett in "The First Battles of the Revolutionary War" (1825). Everett argues that American colonial legislatures of the 1770s exhibited the bravery and eloquence of Grecian and Roman councils, yet he also insists that martial epic heroes were barbaric. In Everett's view, a truer heroism was shown by the freeholding farmers in 1775, who yielded to battle heroics only to preserve their underlying commitments to liberty and Christian civilization. His term for such men is "citizen heroes."[84]

The desire to redefine heroism as a civic vision made possible by momentary valor explains the repeated comparisons of worthies of the Revolution to Cincinnatus, the patriot who abruptly left the plow to defend his land, but whose physical heroics did not alter his civilized values. Searching in recent epic poetry for a suitable precedent, literary Americans found it in Richard Glover's *Leonidas* (1737), a blank-verse epic popular throughout the eighteenth century. Glover had portrayed Leonidas as a valiant defender of Greek liberties who offered his life for his country, and who died after the successful defense of his people at Thermopylae, where his tiny band of citizen warriors subdued the invading Persians. By likening Washington to Leonidas, writers as varied as Fisher Ames, Parson Weems, Edward Everett, and Robert Treat Paine all indicate how extensively the flattering parallel had been noticed.

The most forceful assertion of the similarity was made by Lord Byron. The eighth canto of *Don Juan* opens by angrily attacking the unending bloody consequences of the archaic ideal of martial heroism. Byron then cites two exceptions to his generality:

> And such they are — and such they will be found:
> Not so Leonidas and Washington,
> Whose every battle-field is holy ground
> Which breathes of nations saved, not worlds undone.
> How sweetly on the ear such echoes sound!
> While the mere victor's may appal or stun

The servile and the vain – such names will be
A watchword till the Future shall be free.[85]

The presence of so earnest a statement in a poem rightly known for sophisticated scurrility and scorning of the epic is itself a revelation. Evidently, not all heroes were made merely for bards to sing. For Byron as for post-Revolutionary Americans, military glory achieved in the defense of popular liberty remained a valid possibility for heroic song.

An American poet who attempted heroic verse without conceiving of his hero as a combination of libertarian gentleman and unwilling general was likely to incur ethical difficulties. The first completed and published heroic poem dealing directly with the Revolutionary War is *The Columbiad* (1795), written anonymously by "A New-Jersey Farmer" who has been identified as Richard Snowden. Snowden's poem consists of forty-six pages of heroic couplets divided into thirteen cantos. It has an invocation, a nominal hero (Washington), a great action (the Revolution), and supernatural agents (Columbia and Liberty). Snowden includes catalogues and epic similes, and ends with a prophetic vision of America's rising glory. Because Washington embodies a wholly military model of heroism, however, the farmer-poet is reluctant to present him directly to the reader. Consequently, Snowden's role is to be only a "declamatory gazeteer" who doggedly follows the course of the Revolution from Lexington through Yorktown, devoting one short canto to distant celebration of each battle.

Snowden is troubled by the morality of his poetic undertaking. Although he hymns American military victories, and praises the courage of patriots, he frequently insists that war is unholy and detestable, that peace is lovely, and that the sweet retreat of the rural life is preferable to all worldly glory. He praises local militia for being "Like mighty Ajax in great Homer's song," yet warns his reader in a footnote that "real happiness is to be found in the cottage of the farmer."[86] Epic conventions impel him toward a martial definition of heroism that he cannot accept. Because Snowden is unable to conceive an epic hero suitable to a land of Christian farmers, his poem can have no vivid central figure to sustain it.

V. A HERO FOR AN AGE

During the 1790s the most influential of American critics, Joseph Dennie, quoted Light Horse Harry Lee's phrases in calling for "some future Homer to erect *monumentum aere perennius* to the memory of him whom our fathers have proclaimed 'first in war, first in peace, and first in the hearts of his country.' "[87] Walter Marshall McGill was eventually to write the verse epic Dennie had in mind, but the first full portrayal of Washington in epic clothing was penned by a writer Dennie would have

scorned even to review. Mason Locke Weems, unlike McGill, had no
Homeric pretensions, but he did have a bookseller's eye for popular responses. Shortly before Washington's death in 1799, Weems set about
creating the first edition of *The Life of Washington,* a work that went
through eighty-four printings between 1800 and 1829, and remains one
of the essential pieces of American hagiography.[88] As Jay Fliegelman has
shown, Weems's Washington is a figure claimable by Ancients and Moderns, by prodigal sons whose disobedience secures their fathers' affection, as well as by fathers who wish to free their sons from bondage.[89]
Weems's Washington is also, however, a nearly exact embodiment of
the new nation's redefinition of the epic hero. Weems's biography shows
us, in crude and comic outline, the literary problems of rendering America's heroic self-image. Whenever Weems sets out to humanize Washington as a Christian farmer, he tells colloquial anecdotes that reduce Washington to a Man of Sentiment. But whenever he attempts to portray
Washington as a martial hero, his polysyllabic straining after grandeur
ends in bombast. Different prose styles create two Washingtons who
never cohere.

Weems's first chapter protests that the popular image of Washington
as a martial hero, demigod, and unequalled orator is essentially false. The
private virtues of "piety and patriotism," "industry and honour" (5),
were Washington's exemplary heroic qualities. Of the sixteen chapters
in Weems's biography, however, only the first four and the last three are
concerned with the private virtues of the inner man. The middle nine
chapters comprise a prose narrative of American achievements during
the wars of 1756 and 1776. Many of these pages memorialize battlefield
heroics at which Washington was not present. Whenever Washington
does reemerge at the foreground of the narrative, the virtues Weems
attributes to him are those of a warrior, a demigod, and an orator.

Either Weems believed that the Revolutionary War truly deserved
martial glorification or he shrewdly recognized that most of his readers
really preferred the slaughtering of redcoats to eulogizing virtue. At the
beginning of the second chapter, Weems assures his readers that "the
furniture of this vast continent, where the Almighty has reared his cloud-
capt mountains, and spread his sea-like lakes and poured his mighty rivers, and hurled down his thundering cataracts in a style of the *sublime,*
[is] so far superior to any thing of the kind in other continents, that we
may fairly conclude that great men and great deeds are designed for
America" (6). The mantle of heroism descends upon young George when
he throws a stone across the Rappahannock and outstrips fellow Virgin-
ians in games and contests. On the battlefield, Weems's Washington drives
a chariot, not a carriage; he leads Myrmidons and directs legions. Weems
purports to condemn war, yet he relishes his battle sequences, precedes

them by councils of chieftains, and leaves his battlefields to birds of prey. Like Aeneas, Washington knows that his cultural mission is to create a new state under divine aegis. For Weems, however, assertions of providential will are not enough; he must have modern celestial machinery. Death appears on the field amid Braddock's troops: "LIBERTY, heaven-born Goddess" (69) appears at Lexington; Brittania is seen weeping on the cliffs of Dover after Burgoyne's defeat; and the Genius of Columbia intervenes to thwart André.

Completing the military narrative leading to the triumph of Yorktown places great strain upon Weems's conception of heroic character. Weems claims that Washington exemplifies "that TRUE HEROIC VALOUR which combats malignant passions – conquers unreasonable *self* – rejects the hell of *hatred,* and invites the heaven of *love* into our own bosoms" (191). Elsewhere, however, Weems exalts Washington by likening him to Jupiter Conservator, Mars, Achilles, Hercules, and Alexander – among others, and in that order. To substantiate Washington's Christian heroism, Weems portrays his hero weeping over the enemy dead, forgiving Hessian mercenaries, and humanely sparing the British at Yorktown. The Washington who prepares for combat, however, is an altogether different figure. In an epic simile of charmingly absurd grandiloquence, Washington is seen inspiring his troops before the battle of Trenton:

> As the big lion of Zara, calling his brindled sons to battle against the mighty rhinoceros, if he mark their falling manes and crouching to his side, instantly puts on all his terrors – his eyes roll in blood – he shakes the forest with his deepening roar, till, kindled by their father's fire, the maddening cubs swell with answering rage, and spring undaunted on the Monster. Thus stately and terrible rode COLUMBIA'S FIRST AND GREATEST SON, along the front of his halted troops. (84)

Washington's ferocity may be an act, but Weems is quite content to impress his readers with Washington's leonine qualities. The demand of Kamesian epic convention (a simile must magnify its referent) conflicts with the Christian piety Weems claims to affirm.

After Weems has followed General Washington through the Peace of Paris, the ideal of heroic behavior shifts again. Weems praises Washington for qualities shared by no epic warrior: renunciation of power, love of plain living, and distrust of ceremony:

> To establish in his country the golden reign of liberty was his grand wish. In the accomplishment of this he seeks his happiness. He abhors war; but, if war be necessary, to this end he bravely encounters it. His ruling passion must be obeyed. He beats his ploughshare into a sword, and exchanges the peace and pleasures of his farm for the din and dangers of the camp. Having won the great prize for which he contended,

> he returns to his plough. . . . The *useful citizen* is the high character he
> wishes to act – his sword turned into a ploughshare is his favorite in-
> strument, and his beloved farm his stage. (128)

For two generations of readers, Weems thus defined the ruling passion
of the American hero as a Christian devotion to liberty so disinterested
that it allowed for war as a temporary means toward a free republic.
Assuming that his nation would have little future need for warriors, Weems
then recasts his exemplary hero as the "useful citizen," a phrase very like
Everett's "citizen hero."

Weems's heroic model – warrior, farmer, statesman, Christian, libertarian, reverential son, and sonless father – is a monster of virtue who
seems as incredible to us as he seemed credible to Weems's eager buyers.
Yet we cannot conclude that Weems was a literary *naif*, nor that his ov-
erwriting reflected intended mockery of epic. Amid all the exaltation of
Revolutionary heroes, Weems shrewdly perceived that many Americans
were eager to confuse the epic hero with the perfect man. Although Herculean valor and useful citizenship made strange bedfellows, Weems never
hesitated to ascribe them to one hero, because his readers wished to believe that the mélange had been historical. Knowing that conventions of
epic poetry were the accepted garb for heroism, Weems simply transferred them to prose, without worrying whether they were suited to the
private virtues of the Christian farmer. When those conventions led him
to glorify conquest, Weems cheerfully packed in as much sublime bloodshed as he could muster, sensing that his audience would appreciate it.

As the nineteenth century began, there seemed to be no way of cap-
turing the stature of Washington without the analogies of heroic poetry.
When John Blair Linn sought a model for his own prose elegy for Washington, he clearly believed that Weems's way might make for a popular
sermon, but not sublime prose. Having asserted in his essay "The Early
Poetry of Greece" (1796) that Homer had sung "the simplicity, virtue
and magnanimity of the heroic age" in verse of a "perfection which has
never been surpassed,"[90] Linn despaired of imitating Homer himself. Instead, he opted for a probably workable modern idiom and published
The Death of Washington: A Poem in Imitation of the Manner of Ossian (1800).
Fingal/Washington rescues Braddock's troops, triumphs at Princeton and
Yorktown, establishes a peaceable kingdom, and then passes on, "the
last of his race," newly renamed "Chief of Vernon" because "Thine arm
was like a falling tower. Thy deeds were mighty among the deeds of
heroes."[91] It does not matter that Linn could spin out the terse mono-
syllables of melancholic pseudoprimitivism at least as well as Macpherson. To situate dying bards, bossy shields, and windy mead halls along
the Potomac resulted in anachronisms so painful that the sad close of
Washington's death can arouse only relieved laughter. Despite Parson

Weems's sermonizing (or perhaps because of it), his joyful way of throwing epic clothing over Washington proved far more acceptable to his contemporaries.

Whether Weems was aware of the inconsistent virtues of his hero, whether he believed in his creation, or whether he was only exploiting it, is not ultimately of much importance.[92] The saleability of the *Life of Washington* reveals an eager popular appetite for didactic works that could cast a republican, soldier–farmer gentleman into quasi–epic mold. We regard the verse epics of the early Republic as the dinosaurs of their day, but in substance, and even in mode, they were attempts to meet the most current of expectations.

2

FREEDOM'S HEROES

The epic poem has always been, as Milton knew, "of highest hope and hardest attempting,"[1] but creating the American epic posed problems of adaptation that were beyond promise of solution. As long as the word "epic" connoted "long, heroic narrative poem," new wine would almost surely be poured into old skins. Convinced that the future of a Christian agrarian republic was the higher argument, American poets were drawn toward static prophecies of utopia, while basing their slim narratives upon epic models that had exalted martial heroism. The Rights of Man were somehow to be affirmed through such essentially elitist conventions as the councils and single combats of chieftains. Neither of the approved meters was appropriate. The closed couplet, admirably suited to antithesis and irony, was now to serve as the medium for extended panegyric. The sublimity of Miltonic blank verse was to be applied to wholly human and earthly actions without incongruity or bombast. Although epic tradition encouraged the exalting of individuals, American readers were to accept the premise that the hero is all of us, in potential if not in present fact.

While recognizing the failings of American epic poems, it is now time to look beneath them, to attend more closely to the vision of New World culture these poems contain, and to consider carefully the process by which these poems were brought to their completion. Ridiculing without reading the poems of Dwight, Barlow, and "Pop" Emmons has long been a convention in itself, a way of disguising a nationalist literary inferiority complex by disassociating ourselves (as presumably perceptive modernists) from all those failed national poems. It has been forgotten that many of the same problems and literary failings afflicted British epic poems of the same era. Moreover, a hurry to display aesthetic condescension has blinded us to the merits that poetry of cultural persuasion can sometimes possess. The best and most important of these poems, Barlow's *The Columbiad,* has received the severest drubbing. Our sense

of embarrassed nationality has also blinded us to a crucial distinction between two generations of epic poets. Dwight and Barlow were attempting to write two opposite kinds of New World epics, but neither was a chauvinist waving a literary flag for thirteen United States. Both were international republicans who saw the American nation as the beginning of a new era. Only after 1815 did a narrower nationalism arise in which heroic virtue was confined within the ever-expanding borders of the Republic.

I. TYPOLOGY AND EPIC

Ever since William Cowper ridiculed *The Conquest of Canaan* for portraying the American Revolution by means of a biblical narrative,[2] criticism of Dwight's poem has centered upon the crucial question of the author's intent. Three perceptive readers have disagreed in their conclusions. Leon Howard claimed that, by modernizing barbaric manners, Dwight almost unknowingly turned Joshua into "so perfect a representation of the American ideal hero that later readers have persisted in confusing him with George Washington."[3] Howard thus accepts Dwight's peeved disclaimer: "I presume the Reviewers have thot [*sic*] the writer destitute of every Critical idea, to have imagined the *Conquest* of a country a proper event, under which to allegorize the *defence* of another country."[4] Kenneth Silverman has contended that "Dwight probably did intend writing a patriotic allegory" and cites passages that establish parallels between Washington and Joshua, the Israelites and the Americans, the Canaanites and the British.[5] Lawrence Buell has recently contended "to the extent that the poem does reflect current events, they take on meaning through their resemblance to their scriptural antecedents, rather than vice versa."[6] The issue of Dwight's mediation between past and present will not be clarified, however, until more consideration is paid to the calendar by which the poem evolved. Three questions arise that must precede determination of possible allegory. First, why did Dwight initially choose the conquest of Canaan as the subject for his epic? Second, why should the grandson of Jonathan Edwards have written a sustained allegory, after generations of New Englanders had become accustomed to a typological interpretation of Old Testament history? Third, how did the onset of the Revolution alter the way in which Dwight perceived his poem?

According to Dwight's own words, which there is neither evidence nor reason to doubt, "the poem was begun, in the year 1771, & written out, several times, before the year 1775. . . . All the essential parts were finished, before the war began & the poem advertised for the press, during the first year of the war."[7] Is it likely that a nineteen-year-old tutor at Yale College, who knew little about Virginia, would concoct an elab-

orate allegory on the Revolutionary War, with George Washington as its disguised hero, five years before the war began? While revising the poem between 1776 and its publication in 1785, Dwight was surely struck, as he said, by "a considerable resemblance between the case of the Israelites, & that of the Americans."[8] Furthermore, the text proves that, during the war, Dwight made changes and additions to the poem that explore this resemblance. A Revolutionary allegory, however, could have formed no part of Dwight's original intent in 1771, and has very little place in his published poem. Dwight had read Voltaire, Kames, and Blair, all of whom had contended that allegory and epic were oil and water. He surely knew Addison's famous censure of Milton for intruding the figures of Sin and Death in *Paradise Lost*.

The only guide to Dwight's original purpose is "A Dissertation on the History, Eloquence and Poetry of the Bible," published one year after Dwight began work on his epic. There Dwight contends that the Bible contains poetry more sublime than Homer, more correct than Virgil, and more moral than either of them. Old Testament prophets could animate nature while showing how divine power acts in history without visible hand. Biblical history remains superior to classical epic because biblical narratives are revelations of God's timeless will. Acknowledging that the sixth *Aeneid* is great prophetic poetry, Dwight nonetheless insists that it is full of "wild conjectures" and now irrelevant comments on Rome and her empire. Because the Bible offers models of heroic ethics and prophecies of eternity that we Moderns share, "every one of us is infinitely more interested in the subject, than the Romans were in that of Virgil."[9] As he began his epic, Dwight was evidently convinced that only a subject from the biblical past afforded an action sufficiently revelatory and sublime for a New World epic. If he believed that no event worthy of the epic had transpired in the West, he kept his doubts to himself.

These modest challenges to epic theory are carried through in the completed poem. Joshua's conquest of the Canaanite tribes allows Dwight to describe sublime providential acts with a free hand. Apart from one dimly described angel, Dwight restricts his machinery to the storms, meteors, and other secondary causes by which Jehovah shows that building the promised land in Canaan fulfills the divine plan. Near the end of the poem, Joshua is led atop a high hill and granted a six-hundred-line prophecy of the Millennium, the Conflagration, the Last Judgment, and the Consummation of all things, as well as a final view of heaven. The Seraph shows Joshua that in the New World "Empire's last and brightest throne shall rise; / And Peace, and Right, and Freedom greet the skies."[10] The Seraph even predicts that "Law," "union'd Choice," and "Commerce" will make America into "new Canaan's promis'd shores" from

which all lands will be regenerated and the Millennium begin. But the "New Canaan" nonetheless is a clearly separable concern that occupies one hundred lines in the last book of a very long poem about the Old Canaan.

While selecting his subject, Dwight surely attended closely to the dictates of Lord Kames, who had insisted that a worthy epic poem must describe past heroic actions in an elevated style. In 1771 Dwight would have been unlikely even to consider an American subject, especially when he read Kames's warning, "After Voltaire, no writer, it is probable, will think of erecting an epic poem upon a recent event in the history of his own country." The epic poet, according to Kames, should "avoid the familiarity of persons and events nearly connected to us," and select a subject distant in time and place, so as to ensure "dignity and elevation."[11]

Having chosen a biblical subject not exhausted by Milton, but readily adaptable to the generic prescriptions of contemporary critical authority, Dwight set out to complete an epic poem, with the Book of *Joshua* as his source, and the examples of Homer, Virgil, and Milton as his predecessors. Beginning in medias res and at the nadir of his hero's fortunes, Dwight decided to versify chapters 7–11 of *Joshua,* which recount Joshua's conquest of Ai and defense of the Gibeonites. Those particular chapters consist of a sparse narrative of Joshua's brutalities, together with descriptions of his clever political maneuvers and catalogues of the conquered. Dwight could have known little about Israel or about hand-to-hand fighting in heroic times, yet he had set himself the task of turning four short chapters of biblical narrative into at least ten 600-line books of closed couplets.

The difficulties of such an undertaking, which might have defeated any poet, were entirely too much for Dwight, who lacked the ability to transform through imitation. From Milton came the subject and the diction, Pandemoniumlike councils, prelapsarian lovers named Irad and Selima, and the long concluding prophecy. From Dryden's *Aeneid* came Joshua's half-reluctant obedience to the divine command of conquest for the benefit of future generations. From Pope's *Iliad* came Dwight's many battle scenes, though Dwight overlooked Pope's tribute to the variety of Homer's descriptions of warfare. Dwight's warriors, provided with forever-glowing eyes, refulgent helms, crested plumes, and moonlike shields, speed their javelins, flash their falchions (an alliterative phrase Pope had used sparingly) and hurl themselves upon the enemy. The windy plains Dwight recreates before the wall of Ai and Gibeon are covered by nightfall with "corses innumerable" in a "purple flood" which is often ankle deep. Literary immaturity is not, however, the only cause of such borrowing. For an American to have so completely recast a biblical nar-

rative through the lenses of the three great epic poets shows an absolute trust that Western civilization is ultimately all one, and all available to its youngest inheritor.

Transforming admired passages of blank verse into closed couplets proved especially troublesome. Compare Milton's account of God's creation of the beasts to Dwight's:

> The Cattle in the Fields and Meadows green:
> Those rare and solitary, these in flocks
> Pasturing at once, and in broad Herds upsprung.
> The grassy Clods now Calv'd, now half appear'd
> The Tawny Lion, pawing to get free
> His hinder parts, then springs as broke from Bonds,
> And Rampant shakes his Brinded mane.[12]

> He spoke; and, wondering, from disparted plains
> In throngs unnumber'd rose the bestial trains:
> Gay steeds exulting pranc'd the vernal field;
> The lion glar'd, and mid the gazing throng
> Shook his rough mane, and grimly stalk'd along.[13]

Milton shaped his lines to emphasize the miracle of God's creating beasts out of the earth. Three metrically even lines describing a static pastoral life lead to the striking image of clods turning into calves, and finally to highly visual lines that rhythmically convey a struggle to be free. Metrical accents fall on active verbs ("upsprung, pawing, springs, shakes"), while alliteration and assonance draw the reader toward the wonder of clods calving. Milton's showing that God created the lion free in motion illustrates his belief that God created man free in will.

Dwight follows the order of Milton's images, but his serviceable couplets have no purpose other than as a catalogue. We are reminded of the miracle of animation only by the tortuous word "disparted," not by images that convey the transforming of earth to beast. Dwight is content simply to list the different attributes of animals: harmless flocks, gay steeds, and grim lions. Every noun has its adjective. Milton's words are heightened in a reach for even greater sublimity: "Broad herds" become "flocks unnumber'd," and "Meadows green" a "vernal field"; to make Nature continually purposive, the Tawny Lion now must glare and stalk.

A long poem in heroic couplets poses a problem of metrical monotony that no poet can wholly solve. The last verse paragraph of *The Conquest of Canaan,* containing 24 lines and 120 poetic feet, consists of 107 iambs, only 13 spondees or trochees, no anapests or dactylls, only 10 caesuras, and only 1 run-on line. In every one of the 24 verses, the last three feet are iambs. Closed couplets of such regularity, continued for some 9,000 lines, using a limited range of end rhymes, and filled with an equally limited vocabulary of sublime archaisms, only congeal one's feel-

ing and bewilder one's mind. Dwight had mastered the pattern, but forgot Pope's saving exceptions:

> Chariots on Chariots rowl; the Clashing Spokes
> Shock; while the madding Steeds break short their Yokes.
>
> Loud sounds the Axe, redoubling Strokes on Strokes.
> On all sides round the Forest hurles her Oaks
> Headlong. Deep-echoing groan the Thickets brown;
> Then rustling, crackling, crashing, thunder down.[14]

Dwight's imitation of Pope's medium cannot rise to such effects. By opting for harmony, Dwight achieved only a numbing uniformity.

The importance of Dwight's poem rests upon his attempt to make his heroic narrative both biblical and contemporary in its morality. Dwight's preface defends his epic on the grounds that "the poem is uniformly friendly to delicacy, and virtue" (18). The virtues portrayed, however dear to the eighteenth century, are also supposedly universal: "In the best characters, [the poet] has endeavored to represent such manners, as are removed from the peculiarities of any age: elevated without design, refined without ceremony, elegant without fashion, and agreeable, because they are ornamented with sincerity, dignity, and religion" (17).

The book of *Joshua* poses no small obstacles to a poet who would commend elevation, refinement, elegance, religion, and sincerity. The biblical Joshua had been an extremely able general bent upon fulfilling Jehovah's command that the Israelites conquer Canaan. After a rebellious follower named Achan stole Israelite plunder, Joshua burned and stoned Achan's family. The biblical Joshua enticed the men of Ai beyond their city walls, slaughtered them, took the city's spoil, murdered all the inhabitants, hung the king, and displayed the king's body at the city's gates. Certain repeated phrases of the biblical narrative remain in the reader's mind: "left none remaining"; "utterly destroyed all that breathed, as the Lord God of Israel commanded"; "Be strong and of good courage."

If Dwight were to adhere to the biblical account, he would write an epic that was antiquarian in content and barbaric in morality. If he were to recast Joshua and the Israelites as men of modern virtue, he would falsify the Old Testament and abandon his belief that biblical subjects were preferable because they were true. Dwight chose to see new decency in old butchery, to justify needed changes in his preface, but to write his verses assuming that his modernization had been historical truth. Instead of burning kings, Dwight's Joshua forgives those who betray him. He consoles sick troops, cares for orphaned war victims, and weeps over slain soldiers. A man of reason who detests war, Joshua emerges as a fatherly defender of human rights:

> Patient, serene, as ills and injuries tried,
> Meek without meanness, noble without pride,

Frank yet impovious [*sic*], manly yet refin'd,
As the sun watchful, and as angels kind,
His Maker first, his conscience next he fear'd,
All rights kept sacred, and all laws rever'd. (154)

Whenever the biblical Israelites had not exemplified the virtue of refinement, Dwight tacitly rewrote scripture. In the Bible, Achan had been
apprehended, sentenced, and stoned by Joshua himself; in *The Conquest
of Canaan,* a contrite Achan is reluctantly sentenced to a merciful death
by Joshua, whose "feeling mind / To crimes was gentle and to misery
kind" (107).

Dwight surely could have found a biblical subject equally heroic but
more adaptable to modern virtues. He probably chose the conquest of
Canaan because it could readily serve as a type prefiguring the new Israel.
Generations of New England Puritans had regarded their ancestral experiences through the paradigm of *Exodus,* seeing Anglican persecutors
as Egyptians, Puritans as the Chosen Israelites, the Atlantic Ocean as the
Red Sea, and America as Canaan. Dwight's first published poem,
"America," already circulating in manuscript when he started his epic,
had ended with a celebration of the Millennium to be realized on Western
soil. Although America itself might offer no subject grand enough for
an epic poem, the book of *Joshua* afforded an opportunity to kill three
birds with one epic tome. Dwight could draw from the well of the biblical sublime, heed Lord Kames's dictum about subjects from the past,
and simultaneously imply a new world analogy.

An implied analogy cannot sustain an allegory. The tenth book of
Dwight's poem, the only part that is often read, distinguishes between
the old Canaan, which has been Dwight's subject, and the new Canaan,
whose future is told in prophecy. America is to become "the last retreat
for poor, oppress'd mankind," a land whose "spacious plains," "rich
vallies," and "sky tall mountains" will provide the resources for a wealthy
empire (273). If Dwight had been writing an allegory, his prophecy would
have been both superfluous and confusing. The way Dwight reorders
history in the tenth book reveals that Canaan was intended to be no less
but no more than a type for America. After describing the destruction of
Jerusalem, Dwight shifts immediately to a related but separate event,
Columbus's discovery of America. Because in 1492 "a new Moses lifts
the daring Wing, / Through trackless seas, an unknown flight explores /
And hails a new Canaan's promis'd shores" (273–4), 1400 years of presumably inconsequential human history can simply be erased from the
divine record. The rise of the new Canaan grows from the conquest of
the old but is not synonymous with it; the New World's importance is
to initiate a Millennium that is universal and scriptural. The order of
Sacvan Bercovitch's claim, "Ultimately, Israel's conquest of Canaan is

confirmed and consecrated by what it tells of America's mission," should perhaps be reversed.[15]

After Dwight had completed at least two drafts of his poem, battle broke out in Lexington and Concord. Three months after subscription advertisements had appeared in newspapers, independence was declared and publication became financially impossible. By 1784 the British were defeated, American independence was recognized, but Dwight's poem was yet unpublished. Dwight must have felt – to put it kindly – discomfited. Doubtless he reassured himself that no epic could be written on a recent, familiar subject. He must also have believed, however, that the New World Millennium was soon to begin, and that an accident of history had prevented him from directly singing the great event that had made it possible.

Calls for an epic poem on the Revolution had already appeared in journals while *The Conquest of Canaan* was in press. When writing his preface, Dwight thus needed to assert his claim for primacy while defending his subject. He began by claiming, quite justly, "This poem is the first of the kind, which has been published in this country" (17). He closed by pleading that, whatever faults his poem might have, the poet had endeavored to please his countrymen and had "thrown in his mite, for the advancement of the refined arts, on this side of the Atlantic" (18). The defensive phrase "thrown in his mite" suggests that a first American epic should be its own justification. Although acknowledging some changes in the biblical account, Dwight confronted his now problematic choice of subject: "It may perhaps be thought the result of inattention or ignorance, that he chose a subject in which his countrymen had no national interest. But he remarked that the *Iliad* and *Eneid* were as agreeable to modern nations, as to the Greeks and Romans" (17–18). Unable to admit that his epic had missed out on the Revolution, Dwight defended his poem by yet another shaky argument. As the "Friend" essays show, Dwight knew that the epics of Homer and Virgil had gained resonance because they recounted ancestral heroics known to their peoples. He, by contrast, was an eighteenth-century American trying to revivify a Hebraic historical event that had transpired slightly more than 3,000 years before.

As the war for independence proceeded, Dwight must have recognized that the "elevated, . . . elegant and refined" traits of his Joshua were exactly suited to the emerging national model of heroism. His poem, however outdated in subject, was prescient in its Manners. But was there not also an increasingly clear similarity between the American political situation in the late 1770s and the Israelites' political situation in the first book of his epic manuscript? A great warrior and statesman, attempting to unify scattered tribes, and to found a millennial empire according to

divine command, faced widespread defection after initial defeats in battle. Perhaps the analogue between the millennial expectations of the old
and the new Canaan could now be extended to include direct parallels
between Joshua and Washington, Egypt and England, cowardly Israelites and American traitors.

The first book of *The Conquest of Canaan* bears clear evidence of revision to incorporate these parallels. The insidious Hanniel tries to persuade the Israelites to return to Egypt, land of ease, civilization, and protective monarchy, a place where "With die refulgent crimson vestures
glow, / And robes of kings succeed this garb of woe" (30). Hanniel then
urges the Israelites to pay tribute to the Egyptian king because those
"who share the blessing must the tax supply" (31). Joshua's forceful re-
futation of Hanniel is couched in terms pertinent to the American republic, but not to biblical Israel:

> Then o'er wide lands, as blissful Eden bright,
> Type of the skies, and seats of pure delight,
> Our sons, with prosperous course, shall stretch their sway,
> And claim an empire, spread from sea to sea:
> In one great whole th'harmonious tribes combine;
> Trace Justice's path, and choose their chiefs divine;
> On Freedom's base erect the heavenly plan;
> Teach law to reign, and save the rights of man. (42)

Joshua's soldiers, unlike their biblical predecessors, have no interest in
plunder or finery; such lines as "Plain, generous manners vigorous limbs
confess, / And vigorous minds to freedom ardent press" (41) connect
gentlemanly simplicity with libertarian politics.

After book one, Dwight virtually ceased making pointed comparisons
to republican triumph in America. Either he tired of revision or he recognized that so forced a political analogue could not be sustained. Israel
was not New Jersey, Joshua was no republican, and Jabin was not an
imperial monarch depriving Jewish colonials of their constitutional rights.
Instead of following his analogy through, Dwight reshaped Joshua as a
republican in book one, left him an eighteenth-century gentleman thereafter, dropped explicit American allegory, and then dedicated his poem
"To his Excellency, George Washington Esquire, Commander in chief
of the American Armies, the Saviour of his Country, the Supporter of
Freedom, and the Benefactor of Mankind" (15).

Despite all of Dwight's care to modernize manners and point up republican parallels, only British reviewers recognized his occasional analogies. Because American readers expected Washington himself to be the
hero of any American epic, they condemned Dwight's poem as antiquarianism whenever they bothered to read it. Trying to defend Dwight's
effort three years after publication, Noah Webster had to admit that

Americans did not "take any uncommon interest in the poem."[16] Joseph Dennie regretted that Dwight's "powers have been lavished on a subject which, no longer possessing general interest, is not likely to attract general attention, or promote the welfare of mankind."[17] A reviewer for the *Analectic Magazine,* writing in 1817, ascribed Dwight's failure entirely to his not "selecting a subject for an epic connected with the history of his own country."[18] Samuel Knapp ignored Dwight's purpose when he charged that the poet, "although constituted for epick grandeur," had been misled by his piety into an antiquarian bypath: "There was no novelty in the vengeance of heaven pouring its chastisements upon a wicked nation."[19] Echoing the growing nationalistic commonplace that Dwight had been "by no means happy in the choice of his fable," Bryant noted that "the work would not sell, and loads of copies yet cumber the shelves of our booksellers."[20]

The least sparing of Dwight's critics was his predecessor as President of Yale, Ezra Stiles. In 1781, when Dwight had been at work on his epic for ten years, Stiles wrote a five-leaf entry on Dwight in his diary, then ripped it out, leaving for posterity only the slur that Dwight intended his writing "to make his fortune, by procuring some office." Stiles then noted "it is natural to suppose such ideas play in his mind respecting his own Work of Genius as probably surpassing Homer and Milton." When Dwight's Work of Genius was finally published, Stiles disposed of it with the devasting comment "I bo't Mr. Dwight's Conquest of Canaan just printed 8/. It has been in writing from 1776 to 1785. Nonum prematur in Annum."[21] Stiles's kindest and last word on the poem is a footnote he added to John Trumbull's ranking of epic poets. Noting that Trumbull had rated Dwight ninth, below Ossian and Spencer but above Lucan, Ercilla, and Statius, Stiles commented "A proper Correction might fix it here or perhaps raise it. Its present faults will endanger its sinking at least two Deg. lower."[22]

When Dwight had written his poem, he had modernized heroic Manners but not epic form. Proposition, invocation, similes, councils, single combat, prophecies, Miltonic diction, and heroic couplets had all been conspicuously present. By the late 1780s, however, Dwight needed to believe that his epic had not been well received because it had broken rules precious to narrow-minded readers. His poem "The Critics" (1785) ridicules reviewers who would judge today's greyhound by the merits of yesterday's cur. The fourth of Dwight's essays, titled "The Friend" (1789), criticizes neo-Aristotelians who erect a single specimen into a class and demand that all modern epics be exactly like *The Iliad.*

There is no evidence that anyone ever criticized *The Conquest of Canaan* for disobedience to Aristotle, Le Bossu, or Kames. The reason for Dwight's curious self-defense must be sought in Dwight's essay itself:

> In our own happy state of society, disjoined from the customs and systems of Europe, commencing a new system of science and politics, it is to be ardently hoped, that so much independence of mind will be assumed by us, as to induce us to shake off these rusty shackles, examine things on the plan of nature and evidence, and laugh at the grey-bearded decisions of doting authority.[23]

To his credit, Dwight now senses the need for a new epic form even though he has no power to describe it. His need to look back upon his poem as an American experiment damned for its novelty is an understandable rationalization. Knowing that his completed epic was dead on his hands, and that he could not make it new, Dwight turned from reifying America's cultural maturity to ministering the Word and to building Yale College. As his epigraph and epitaph for *The Conquest of Canaan,* he slightly altered a couplet from the "Essay on Criticism":

> Fired at first with that the Muse imparts
> In fearless youth we tempt the height of Arts.[24]

By dropping the plural from Pope's phrase "heights of Arts," Dwight admitted, albeit tacitly, that his particular rashness had been a matter of the literary epic.

One of the few contemporaries who seems to have read Dwight's entire poem was Philip Freneau. Expecting that the great American epic would concern the Revolution directly, Freneau was not prepared to look kindly on Dwight's kind of effort. In 1790 he wrote a satirical essay "On Epic Poetry" that resembles Pope's "A Receipt to Make an Epic Poem" and takes *The Conquest of Canaan* as its model and victim. Freneau proposes a few easy rules for attaining "the very pinnacle of poetical fame" without having to tax the brain or observe nature. His first rule is to purchase Pope's *Iliad* and *Odyssey,* Dryden's *Aeneid,* and any epic of Blackmore, and "Read these over night and day (and do not forget to put them under your pillow at night) till you have got the complete sing-song-Heroic in your head." Second, the epic bard must choose a Fable, preferably from his school-satchel, or, if his satchel is empty, from "ancient Jewish history." The Old Testament is a better treasure-trove of subjects than the New because "there can be no true Epic poem without plenty of *butchering* work." Third, "No epic poem can be a good one wherein the dreams and nonsense of antiquity have not a preference given to them over modern rationality." Therefore, an epic bard had best recreate the Ptolemaic universe (here Dwight had usually followed Milton) and must represent God as "taking one side in the miserable quarrels and savage contentions of this earth."[25]

Freneau refused to grant Dwight's poem a merciful oblivion. In the 1795 edition of "The Rising Empire," Freneau claimed to have unearthed the true rising glory of that *Terra Vulpina* known as Connecticut:

Bards of huge fame in every hamlet rise,
Each (in idea) of Virgilian size:
Even beardless lads a rhyming knack display –
Iliads begun, and finished in a day!
Rhymes, that of old on Blackmore's wheel were spun,
Come rattling down on Greenfield's reverend son;
Madly presumed time's vortex to defy!
Things born to live an hour – then squeak and die.[26]

Freneau's contempt for Dwight may well have been based as much upon
a personal literary regret as upon aesthetic discrimination, political enmity, or envy of Dwight's comparative eminence. Freneau's longstanding support for an American Homer and for a heroic poem on "the real
revolution" had not led him to attempt the epic himself. Even if Freneau
harbored such a desire, the exigencies of his later life left him no time.
Only three years after *The Conquest of Canaan* had appeared, Freneau's
persona in a series of familiar letters, Robert Slender, had bluntly advised
would-be American authors "I mean to say, in plain language, that you
would make something by weaving garters or mending old sails, when
an Epic poem would be your utter destruction."[27]

    If Freneau had detected Dwight's attempt to provide a modern ana-
logue for ancient history, he chose to ignore it. Post-Revolutionary
Americans of Jeffersonian allegiance were likely to perceive history as a
linear progression toward 1776 rather than, in Puritan fashion, as a series
of typological parallels. The ridicule Freneau heaped on Dwight nonetheless infers, by inversion, a "receipt" for a worthy modern epic. It
would be a poem on contemporary history, without butchery, Gods,
machinery, miracles, or near worship of Washington. Most important,
it would avoid the sense of meaningless flux, of common lives endured
in vain, that Freneau somehow detected in *The Conquest of Canaan*. Freneau thought he had discovered such an epic in a now lost *Columbiad,* a
work "where fable cannot usurp the place of historical fact, and where,
from the recency of events, the license of imagination must necessarily
be controuled [*sic*], in order to effect, what is wished, A REPUBLICAN
POEM, on the events of the American Revolution."[28] When in 1807 Joel
Barlow published his own *Columbiad,* with more publicity and at greater
expense than any American literary work of its era, Freneau's demand
was answered.

II. A REPUBLICAN EPIC: NO WAR, NO NATION?

    By the time Barlow began his first ambitious poem, he was ready
to brave a subject both contemporary and international. While at Yale,
Barlow had been timidly urged by his tutor, Joseph Buckminster, to
write a biblical epic on Joseph, on Cain and Abel, or perhaps on Daniel.[29]

In the late 1770s Barlow wrote sixty couplets of an epic on the conquest of Babylon by Cyrus the Great[30] – a subject whose similarity to the conquest of Canaan is revealing. By 1779, however, Barlow had decided that the deeds of Columbus were the proper subject for New World epic, and had drawn up a plan for a heroic narrative based upon the voyages of discovery. After soliciting and receiving Timothy Dwight's approval for this revised plan, Barlow was invited to serve as an "usher" in Dwight's school in Northampton.[31] For reasons we can only surmise, Barlow then changed the genre and structure of his poem. Rather than an epic narrative describing Columbus's deeds, Barlow committed himself to a prophetic poem in which an angel would recount to Columbus the glorious consequences of the western discoveries. Adhering closely to this revised plan, Barlow wrote *The Vision of Columbus* between 1779 and 1787; he was intending, in his words, a poem "rather of the philosophic than epic kind."[32]

Barlow's retraction probably suited both poets. Although Dwight had small desire to yield epic laurels to his protegé, Barlow was reaching the conclusion that Columbus's four voyages were too remote and too closed to be the subject for a modern heroic poem. By conceiving *The Vision of Columbus* as a philosophic poem, however, Barlow was still deferring to accepted generic categories. Twenty years later, after Barlow's commitment to the French Revolution, the failure of Dwight's epic, and the mutual cooling of their friendship, Barlow's first and highest literary hope was rekindled in more daring ways. Returning to America in 1804, Barlow was unwilling to allow his major poetic effort to remain a philosophic poem that had been dedicated to Louis XVI, and had attributed greatness of spirit to God's grace rather than human reason. The subject Dwight had believed to be the essence of epic no longer seemed to Barlow to be heroic at all:

> The Jews, when led by Moses out of Egypt, were not only uncivilized, but, having just risen to independence from a state of servitude, they united the manners of servants and savages, and their national character was a compound of servility, ignorance, filthiness and cruelty.[33]

The Vision of Columbus, Barlow now believed, had always been exactly the kind of poem that pointed toward a wholly new heroic code for the epic. Appropriate revisions would of course be needed, but contemporaries needed to know that spiritual freedom and republican politics were far more than "philosophy"; they were the substance and source of modern heroism.

To conceive of a visionary political epic, whether such a poem is viable or not, requires imagination and daring. Barlow had both traits, but his ambitions were surely encouraged, more than has been realized, by the advice and writings of William Hayley, sometime friend of both

Cowper and Blake, and biographer of Milton. In 1791 Barlow sought out Hayley in England to inquire about revising *The Vision of Columbus*. Hayley complimented Barlow's poetic promise and his republicanism, urged Barlow to compress *The Vision of Columbus,* and sent Barlow a set of his own works.[34] At the time when his revolutionary enthusiasm was most intense, Barlow was thus exposed to the substance, and probably the words, of Hayley's "An Essay On Epic Poetry" (1782), a five-epistle prospectus in heroic couplets calling for a contemporary epic poem. Attacking all rules as a chaining of originality, Hayley yearned for the Englishman who would "turn where Milton flames with Epic rage," release "Freedom of thought and Energy of mind," and write a poem showing how "Liberty arrayed in light serene" had blessed England's historical progress since the times of Alfred the Great. Such a poem, Hayley insisted, would show how the "Epic trumpet, in a modern hand," can "Still make the spirit glow, the heart expand."[35] Hayley's ideas were exactly suited to the task of revising a poem like *The Vision of Columbus* into an epic. To reveal that Liberty now resided in the New World rather than England would update Hayley's nationalistic assumptions about freedom's destiny. Hayley had nowhere provided Barlow specific guidelines toward compressing his poem into an epic, but the direction of Hayley's "Essay" was tonic indeed.

When Barlow finally began his revisions in 1804, his beliefs about heroism and epic poetry had become far more rebellious than anything Hayley had entertained. The last book of *The Columbiad* contains a thirty-line evocation of a prophet poet who will overturn the values of heroic literature. Any lasting contemporary epic must embrace "the aspiring genius of the age," the universal force of progress that subsumes legal equality, political freedom and human reason. Subjects once deemed essential to epic are henceforth to be totally discarded:

> For him no more, beneath their furious gods,
> Old ocean crimsons and Olympus nods,
> Uprooted mountains sweep the dark profound
> Or Titans groan beneath the rending ground.
> No more his clangor maddens up the mind,
> To crush, to conquer, and enslave mankind,
> To build on ruin'd realms the shrine of fame,
> And load his numbers with a tyrant's name.[36]

Such an attack on martial heroism far exceeds those of Brockden Brown, Freneau, Hayley, or Southey. No credible epic can include machinery; no moral epic can concern war; no beneficial epic can make a shrine of individual renown.

These demands are the logical end of a cogent argument Barlow has sustained against the unholy triad of religion, the heroic age, and epic

poetry. Fear of the unknown and of natural disasters ("blind credulity on all dark things" [722]) had led primitive peoples to create gods. Worship of such "furious" gods only rendered believers more servile and superstitious. Servility of spirit led both to institutional religion and to the feudal orders of society. Feudal societies, whether of Homeric Greece, Virgilian Rome, the Middle Ages, or Cortes's Spain, could only be perpetuated by promoting wars. Cloaked in rhetoric of glory and honor, wars allowed gold to be grabbed for gods, masters to brutalize serfs, and larger masters to dominate smaller masters. Associating heroism with war has remained the most seductive way of reinforcing tyranny and ignorance. Man's greatest medium for changing society's attitudes, epic poetry, has repeatedly betrayed its promise. Instead of serving mankind, the epic has reclothed old barbaric power in new aristocratic dress. Taken collectively, these ideas suggest that the immense historical panorama of *The Columbiad* has a dark underside complementing the political enlightenment proclaimed on its surface. When we look beneath Barlow's surety about republican political progress, his poem's rendering of Euro-American history repeatedly portrays feudalism, war, priestcraft, and epic poetry all working together to halt the inner growth of mankind.

Only a new epic, Barlow nonetheless believed, could exert the prestige and power needed to overturn the old epic values. A new epic could lead man toward ending war if it could demonstrate that nationalism as well as any theological basis for morality must both be discarded:

> Far nobler objects animate his tongue
> And give new energies to epic song;
> To moral charms he bids the world attend,
> Fraternal states their mutual ties extend,
> O'er cultured earth the rage of conquest cease,
> War sink in night and nature smile in peace.
> Soaring with science then he learns to string
> Her highest harp and brace her broadest wing,
> With her own force to fray [*sic*] the paths untrod,
> With her own glance to ken the total God. (763)

Nationalism, once a healthy force for breaking up medieval city-states, can now serve only to prolong war's ever more destructive power. International progress will never be advanced through promoting the religious creed of any one culture, even if that creed is true. As Walt Whitman and Hart Crane were to assert, theology must give way to experiment, and heroic poetry must assimilate science and technology. In Barlow's lines, empirical science becomes the epic poet's companion muse; only these two together might "ken the *total* God" (italics mine).

God is mentioned so infrequently in *The Columbiad* that the reader, growing accustomed to associating divinity with the force of progress,

experiences the word as an obtrusive personification. Barlow grants the biblical account of man's origins as little space as America's Puritan plantations. World history leads toward 1776, not because heroic yeomen threw off oppressive redcoats, but because the Revolution had revealed that republican politics was Man's new trinity. The American Constitution is the world's document:

> Based on its rock of right your empire lies,
> On walls of wisdom let the fabric rise;
> Preserve your principles, their force unfold,
> Let nations prove them and let kings behold.
> EQUALITY, your first firm-grounded stand;
> Then FREE ELECTION; then your FEDERAL BAND;
> This holy Triad should for ever shine
> The great compendium of all rights divine. (699)

Dwight's and Barlow's epics both culminate in a vision of a worldwide Millennium begun in America, but Barlow's is wholly secular, more appropriate to the twentieth century than to the eighteenth. International commerce, free trade, and technology are mankind's best hope for stopping war. If America can rid herself of slavery, and if the New World's "holy Triad" is accepted by other peoples, the world's nation-states will delegate their authority to an international league that alone should possess peacekeeping forces. Technological progress, fortunately, is sure to continue even though popular attitudes will lag behind them. The reception of Barlow's own poem proved his surmise correct. Smarty reviewers for *Port Folio* and the *Boston Review* mocked Barlow for fantasizing such absurdities as the Suez canal, the Panama canal, flying machines, underwater ships, desert irrigation, and a scientifically devised universal language. (As the twentieth century ends, we might hope that the rest of Barlow's international vision can be realized before we collectively perish without it.)

Although the "Preface" contends that *"The Columbiad* is a patriotic poem; the subject is national and historical" (375), Barlow challenges Americans who define patriotism in terms of political borders. As geographical determinists customarily did, Barlow describes the land before its history, but his land is neither Plymouth's rocky shore nor Virginia's warming strand. Using a perspective best described as a pan-American pan shot, Barlow first places his reader at the Isthmus of Panama, then draws the reader ever upward until all of North and South America are seen as one land mass ordained by Nature to be one western hemisphere, one New World (424–30). The first crucial event in America's history is Cortes's terrifying and bestial obliteration of Aztec culture. Barlow's third book, telling of the combat between two fictive Inca chieftains named Rocha and Zamor, is intended neither as a diversion nor an extractable

"episode." Manco Capac, legendary founder of Inca civilization, allows himself to be perceived as a sun god in order to build a humane community. The mountain chieftain Zamor's jealousy of Capac's achievement leads him to foment tribal rage for war against Capac's son Rocha. To Barlow, Manco Capac represents the highest possibility of a heroic age culture. By picturing Zamor's and Rocha's oblations, sacrifices, and single combat, Barlow can include an epic combat from the heroic age, yet simultaneously show how, after Pizarro's conquest, heroic age culture must be superseded by a new heroism far excelling Pizarro's.

By retaining the consequences of Columbus's discovery as his epic subject, Barlow largely avoided the antiquarian fakery and strained parallelism all too apparent in *The Conquest of Canaan.* His subject, he believed, would be cherished by forward-thinking republicans everywhere, and would allow him to use his wide historical knowledge and his proven gifts for a poetry of ideas. Most important, he had redefined the aims of the epic both to make them serve a secular literary ministry, and to provoke new thinking about the genre.[37] Nonetheless, the immediate problem of refashioning the lines of an old poem remained. How could the consequences of discovery be effectively reworked into a recognizably epic poem? For Barlow, heroism resided in the force of republican progress, not in any single man. But he still sensed that his epic needed a "fable," one action that could sustain narrative interest while allowing him to survey three hundred years of Western history. The structure of his earlier philosophic poem had been a vision in which Columbus, despairing in a Spanish prison, had been consoled by historical prophecies. Could he now lay valid claim to a fable for his long historical vision so long as Columbus, however passive he might be, was nominally its hero?

Barlow's revisions often succeeded in their reworkings of particular epic conventions. His invocation to "Almighty Freedom" clarifies both his hardheaded international purpose ("To teach all men where all their interest lies") and the new inner resources needed by modern writers of epic: "Strong in Thy strength I bend no suppliant knee, / Invoke no miracle, no Muse but Thee" (414). By restricting machinery to occasional personifications and place gods, all events become traceable to human or environmental causes.[38] When the gory demon "WAR" stalks across the Atlantic from Britain in 1776, Barlow clearly relishes a threefold defiance of tradition: the juxtaposition of feminine Freedom to masculine War, his ironic redoing of the *Translatio Imperii,* and a modern recasting of Milton's figure of Sin. (Barlow's War has two incestuous offspring named Famine and Pestilence.) Virgilian visits to Avernus and Miltonic visits to Hell are mere "fraudful drama" (726) compared to the tangible horrors of a British prison ship. The climax of supposedly na-

tional triumph in *The Columbiad* is the joyous funeral pyre following Cornwallis's surrender, a pyre upon which all the flags of now outdated nationalism are thrown.

Such successes seem regrettably incidental when set beside Barlow's failure to lend old conversational interchanges any new intensity.[39] Columbus and the angel, appropriately renamed Hesper,[40] remain nothing but the shuttle and the loom upon which the threads of republicanism can be woven. Professing libertarian Deism, they agree about everything they discuss, thereby precluding any hope of an enlivening debate. In the "Preface," Barlow argues that the form of a vision was particularly suited to his higher argument:

> Most of the events were so recent, so important, and so well known, as to render them inflexible to the hand of fiction. The poem, therefore, could not with propriety be modelled after that regular epic form which the more splendid works of this kind have taken, and on which their success is supposed in a great measure to depend. The attempt would have been highly injudicious; it must have diminished and debased a series of actions which were really great in themselves and could not be disfigured without losing their interest. (376)

For Barlow as for Freneau, the "real" greatness of the "actions" of the Revolution was mental, not martial. Barlow clearly hoped to avoid the absurdity of picturing American Revolutionaries in neo-Virgilian dress by invoking them within a prophetic vision that supposedly originated in 1505. Perhaps sensing that he was offering weak rationalizations for an insoluble problem, Barlow contended "the form I have given to the work is the best that the subject would admit" (376). His worry about forsaking "regular epic form" only draws attention to one unflattering difference between a modern vision and an old narrative. As long as Freedom must act through man, Hesper and Columbus can initiate and achieve nothing as heroes of the poem.

Barlow's lines on Sir Walter Raleigh illustrate how his ideological determinism blocked the cumulative heroic effect essential to epic:

> The Seraph spoke; when full beneath their eye
> A new form'd squadron rose along the sky,
> High on the tallest deck majestic shone
> Sage Raleigh, pointing to the western sun;
> His eye, bent forward, ardent and sublime,
> Seem'd piercing nature and evolving time;
> Beside him stood a globe, whose figure traced
> A future empire in each present waste;
> All former works of men behind him shone
> Graved by his hand in ever during stone;
> On his calm brow a various crown displays
> The hero's laurel and the scholar's bays;

> His graceful limbs in steely mail were drest,
> The bright star burning on his lofty breast;
> His sword high waving flasht the solar ray,
> Illumed the shrouds and rainbow'd far the spray;
> The smiling crew rose resolute and brave,
> And the glad sails hung bounding o'er the wave. (539)

Once Barlow's purpose is understood, such a passage contains no absurdities poetic or historical. Factual accuracy involving the Roanoke expedition is not at issue here, because Barlow's intent is to picture the significance of Raleigh's character within the total perspective of empire's westward course. To individualize Raleigh would distract the reader from seeing him as a personification of the Renaissance fusion of soldier and scholar. Pointing toward the New World, Raleigh comprehends history within his *History,* but has mentally left the lesser past behind him. The only failing of Barlow's verse paragraph is that, as a whole, it never conveys the sense of movement that is its very subject. There is nothing Barlow's Raleigh can do except to pose with eye, arm, and globe frozen in a marmoreal tableau. His function is simply to be there when Hesper lifts – and then drops – the appropriate historical curtain.

As the beads on Barlow's historical string accumulate, the genre to which Barlow's epic originally belonged reemerges with painful clarity. *The Columbiad,* like *The Vision of Columbus,* is one immense "rising glory" poem made up of many smaller ones. Beginning with his Yale commencement orations, Barlow's writing of verse had been so closely aligned to this proleptic genre that he may have become incapable of sustaining a representation of human action when writing about matters of cultural destiny. Like the rising glory poem, *The Columbiad* has an exalted subject but no story, great names but no characters, and heroic achievements seemingly free of human risk.

By striving to make an epic out of republicanism, rather than a heroic republican, Barlow may have been attempting an impossibility. Lukacs offered a compelling argument for the inevitable failure of any epic like *The Columbiad:*

> For the epic, the world at any given moment is an ultimate principle; it is empirical at its deepest, most decisive . . . base; it can sometimes accelerate the rhythm of life, can carry something that was hidden or neglected to a utopian end which was always immanent within it, but it can never, while remaining epic, transcend the breadth and depth, the rounded, sensual, richly ordered nature of life as historically given. Any attempt at a properly utopian epic must fail because it is bound, subjectively or objectively, to transcend the empirical and spill over into the lyrical or dramatic; and such overlapping can never be fruitful for the epic. [41]

Lukacs's generality does not apply to Christian narratives like *The Divine Comedy* or *Paradise Lost,* but it shows why no rising glory poem could ever achieve the effect of epic. Barlow's need to trace the avatars of freedom led him constantly away from the "sensual, richly ordered nature of life" whose texture is so wonderfully inescapable in the Homeric poems. Whitman, no less committed to heroic republicanism than Barlow, was to insist upon reaching it through present, sensual experience.

In his republican epic against war, Barlow had to confront the fact that the New World's first republic had been created through war. Six hundred lines describing Revolutionary battlegrounds were to be added to *The Vision of Columbus* to form *The Columbiad*'s new sixth book. Although Barlow warned against Homer's power "to inflame the minds of young readers with an enthusiastic ardor for military fame" (378), the justice of the Revolutionary cause led Barlow to sound the trumpet himself:

> So leapt our youths to meet the invading hordes,
> Flame fired their courage, freedom edged their swords.
> Gates in their van, on high-hill'd Bemus rose,
> Waved his blue steel and dared the headlong foes.[42]

Evidently troubled by his need to glorify inglorious war, Barlow attempted an ingenious compromise. He would devote four hundred lines to the Battle of Saratoga, treat it as the climactic battle of the Revolution, and compare American farmers to Leonidas's footsoldiers defending Liberty at Thermopylae. The martial hero of Saratoga, fortunately, had been Benedict Arnold. Although Arnold's courage had gained victory, the future traitor could be both aggrandized and denounced in an eight-line epic simile likening him to bloodthirsty Achilles (632). Washington would thus be absent from the poem's major bloody field, an American victory could be celebrated, and descriptions of battle preceded by admonitions about "the false glare of glory" (623). Yet Barlow was not as personally immune to the appeal of battle heroics as his principles suggest. With regard to epic weapons, his "Preface" boasts that we Moderns have won the Battle of the Books: "in a general engagement, the shock of modern armies is, beyond comparison, more magnificent, more sonorous, and more discoloring to the face of nature, than the ancient could have been; it is consequently susceptible of more pomp and variety of description" (386).

Barlow, like Whitman, accords heroic potential to the common man. Moreover, Barlow anticipates Whitman's discovery that the one epic convention fully suitable to a democratic poem with no single hero, action, or deity is the catalogue. In *Leaves of Grass,* catalogues are made up of timeless facts of American life that are as available to future readers as

to the poet. Barlow's catalogues, like Homer's, still memorialize special achievement, thereby conflicting with the poet's commitment to the Republic's potential for a heroic equality. A characteristic example is Barlow's roll call of the Continental Congress:

> Wythe, Mason, Pendleton, with Henry join'd,
> Rush, Rodney, Langdon, friends of humankind,
> Persuasive Dickinson the farmer's boast,
> Recording Thomson pride of all the host,
> Nash, Jay, the Livingstons, in council great
> Rutledge and Laurens hold the rolls of fate. (508)

To replace Homer's ships with the Republic's architects is not enough. Lists of Jays, Rutledges, and Livingstons do not evoke a civilization "Where homebred freemen seize the solid prize / Fixt in small spheres, with safer beams to shine, / They reach the useful and refuse the fine" (704).

Selecting a language appropriate to the new epic resulted in similar incongruities. Barlow's "Postscript" rightly argues that "the uniform tendency of our language is towards simplicity as well as regularity" (856). As he revised, Barlow tried to achieve both republican plainness and epic sublimity. New reflections upon cultural change were written in clear, serviceable couplets, but hortatory or descriptive passages were filled with new words of such "simplicity" and "regularity" as "Azotic, muriatic, homicidious, petrific" and "ludibrious." Answering the call for an American sublime, Barlow expanded his sixteen-line description of the Mississippi into a fifty-two-line personification filled with useless alliteration ("Then stretching, straitening south, he gaily gleams / Swells thro the climes and swallows all their streams" [445]).

Barlow had the modesty and literary taste to admit, in a public letter, "My book is not a work of genius."[43] Hoping that a republican poem might succeed through the integrity of its ideas, he wrote Jefferson "As a poem of the Epic character it can never rank high. As a patriotic legacy of my country, I hope it may prove acceptable."[44] When Barlow wrote his preface, he could only hope that republican persuasion would somehow not depend upon literary quality: "There are two distinct objects to be kept in view in the conduct of a narrative poem: the poetical object and the moral object" (377). By insisting that his purpose had been "altogether of a moral and political nature" (389), Barlow reveals that, for him, to have expressed the New World's deepest ideals in epic form was sufficient. No remark is more characteristic of him than his comment "Why should we write at all, if not to benefit mankind?" (480). For us to smile at his question is to admit that literature's power of public persuasion has vanished. Whatever its poetic deficiencies, Barlow's long-labored *Columbiad,* a secular epic that exalts Freedom into a religion, is a compelling prophecy based upon a wide assimilation of cultural beliefs.

No other work of its era so comprehensively expresses that transitory moment in which the hope for one genuinely New World seemed plausible.

Although *The Columbiad* was sufficiently popular to have four American, one French, and one British edition by 1825, it received uniformly unfavorable reviews from all major American literary journals as well as the *Edinburgh Review*.[45] Francis Jeffrey's estimate was the least unjust: "As an Epic poet, we do think [Barlow's] case is desperate; but, as a philosophical and moral poet, we think he has talents of no ordinary value."[46] American critics, who hoped for their American Homer and dreaded another failure, showed no mercy.[47] All agreed that Barlow's fable was boring and that his couplets were insufficiently varied. Thereafter, however, the poem was damned for many contradictory faults: archaic language, prosaic modern language, lack of machinery, absurdity of machinery, no action, excess of action, too international a subject, too national a subject, slavish imitation of epic models, fatal disregard for epic models. The *Boston Review and Monthly Anthology* hooted at Barlow for breaking a list of epic rules; the *American Review* criticized the poem but commended the poet for recognizing that the old rules were unsuited to a new subject. The reviewer for *Port Folio,* a journal customarily derisive of the notion of an American epic, regretted that Barlow had not written a heroic narrative about Columbus himself, and provided a three-paragraph outline for an American Virgilian epic in which Columbus would "shadow forth" the heroic qualities of Washington.

Behind the telling literary criticisms, there surely was some Federalist animus against Barlow's politics, and some New England animus against his slighting of the Puritans' contributions to Freedom. In the main, however, the reviews demonstrate that Barlow's confusion about the form of a republican epic was widely shared. Unsure of how Barlow's attempt could be bettered, most critics were content to ridicule a poem that was evidently to be considered a national embarrassment. When James Russell Lowell wrote an article on "Nationalism in Literature" (1849), *The Columbiad* was still a ready source for cheap wit: "Joel Barlow made the lowest bid for the construction of our *epos,* got the contract, and delivered in due season the *Columbiad,* concerning which we can only regret that it had not been entitled to a still higher praise of nationality by being written in one of the proposed new languages."[48]

Barlow's ignominy prompted the first outright denial of the possibility that any worthy epic could be fashioned from American materials. Fisher Ames's forceful essay titled "American Literature," written two years after *The Columbiad* was published, measures the likelihood of an emerging American genius solely by comparing the societies of Homeric Greece and republican America. Although Ames reveres Homer, he has

no illusions about human behavior in the heroic age: "if victors, they despoiled their enemies of every thing; the property was booty, and the people were made slaves."[49] To Ames as to Barlow, epic poetry has always concerned cultures that are vicious, aristocratic, unjust, and transitory. Yet Ames does not, like most Americans, wholly condemn the heroic world: "The Greeks seem to us a race of giants, Titans, the rivals, yet the favourites of the gods" (461). Ames admires cultures that demand that their heroes prove their superiority through deeds. Consequently, he believes that good heroic poetry can emerge only under certain cultural conditions: Homer and Virgil were writing for a patriotic audience that still shared qualities of the heroic age.

Convinced that great literature depends on the power of the moment as well as of the man, Ames dismisses the notion that a literary genius is impossible in America, and claims that "the same causes that made Greece famous would . . . make our Boeotia sprout and blossom like their Attica" (463). None of the causes, however, is present. The age of printing has made poetry a solitary amusement rather than a means to forge a communal belief. Political democracy is antithetical to epic because democracy subverts hierarchies of merit and proscribes a literary aristocracy. Any society that holds money and commercial success in highest esteem cannot evolve a bard whose appeal to honor will be convincing.

A modern epic poet, Ames concludes, has nothing to write about:

> Homer wrote of war to heroes and their followers, to men who felt the military passion stronger than the love of life; Virgil, with art at least equal to his genius, addressed his poem to Romans who loved their country with sentiment, with passion, with fanaticism. It is scarcely possible, that a modern epick poet should find a subject that would take hold of the heart, for no such subject worthy of poetry exists. Commerce has supplanted war as the passion of the multitude; and the arts have divided and contracted the objects of pursuit. (467–8)

In Ames's view, anyone who now attempts an epic faces impossible choices. If he undertakes to imitate Homer, he will bore contemporaries with patent fakery: "Another *Iliad* would not be undertaken by a true genius, nor equally interest this age, if he executed it" (462). But if he undertakes an epic about the commercial and democratic present, he deludes himself that mediocrity can be heroic. Ames may not have Dwight in mind for the first alternative, but he has his model for the second: "To enter the lists in single combat against Hector, the Greeks did not offer the lots to the nameless rabble of their soldiery; all eyes were turned upon Agamemnon and Ajax, upon Diomed and Ulysses. Shall we match Joel Barlow against Homer or Hesiod?" (465).

No contemporary American had a greater understanding or admiration for Homer and Virgil than Fisher Ames. "American Literature" is

filled with refreshingly hardheaded perceptions about the society of a heroic age and the difficulties of adapting the epic to contemporary American culture. Ames's argumentative strategy – to associate American literary achievement with a great epic poem and then to foreclose all hope of achieving it – gives his essay an effective air of gloomy eloquence. Like Ames's vehement Federalism, however, his literary conclusions are frozen by his love of aristocratic tradition. He can prove that eighteenth-century America is nothing like Homeric Greece, and that Pope's *Iliad* is a wretched model for a republican epic. He cannot imagine, however, that a poet might find commerce and democracy to be heroic, and might evolve new literary techniques to celebrate them. For Ames, the epic genre has been forever defined by *The Iliad, The Odyssey,* and *The Aeneid;* no long poem that does not closely resemble these three could possibly be an epic. It is revealing that John Milton's name never appears in Ames's essay.

During the immediate aftermath of Barlow's failure, the more common tone among those who denied the possibility of an American epic was one of chagrin rather than contempt. In 1815 Walter Channing, brother of William Ellery Channing, wrote an article for the *North American Review* titled "Reflections on the Literary Delinquency of America." He bluntly concluded that "In the most elevated walk of the Muses, the Epick, we cannot hope for much distinction."[50] Assuming that the Revolution is America's heroic subject, Channing argues that the event is too recent, too familiar, and therefore, as a newly published poem has shown, too uninteresting.

In the late 1820s James Hillhouse wrote a thirty-page essay with the unwieldy title "On Some of the Considerations Which Should Influence an Epic or a Tragic Writer in the Choice of an Era." Hillhouse rehearses the arguments of Ames and Channing, but applies them to a different end. A Modern neither can nor should attempt to recreate the heathen, deterministic world of Homeric epic. *The Columbiad* has proven that republicanism does not make an epic, that "the spirit in which our fathers opposed the late hazards resembles the stern intrepidity of Regulus . . . not the effervescence of a passionate young hero in the field of glory."[51] Authors who would seek heroism in contemporary American life are warned that "the quiet, moral intelligent community, where tranquility flourishes under the shadow of the law, where one happy neighborhood represents every other, offers nothing to the Epic or Tragic Muse" (95). Hillhouse retains sufficient hope for an American genius, however, that he finally ignores his own warning about antiquarianism and conflates tragedy and epic with medieval romance. The true era for either an American tragedy or an American heroic poem, he says, is the English Middle Ages, which affords opportunities for displaying Christian vir-

tues, chivalric love, crusades, and tournaments of single combat. It is perhaps fortunate that Hillhouse's call to adapt the matter of *Ivanhoe* into an American heroic poem was not answered in his century.[52]

Ames, Channing, and Hillhouse were all privileged New Englanders who could not shake the assumption that the Revolution was the only conceivable topic for an epic on a national theme. By 1815 they were rapidly becoming out of date. The successful conclusion of the War of 1812 and the opening of trans-Allegheny regions to settlers offered new possibilities for epic treatment. Paulding was the only Eastern writer to attempt a heroic poem after 1815, and his concern was to be western settlement. Gentility of class prevented Ames, Channing, and Hillhouse from considering the West as the seedbed of heroism, even though individual deeds of courage might admittedly have been done there. Bryan, Paulding, and Emmons, by contrast, were all aware that the common American of the 1820s or 1830s was more likely to be moved by the heroism of conquering the land than by more recollections of neo-Virgilian gentlemen creating the world's republic in Philadelphia. Their oversight was of quite another kind. Shouldering the task of creating a western epic with the old gravity of Dwight and Barlow, they ignored the new tradition of American mock epic that had grown up around them.

3

FREEDOM'S FOOLS

Until the very end of the eighteenth century, the newly popular genre called mock-heroic or mock-epic was regarded as the inverse, not the opposite, of the epic. Unlike the travesty, the mock-epic was not intended to mock the epic, but to ridicule human pretense by dressing up "trivial causes" in the full panoply of epic conventions. The mock-epic could be understood and appreciated only through the epic. Mock-heroics had appeared, not when writers believed the epic to be absurd, but when they sought to expose the folly of heroic pretense among combatants – or writers – who were not worthy of the grandest of literary forms. The mock-epic thus followed the epic in time, yet was its dependent and complement. It surfaced when the epic was still regarded with high admiration, but when its grand subjects seemed to be above small-minded contemporaries.[1]

Epic and mock-epic were thought to have had one origin, even one author. Homer and Virgil, it was assumed, had successfully sung "The Battle of the Frogs and Mice" and "The Gnat" because they had also sung Achilles' wrath and Aeneas' *pietas*. England's great Moderns seemed, however, to have ominously reversed the priorities of their Ancient models. "MacFlecknoe" and "Absalom and Achitophel" had established the English mock-epic, yet Dryden's great heroic work remained his translation of Virgil, whereas his cherished project for his own epic on King Arthur or the Black Prince remained unwritten. Perhaps Pope's *Iliad* truly had, as Johnson claimed, "tuned the English tongue," but Pope's own creative achievements in heroic poetry were "The Rape of the Lock" and *The Dunciad*. His long-planned epic on Brutus, in which England's founding would be ascribed to beneficient government and reasoned tolerance, was never to be written. Although Blackmore and Southey, Dwight and Barlow, were to complete revisionist kinds of epics that remain hard to praise, the dominant poets of the Augustan era had trans-

lated the ancient epics, postponed their own, and diverted their laughter and venom into mock-heroics of astonishing artistry and force.[2]

By the time Americans like Trumbull, Barlow, and Irving were reading Kames's *Elements of Criticism,* the mock-epic had already become a literary tradition with its own critical issues. In addition to Dryden's and Pope's poems, there had appeared, among many others, Garth's *The Dispensary,* the short Latin mock-epics of Addison and Holdsworth, Churchill's *The Rosciad* and, above them all, Nicholas Boileau's *Le Lutrin,* as translated by John Ozell in 1708 with the subtitle "a Mock-Heroic Poem." Here was a tradition of accomplished narrative poems, all written in heroic couplets, all rendering a low subject in high epic style, all parodying[3] epic type scenes, and all maintaining that suspension of contempt, that ironic pretense of heroic stature, which provokes laughter at incongruity. The difficulty with such a generic model for the mock epic, however, was the immense popularity of Samuel Butler's *Hudibras* and its many imitators. Butler had created another kind of mock-heroic in which a seemingly high subject was lowered by comic tetrameter rhyme, slang and off-rhyme, raillery, and sheer invective. The couplets of Boileau and Pope exposed pretense and vanity by describing them in the familiar admired manner. Butler's trivializing metric and disregard for narrative implied that heroic verse and epic convention were at best outmoded and possibly discardable.

Although the two forms overlapped in poetic practice, they were sufficiently distinct to provoke constant critical discriminations between them. Models of mock-heroic were advanced under the guise of determining the subgenres of burlesque. Influential critics tended to denigrate Hudibrastics, elevate the mock-epic, and thereby salvage a future for the epic. Joseph Addison declared that "Burlesque is . . . of two kinds, the first represents mean Persons in the Accoutrements of heroes [Garth, Pope, Cervantes], the other describes great Persons acting and speaking, like the basest among the People [Lucian, Butler]." Acknowledging that the general reader is "wonderfully pleased" with Butler's tetrameter rhyme, Addison nonetheless disparaged *Hudibras,* while striving to seem impartial: "It is a Dispute among the criticks, whether Burlesque Poetry runs best in Heroic Verse, like that of the *Dispensary,* or in Doggerel, like that of *Hudibras.* I think where the low Character is to be raised, the Heroic is the proper Measure, but when an Hero is to be pulled down and degraded, it is best done in Doggerel." Addison's influential condemnation of Hudibrastics as "Doggerel" probably derived from Dryden, who had written that eight-syllable Burlesque rhyme "makes a Poet giddy with turning in a Space too narrow for his imagination." Moreover, the forceful contrast Addison established between two kinds of burlesque was

itself derivative; it restates a distinction made by John Ozell three years earlier:

> Monsieur *Boileau* calls this poem of his *Heroi-Comique,* Mock-Heroic; that is, a ridiculous Action made considerable in Heroic Verse. If I distinguish right, there are two sorts of *Burlesque;* the first where things of mean Figure and Slight Concern appear in all the Pomp and Bustle of an *Epic* Poem; such is this of the *Lutrin*. The second sort is where great Events are made Ridiculous by the meanness of the Character, and the oddness of the Numbers, such is the *Hudibras* of our Excellent *Butler*.

Ozell and Addison, though they slight Butler to differing degrees, both wish permanently to separate the two kinds of heroi-comical writing.[4]

By the late eighteenth century, these judgments tended to harden further. Feminine endings, off rhyme and comic rhyme were thought to be the province only of the low burlesque. Cervantes was praised for maintaining his ironic praise of Don Quixote's chivalric heroism. Fielding's notion of the "comic epic poem in prose" admitted broad linguistic burlesque only at select obvious moments such as battle scenes. Joseph Wharton's discussion of comedy singles out *Le Lutrin, The Dispensary,* "The Rape of the Lock," and *The Dunciad* as works which "by assuming the form of the epopea . . . have acquired a dignity and gracefulness, which all satires delivered merely in the poet's own person must want." By the time of James Beattie's "Essay on Laughter and Ludicrous Composition," contemporary with Trumbull's *M'Fingal,* "Mock-Heroic" and "Burlesque" became separate categories, with *The Dunciad* serving as the model of the first, *Hudibras* of the second. Beattie's judgment upon the two kinds can hardly be described as impartial: "Solemnity is the character assumed by the mock-epic poet; he considers little things as great, and describes them accordingly – the *burlesque* author is a buffoon by profession."[5]

The rise of mock-epic to popularity in the early eighteenth century had been preceded by an age of travesties, the most famous being Scarron's *Virgile Travestie (1664)*. The proximity of travesty to mock-epic, together with the need to save serious epic for the future, prompted poet-critics to try to sever the tone of the epic poem from the tone of the mock-epic. The epic was to be perpetually dignified and serious, the mock-epic perpetually ludicrous. Dryden objected to witticisms because they were "not only below the dignity of Heroick Verse, but contrary to its Nature; Virgil and Homer have not one of them." The "Postscript" Pope wrote for *The Odyssey,* his last statement on Homer, acknowledges that mock-epic derives from both the form of the epic and the spirit of Cervantes. And yet, Pope insists upon separating epic from mock-epic because of their opposite, yet internally uniform tone: "The

use of pompous expression for low actions or thoughts is the true sublime of *Don Quixote*. How far unfit it is for epic poetry appears in its being the perfection of the mock epic." The true epic poet, Boileau had declared, *"Orne, élève, embellit, aggrandit toutes choses."* No touch of the comic, said Boileau, should ever enter into the characterization of the epic hero:

> *En valeur éclatant, en vertus magnifique:*
> *Qu'en lui, jusqu'aux défauts, tout se montre héroïque.*

The force of the combined opinions of Dryden, Pope, and Boileau can be seen throughout the century in commentary upon adapting the epic to comic purpose. Richard Cambridge's preface to his mock-epic *The Scribleriad* (1751) argues that, although "A Mock-Heroic poem should, in as many respects as possible, imitate the True Heroic," an absolute separation of tone and mood should be maintained. Whereas the epic must always be serious, the mock epic must never be flippant: "A mock-heroic poem should throughout be serious, because the originals are serious; therefore the author should never be seen to laugh but constantly wear that grave irony which Cervantes only has inviolably preserv'd." Only burlesques of lower kinds forsake pentameter couplets or indulge in direct authorial raillery.[6]

For an American author of satirical disposition, this mock-epic tradition provided a foothold even more tenuous than its epic counterpart. American writers of serious epic knew they somehow had to adapt Milton to American ground, but they took comfort in the fact that Milton had been a Puritan, a revolutionary, a hater of tyranny. The subjects and forms of the great recent mock-epics had been, however, truly foreign. The mainstay of the high-burlesque, the mock-epic proper, had been satire directed, not against the heroic code of war, but against bad writing itself, the goddess of Dulness as She had reappeared in contemporary literature and thought ("MackFlecknoe," *The Dunciad, The Scribleriad, The Rosciad,* and, eventually, *Don Juan*). American writers, however, were so sensitive to the need to demonstrate cultural maturity that the prospect of satirizing the little literature they did have was not tolerable. Clerical disputes of the institutional kind mocked in *Le Lutrin* scarcely existed in America because of spare protestant liturgy and pluralism of churches. The beau monde of Belinda and the Baron, Sir Plume and Clarissa, had sustained the most beloved of all mock-epics, but satirizing some nonexistent American equivalent of Hampton Court seemed pointless and pallid. Least promising of all was the model of *Hudibras*. As *Modern Chivalry* was to prove, it was possible to send American counterparts of Sancho and the Don, Ralph and Hudibras, out on the New World's open roads, but it would have helped to have had varied institutions to sustain

the satire. Although Cervantes had mastered the psychology of heroic illusion, Butler had adapted the Quixotic situation in order to ridicule – of all targets unacceptable to many American readers – the piety of the Puritan.

The one fresh subject open and vital to writers of American mock-epic was republican politics or, more particularly, the assumption of historical progress that accompanied republican revolution.[7] With the sole exception of Barlow's "The Hasty Pudding" (1793), all of the era's achievements in mock-heroic literature would arise from the need to place "republican progress' in its historical perspective. *M'Fingal* (1775, 1782), *The Anarchiad* (1785–6), *Modern Chivalry* (1792–1815), and *The History of New York* (1809) return again and again to the same issues: whether law can restrain demagoguery, whether a republic can withstand popular stupidity and violence, whether reason can subdue desire, whether historical change can be called progress. The creators of these flawed yet inventive works were lawyer-authors whose classical education and skeptical Federalist mentality found appropriate literary outlet in adapting known mock-heroic genres. Like American writers of serious or sublime epic, they poured the new wine of revolutionary politics into modified old forms – heroic burlesque and the Cervantic novel. These mock-heroic genres freed American writers to deal with their present realistically and their past skeptically. Republican greatness no longer had to be demonstrated through assertion or example; it could be tested, played with, enjoyed. American mock-heroics achieved literary and popular success, not only because Trumbull and Irving had impressive comic talent, but because their essential subject, the illusion of Revolutionary progress, touched a latent popular fear in nonthreatening ways. The mock heroic genre, itself derivative from epic, encouraged its practitioner to vent a skepticism that could be dismissed as literary fun.

In the 1770s the choice of mock-heroic form proved to be as vexing as the choice of content. Although the heroic couplet was an Old World meter, it had proven at least usable for Dwight's and Barlow's epics because it was applied to heroic characters from the biblical or Euro-American past. To create contemporary Americans who were speaking the language of Pope's *Iliad* was increasingly likely to prompt mockery of the poet rather than his characters. Butler's medium thus seemed more appropriate. In a manner ultimately prophetic of Mark Twain, Hudibrastics had used common language to ridicule the elevated language of pretentious people. Its running rhymes allowed for digression in ways appropriate to a comparatively unformed world. But Hudibrastics also exposed a poet of the 1770s to disadvantages. Hudibrastics was clearly regarded as the low form of burlesque, therefore a compromising choice for an American intent upon a substantial comic poem. Even worse, the

popularity of *Hudibras* had steadily declined as the importance of its topical associations with the Puritan Interregnum had gradually faded.

II. "OPPOSING WINDS IN AEOLUS' CAVE"

The literary precocity of John Trumbull was as evident in his
critical acuity as in his creative wit. Although he fleetingly contemplated
a serious epic as an adolescent, he knew instinctively that his friend
Dwight's *The Conquest of Canaan* was a poem of obscure metaphor, gar-
gantuan prolixity and "glowing patchwork"; the dozing reader had best
obtain a lightning rod to help him survive the storms that arrive in every
book. Trumbull knew the works of Boileau, Churchill, and Sterne, as
well as Homer, Milton, and Lord Kames. As early as 1775, he perceived
the celebrated "M'Pherson" to be only "a Scotch ministerial scribbler"
who had written "Fingal, an antient Epic Poem, *published as the work of
Ossian*" (italics mine). Aware that he was "the first, who dared by Satire
to oppose the party of controversial Scribblers, & set this part of America
an example of the use of Ridicule & Humour," Trumbull knew that, in
writing *M'Fingal*, he faced a choice between low and high burlesque,
between Hudibrastics and mock-epic. His compromise, characteristi-
cally deft, was immediately apparent to any contemporary who knew
why Butler's and Pope's poems were thought not to mix. *M'Fingal* was
to be written throughout, Trumbull insisted, in "the affected jingle of
Hudibrastic rhymes," though of Swift's and Churchill's kind. But the
poem as a whole would be, as the subtitles of the 1775, 1782, and 1820
editions all proclaim, "a modern epic poem." Low and high burlesque,
Trumbull evidently believed, would in *M'Fingal* be made one.[8]

Reasons for Trumbull's choice can be traced in extant letters. In May
of 1775, Silas Deane wrote to Trumbull to solicit a burlesque that would
ridicule General Gage's military posturings in tactical detail. Trumbull's
demurrer shows his preference for a different kind of poem:

> The whole subject is so merely a *Nothing,* that it must be a kind of
> Creation to make anything of it. Yet to give a narration of Facts, leaves
> no room for Invention – I mean for Fiction, which is of as much Ad-
> vantage to a humorous as to a serious poem – Witness Hudibras, the
> Rape of the Lock, the Dispensary, the Lutrin – all, Poems of unequalled
> Humour, which owe half their beauties to the graces of Fiction – Be-
> sides, would not the high burlesque, the style of the Dunciad, for in-
> stance, suit this subject better than the low style of Hudibras, & be
> easier adapted to a serious turn in a subsequent canto, according to your
> plan of varying the Style in different parts.[9]

The end of this passage returns to the familiar distinction between high
and low burlesque, but its beginning conflates the two subgenres within
a much wider one of inventive verse comedy. Although Trumbull would

decide, finally, to retain "the low style of Hudibras," *M'Fingal* was to be a wholly fictitious though representative narrative, free of all those commitments to presumed historical fact that often make Dwight's and Barlow's couplets seem straightened and absurd. Unlike Beattie or Cambridge, Trumbull believed that the high burlesque could allow for a greater flexibility of tone. The weightier "subsequent canto" he refers to would become canto three of the 1782 edition, in which M'Fingal's strictures against rebel violence and demagoguery would indeed take a "serious turn."

Six months later, once Cantos One and Two were finished in draft, Trumbull wrote to John Adams declaring that the characters of Honorius and M'Fingal, as well as the description of the town meeting, were true to all Whigs and Tories because they were true to none in particular. His letter also suggests why he finally chose to abandon heroic couplets in favor of Hudibrastics. As in *The Progress of Dulness,* Trumbull wished to attain "a mixture of Irony & Sarcasm under various Characters & different styles," a flexibility presumably less available in the sustained couplets of the mock heroic, where irony would be continual, but direct sarcasm would seem obtrusive.[10]

Trumbull's motive for insisting that a "modern epic poem" could be written in Hudibrastics was finally acknowledged in the 1784 letter he wrote to the Marquis de Chastellux, a letter Trumbull printed as a statement of intent in his *Collected Poems* (1820). Although *M'Fingal* had been written in Hudibrastic couplets, Trumbull insisted that "In the style I have preferred the high burlesque to the low (which is the style of *Hudibras*), not only as more agreeable to my own taste, but as it readily admits a transition to the grave, elevated or sublime." His poem was not mere Butleresque raillery, but the true mock-heroic burlesque, "a Poem which from its nature must in every part be a parody of the serious Epic."

Anyone familiar with Butler's poem can well understand why Trumbull declared that good parody must apply "in every part." Until *Don Juan* was to make a literary virtue of not planning a narrative, Butler's *Hudibras* remained the most ill-shaped, digressive, and sprawling of mock-heroic tales. To Trumbull "this [burlesque] kind of poetry, as well as the sublime, demands a regular plan and design." However varied a mock epic might be in tone, it must be "sprightly," unified, and short. In his letter, Trumbull attacked even the best high burlesques for their "irregularity and deficiency" in design. *Le Lutrin* and *The Dispensary,* he contended, are essentially unfinished; the fourth book of *The Dunciad* has "scarcely any connection with the former parts, either in manner or design." A clearly balanced narrative, Trumbull believed, was essential to reinforce a proper balance of satiric attitude; his purpose in *M'Fingal* had been not merely to ridicule Tories, but "with as much impartiality as

possible, [to] satirize the follies and extravagancies of my countrymen, as well as of their enemies."[11]

Trumbull had good reason to be proud of his "regular plan and design." His four cantos make up a poem less than half the length of *Hudibras*. Because Trumbull knew that Butler's off-rhymes were striking in single couplets, but fatiguing in a long poem, he used them much more sparingly than he had in *The Progress of Dulness*. Butler's lengthy mockery of Puritan jargon is pared away; M'Fingal's political bluster refers to known events in inflated but accessible speech. From the outset, Trumbull planned his entire narrative to end with M'Fingal's sneaking away to Boston, a comic cowardice "to which event every incident in the poem tends."[12] The shape of the narrative thus justifies Trumbull's claim upon a high mock-epic parody, even though it is in Hudibrastic meter. Cantos One and Two ("The Town Meeting") parody the epic council and the feast; Canto Three ("The Liberty Pole") parodies ceremonies of libation and sacrifice, then climaxes in a single combat replete with comic machinery and a weighing of Jove's scales; Canto Four brings M'Fingal to Pandemonium (Tories in the cellar) and ends with Malcolm's parodic vision of the demise of Tory Empire. John Trumbull not only had the best ear of any American poet of his generation; his compact narratives show that, unlike Dwight or Barlow, he always knew when to stop. The Horatian epigraph Trumbull chose for the first complete edition of *M'Fingal* makes the point forcefully: *"Est brevitate opus, ut currat sententia, neu se / Impediat verbis lassas onerantibus aures."*[13]

A longstanding critical opinion argues that the first two cantos, avowedly patriotic in their satire of Tory insolence and stupidity, were occasioned by the promptings of revolutionary duty; in the last two cantos, completed seven years later, M'Fingal expresses Trumbull's fears that violence and demagoguery might be becoming a tradition of the new nation. Although it would be folly to deny that M'Fingal's speeches in Book Three, while he is being tarred and feathered, acquire the dignity of deserved outrage, this familiar interpretation exaggerates Trumbull's immediate political motivation and divides a well designed narrative into halves. Trumbull's account of the poem's genesis was quite different: His narrative had been planned as a whole in 1775, his purposes had been primarily literary ("I hoped to write a burlesque poem which your Boileau would not have condemned"[14]), and his intent had always been to satirize both Whigs and Tories. The validity of his three claims can be shown by considering the poem's "Action," those moments in which our response to narrative depends upon Trumbull's parody of epic conventions. At issue here is more than a question of the poem's formal unity or of Trumbull's consistency of political attitude. Those who insist upon a Republican Trumbull in Cantos One and Two, and a Federalist

Trumbull in Cantos Three and Four, assume that Trumbull believed sufficiently in the force of political ideas to wish to write shifting comic
propaganda. Close study of *M'Fingal* suggests that the entire poem developed from the assumption that men are driven to public actions by
selfishness and mob instinct, not by political creed of any persuasion.

Although relishing the comedy of the literary word, Trumbull's mock-
epic satirizes the folly of the political word. His invocation, which appears as a "preface" some four hundred lines into the fist canto, is to the
meetinghouse scribe who, with Echo as his clerk, doggedly takes down
the words of M'Fingal and Honorius while they try to address the crowd.
This Muse is, of course, a mock version of the poet himself, who excuses
his tiresomeness by proclaiming:

> And tho' the speech ben't worth a groat,
> As usual, 'tisn't the author's fault,
> But error merely of the prater,
> Who should have talk'd to th' purpose better. (116)

We may doubt whether Honorius's speeches were ever intended to serve
as inspirational patriotic truth. Like his name, these speeches assume a
gravity that only renders their correctness tedious, if not priggish; certainly the poet never directly sanctions them. M'Fingal's comic bluster
effectively satirizes Tory allegiance, not because aristocracy is evil, but
because he unwittingly exposes the reality of British oppression through
his own malapropisms and stupidity.

The thrust of Trumbull's narrative subverts political rhetoric of both
parties. Neither the Whig nor the Tory listens to the other's speeches,
nor does either provide reasoned rejoinders. The people who throng the
meetinghouse ("Beneath stood voters of all colours / Whigs, tories, orators and bawlers" [108]), attend to neither speaker. Honorius and then
M'Fingal are hissed and shouted down. Trumbull's poem begins in medias speech because, for the mob that fills the meetinghouse, words followed by fitful brutalities are the only kind of concerted "action" that is
possible. The first two cantos parody the opening council speeches of
The Iliad in order to establish a contrast between Greek chieftains, whose
speeches at least were heeded, and the American meetinghouse, where up-
roar reigns. Before the speechifying begins, the poet describes the moods
of the crowd as "Opposing winds in Aeolus's Cave" (108). After the two
cantos of debate are concluded, Trumbull provides appropriate similes:

> Like Aesop's times, as fable runs,
> Where ev'ry creature talk'd at once,
> Or like the variegated gabble
> That craz'd the carpenters of Babel
> Each party soon forgot the quarrel,
> And let the other go on parole. (152)

The immediately preceding lines had pictured the onset of the Realm of Chaos and Night over the meetinghouse, a tumult leading the great M'Fingal to draw his sword, threatening to do something. The god hovering over the field of battle is Victory, seen only by the bard, who prepares to join the strongest (loudest) side. Whether Honorius's speeches are just is finally a pointless question because the events of Trumbull's Revolutionary world are not determined by ethical principles of any sort.

The Third Canto, which contains the epic's Action, elicits a playful curse on all political houses. Trumbull accounts for M'Fingal's rage at the liberty pole by mocking the Whig's sacred symbol through seemingly aggrandizing comparisons: "Like spears at Brobdignagian tilting / Or Satan's walking-staff in Milton" (153). The people's rage against M'Fingal, in turn, is not fed by political belief but by "ceremonies of libation," draughts of flip needed to stimulate "the quintessence of public spirit" (154). However plausible M'Fingal's warnings about liberty becoming license may sound, he has no justification for proclaiming the riot act simply because he believes them.

It is, in fact, M'Fingal's proclamation of the riot act that causes the riot, a melée of stones, fists, and bottles that Trumbull offers as America's equivalent of an epic battle. Although M'Fingal's hour of courage, his *aristeia*, is inspired only by his rusted militia sword and ephemeral rage, he so intimidates the Whig heroes that he nearly fells the liberty pole. The climactic single combat inevitably follows, a combat explicitly parodic of Homer, Virgil, and Milton (164). The chairman of the Committee of Safety challenges M'Fingal to fight, the spade against the sword, while Jove weighs the fates of both in his golden scales. Lacking all political integrity, the chairman's courage can derive only from the machinery of the epic poem; he is in fact not the chairman but some heavenly power descended in his shape ("Whether 'twere Pallas, Mars or Iris / 'Tis scarce worth while to make enquiries" [163 – 4]). After M'Fingal flees in terror, then pauses to pick up a small un-Homeric stone, the climax of the poem follows:

> The deadly spade discharg'd a blow
> Tremendous on his rear below;
> His bent knee fail'd, and void of strength
> Stretch'd on the ground his manly length;
> Like antient oak o'erturned he lay,
> Or tow'rs to tempests fall'n a prey,
> And more things else – but all men know 'em
> If slightly vers'd in Epic Poem." (167)

To have rhymed "all men know 'em" with "epic poem" is a timely subtlety, at once smiling at his generation's worried familiarity with epic, while implying that the old form is wholly inappropriate to a world of

revolutionary agitation. The Action of low farce and the diction of the high burlesque here fuse in Hudibrastics that, line by line, parallel the Homeric sequence of epic combat. Trumbull manages to mock his contemporaries' expectation of inappropriate conventions without in any way satirizing the poems that long ago established them.

The remainder of the narrative allows no opening to political virtue. M'Fingal stands "heroic as a mule" (168) defying the rabble to do their worst. When he is sentenced to be tarred, feathered, and ridden from town, not because of any criminal deed, but because he is "The vilest Tory in the town" (171), M'Fingal promptly turns coward, running to where "The Tory Pandemonium muster" in his own cellar (177). Trumbull's underworld is a place for fearful losers rather than for the morally lost. When M'Fingal prophecies, quite plausibly, that the mob will tar, feather, and dispossess Loyalists everywhere, he makes his own experience representative in exactly the way Trumbull desired. Malcolm's lengthy prophecy of Tory demise and Whig triumph, extending from Burgoyne's surrender to Cornwallis's, parodies both Michael's prophecy to Adam and, in turn, Hector's appearance in Aeneas' dream. The second Troy and the fortunate fall to be found at the end of Trumbull's poem are, as one might expect, a prospect of the rising glory of America in which Tories will have no part. But it is crucial to remember that Malcolm's panegyric is short compensation at the end of a narrative dominated by idle rhetoric and mob volatility. Trumbull's note tells us that Malcolm's prophecy of an "American empire proud and vaunting" (210) reflects only the viewpoint of an embittered Scot who "thinking his merits and sufferings unrewarded, appeared equally malevolent against Whigs and Tories" (180). According to Malcolm, America's ascent to "glory, wealth and fame" will be based on rising commerce and a strong navy, rather than on respect for republican law (210).

Trumbull ends the narrative with M'Fingal's "grand retreat"; after hearing of the Tories's eventual defeat, M'Fingal sneaks out a cellar window, creeps away from the advancing Whigs, "And crawling slow in deadly fear / By movements wise made good his rear" (211). M'Fingal's retreat to Boston, like Howe's retreat from Boston, shows the British posterior to the world. Trumbull concludes his poem, however, with an epic simile that generalizes the significance of the narrative far beyond the Revolutionary War. Just as M'Fingal has crept away from his Tory cohorts:

> So when wise Noah summon'd greeting
> All animals to gen'ral meeting;
> From ev'ry side the members sent
> All kinds of beasts to represent;
> Each from the flood took care t'embark,

> And save his carcase in the ark;
> But as it fares in state and church
> Left his constituents in the lurch. (211 – 12)

These last lines suggest the universal inevitability of political desertion: We human animals, of any persuasion, will always act to save our carcases during floodtimes. If Trumbull's blithe skepticism is aimed at any particular polity, his simile suggests it is American democracy rather than British aristocracy. Noah is summoning all the animals to a general meeting; every region has sent representatives according to its interests. The new republic may choose to separate church and state, but the defining political act within both groups will be to sacrifice the interests of constituents to the interests of self. Judge John Trumbull's eventual vocational preferences are all implied here: One may honorably retreat from revolutionary Boston if one serves justice with a pen; literature can at most dispel melancholy through hooting at human folly; civil statutes, however, will prove to be the individual's only defense against the violent vagaries of mass opinion.

In genre and in political tone, Trumbull struck compromises that could both serve and survive the Revolution. Because the ignominy of the Tory is kept at the forefront, his poem was understandably read as a goad to Whig commitment. Its display of the brutalities of popular excess provided quotations for Republican as well as Federalist newspapers for years. Trumbull's farcical parody of epic conventions was so broad and genial that the poem would continue to be entertaining as long as Homer, Virgil, and Milton were staples of American education. By 1830, *M'Fingal's* thirty editions had given it, as Samuel Kettell remarked, "a greater celebrity than any other American poem." Nor was it surprising that by midcentury the popularity of America's famed mock-epic would wane together with the stature of epic poetry.[15]

The disappearance of *M'Fingal* from the canon is a loss that reflects diminished familiarity with Trumbull's epic models. What has dropped from view is the remarkable skill of Trumbull's parodies. To Americans intent upon America's rising glory, few lines in *Paradise Lost* were more important than the introduction of Michael's prophecy to Adam:

> Ere thou from here depart, know I am sent
> To shew thee what shall come in future day
> To thee and to thy Offspring. . . . Ascend
> This Hill . . . But to nobler sights,
> *Michael* from *Adam*'s eyes the Film remov'd
> Which that false Fruit that promis'd clearer sight
> Had bred; then purg'd with Euphrasie and Rue
> The visual Nerve, for he had much to see;
> And from the Well of Life three drops instill'd.[16]

As Malcolm the Tory prepares to show M'Fingal the future catastrophe of their race, he announces:

> As shown by great archangel, Michael,
> Old Adam saw the world's whole sequel . . .
> So from this stage shalt thou behold,
> The war its coming scenes unfold, . . .
> But first my pow'r for visions bright,
> Must cleanse from clouds thy mental sight
> Remove the dim suffusions spread,
> Which bribes and sal'ries there have bred
> And from the well of Bute infuse,
> Three genuine drops of Highland dews,
> To purge, like euphrasy and rue,
> Thine eyes, for much thou hast to view. (182)

By citing Michael's speech in a mock-epic simile, Trumbull demonstrates the self-consciousness of the entire epic tradition. Malcolm's self-imposed duty to imitate Milton's Michael lends an elaborately fictive quality to anything he might say. The similarities between the passages lead only to differences. Just as Michael's mount has dwindled to Malcolm's cellar stage, so do Milton's specific phrases ("Euphrasie and Rue," "had much to see") serve to trivialize the Tories' political night because they have been compressed into the jingle of Hudibrastics. The film over Adam's eyes, once caused by the false fruit of forbidden knowledge, is now caused by the blindness of political bribery. When Michael's Well of Life is supplanted by Malcolm's well of Bute, there seems scant hope for moral or spiritual vision in any form. Although the townspeople in Trumbull's poem believe themselves to be elevated by political controversy, their wordy protestations of republican destiny show their laughable, secular egoism. Readers wearying of the many recent prospect poems on America's rising political glory most surely were delighted at Trumbull's implied satire of the genre.

III. IMPROVISINGS

From October of 1786 to May of 1787, while Humphreys, Barlow, Hopkins, and Trumbull were writing ten of the twelve numbers of *The Anarchiad*, regional anarchy seemed to portend the fall of the four-year-old republic. Creditors in Rhode Island were refusing to allow farmers to repay debts, contracted in specie, with paper currency inflated one thousand percent. In Massachusetts, where gold currency remained, approximately one thousand farmers were jailed for debt. Five county courts had been closed by mobs of farmers who neither would nor could meet their obligations. In January of 1787, Daniel Shays, former captain of a patriot regiment, led an attack of 1,100 farmers upon the Springfield

Arsenal, only some fifty miles upriver from Hartford, where the four Wits were singly and/or collectively serializing *The Anarchiad*.

These circumstances explain, if not excuse, the failing of an intermittently brilliant poem. Whether derived from *The Rolliad* or not, the narrative frame of *The Anarchiad* cleverly satirizes the new nation's need to devise a heroic past. A nameless editor breathlessly announces that among "the relics of antiquity" recently recovered from western mound builders, "I was overjoyed to find a folio manuscript which appeared to contain an epic poem, complete." This pedantic editor, unable to distinguish between epic and mock-epic, proceeds in his headnotes to assure the reader that *The Anarchiad* obeys all the rules of epic poetry. Having discovered that his text is subtitled "a Poem on the restoration of Chaos and substantial Night," he then accuses "the celebrated English poet, Mr. Pope" of plagiarism from the great American ur-epic, "the most perfect . . . model of all subsequent epic productions."[17] Such a frame offered the Hartford poets many advantages: It allowed for satire on the pedantry of rules critics; *The Dunciad* could be pointedly imitated yet adapted to American ground; succeeding numbers could follow the changing course of Massachusetts anarchy; above all, the entire poem could imply that the true American epic was only to be, after all, a mock-epic, a high burlesque in which demagogues and debtors masked themselves as revolutionary heroes.

Ironically, this openness of form allowed the faults of American epics to creep into American mock-epic. The opening number, deservedly popular, prophesies in ten couplets how the bluster of Shays shall enable Anarch to restore Chaos and Night by inducing the citizenry no longer to believe in a law or a constitution. Supposedly drawn from *The Anarchiad's* eighth book, "The Book of Vision," these lines are a dark, comic inversion of every solace that contemporary poems on America's rising glory were offering. After the first number, however, *The Anarchiad* merely repeats its prophetic warnings in ever shriller terms while the contemporary crisis worsened. Instead of a mock-epic narrative, *The Anarchiad* becomes a series of diatribes in which Anarch, Wronghead, Tweedle, and Hesper reveal, often without any irony, the dark powers of mob rule, paper money, illiteracy and demagoguery. Heroic games, single combat, and climactic battles are referred to, but never appear. Unlike *M'Fingal,* but like *The Columbiad, The Anarchiad* never strays from prophetic speechifying long enough to devise a dramatic action that might enliven it. Variety is obtained only by throwing in a "miscellaneous" "Ode on the Genius of America" and a "miscellaneous" mock elegy on William Wimble, both written in other meters. *Ad hominem* attacks increase as the comedy of generic parody fades. The last two numbers, written after Shays's rebellion had been quelled, concern a visit to the

underworld in which the preeminent villains are democratic politicians who rage for the Millennium, and foreign savants who exult in America's degeneracy. Such an ending, utterly inconsistent with previous numbers, shows the eventual bankruptcy of allowing a mock-epic to serve as propaganda against present political crises.

Blatantly topical in subject, the verse of *The Anarchiad* ironically comes to life, not in its numbing invective, but in literary allusion. Assuming that any reader must know the famous ending of *The Dunciad* ("Lo! Thy dread Empire, Chaos! is restor'd; / Light dies before thy uncreating word"[18]), the American poets politicized it to serve as the climactic couplet of their first number: "Thy constitution, Chaos, is restor'd; Law sinks before thy uncreating word" (5). Pope's literary Dulness has evidently become the lesser evil. The Word America needs is one of Law, but the only constitution restorable through popular clamor is the constitution of Chaos, rather than the Constitution creating federal unity.

After gratuitous drubbing of the Comte de Buffon and Abbé Raynal, *The Anarchiad* concludes with an equally effective parody of the ending of Pope's "Messiah." Pope describes Christ's arrival to consummate a Deistic Millennium:

> No more the rising *Sun* shall gild the Morn
> Nor evening Cynthia fill her silver Horn,
> But lost, dissolv'd in thy superior Rays;
> One Tyde of Glory, one unclouded Blaze,
> O'erflow thy Courts: THE LIGHT HIMSELF shall shine
> Reveal'd; and God's eternal Day be Thine.[19]

In the last lines of *The Anarchiad,* the seer of the American underworld, one "Merlin of the West," warns scribbler Tweedle about the combined dangers of popular demagoguery and bad writing, which will usher in Anarch's Millennium:

> No more shall glory gild the hero's name,
> Nor envy sicken at the deeds of fame;
> Virtue no more the generous breast shall fire,
> Nor radiant truth the historic page inspire;
> One tide of falsehood o'er the world be spread,
> In wit's light robe shall gaudy fiction shine,
> And all be lies, as in a work of thine. (77)

Here again the artistry lies in parodic allusion, rather than the lines themselves. Pope's apocalyptic terminology is reworked into a satiric welcome of the coming of literary and political darkness. In the New World's duncedom, both Cynthia and Christ drop away, to be supplanted by demagogue Tweedle and a wasteland defined only by what has been lost. (The American underworld of *The Anarchiad* is called simply "The Land of Annihilation.") To the American poet, the direst threat is the prospect

that a "hero's name" and "deeds of fame" will become irrelevant amid a rising tide of egalitarianism. As in American panegyrical poems, the future rouses the poet's voice to a climax based on rhetoric rather than deed. Instead of striving for the comic irony of the high burlesque, as *M'Fingal* had done, *The Anarchiad* links "wit's light robe" with "gaudy fiction" and projects them both into the night of the Republic. As a mock-epic, *The Anarchiad* may not have one intentionally comic verse within it.

At century's end, when distinctions among genres were obviously breaking down, American experimentation in comic forms went beyond Trumbull's attempt to mingle high and low burlesque. Joel Barlow's "The Hasty-Pudding" (1793), repeatedly classified as a mock-epic, mocks neither the rural America of cornmeal mush, nor the counterworld of French Revolutionary politics, nor the conventions of epic poetry. After an opening Proposition and Invocation, mock-epic conventions virtually disappear from Barlow's poem, which has neither battle nor narrative, hero nor council. "The Hasty Pudding," like John Phillips' "Cyder" or John Gay's "Wine," praises the consumptive pleasures of a day-to-day world that is aheroic rather than antiheroic. More akin to pastoral than to mock-epic, "The Hasty Pudding" makes only rare and playful allusions to the heroic world of epic poetry. By rejecting sublime European themes ("Ye Alps audacious . . . Ye Gallic flags . . . I sing not you"),[20] Barlow implies, perhaps unintentionally, that the daily life of the New England farmer contains nothing heroic, contemptible, or ridiculous, however much it may be enjoyed.

The innovation in Barlow's poem lies in its sustained sexual punning, rather than in its smiling at the rules men devise for making poetry or pudding. Such punning was quite in character. When Barlow was fifty-eight years of age, exiled in Poland from his wife Ruth's bed, he wooed her through playful language linking place to sexual power: "I love my darling, first-begotten, longbeloved wife better & more & harder & softer than all the Poles between the south pole and the north pole."[21] The "softer theme" promised in the proposition of "The Hasty-Pudding" is an unspecified "virgin theme," "fruitful, rich, well suited to inspire / The purest frenzy of poetic fire" (87). The growing, harvesting, and eating of maize then serves as one prolonged metaphor for the risings of sexuality. As the corn grows

> "Then start the juices, then the roots expand;
> Then, like a column of Corinthian mould,
> The stalk struts upward, and the leaves unfold;
> The bushy branches all the ridges fill,
> Entwine their arms and kiss from hill to hill. (94).

Husking parties are occasions for rural swains to reap their own harvests (96). After the epic weapon of the spoon is prepared, the eater readies himself "With ease to enter and discharge the freight" (98). The last lines of the poem describe the eater's climactic ecstasy:

> Just in the zenith your wise head project,
> Your full spoon, rising in a line direct,
> Bold as a bucket, heeds no drops that fall,
> The wide mouth'd bowl will surely catch them all. (98)

During the many years in which "The Hasty-Pudding" was to be condescendingly praised as Barlow's one successful poem, one wonders whether appreciation of it truly depended on its meager "mock-epic" qualities.

Joel Barlow's struggle to attain convincing heroic verse was to succeed only momentarily, at the very end of his life, when he set aside the American epic and all generic categories. "Advice to A Raven in Russia" (1812), written after Barlow had seen the devastation following Napoleon's retreat from Moscow, releases hatred through the ironic mask of impartial advice. To Barlow, Bonaparte's wars marked the annihilation of all he had ever dreamed. Napoleon was the republican turned emperor, a militarist who had sacrificed the Rights of Man to tyranny, and then reduced Europe to a plain of carnage. Napoleon had, in sum, made Europe the opposite of everything the New World still might become. But instead of denouncing Old World feudalism in the manner of *The Columbiad*, Barlow selected the grimmest of epic motifs – the bird of prey – and impassively debated wartime strategy. The sardonic mode of the poet's "Advice" (Fly South for warm meat this winter; next year carrion will be everywhere) belongs neither to the epic nor to any species of burlesque. The spectacle of Napoleonic devastation had led Barlow to contemplate previously unimaginable horror in new ways. Into the open eyes of frozen soldiers' corpses, Barlow projects the possibilities of divine injustice and worldwide cataclysm:

> The frozen orb, preserving still its form
> Defies your talons as it braves the storm,
> But stands and stares to God, as if to know,
> In what curst hands he leaves his world below.[22]

Though Barlow here attains the terrifying sublimity that had so long eluded him, the grandeur of his poem grows from his rage at the betrayal of republican values rather than from his elation at their fulfillment.

Like Dwight, Freneau, and Trumbull, Brackenridge turned away from a youthful assault upon the epic. Instead of continuing to anticipate a Homer and a Milton rising in America, Brackenridge increasingly la-

mented popular indifference to literary ambition, and warned any son of
the Revolution against a career in letters. The source of Brackenridge's
belief that Cervantes, not Homer, was the appropriate model for a vast
American work lies, however, in the politics of class conflict, rather than
in personal frustration at a failed epic endeavor. Brackenridge's contempt
for the western Pennsylvania representatives whose planned absence prevented the quorum necessary to ratify the federal Constitution was reinforced by his class contempt for William Findley, the Irish weaver who
had led them.[23] For Brackenridge, an American satire thus became fea-
sible at the moment when demagoguery, ignorance, and ambition, in-
vested in an ethnic inferior, gained political viability at the expense of a
responsible and educated elite.

The four volumes of *Modern Chivalry* surely are, as Robert Ferguson
has shown, an essential index of the shift in American ideas about law
and politics between 1792 and 1815. As a work of literature, however, it
is at once less coherent in form and even more mechanical in situation
than *The Columbiad,* which is considerably shorter. *Modern Chivalry* began as Hudibrastic poem, "The Modern Chevalier," which Brackenridge believed had considerable "felicity of imitation." Because, as he
admitted, others found his Hudibrastics tiresome, he switched to "the
prose of Cervantes" simply because it provided "a more humble and
might be a safer walk." The "adventures" of Captain Farrago and Teague
O'Reagan consist of little but repeated instances of Teague's attaining a position above his ability, a threatening elevation from which he is
sure to be rescued by the worthy Farrago. Brackenridge is too determined upon class distinctions to allow his gentleman to tilt at a windmill,
or his rogue to be perceptive and affectionate. Instead of parables about
man's need for illusion, Brackenridge gives us judgmental satire of the
Republic's crudities. Unable to shape narrative toward a significant comic
conflict, Brackenridge devises onesided dialogue or, more commonly,
sermonizes directly to the reader. Essayistic digressions, which Fielding
had concentrated in the first chapter of the books of *Tom Jones,* may be
found almost anywhere, and nearly everywhere, in *Modern Chivalry.*[24]

The interminable sprawl of *Modern Chivalry* is partially caused by
Brackenridge's bewilderment over genre. *Modern Chivalry* is neither a
novel nor a book of travels, neither mock-epic nor mock-romance, neither high nor low burlesque. The term "prose satire," which Brackenridge does not use, would have suggested an appropriate range of tone,
but no narrative design. The author refers to *Modern Chivalry* simply as
"this book" (4), "a treatise" (44), "this work" (76) or, finally, a "caricature" (803). By ignoring known generic categories, Brackenridge found
himself in an open literary field. Lacing the ability to devise a new form,
he resorted to mechanical repetition of one situation, gaining incidental

satiric successes at the expense of shapeless verbiage. After eight hundred pages and nearly thirty years, Brackenridge's concluding apology shows a sad candor:

> I cannot think it will do harm. It contains a good deal of moral senti-
> ment, the result of my own reading, observation, and experience. . . .
> If I were to go over the same ground again, I would make one word do
> where two were used. The fact is that I have spoken upon subjects I did
> not understand, and had an ambition to display oratory. In correcting
> the errors of ambition for place, or the mere display of powers, this
> book may be of service in a republic. (803)

Like Barlow apologizing for *The Columbiad,* Brackenridge claims that literary merit is secondary to republican duty, in part because of his own failings of artistry. Rebelling against the boundaries of genre, neither author was able to turn new freedom to literary advantage. Ironically, the first American writer to do so was that supposed traditionalist Washington Irving. *The History of New York,* far more daring than *M'Fingal* in its conflation of comic forms, provided a new kind of mock-heroic American literature. Whereas Trumbull had been wary of any political idea, Diedrich Knickerbocker confronts the possibility that all of "history" and all of "progress" are comforting lies men need to impose upon the chaos of time. By subsuming the mock-epic and mock-romance within an ostensibly heroic history, Irving was able to give coherent literary shape to the possibility of an anarchic present.

IV. HISTORIAN WITH TWO URNS

Melville's Ishmael and Irving's Knickerbocker are bachelors who condescend to women, pedants who mock pedantry, historians who laugh at their sources, encyclopedists who distrust the reality of fact. Their narratives center around heroes of similar qualities. Wooden-legged Peter Stuyvesant, likened in mock-epic simile to the grampus and the bear, rages in solitary, futile defiance of malignant powers without and lesser men beneath. Despite Stuyvesant's bluster and Ahab's vaunt, their commitments to one-man rule are honest and open, backed up by the physical courage integral to an old heroic code. In the face of their own ruin, a jaunty indifference to metaphysical answers and a Rabelaisian pursuit of sensual pleasure often seem, to Knickerbocker and to Ishmael, man's only and best recourse. Although Melville wrote Duyckinck in 1851 that Irving seemed a "grasshopper" compared to Hawthorne, Melville was to resume reading Irving's books in 1853; more important, he had read the Knickerbocker *History* in 1847 at the very time he was reading Rabelais. Irving's comic masterpiece, like *Moby-Dick,* absorbs literary genres, then mocks its own successful effort to supersede them. Although Irving was later to apologize for Knickerbocker's impudent ridicule, and to trim

his career into safer sentimental and patriotic modes, the Knickerbocker *History* remains a pivotal work in the literature of the new nation. It is at once the culmination of earlier mock-heroic burlesques on American politics and the beginning of that almost unclassifiable mode of mock-epic and epic that Melville and Whitman were to push beyond all limits.[25]

The newly discovered "eighth" labor of Hercules, Knickerbocker tells his reader, has been to write the *History of New York*. Needing to pay his long-overdue bill at the Columbian Hotel, Knickerbocker becomes the presiding mock-hero of the history he creates. His immense literary labor on behalf of his inconsequential Dutch ancestry parodies a filiopietistic duty assumed by his generation of Americans – to sing the heroism of seventeenth-century settlers as the germ of Revolutionary virtue. Historians and orators were expected to show how the courage of the founding fathers, traced back to the first generation, affirmed the progress of history into reasoned republicanism. Behind the mask of fussy, harmless old Knickerbocker, Irving could satirize these comforting patriarchal assumptions, portraying Christian settlement as bumbling greed, Indian conversion as a land grab, and self-government as the opening wedge of demagoguery. The more Knickerbocker protests his concern for his ancestry, the more he ridicules it. Mock-epic conventions proliferate as Knickerbocker discovers how little there is to write about. As the era of "Walter the Doubter," gives way to "William the Testy" and to "Peter the Headstrong," Knickerbocker's ordering of colonial regimes reverses contemporary assumptions about progress. The Knickerbocker *History* thus becomes both a subversive comedy about generational decline and "the first American book to question directly the civic vision of the Founding Fathers."[26]

To cushion the threat of his subversion, Knickerbocker at first turns history into mock-heroic burlesque, thereby obscuring any clear boundary between past fact and literary artifice. He invokes "Apollo and his whole seraglio of Muses" (449) to witness that his embellishments follow the approved method of modern historians, then defies any detractor to write a more accurate account. Knickerbocker aggrandizes Hendrik Hudson's discovery of New York Bay by comparing him to Jason and the Argonauts, who are then promptly called "a mere gang of sheep stealers, on a marauding expedition" (428). Ostensibly worried that Dutch heroism needs literary aid, Knickerbocker laments that he lacks "the privileges of Dan Homer and Dan Virgil to enliven my narration" with Olympians, giant Lystrigonians and, most especially, "honest old Neptune" (428). Fifteen pages later, Knickerbocker pulls out all his literary stops for the grand moment of Manhattan's settlement. He likens Dutch wanderings to "the oft sung story of the Eneid," compares Hellgate to

Carybdis, and sends his Dutchmen cruising past "as many Lystrigonians and Cyclops and Syrens and unhappy Didos, as did ever the pious Eneas" (444). The lost Dutchmen finally found their city when their "canoes" are washed ashore by the timely arrival of half a dozen potent billows sent by nonexistent "old Neptune" (445).

Unlike older forms of low and high burlesque, the satire of such passages is aimed in every direction simultaneously, including the writer's. Aeneas the founder of Rome, Knickerbocker knows, was a cowardly womanizer with his eye on the main chance. Aeneas' New World counterparts, the Dutch founders of New York, were sleepy, lovably incompetent sensualists. Notions of a divine mission guiding the rise and fall of civilization are the delusions of epic poets and historians, who have devised preposterous machinery to shore them up. Instead of serving as a standard by which to judge the triviality of the present, Dan Homer and Dan Virgil are themselves ridiculed because their highflown conventions are outmoded, and their view of the world is a lie. Above all, however, Irving's mock-epic satirizes the contemporary reader who expects a heroic history in quasi-epic clothing. Knickerbocker introduces his reader to "the golden reign of Wouter Van Twiller" by an opening account of "the grand council of New Amsterdam" (468). Anticipating Homeric speech by libertarian forefathers, the reader hears only the snores of fat burgomasters. Lest his Manhattan readers assume that generational progress must have washed away their low commercial origin, Knickerbocker likens the Dutch grand council to New York's Board of Aldermen. Legislative chambers, new and old, are governed by Walter's gold-lettered maxim, "The sow that's still / Sucks all the swill" (472). Forward-looking republicans are laughingly shown why Walter Van Twiller's era was indeed the closest approximation of the Golden Age that New Amsterdam and New York will ever know. Happily innocent of the legal wrangling of William the Testy (Thomas Jefferson), Walter the Doubter never doubted that human comfort should take precedence over political words.

As the legends of Sleepy Hollow and Rip Van Winkle attest, Diedrich Knickerbocker repeatedly associates the fall from paradise with the onset of a political mentality that replaces a world of infantile sensual gratification with the adult problems of moral and societal governance. As the reader learns how William the Testy introduced representative government, legal precedent, education, and political debate to New Netherlands, the torpor of Walter the Doubter acquires a regressive appeal. The visible follies and hidden selfishness of the new world of politics become associated with the changed Revolutionary world of Kieft's (Jefferson's) administration. The figure of Peter Stuyvesant gathers significance because he arrives in New Netherlands exactly at the moment when this

shift has become clear. For Knickerbocker, Stuyvesant embodies the possibility of turning the present world of committee policy far backward in time, beyond the sleepy expediency of the burgomasters, to a world of personal decision and courageous deeds. Stuyvesant's arrival thus shifts Irving's history from both low and high burlesque toward an embarrassed elegy.

Although the eras of Walter and William demanded only one book each of Knickerbocker's *History*, Peter Stuyvesant dominates the last three books. "The best of our ancient Dutch governors," Stuyvesant is half-facetiously introduced as "a combination of heros" who possesses the strength of Ajax, the stature of Hercules, the wrath of Achilles, and the integrity of Charlemagne, together with one less-expected virtue, "a sovereign contempt for the sovereign people" traceable to Plutarch's Coriolanus (565). Knickerbocker's admiration is evident in such phrases as "my favourite hero, the gallant Peter Stuyvesant" (643). Like Israel Putnam, to whom he is twice compared, Stuyvesant displays the solitary political and military courage that Americans, in presumably rare moments, were to display during the Revolution. Although Stuyvesant embodies Knickerbocker's yearning to reverse the decline of an increasingly political world, Stuyvesant also possesses personal virtues Knickerbocker associates with the Revolution:

> If from all that I have said thou dost not gather, worthy reader, that Peter Stuyvesant was a tough, sturdy, valiant, weatherbeaten, mettlesome, leathernsided, lion hearted, generous spirited, obstinate old "seventy six" of a governor, thou art a very numscull at drawing conclusions. (567)

"Old seventy six," it seems, proves his integrity by remaining resolutely opposed to any form of popular sovereignty.

Knickerbocker unfolds Stuyvesant's deeds as if the script formed a climacteric of heroic truculence. After throwing Kieft's entire "meddlesome" cabinet out of office (569), Stuyvesant quells further internal opposition by the force of his physical presence and sheer will. He promotes commerce, opposes lawyers, builds fortifications, fixes the Connecticut boundary, and defies the aggressions of the Council for New England. Knickerbocker makes no mention of seemingly puritanical policies of the historical Stuyvesant: his measures to control taverns, to promote the Dutch Reformed Church, to define legal slavery, or to regularize land purchases from the Indians.[27] Instead, Knickerbocker's Stuyvesant proceeds from personal conviction to physical act without any political mediation whatever. As the "gallant old Governor" leads out his troops to combat the Swedes, Knickerbocker remarks, with a rare absence of irony, "There is something so captivating in personal bravery, that, with

the common mass of mankind, it takes the lead of most other merits" (637).

The end of Knickerbocker's elaborate display of Stuyvesant's stature is to show that "personal bravery" has become an insufficient, even absurd anachronism in a newly politicized world. Knickerbocker ends Books Six and Seven with public confrontation between Stuyvesant and two opposite kinds of enemies, both defined through ethnic stereotypes. The foreground of the mock-epic action, New Amsterdam's conquest of New Sweden, culminates in Book Six, Chapter Seven, describing Stuyvesant's capture of Fort Christina, "the most horrible battle ever recorded in poetry or prose" (648). The immortal deities, newly arrived from Troy, "all itching to have a finger in the pie," deploy themselves in appropriate modern guise: Venus, "a blear eyed trull," parades along the battlements of Fort Christina, while "ox-eyed Juno" displays herself on a Dutch baggage wagon; Mars is a drunken Swedish corporal, Minerva "a brawny gin suttler"; Apollo, preparing to sing the epic event, trudges along in the rear "as a bandy-legged fifer, playing most villainously out of tune" (648–9). After feasts and councils, catalogues and armings, the Dutch warriors, devastated by Swedish attack, withdraw to their neighboring tavern, whence they are persuaded to return to the field by the gallant Peter. Challenging Swedish General Rinsing to single combat, Peter deflects Rinsing's sword thrust with his crown, fells Rinsing with his "sturdy stone pottle," and then retires, covered with glory, from a field upon which no one was killed.

Irving's burlesque suggests that the ancient epic was never more than today's mock-heroic history, because Troy was never more significant than Fort Christina. Venus and Juno were never more than military whores – Helen projected into the Heavens. The kinds of glory promoted by epic bards have always been "villainously out of tune" with the reality of war. The surest of all martial merits is revealed to be not valor, but hardheadedness. As Rinsing's sword pierces Peter's helmet, but not his cranium, Stuyvesant finally earns his epic epithet ("Hart-kopping Piet" or "Peter the Headstrong"). The reader, however, is left to wonder exactly where on the modern scale of mock-heroic virtues sheer intransigence shades into stupidity.

Like similar burlesque battles in *Joseph Andrews* and *Tom Jones,* the conquest of Fort Christina is initially presented as farce detachable from the immediate narrative context. In Book Seven, however, Knickerbocker shows us that gestures of heroic conquest have lasting historical consequence. While Stuyvesant is away earning mock-heroic laurels in New Sweden, the "Amphyctionic Council of the East" (The Council For New England) secretly arranges with Charles II to subjugate New

Amsterdam through a land grant backed up by ministerial bravado and a surprise invasion. Although Knickerbocker had declared that New Amsterdam's fall was to be brought about by the *Parcae* (565), the conquest ultimately results from English expansionism, Puritan deceit and Stuyvesant's own "intolerable hunger for martial glory, which raged within his very bowels" (642). Stuyvesant's stubborn courage enables him to put down the swords of stolid Swedes, but leaves him helpless before the words of cunning Yankees. When Stuyvesant journeys to Hartford to challenge the head of the Amphyctionic Council to single combat, its director smilingly declines, knowing that conquest now proceeds by immigration, conspiracy, and rhetorical gesture. In a world where lying words are the ruling weapon, Stuyvesant's honest courage makes him a sure loser.

Rather than lamenting the end of old heroic virtue, Knickerbocker concludes his portrayal of Stuyvesant by puffing him into a pretentious relic. Although all other Dutch citizens quickly acquiesce in the English takeover, Stuyvesant refuses to capitulate, withdrawing into the upstairs room of his mansion "like a giant into his castle" (716). Knowing that New Netherlands has been lost, Stuyvesant nonetheless prefers to aim his own blunderbuss against the world rather than to sign a treaty whose words only acknowledge reality. Although at first such stubbornness "struck even the ignoble vulgar, with awe and admiration" (716), Stuyvesant soon learns that he has no cause to sustain. By finally signing the vile paper, Stuyvesant reduces his contentiousness to a foolish gesture. To forestall any melancholy over the end of heroism, Knickerbocker follows Stuyvesant's surrender with mock reflections upon his own role as "historian of sensibility." Contemplating "the decline and fall of your renowned and mighty empires," Knickerbocker knows that he too "has reduced his impetuous grief to a kind of manual" (718). To elegize Gibbon's Rome or Irving's New York seems equally phony after Knickerbocker enjoins the reader "You who have noses, prepare to blow them now" (718).

In ways still unrecognized, Washington Irving used the mock-heroic genre to assert ideas about literary artifice that are as old as Sterne, as new as Nabokov and Post-Modernism. The world exists for writers to create: "Cities, empires, plots, conspiracies, wars, havock and desolation, are ordained by Providence only as food for the historian" (380). Writers not only control the past; they first imagine it and then persuade readers that their imaginings are true (553). Only authors create heroes and only authors mourn for them (563). Like God, the writer of mock-heroic history is an able architect who devises for us, not reality, but a theater (398). People do mighty deeds to obtain fame, which is "half a page of dirty paper" (662). As the art of literary imagining developed,

mimesis was long ago replaced by a set of falsifying literary conventions readers have learned to anticipate (511). In order to fabricate his own nest, each author must first tear everyone else's nest to pieces (409).

Such possibilities lead Diedrich Knickerbocker to a gay, defiant skepticism about the historical endeavor upon which he and his reader are engaged. Because he is "lugging forth the character of an almost forgotten hero," Knickerbocker taunts his reader with the reminder that Peter Stuyvesant must be either a "spurious fabrication of his own" or else a "dismembered fragment" dressed up in "false trappings" (502). "With one flourish of my pen," Knickerbocker exults, he can eliminate his readers' ancestors or exalt a coward by concocting a battle (553). Once the past is known to be artifice, Knickerbocker self-consciously becomes the Jove of his own mock-Homeric history, doling out misfortunes and blessings to New Netherlands from the "two huge tuns" of his inkwells (533). Peter Stuyvesant eventually becomes an art form, "altogether one of the most commanding, bitterlooking and soldierlike figures, that ever strutted on canvas" (608). Stuyvesant's character is a literary collage made up of Hercules, Achilles, Charlemagne, and Coriolanus; he exists only because the reality of his literary prototypes has been assumed: "Had not Homer tuned his lofty lyre, observes the elegant Cicero, the valour of Achilles had remained unsung. – And such, too, after all the toils and perils he had braved, after all the gallant actions he had atchieved [sic], such too had nearly been the fate of the chivalric Peter Stuyvesant, but that I fortunately stepped in and engraved his name on the indelible tablet of history, just as the caitiff Time was silently brushing it away forever" (661).

Whenever Knickerbocker pens similar passages, heroism and mock-heroism lose all reality as social values, and become one man's imaginings, infinitely shiftable at will.[28] As Knickerbocker prepares for "the most horrible battle ever recorded in poetry or prose," he remarks that the battle will be anything he makes of it. After all, if Homer lied about essentials, why not Knickerbocker? "I can drive [my] antagonist clear round and round the field, as did Dan Homer most falsely make that fine fellow Hector scamper like a poltroon around the walls of Troy; for which in my humble opinion the prince of Poets deserved to have his head broken" (644). Knickerbocker's reader is thus made ever wary of the "lofty and gigantic mode in which we heroic writers always talk of war, thereby to give it a noble and imposing aspect" (607). But his reader is made equally conscious that the mock epic is only another, equally suspect, set of conventions. While Swedes and Dutchmen prepare for battle, Knickerbocker declares "Therefore stand by for broken heads and bloody noses! my pen has long itched for a battle – siege after siege have I carried on, without blows or bloodshed; but now I have at length got

a chance" (644–5). Knickerbocker's "chance" has, of course, nothing to do with any event of the past; it depends solely upon the literary placement of a climactic, mock-epic scuffle. In Irving's view, republican America has become so removed from the heroic age that the reality of New Netherlands must rest on Knickerbocker's debunking of his reader's literary experience.

Knickerbocker is forever on the verge of openly admitting that words, especially his own, connect to nothing but their own literary precedents. In the midst of his introductory mock cosmology, Knickerbocker likens ideas to balloons which, inflated by the vapours of the imagination, soar away to the moon (397). The patriotic author, "weeping and howling in prose, in blank verse, and in rhyme . . . inflates a nation with sighs it never heaved" (563). Knickerbocker professes to worry that his countrymen, admiring the ways of William the Testy, are now sustained only by their own hyperbole; America has become a land of "statesmen, orators, civilians and divines who by dint of big words, inflated periods, and windy doctrines, are kept afloat on the surface of society, as ignorant swimmers are buoyed up by blown bladders" (534).

Metaphors likening language to a balloon or bladder, inflated with gaseous nothing, culminate in the epic simile Knickerbocker finally applies to the decline and fall of the Dutch dynasty:

> Thus have I seen a crew of truant urchins, beating and belabouring a distended bladder, which maintained its size, uninjured by their assaults – At length an unlucky brat, more knowing than the rest, collecting all his might, bounces down with his bottom upon the inflated globe. – The contact of contending spheres is aweful and destructive – the bloated membrane yields – it bursts, it explodes with a noise strange and equivocal, wonderfully resembling thunder – and is no more. (720)

Knickerbocker's scatological analogy applies both to the Dutch dynasty and to the man who has now completed its history. It is Knickerbocker who has made a "distended bladder" of gaseous words from the scantiest of historical sources. It is also Knickerbocker who, as an "unlucky brat," has forever delighted in puncturing the "inflated globes" he has blown up for our enjoyment. Just as the Dutch dynasty leaves nothing behind after its noisy explosion, so Knickerbocker's *History* may have left nothing but the spirit of ridicule it has blown forth in every direction.

In its amiable jesting and insistence on the artifice of literature, Irving's mock-epic is the American counterpart to *Don Juan*.[29] Like Byron, Irving laughs away established ideas about the reality of heroism and the mimetic possibilities of epic. Neither the American reading public nor Irving himself was prepared, however, to entertain the nihilistic jests hidden behind Knickerbocker's fussy pedantry. When Geoffrey Crayon resurrects the past, he prefers nostalgia to impudence. Irving's Washington

would be a supposedly historical exemplar, rendered with all the filiopie-
tism Irving's culture – and his own later eminence – demanded. Not
surprisingly, Irving's apology for the Knickerbocker *History* is perilously
close to a retraction. Even Bryant's elegiac tribute ("Of all mock heroic
works, Knickerbocker's *History of New York* is the gayest, the airiest and
the least tiresome") reduces Irving's achievement into a safe spoof on
quaint colonials.[30]

Nonetheless, the popularity of the Knickerbocker *History* in its time
testifies to an important paradox in the development of American heroic
literature. A serious imitative epic was what the new nation demanded
for cultural self-justification. When such poems were published, however, they proved to be an embarrassment few would read. New forms
of mock epic like *M'Fingal*, "The Hasty-Pudding" or the Knickerbocker
History often drew upon deeper sources of creative imagination, and remained of lasting interest among contemporaries. Nonetheless, it was
still commonly assumed until mid-century that the mock-epic was a form
separate from and inferior to the serious epic. Noah Webster's short definition of "Burlesk" completely ignored the older distinction between
mock-epic and burlesque by grouping Scarron, Boileau, Butler, and
Trumbull as writers all of one kind. The word "epic" however, prodded
Webster into a grave enumeration of literary conventions, derived from
Kames and the *Brittanica,* that concludes "The end is to improve the mor-
als and inspire a love of virtue, bravery and illustrious actions." A few
sentences after Samuel Kettell acknowledged that *M'Fingal* had enjoyed
"a greater celebrity than any other American poem," he warned "Burlesque poetry is but an inferior species of composition, and the masters
of it can claim but a second place in the temple of the Muses." The
serious epic, to the many people of Kettell's persuasion, still existed to
exalt heroism, whereas the mock-epic existed to ridicule folly. The contrast of tone between *The Columbiad* and the Knickerbocker *History,* between *The Conquest of Canaan* and *M'Fingal,* seemed only to confirm the
total separation of epic panegyric from mock-epic satire. As long as readers like Kettell believed that it was "a prostitution of poetry to busy it
with the faults and follies of men," an American didactic epic, purged of
authorial humor and its hero's failings, would continue to be sought as a
needed, literary centerpiece.[31]

4

A WHITE ACHILLES FOR
THE WEST?

Dixon Wecter once remarked that "The winning of the West is the great fantasy of our Republic. It is the epic which the folk mind has looked upon as more truly American than the settlement of Jamestown and Plymouth, the spacious life of the old plantation, or the building of stone and steel."[1] Although Wecter did not mention the American Revolution, his claim about "the folk mind" remains useful both in the loose sense of the word "epic" (a heroic cultural achievement) and in the restrictive sense of a literary genre. In a similar vein, Constance Rourke claimed that the Promethean exploits of the Davy Crockett stories formed an oral folk epic for nineteenth-century settlers.[2] If we update the context of such claims, their essence can be seen to remain valid. Since outer space has become America's new frontier, the durability of media series (Space Cadet, Star Trek, Star Wars) centering on exploration seems to indicate that the appeal of venturing into the unknown has far outlasted flurries of interest in the Revolution, the plantation myth, or city builders.

Throughout the nineteenth century, literary figures from the West drew up plans for never written epic poems that would describe the heroism of crossing the frontier. In an 1854 issue of *The Pioneer or California Monthly,* Edward Pollock argued that a great epic could and should be written on Western man and Western scenery.[3] Bret Harte, who felt that the gold rush was "an era replete with a certain heroic Greek poetry," considered *The Luck of Roaring Camp* to be a collection of "materials for the *Iliad* that is yet to be sung," and wrote Howells that he contemplated writing "that great epic poem . . . truly American literature for which the world is anxiously waiting."[4]

After the frontier was officially declared at an end, there arose a demand to memorialize the conquests of all the forgotten, presumably Teutonic, settlers. Frank Norris's desire to complete "a big Epic trilogy," "some great work with the West and California as a background,"[5] is in part attributable to his regret that the West had become

94

the literary property of the dime novel. In his essay "A Neglected Epic," Norris berated both "well-bred gentlemen in New England," who thought that only Norse or German legends were suitable to epic, and the ghost writers for Erastus Beadle, who had falsely described Western settlers as "desperadoes" or "harlequins . . . in fringed leggings":

> The great figure of our neglected epic, the Hector of our ignored Iliad, is not, as the dime novels would have us believe, a law-breaker, but a law-maker; a fighter, it is true, as is always the case with epic figures, but a fighter for peace. . . . We have taken no account of the brave men who stood for law and justice and liberty, and for these great ideas died by the hundreds, unknown and unsung – died that the West might be subdued, that the last stage of the march should be accomplished, that the Anglo-Saxon should fulfill his destiny and complete the cycle of the world.[6]

As in American heroic literature from Mather to Benét, Norris's western Hector is no single hero, but the hundreds of "brave men" who together fulfilled the progressive imperatives of history.

Norris's racial assumptions are baldly restated in an anonymous, un-dated pamphlet titled "The Epic of the West: Its Hero." The author re-counts achievements of Western civilizers from Daniel Boone through the completion of the Transcontinental Railroad, and insists that all these heroes have embodied the aggressive spirit of German liberty. Because both the Indian and the wilderness have been wholly conquered, Amer-ican citizens may be sure that previous epic subjects have been superseded: "There is yet to appear some poet immortal who shall praise the most valiant hero whose epic deeds did ever bless mankind, the western pi-oneer."[7]

Amid the increasingly aggressive nationalism that developed after 1815, today's winning of the West seemed a more promising epic theme than yesterday's Revolution. Pioneers crossing the Alleghenies could collec-tively embody recent, national proof of Empire's westward course. For-tunately, the pioneer could be imagined as a classless commoner freed of the gentlemanly origins of Revolutionary fathers. Without regard for Indian occupancy of western lands, the white pioneer's act of settlement was conceived as a voyage of discovery through and across the pristine sublimity of mountain barriers. Indian warfare could provide the hand to hand battles that were advancing white civilization against the barba-rism of the heroic age. The long journey of the settler, ending in con-quest and displacement of the infidel, could thus be refashioned as the outgrowth of a particular epic motif leading back through Camoens and Tasso to Virgil. Not the least advantage of the Western subject was its appeal to familial virtues, including family ownership of land. Authors of epics on the Revolution had isolated male achievement from all private

contexts; the act of settlement encouraged poets to picture the migrating family acting together.

Among literary patriots, the failure of *The Columbiad* served only to make the need for a truly national epic more acute. The *Analectic Magazine* warned any American poet intent on an epic against launching out beyond his depth, yet still concluded "We by no means despair of seeing produced among ourselves, in the fullness of time, an heroic poem which shall rival in sublimity and beauty, and surpass in interest and instructiveness, any [sic] the most excellent and admired, of which the world is in possession."[8] A less patient critic complained "We have as yet, indeed, no national poet, no writer who, like Homer or Milton, stands out in a strong light as a representative of American humanity in its greatest perfection."[9] International republicanism was clearly falling out of fashion. Orestes Brownson's concern for the class struggle did not prevent him from opening an 1839 address on American literature by noting "There is no great poem of American origin, unless we call Barlow's Columbiad such, – our only national epic."[10] In spite of its continental literary interests, the *North American Review* longed for "a poem in ten books or cantos, or even in six" that might stand beside, and preferably update, Barlow's "venerable production."[11] A common regret of the 1830s was that William Cullen Bryant, bard of our prairies as well as our woods, had not yet attempted to write the national epic.[12]

Westerners were elated by the new epic subject. Thomas Peirce of Cincinnati, author of *The Muse of Hesperia* (1823), was certain that a Western bard had subjects for "a loftier, nobler song" than his Eastern predecessors. Peirce provided a verse list of possible subjects including Jackson's victory at New Orleans, Perry's victory on Lake Erie, the growth of commerce in Kentucky, or the conquest of plains Indians by pioneers who "Met and chastised for barbarous deeds / Their savage foes."[13] Timothy Flint, however, was astute enough to recognize that the epic of the West had better concern a settler of humble origin who had already become a national legend: "The adventures of Daniel Boon [sic] would make no mean show beside those of other heroes and adventurers. But although much has been said in prose, and sung in verse, about Daniel Boon, this Achilles of the West wants a Homer, worthily to celebrate his exploits."[14] To none of these literary projectors does the idea ever occur that the Indians might have sung their own epics, or might be the heroes of a white writer's epic. Instead, their cultural vision narrows to a cruel intensity. The settler with his family stands both for Civilization and Nation; beyond is only the Other to be destroyed.

These literary and cultural needs inevitably produced such conceptually similar poems as Daniel Bryan's *The Mountain Muse* (1813) and Paulding's *The Backwoodsman* (1818). Bryan's hero is Daniel Boone and

his heroic subjects are the settlement of Kentucky, the removal of the Shawnee Indians from Ohio, and the glorious future of western civilization. Paulding's hero is a hypothetical settler named Basil, and his heroic subjects are the settlement of the Ohio River valley, the removal of the Shawnee, and the benefits of agricultural freehold. Both of these pioneer heroes, confined by repressive Eastern policies of land tenure, migrate across the sublime Alleghenies, establish footholds of civilization along the Ohio, and lovingly bring their families into their new lands. The climactic action of both poems is the defeat and removal of Indians who retain only the evil qualities of Milton's Satan. The pioneer hero, representing an all-white nation, is never tempted to value red culture. Consequently, the lasting threat to the Republic's future in these poems is not the Satanic Indian villain, always defeatable in war, but the white renegade who aids him, and who has reverted, in ways we are assured are atypical, to the cruel animality of the savage. For the white hero, any brutality that will erase the red brute becomes a sad necessity; only the white brute requires the nonexistent restraint of legal statutes.

Describing the ways of the pioneer allowed a poet to rework epic type scenes, but embracing the heroism of the common man did not. Knowing that the world of Pope's *Iliad* did not readily prompt thoughts of Boonesborough or Marietta, Bryan and Paulding faced problems of poetic form no less formidable than those of Dwight and Barlow. Daniel Boone must be made to speak in blank verse and Basil's tale must be told in heroic couplets. And yet, although both poems have invocations, propositions, single combat, and one or two epic similes, neither poet attempted to sustain epic conventions. After beginning *The Mountain Muse* with a council in which Truth, Enterprise, and Zeal select Boone to be Civilization's hero, Daniel Bryan descends to chronicling, in the words of his subtitle, "The Adventures of Daniel Boone." Paulding's poem shifts in the exactly opposite direction. After ridiculing epic and chivalric poetry in his first book, Paulding fills out his poem with as grandly heroic a battle as his subject permits.

Unlike Dwight or Barlow, Paulding and Bryan are so suspicious of the epic that they have difficulty completing their poems. Written without a firm narrative plan, their poems are dragged out to six and seven books respectively. The endurance of pragmatic settlers seems so admirable to both writers that they become ashamed of wasting time composing poems to portray it. Although Bryan and Paulding resent the epic's associations with aristocrats and leisure, they remain in awe of a genre they cannot transform. Sensing that their heroes might scorn the very poems that commemorate them, neither poet directly declares that his poem is an epic.

I. THE MOUNTAIN MUSE

Within ten years of his death, Daniel Boone had been praised as an empire builder bringing civilization to the wilderness, as a simple philosopher of primitive nature, and as a rebel against the confinements of civilization.[15] Because the historical man had been a surveyor, road builder, sheriff, Indian fighter, solitary explorer, hunter, trapper, state representative, and landowner, Boone's life could be shaped to fit whichever of these three images suited the prejudices of the beholder. The source Daniel Bryan dutifully followed, John Filson's "The Adventures of Colonel Daniel Boone" (1784), had portrayed Boone as a highly literate gentleman who loved the wilderness he sought to conquer.[16] The motives Bryan attributes to Boone, however, suggest that Bryan is almost as much an admirer of unspoiled nature as a spokesman for the march of progress. Instead of resolving these inconsistencies, Bryan endows Boone with expansionist purpose in one adventure and primitivist feeling in another.

Bryan's public purpose is made unmistakably plain in his first book. During a heavenly council atop the Alleghenies, the Guardian Geniuses of American – Truth, Zeal, Humanity, and Enterprise – all agree that refinement, with its civilizing hand, shall smooth away natural crudities, make the desert flower, and create a "bless'd Asylum for sweet liberty."[17] Truth declares that the fertile western lands shall not be wasted upon "scattered hordes / Of rude predaceous men, who feed on blood," while polished millions starve in European slums or crowded Eastern cities (28). Lest any reader conclude that pity for the Indian might be humane, Bryan arranges for Humanity to warn the council against savage atrocities and to conclude:

> The task, the Godlike task be ours, that wretch
> In bright Refinement's golden crucible
> To melt, to decompose and sublimate! (31)

The task of civilizing falls to Daniel Boone, not primarily because of Boone's skills as a pathfinder, but because he embodies Humanity:

> The great, ennobling virtues of the soul;
> Benevolence, Mercy, Meekness, Pity, Love;
> Benignant Justice, Valor lion-like,
> And Fortitude, with stoic nerves endow'd. (41)

According to Bryan, Boone felt his "keenest grief" on the day when, determined upon his historical mission, he was "constrained to leave domestic bliss, / the sweet endearments of connubial love" (55). During the last meeting between Daniel and his Rebecca, a meeting meant to recall Hector and Andromache, Aeneas and Dido, Boone informs his wife that he is commanded, not only to "scatter knowledge through the Heathen wilds," but to "mend the state of Universal Man" (59).

Once the narrative begins, Bryan finds himself hard pressed to provide Boone with deeds suitable to such grand purposes. Boone kills
panthers, frightens away stampeding buffalo, and twice rescues genteel
maidens from lascivious captors. He cleanses the dens of white renegades
called the Allegheny Robbers and dutifully brings his captives back to
criminal trial. The "Stygian dungeons" in which the robbers live provide
Daniel his chance to visit the underworld, a hell in which the white man
has reverted to the barbarous life of hunting (99). In the sixth and seventh
books Bryan celebrates the most heroic acts to be found in Filson's account. Daniel directs the nine-day defense of Boonesborough against
redcoats, white renegades, and their Indian myrmidons. Bryan invents a
Satanic Indian chief named Coluxso and sends him into single combat
against Daniel. The poem concludes with the providential burning of
Shawnee crops, the leveling of Shawnee towns by pioneers, and the expulsion of the red man from the Ohio River valley.

Because Bryan does not allow Boone to speak while performing these
deeds, the reader must assume that such feats "mend the state of Universal Man" and exhibit Boone's "Benevolence, Mercy, Meekness, Pity,"
and "Love." We simply see Boone doggedly carrying out his appointed
tasks with no apparent emotion and certainly without inner doubt. Bryan's
fourth and fifth books, however, portray a different hero. Surrounded
by the "grape-empurpled groves" of the Kentucky wilderness, Boone
abandons his divine mission (117). He walks through his western Eden
enraptured, "like the primary lord of Paradise . . . bestowing *names* on
streams and founts, / On plants and places yet anonymous" (144). In the
midst of New World sublimity, Boone decides that no city's pomp, polished art, or richest commerce could delight him half as much as the
world of wild luxuriance – "Sublime, majestic, beauteous, splendid, fair"
– which is all about him (134).

Boone's only declaration of inner feeling occurs in this Edenic contest:

> Innocence on timid pionions flies
> To Nature's Solitudes and sweet retreats,
> From the turmoil of Vice-enveloped crowds.
> 'Tis there the soul with passions undisturb'd
> In philosophic converse with *herself,*
> Can ascertain her energies divine,
> And exercise them in exalted thought –
> 'Tis there the mind with animated eye,
> Beholds her intellectual *currents* roll,
> Unruffled and serene. (128–9)

Only in pure wilderness does the soul's divine energy emerge, thereby
releasing the imagination needed to reshape Nature herself. In diction
and idea, Bryan's passage suggests an admiring reading of "Tintern Ab-

bey." Although Bryan cannot allow "Nature's Solitudes" to impede "Refinement's golden crucible," this passage suggests that the shaping power of the poetic imagination may constitute the truly heroic act. Whitman, Hart Crane, and William Carlos Williams, extending the ordering power of discovery to the reader, were to regard Bryan's momentary idea as the essence of a modern heroic poem.

Immediately after Boone's return to frontier clearings, he reassumes his mission to refine and to civilize. Without a moment's hesitation, he accepts appointments as surveyor, sheriff, and militia captain in order to build roads and construct forts. His criticisms of civilization and his exposure to Nature's God seem never to have occurred. Bryan evidently could not permit Boone to question whether the triumph of commerce was compatible with his love for the Kentucky Eden. Convinced that both the sublimity of nature and the spread of empire were epic themes, Bryan saw no way to combine them. Believing that an epic poem must wholly celebrate its culture's values, Bryan could not conceive of the solitary, pure, and embittered backwoods hero who would give significance to the Leatherstocking Tales.

The contradictory virtues that Bryan ascribed to Boone are all tellingly unhistorical. John Bakeless's careful and thorough biography of Boone shows that Bryan's hero was neither a romantic motivated by natural piety, nor a self-declared pathfinder for civilization. The historical Boone was an excellent woodsman, but never the organizer of any settlement expedition. He entered personal claims for tens of thousands of acres in Kentucky and Missouri, but never considered himself the standard bearer of progress.[18] Although Boone dearly loved outwitting Indians, there is no evidence that his heart was attuned to the God in Nature. His revolutionary patriotism was fitful and he disliked farming almost as much as land-robbing lawyers.

Bryan's Boone has read Milton and Cowper. He speaks and is praised in blank verse filled with inversions, personifications and such coined words as "nubilous," "caliginous," "idoneous," "grumous," and "temerarious." A letter written by Lieutenant Colonel Boone to the Governor of Kentucky in 1791 provides a sample of the historical man's powers of self-expression. Boone is offering to carry defense ammunition free of charge if he is awarded a contract to sell flour to the troops:

> Sir,
>
> as Sum purson Must carry out the armantstion to Red Stone if your Exelency Should have thought me a proper purson I Would undertake it on Conditions I have the apintment to vitel the Company at Kanhowway So that I Could take Down the Flower as I paste the place. I am your Exelency most obedent omble Sarvent,
>
> Dal Boone[19]

Bryan endows the writer of this letter with "play of mind," "sensibility," "urbanity," "mild address," and a "fine intellectual face" (121).

Because Daniel Bryan had talked with Boone a number of times before Boone's removal to Missouri, Bryan's magniloquent and refined hero can only be an artifice created for personal needs or for coastal readers.[20] During his last years, Daniel Boone either tried to read *The Mountain Muse,* or arranged to have the poem read to him. Regretting that he could not sue his nephew for slander, Boone said that "such productions . . . ought to be left till the person was put in the ground."[21] This comment may be the only instance in literary history of a cultural hero remarking on the epic poem made of his exploits. Although it may not be impossible to make a credible epic hero out of a contemporary, Bryan's poem had shown that Timothy Flint had been a trifle hasty. A poem worthy of Homer or Milton could not be fashioned from the adventures of Daniel Boone. Coastal reviewers were not conned but Southerners were dismayed. Finding himself "amused to be hunting a wild American poet," a reviewer for the *Analectic Magazine* gleefully announced that Bryan's poem "needs nothing but a little exaggeration to be heightened into broad caricature."[22] Simms tried to find something salvageable among Bryan's "truly barbarous mortals" and his "innumerable spirits readily coming whenever called"; his highest praise was that "some good poetry might be got out of it, – but to young men, it is but dangerous travelling in the woods."[23]

II. THE BACKWOODSMAN

Daniel Bryan probably avoided the term "epic" because he recognized that his verse could only be unfavorably compared to its Miltonic model. Paulding avoids the word "epic" because he explicitly links both the subject matter and the conventions of the genre with feudal overrefinement. His essay pleading for a "National Literature" (1820) rejects the world beyond American borders. "Misled by bad models," Americans have blindly preferred "antiquated machinery" to "Rational Fictions" that will "honour the adventurous spirits who first sought, explored, and cleared this western wilderness." "Mere romance-writers" like Byron and Scott are not wanted in America, because they would continue to make chivalric heroes out of border outlaws and rakish gentry. The matter of Puritan plantation, however, is not sufficiently national and is so tainted with witchery that it might tempt an American to reintroduce "gothic or Grecian machinery."[24] Paulding declines to specify America's chosen heroic subject because "National Literature" is a tacit apologia for *The Backwoodsman,* published two years earlier. The sixth book of Paulding's poem had expended some two hundred lines

distinguishing true from false heroism. The hero of European bards will forever be a warrior who "pants on tiptoe for bright Glory's crown" and thereby "makes a desert of one half the world." The "nobler heroism" is to be a hardy freeholder, indifferent to fame, who "quits all the dear domestic joys of life, / Home, harvest, happiness and honest wife" in order to rid his God-ordained plot of land from invading savages and absentee land-claimants. The exchanges of commerce, which had promoted international liberty in Joel Barlow's world, only impede the freedom of Paulding's hero. The backwoodsman's isolation enables him to exercise heroic free will and rise above the political concerns of epic councils, where man becomes "a dull machine, / Mov'd like a puppet in the mimic scene, / Rein'd or impell'd by Power's resistless force."[25]

Such belligerence implies that the western muse will never evolve through the *Translatio Imperii,* but can exist only through defiance of everything the old muses have created. In his preface, Paulding calls his poem an "experiment" because he has abandoned "his original intention in the construction of a regular plan." Accordingly, *The Backwoodsman* contains no divine machinery, not even the allegorical personifications to which Barlow and Bryan had resorted. Paulding invents no heavenly or Satanic councils, no visits to the underworld, no feasts, and no catalogues. Scorning events that might smack of extraordinary romance, Paulding refuses to trivialize Basil's westward migration with the kinds of "adventures" Daniel Bryan had included. Although Paulding retains the heroic couplet, invocations, and an occasional epic simile, his diction is refreshingly free of coined adjectives, awkward inversions and bombast. By discarding almost all the old conventions, Paulding became the first American poet to confront the opportunity and the burden of creating an indigenous heroic poem. In the words of Williams's epigraph to *Paterson,* Paulding was intent upon "A reply to Greek and Latin with the bare hands."[26] The ending of his invocation shows that Paulding felt himself on uncharted seas: "Come then, neglected Muse! and try with me / The untrack'd path" (9).

In the midst of any peril, Bryan's Boone had possessed every skill. To make him representative, Bryan had blithely claimed that the western states now stand "with glories of ten thousand Boones emblazed" (232). Paulding wishes his poem to be above such cheap plots and transparent falsities; he must find the nation's hero in the unknown commoner and ordinary deeds. An exemplar for Americans only, "our hero" is immediately claimed to be "like true Yankee lad" (9) in his concern for family, liberty, and freehold. In order to keep Basil as representative as possible, Paulding provides him with no heritage, no surname, no individuating characteristics whatever. Throughout the entire poem, Basil is never permitted to utter one word, perhaps because Paulding recognized that a

sturdy democratic farmer speaking heroic couplets might seem preposterous.

Paulding was determined to keep the action of his poem as ordinarily
heroic as his central figure. Throughout the first three books, which describe the westward trek of Basil's family, Paulding resists every opportunity to make the migration dramatic or suspenseful. He draws the most
ordinary picture of settlement he can, then informs the reader of its heroic significance. When the family bids farewell to civilization, the poet
declares:

> A simple scene! yet if we view it well
> 'Twill soon to grander outlines haply swell,
> For here we see, as on a chart unfurl'd
> The destinies of this great Western world.
> So came our ancestors, stern volunteers!
> Who knew the dangers, yet despis'd the fears;
> Thus did they sever many a heart-knit tie,
> Freedom and competence to win, or die;
> And thus their hardy offspring dare to roam,
> Far in the West, to seek a happier home,
> To push the red-man from his solitude,
> And plant refinement in the forest rude
> Thus daringly their glorious race to run
> Ev'n to the regions of yon setting sun. (62–3)

As in this passage, the heroic action of Paulding's poem is nothing more
than one example of the prophecy that prompted it. Basil, repeatedly
called "the pilgrim," is simply a name meant to stand for the collective
force of American farming, a force whose libertarian and landowning
tenets are traced back to 1620, but not before.

Without traditional epic motifs, without episodes that enrich the action, and without a hero of any individual character, Paulding has difficulty sustaining his "experiment." Sometimes he lectures the reader about
the kind of heroism Basil represents. More frequently, he composes verse
paragraphs on topics suggested by western migration: the Moravians,
Indian burial mounds, Revolutionary fathers, Campbell's "Gertrude of
Wyoming," and the sublimities of the landscape. Most often, however,
he resorts to satire. To convince the reader that every pioneer is America's true hero, he prefers to ridicule European heroism rather than to
aggrandize a world of flatboats, stumps, and log cabins. His poem begins
as follows:

> My humble theme is of a hardy swain,
> The lowliest of the lowly rural train,
> Who left his native fields afar to roam,
> In western wilds in search of happier home.
> Simple the tale I venture to rehearse,

> For humble is the Muse, and weak her verse;
> She hazards not, to sing in lofty lays,
> Of steel-clad knights, renown'd in other days,
> For glorious feats that, in this dastard time,
> Would on the gallows make them swing sublime;
> Or tell of stately dames of royal birth,
> That scorn'd communion with dull things of earth. (7)

The repetition of such competent satiric passages ultimately defeats the poem's purpose. Because Paulding cannot or will not invest Basil with any dramatic interest, the reader begins to feel that a glory-hunting warrior or a steel-clad knight might enliven the poem.

To make Basil seem significant, Paulding finally has to compromise his own scorn for aristocracy. "Our hero" the common farmer is elevated to presumably deserved titles:

> Judge, general, congressman, and half a score
> Of goodly offices, and titles more
> Reward his worth, while like a prince he lives,
> And what he gains from heav'n to mortals gives. (174)

At the moment when America's everyman is elected to Congress, his dispensing of gifts becomes an act of noblesse oblige. Would that every "true Yankee lad" could become so princely an equal!

Unable to transform the epic, Paulding became apologetic about his accommodations. In dogged heroic couplets Paulding complains, "Neglected Muse of this our western clime, / How long in servile imitative rhyme, / Wilt thou thy stifled energies impart, / And miss the path that leads to every heart?" (8). At the end of Book Two, however, Paulding suddenly decides that his plain couplets are not sufficiently sublime, the Ohio River deserves a poet who will "track thy wand'rings with a loftier wing, / And in oblivion drown my weaker verse" (54). And yet, a few pages later, Paulding suddenly claims that the legacy of Washington's "spotless, blameless, high heroic name" neither could nor should be conveyed in verse:

> No pen historic, nor the fabling lyre,
> Attun'd to flattery, his deeds require:
> Look in his Country's face, you'll see them there!
> List to her voice, you'll hear them in the air! (78)

In the space of a few pages, Paulding has praised a poetic simplicity he cannot practice, invoked a nobler lay than his, and then declared in verse that verse is superfluous. Legends are not formed, nor epics written, in the midst of such literary and cultural uncertainty.

Paulding's compromised attack upon heroic tradition is most apparent in his apologetic inclusion of warfare. By the end of Book Three, his declared heroic action, Basil's migration to gain a freehold, has been suc-

cessfully completed; martial heroism, we assume, has been superseded by the virtues of peaceful, Christian settlement. Without any preparation, Book Four begins a new heroic action in which Basil's neighbors drive the Indians and the British from the Ohio valley. This conquest, which demands three new books, allows Paulding to invent two diabolic Indian chiefs, tribal councils, bloodthirsty speeches, and a climactic battle with which the poem can end. Although Paulding celebrates the settlers' victory, Basil has no part in it, and is never mentioned for eighty-five pages.

After preparing his reader for a splendid victory in Book Six, Paulding then insists that martial glory is, after all, a barbarous sham:

> Enough of war; its glories and its ills
> The volume of the past, and present fills.
> . . . .
> Why then should I luxuriate in gore,
> And tell of horrors often told before;
> Why should I free my Muse from her restraint
> And with unfeeling coolness pause, to paint
> The quiv'ring limb, the bleeding bosom bare,
> The dripping head, reft of its honour'd hair. (159–60)

After this probably sincere disclaimer, Paulding promptly frees his muse from restraint in a two-hundred-and-seventy-line battle account filled with pictures of scalped maidens, beasts of prey, and such sentiments as "our soldiers hung upon their rear, / And mow'd them like the ripen'd harvest ear" (162).

The subject of Paulding's first three books, together with his claim that America must evolve a democratic kind of heroic poetry, comprise a tentative groping toward the 1855 preface to *Leaves of Grass*. Paulding is the first American poet to try to base a heroic poem upon a virtually nameless common man. His attempt fails, in part because of the verse form, but primarily because Paulding defines heroism as the building of objects (farm, house, and town) rather than an inner attitude. Basil is a bluff commoner who travels his open road to win freedom and dispense good will, but he has no separate self, no delight in self-mockery, no vision beyond his localized world. Paulding's democratic belligerence is real, but Basil's winnings are never extended to Kanuck, Tuckahoe, Cuff, or a Venerealee.

Reviewers of *The Backwoodsman* detected Paulding's compromises, but refused to consider the import of his aims. Aware of Paulding's invocations, heroic couplets, similes, climactic battle, and frequent use of the word "hero," they wrongly assumed that Paulding had intended to write a traditional epic poem, and then condemned him for having failed to do so. Joseph Rodman Drake jeered at "the poet of cabbages, log huts and

gin"; Fitz-Greene Halleck remarked that Homer would never have had the temerity to write *The Backwoodsman*.[27] *Port Folio* complained that Paulding's hero was "no better than a common squatter"; *The Backwoodsman* proves that, in a country where "all is plain, simple, unsophisticated nature," epic poetry has no place: "In such an utter absence of any thing like a hero, or even a suitable scene for a poet's eye to roll upon, it required uncommon nerves and powerful motives to publish an epic lay."[28]

Standards still more traditional were wielded by the *American Monthly Magazine and Critical Review*. Heroic poetry has always dealt with the marvelous, the aristocratic and with "monarchal elevation of character." Paulding's verse is filled with "low and vulgar terms," and his subject is "not altogether suited to the epic strain." Basil may be a worthy man, but he is no hero: "Hewing trees, digging, delving, ploughing, sowing, and reaping, are doubtless, all of them, respectable avocations, but make no very splendid figure in heroic song."[29] At the end of this review, Paulding's poem is advanced as proof that no epic could be written about America's unheroic civilization. Although the familiar form of Paulding's poem made such traditionalist criticism inevitable, his purposes surely deserved a more sympathetic hearing. In a letter to Washington Irving, Paulding sought comfort by claiming a revealing precedent: "My unfortunate poem has been over and over again attacked by the combined powers of wit and dullness. . . . I consoled myself with the example of Milton and appealed to posterity."[30] At the risk of a friendship, the creator of the Knickerbocker *History* could readily have told Paulding why his sober lesson in a pioneer's virtues was never to find fit audience though few.

III.   THE UNDERWORLD OF AMERICAN EPIC

Whatever halting steps Barlow, Bryan, and Paulding had taken toward differing kinds of New World epic were soon quashed by the return of militant imitation. Walter Marshall McGill's *The Western World* (1837) and Richard Emmons's *The Fredoniad* (1827) release zeal for westward expansion through adoring appropriation of Dryden's *Aeneid* and Pope's *Iliad*. Sure that only one republic still counted, McGill and Emmons versified intra-American battles in ways that generated enough chauvinism to extend their epic endeavors almost without end. Advocates of Manifest Destiny as John Louis O'Sullivan would later define it, they saw no need to discover gentlemanly manners within a Joshua, to seek a worldwide republic of peace, or even to proclaim the heroism of the average male. For them, old epic conventions glorifying conquest should be relished, not changed. America's bloody victories, they now knew, had been wholly justified by the expanding powers of the Repub-

lic. Looking back at the two wars that had created the nation was their way of looking forward toward other wars that would enlarge it.

Readers of McGill's *The Western World* quickly learned that any history worth remembering began in 1492, but that "the western world" means only these United States. Desiring to "add something to the stateliness and grandeur of American poesy," and driven by "a love of country almost approaching enthusiasm," McGill completed ten books and 381 pages of heroic couplets recounting the campaigns of the American armies from the Battle of Lexington (Book II) through the Battle of Yorktown (Book X), with George Washington as his hero and Howe and Cornwallis as his villains.[31] As the opening proposition shows, McGill associates the epic with unalloyed patriotism expressed in comparatively simple diction:

> Of revolution, and of empires sing,
> Of haughty tyrants, and the proud king,
> That lifted high his dread oppressive hand,
> To destroy at once, fair Columbia's land.
> Thou plaintive muse, sing thou too of heroes
> Of mighty men who bore the frightful woes
> Attendant on Columbia's day of dread
> And their republic won. (40)

Ignoring the controversies that prompted the war, McGill portrays America as a utopia of increasingly prosperous freeholders invaded by land-hungry royal hirelings. All redskins are fierce savages and every fighting Indian is a British mercenary. Before many of the poem's battles, virginal maidens and white-haired patriarchs gather to send their heroes off to victory. Unifying iconographic images of the Revolutionary War are carefully rehearsed: the Crossing of the Delaware, revelling Hessians in Trenton, Washington on his knees at Valley Forge, and Cornwallis surrendering his sword.

The Western World would retain no interest were it not for McGill's reshaping of the heroic image of George Washington. The benevolent and affectionate father dear to the post-Revolutionary generation is replaced by a figure of older origin but clearer contemporaneity. McGill's Washington is America's "Old Chief," "an ancient giant warrior grave," "Old Washington, now gray in War."[32] In book after book he appears as a dark-browed figure with flashing eyes and a rasping voice who sits astride his war horse, urging his admiring troops to follow him to glory or to death:

> Now Washington prepares;
> From his visage dark, vengeance horrid glares,
> And, as he rides from rank to rank in haste,
> His stern voice sonorous in accents waste

> Its deep tones sounds. His mighty soul awakes
> And, strange, the huge ancient warrior quakes
> Throughout with ancient vigor, while he shouts. (298)

According to McGill, Washington fought primarily to protect freeholders from confiscation rather than to secure the Rights of Man. Something of a rabble rouser, Washington addresses his troops in short, simple phrases and twice warns that the British, if victorious, will rape American women. Worshipping Jehovah rather than Almighty Goodness, Washington can afford no gentlemanly tolerance. Parson Weems would have thought McGill's Washington was only half the man; both Dwight and Barlow would have been repulsed by him.

Washington's age, features, courage, disregard for ideas, and unbending will all correspond to the age's image of Andrew Jackson.[33] In McGill's view, Washington's greatest triumph prefigures Jackson's. Like Jackson at New Orleans, Washington at Yorktown builds his redoubt, places soldiers and helpless citizens behind it, looks out over the sea, and burns to destroy an anticipated British fleet.[34] When McGill's Genius of Liberty prophecies the greatness of America, her concern is the conquest of the trans-Allegheny west, not the rise of republicanism in the New World:

> On plains that once but mighty oaks bore
> I build me cities and towns far and near,
> And there at night the mighty savage cries;
> And where his war whoops in void distance dies,
> There, there, I spread my waving fruitful fields,
> That earth might show, and dark soil yield
> Their abundance. There, the wigwam razed,
> My sons dwell safely, and large cities rear
> Their lofty battlements, and praise to God
> At morn and evening thro' the land is heard. (97)

Washington, imbued with "Liberty" of the most aggressive sort, thus dissolves into the patriarchal force which, by razing wigwams, is bringing crops, cities, and God to western vacancy. The circumstances of publication are the key to McGill's intent. In the year his poem appeared, the aging president had retired to the Hermitage. Published in Tennessee, *The Western World* is dedicated to "the worthy and illustrious citizen of Tennessee, Gen. Andrew Jackson. . . . By his fellow-citizen, friend and obedient servant Walter M. McGill."

Simply to describe Dr. Richard Emmons's mammoth epic *The Fredoniad* is an act of critical cruelty. Its full title is *The Fredoniad; or Independence Preserved: An Epic Poem on the Late War of 1812.* Emmons offers his countrymen what may be the longest poem in English: 4 volumes, 40 cantos, 1,404 pages, some 33,380 lines of heroic couplets – a poem more than twice the length of *The Iliad.* This immense effort is expended to

memorialize the heroics of every American engagement from the surrender of Detroit through Jackson's victory at New Orleans. At least 500
lines are devoted to each of at least 31 separate battles. Emmons's poem
includes a proposition, six separate invocations, visions of heaven and
hell, intervening deities, dreams, storms, single combat, hundreds of epic
similes, numerous councils and catalogues, and references to Homer,
Virgil, Milton, and Ossian. *The Fredoniad* does not, however, have a
hero, unless the nation itself or the idea of independence can be called a
hero. To Emmons, the sheer accumulating of historical events, the mere
amassing of heroic names, is sufficient for epic poetry.

The *Fredoniad* begins with an infernal council in which Satan determines to reinstate monarchy in Columbia by sending his agents, Avarice
and Luxury, to corrupt republican hearts. After two cantos, the Satanic
council adjourns to the top of the White Mountains, whereupon the scene
of the poem predictably shifts to heaven. Fredonia, guardian seraph of
America, sits enthroned in her celestial palace of thirteen pillars, surrounded by Independence, Temperance, Justice, Industry, and other republican virtues. Franklin, Washington, and other deceased patriots,
"couchant on the supernal herb," discuss appropriate counteractions to
the Satanic plot, while the entire Fredonian hall is serenaded by those
"two sons of epick song," Joel Barlow and Timothy Dwight.[35]

The heavenly assembly determines that, although they must not directly aid the Americans (lest the glory of Fredonia's sons be dimmed),
they may intervene to thwart Lucifer's fell designs. Accordingly, Fredonia descends at appropriate moments to restrain Lucifer, whose unceasing schemes on behalf of the British cause account for any temporary
American defeats. Golden-haired Fredonia descends upon Lake Erie clothed
in red, white, and blue robes, surrounded by an angelic choir singing the
Rights of Man and the glories of Franchise. She carries a light-tipped
spear in her right hand and a Homeric shield over her alabaster left arm,
on which are pictured the victories at Bunker Hill and Saratoga, Trenton
and Eutaw Springs. When Satan casts a disguising cloud over the attacking British at Sandusky, Fredonia snatches it away. When Satan hurls
thunderbolts at Americans, Fredonia wards them off with her shield. On
three other occasions, Satan masks himself as a tidal wave, a dusky red
chieftain, and a glittering lord, only to be instantly dispersed by a touch
from Fredonia's gleaming spear.

Emmons's strainings after grandiosity would be unintentionally comic
were they not unrelieved. Albions and Columbians perpetually draw their
falchions; black streams forever pour from the mouth of Death's tubes.
Emmons apologizes for including a minor skirmish of the Battle at
Raisin, but then inflates the skirmish into a cataclysm deserving an al-
exandrine:

Now peals on peals with strength redoubling roar,
The dark-brown earth is glued with clotted gore.
Clouds of convolving smoke obscure the sky –
Steel rings, fires blaze, trees fall, blood streams, and warriors die.
    (I, 119)

To Emmons, all Americans are heroes, but none is a common man. Emmons focuses upon distinguished figures (Shelby, Johnson, Perry, Lawrence), then adds catalogues of forgotten names who are hastily said to be no less heroic. Every epic convention must be both included and heightened. The epic feast, for example, might seem inappropriate to a race of homespun heroes for whom Temperance is a guardian seraph. Emmons, however, manages an epic feast by attributing it to the Indians. After a massacre of white civilians, red devils devour boiling cauldrons of blood spiced with human brains, condors' claws, maiden's breasts, and the tongues of unweaned infants (I, 315–18). In order to write such a passage, Emmons probably assured himself that, in America's great epic, the fascinating atrocities of the Captivity Narrative must reach their apogee.

Only an inexhaustible patriotism could sustain so long a poem with so little of the complex view of life that informs nationalistic epics like *The Aeneid* or *The Lusiads*. Emmons gasps in ecstatic wonder over such undefined abstractions as Liberty, Justice, Union, and Progress. Although Emmons seems to be of the Republican persuasion, he perpetually warns his reader against entertaining any idea that might lead to faction. The third canto offers us the remarkable picture of Thomas Jefferson and Fisher Ames singing sweetly to one another in Fredonia's celestial hall. Unlike its American predecessors, *The Fredoniad* does not even have a vision of what the New World might become. Emmons's only standard of value is America, which is synonymous with Freedom. All an epic bard need do is to dress up newspaper accounts of the war in classical clothing, blacken the English, glorify the Americans, and keep on writing. Emmons recognized that his almost endless string of American heroes and English villains aroused little dramatic interest:

How sad the Muse regrets so few to find
Of Albion chiefs endow'd with noble mind!
Their characters are so begrim'd with wrong
They stain the honour of the epic song. (III, 81)

Emmons can respond to his dilemma neither by shortening his poem nor by inventing one engaging English foe. Because his Muse serves history, she must portray all English commanders as cruel, luxurious aristocrats.

Surely Emmons knew *Paradise Lost* and Pope's Homer sufficiently well to recognize that his own verse, with its wretched rhymes and countless

dashes, was merely doggerel. The prospect of finishing his American epic so enthralled him, however, that he claimed indifference to aesthetic merit. In his various invocations, Emmons confesses to some weariness in completing his task, but not to literary deficiencies. At the beginning of the third volume, he complains "the more I sing, the more boundless seems my song" (III, 5). One volume later he admits that the prospect of completing his last ten cantos "gives inspiration sweet! / It makes my pulse in dancing measures beat" (IV, 3). After Jackson's men have stained the Mississippi with British corpses in Canto Forty, the exhausted Muse can muster only a six-line huzzah to "Virtue, blessed Freedom; – Union, proud Liberty!" (IV, 293). Thus ends an attempt to make an epic poem by heaping up historical details, dressing them in the garb of literary antiquity, and versifying them with unthinking patriotic ardor. One wonders whether an epic of such chauvinistic purpose, imitative excess, parochial vision, and sheer length could have been written in any other time or place than Jacksonian America.

Although Emmons convinced his brother to publish *The Fredoniad* in two sumptuously bound editions, the poem proved indigestible. Even Timothy Flint, whose *Western Review* was committed to nationalistic literature by and about westerners, found that there was nothing to praise, everything to embarrass, in Emmons's effort. In a five-page review, Flint lambasted *The Fredoniad* for its silly machinery, metrical monotony, historical errors, and perpetual bathos.[36] Noting that Emmons prided himself on being a Kentucky commoner, Flint contended that Emmons's "illimitable dead sea" of verse could only have appeared in the land of ringtailed panthers, huge lizards, snapping turtles, and six-boiler steamboats. Flint desired a western epic with Boone as Achilles, but *The Fredoniad* led him to conclude that Dr. Emmons should have devoted his last ten years to professional practicality: "Instead of furnishing the community with an argument against yielding any aid to literary efforts of any kind, [Emmons] might have administered pills, or cut down trees, or made chimneys, and in a thousand ways been usefully, and cheerfully, and gainfully, and honorably employed" (182). Flint here restates the warning that Freneau's Robert Slender had given to American epic poets; now, however, the advice comes after the unfortunate fact.

Flint's admirer Mrs. Trollope, professing to search for any American literature to review, remarked: "The massive *Fredoniad* of Dr. Emmons in forty cantos I never read; but as I did not meet a single native who had, I hope this want of poetical enterprise will be excused."[37] *Domestic Manners of the Americans* made Emmons a laughingstock whenever the poem was recalled. Poe dismissed Emmons with fleeting ridicule.[38] Herman Melville, who probably encountered *The Fredoniad* in Evert Duyck-

inck's library, and who was determined to tout the motives, if not the products, of literary nationalists, offered the kindest possible words for Emmons's effort:

> I was much pleased with a hot-headed Carolina cousin
> of mine, who once said, – "If there were no other
> American to stand by, in literature, why, then, I
> would stand by Pop Emmons and his 'Fredoniad,' and
> till a better epic came along, swear it was not very
> far behind the Iliad." Take away the words, and in
> spirit he was sound.[39]

Melville, already at work on *Moby-Dick* when these sentences were written, had been reading Camoens, Pope's *Iliad,* and *Paradise Lost* in recent years. Apt to be hotheadedly nationalistic at times, Melville nonetheless distances his own response to Emmons by attributing it to a nonexistent Carolina cousin. Nonetheless, Melville's statement shows his sympathy with Emmons's epic ambition, together with his sly disdain for its result ("Take away the words . . ."). No American epic, Melville knew, could ever arise from such imitative drivel, such naive patriotism. Humorless assaults on the high style would no longer do. And so, even though Captain Ahab was closely to resemble Milton's Satan, Melville follows his remarks on Emmons with the caveat "We want no American Goldsmiths; nay, we want no American Miltons."[40]

Overwritten, unread poems like *The Western World* and *The Fredoniad* tempt us to grant Constance Rourke's claim that a folk epic about the West lay in the Davy Crockett stories.[41] Here are anonymous stories of the people, told about a martyred historical figure, stories that had gradually accumulated in at least fifty popular almanacs published in Baltimore, Boston, Nashville, New York, and Philadelphia over a twenty-year period after 1835. The oral rhythms and grotesque dialect of the best tales ("Crockett's Morning Hunt," "Crockett Out-Diving the Pearl Divers") are exactly suited to self-conscious fantasizing about the backwoodsman's powers over the beasts and the elements. The comedy of the Crockett legends depends upon the speaker, listener, and reader all tacitly recognizing that the backwoodsman can subdue nature only through a lie, the more vividly outlandish the better. Beneath the superficial differences of region and subject, the Crockett stories provide us the same mixture of relishing and mocking American's self-assumed giantism that one finds in Knickerbocker's history. Paulding's Nimrod Wildfire, fashioned upon Crockett legends, is a more imposing backwoods hero than Paulding's Basil is ever allowed to be.

But there is good reason why the Davy Crockett stories were never wrought into mock-epic or epic. Consider typical subjects of the almanac stories: Crockett jumps over the Ozarks on his tame bear Death Hug;

Crockett shoots lightning from his eyes to split boulders; Crockett greases some lightning with rattlesnake oil so that he can ride on it to the Rockies; Crockett charms Pacific pearl oysters into opening their shells; Crockett swims up Niagara Falls on his pet alligator; Crockett greases the world's axle to prevent the universe from freezing.[42] Such tales are detachable incidents displaying a solitary male's comic power over nature. They may happen anywhere, anytime, in any order, because there is no connection between the frontier hero and any community or culture, no real link between the historical Whig politician David Crockett and the dreams of frontier power that the almanacs later fashioned from him. An American version of Promethean myth, Crockett's lightning brings no knowledge to mankind. When Melville remarked that Hercules was an "antique Crockett," he placed the Crockett stories in their more appropriate lineage.[43] Even if folk materials had not been commonly regarded as beneath the dignity of the epic poem, the Crockett stories glorified individualism in its most anarchic and merely physical form.

IV. MID-CENTURY ASSAULT

By the 1840s, sixty years of increasingly abysmal epic verse had rendered the very idea of the great American epic ludicrous, especially among astute Eastern writers amused by recent notions of a frontier Homer. Hawthorne, whose pursuit of psychological romance seems completely removed from the issues of heroic literature, nonetheless kept returning to the idea of American epic. His satirical sketch "A Select Party" (1844) pictures the anxiously awaited "American Master Genius" as a poor, classless youth "hewing . . . out of the unwrought granite of our intellectual quarries" America's first great original work, "whether moulded in the form of an epic poem, or assuming a guise altogether new." The Master Genius, like all other figures in the tale, is only a fantasy of the unobtainable. When the Oldest Inhabitant of Fancy's Hall is introduced to Master Genius, the old traditionalist stalks away "observing that a man who had been honored with the acquaintance of Dwight, and Freneau, and Joel Barlow, might be allowed a little austerity of taste."[44] Two years later, Hawthorne was to satirize the American epic once again by claiming to be fearful that the heroic couplet was about to be inflicted upon the Mexican War: "*Is* old Joel Barlow yet alive? Unconscionable man! Why, he must have nearly fulfilled his century! And *does* he meditate an epic on the war between Mexico and Texas, with machinery contrived on the principle of the steam-engine, as being the nearest to celestial agency that our epoch can boast?"[45] Among the most absurd fantasies of that "minor poet" Miles Coverdale is his hope that the residents of Blithedale "must all figure heroically in an Epic poem" for which he will serve as the ghostly muse.[46]

Talented Eastern writers young and old joined in the onslaught. In *A Fable For Critics* (1848), Lowell sneered "There's scarcely a huddle of log-huts and shanties / That has not brought forth its own Miltons and Dantes."[47] Longfellow's Mr. Hathaway, a caricature of a shaggy literary nationalist, struts about proclaiming "We want a national epic that shall correspond to the size of the country; that shall be to all other epics what Banvard's Panorama of the Mississippi is to all other paintings – the largest in the world!"[48] By midcentury, the need to imagine the founding fathers in pseudo-Virgilian garb had finally abated. Irving insisted that his *Life of Washington* was intended to "depict the heroes of Seventy-Six as they really were – men in cocked hats, regimental colors, and breeches, and not classical warriors, in shining armor and flowing mantles, with brows bound with laurel."[49] His preference for writing a restrained, prose biography is surely connected to his perception that "our national songs are full of ridiculous exaggeration, and frothy rant, and commonplace bloated up into fustian. The writers seem to think that huge words and mountainous figures constitute the sublime."[50] If Irving's life of Washington seems dull set beside the Knickerbocker history, part of the cause is Irving's recognition that the intervening generation of nationalists had seen no comedy in literature that puffed up commonplaces into fustian.

The subliterary abyss into which the epic was falling is apparent in James Russell Lowell's reactions to Thomas Harris's 210-page, 16-part mishmash titled *An Epic of the Starry Heaven* (1855). According to the preface, Harris spoke the verses of his "epic" while in a prolonged trance, during which Dante provided him clairvoyance into such heavenly realms as "The Eden of Maternal Affection," "The Heavenly City Beyond Jupiter," and "The School of Love Upon Mercury." Doggerel in sixteen different meters introduces us to a varied brew of numerology, pantheism, phrenology, and prophetic visions of Earth's one universal republic, based upon "A new democracy / A new theocracy / The Priesthood of the Free."[51] Lowell dutifully read through to the end, annotating his copy with the following sequence of marginal comments: "Swedenborg has been whispering in Dante's ear" (38); "Dante is well up with American Literature. He has read Poe, it seems"(42); "Bosh" (48); "What did Dante know of railways?" (68); "Oh bosh! bosh! bosh!" (83); "A kind of land of Cockayne where the birds fly about reading" (83). Six years later, Lowell removed Harris's epic from Elmwood and presented it to Harvard's Houghton Library. The poem was noticed but seems never to have been reviewed.

Lowell's keen sense of literary history led him seriously to consider why the repeated efforts to make a verse epic from New World materials had all failed. In two articles masked as reviews, "Longfellow's *Kavanagh*: Nationality in Literature" (1849) and "James Gates Percival" (1867),

Lowell argues persuasively that no epic worthy of the name could have been written so soon after the winning of independence. Epics are not produced simply because they are commanded to appear for cultural self-justification, nor can living poems, however patriotic, be written by mediocre poets. To Lowell there had been three insurmountable problems: "We were not yet, in any true sense, a nation; . . . we wanted that literary and social atmosphere which is the breadth of life to all artistic production; . . . our poetic forefathers were Joel Barlow and Timothy Dwight."[52] Lowell perceives the absurdity in the long-treasured argument that the American bard will be more sublime than Homer because the Mississippi dwarfs the Scamander. Like Fisher Ames, he argues that democracy is both "altogether too abstract" and too egalitarian to provide materials for an epic poem[53] – arguments valid so long as the word "epic" is applicable only to Homeric or Virgilian models.

Lowell's Cambridge loyalties and somewhat trendy wit led him to dismiss the notion of a Western poet singing "the epos of the New World" as merely a "cheap vision" which "cost no thought."[54] Lowell's commitment to continental literary tradition grew so strong that he refused to admit that works mediating between the Old and New Worlds could succeed. Nationalism is provincialism, but the Old World is too removed for Americans to claim international republicanism. The American West is merely "sham shaggy" and any great American poet "will be original rather in spite of democracy, than in consequence of it."[55] Without pausing to consider the historical fiction of Cooper, Sedgwick, Simms, or Hawthorne, Lowell rehearses the shopworn complaint that America has no "historical and national associations," no "proper youth as a nation," and "no mythic period either."[56] If we must have our American poet, Lowell would prefer him to have as little indigenous crudity about him as possible: "We should expect of the young Western poet that he would aim rather at elegance and refinement than at a display of the rude vigor that is supposed to be his birthright."[57] Faced with the thinness of American culture, the American poet should consider richer, European subjects: 'Prometheus, Coriolanus, Tasso and Tell are ours if we can use them, as truly as Washington or Daniel Boone."[58] Lowell thus returns to the same specious reasoning that had led Hillhouse, thirty years earlier, to call for an American heroic poem on the middle ages. The oddity of Lowell's argument is that it could be used to defend a poem he ridicules, Dwight's *The Conquest of Canaan*. Lowell can provide no example of a successful epic that concerns a foreign culture.

American verse epics were not doomed because of the insufficiently heroic materials of American history, the meanness of democracy, nor the crudity of the West. Their failure is due more to the unsuitable literary conventions they worriedly imitated than to the untempered opti-

mism of their cultural expectations. Many pursued an admirable hope that a new polity and an unspoiled continent might raise common men everywhere to new heroic stature as self-reliant humanitarians, lovers of peace, architects of republican civilization. Concerned that their New World epics be recognizable outgrowths of the old genre, they exalted uncommon heroes and martial exploits in diction and verse forms that became increasingly less applicable to their culture. In 1847 Cornelius Conway Felton, who knew heroic poetry thoroughly, remarked upon the constricting effect literary convention had recently had upon epic poems:

> Modern poets have considered them [Aristotle, Le Bossu, Pope] as comprising the whole substance of the rules which regulate the epic song. Those, therefore, who have aspired to the honor and dignity of this species of poetry, with few exceptions, have imitated, not the essential spirit, but the accidental form, which these productions happened to take; and it must be confessed the majority of modern epics are not very easy reading.[59]

Felton was not thinking exclusively of American epics. If he had been, he would surely have recognized that, for American purposes, the older conventions of epic poetry were inappropriate to republican values.

Visions of rising glory tempted American epic poets to blur known differences between heroic character and human perfection. Joshua, Columbus, Washington, Boone, and Basil are cultural ideals given a name; they are, quite literally, heroes made for a bard to sing. Conversely, the cultural need for villainy blinded American poets to the literary need for a worthy antagonist. Not even Joel Barlow was willing to acknowledge that the demise of Hector, Turnus, and Satan is tragic, that Achilles and Aeneas must knowingly bear immense personal loss if they are to attain undying honor or found an empire.

The prophetic tenth book of Dwight's and Barlow's poems, Basil's pastoral freehold, and the spread of civilization across the West all express cherished hopes of the early national period. In part these epic poems embarrass us because the course of history has made their republican expectations seem unrealizable, and their Republican expectations parochial. But the poetic tone that emerges from declaring their hopes as certainties remains revealingly shrill. Joel Barlow clearly knew where the demand for a panegyrical epic was leading him:

> I joy to raise
> The high toned anthem of my country's praise;
> To sing her victories, virtues, wisdom, weal,
> Boast with loud voice the patriot pride I feel;
> Warm wild I sing; and, to her failings blind,
> Mislead myself, perhaps mislead mankind.[60]

Barlow's country may ultimately be mankind, but he must risk over-praising the Republic as the means of arriving there.

By midcentury, criticism of particular epic poems had widened into ridicule of the very notion of a modern epic poem, whatever its subject. Convincing epic poems, critics concluded, could only concern primitive, martial cultures that moderns know nothing about. Epic poems require machinery but no sane contemporary can believe in its existence. Enlightened Moderns detest war and find sublime diction wearisome. The epic is dying of a shift in literary taste. Heroic couplets, blank verse, personification, and exhortative rhetoric of any kind merely bore contemporary readers, who are moved only by lyrics that express individual emotions in fresh images and a very few stanzas.

American attacks upon the contemporary epic began as early as 1812, seven years after Robert Southey called the epic "degraded."[61] A critic for *Port Folio* declared that "An epic poem seldom succeeds, unless in a barbarous or semi-barbarous age." "Whenever Columbia or Brittania is mentioned, it excites an inclination to doze." The reviewer concludes that "the age of epic poetry is past, unless the critics will consent that machinery shall be considered no longer necessary."[62] Not inclined to be quite so temperate, John Neal concluded that epic poetry was "entirely done with, in this world – and for ever (we hope)."[63] At the outset of his career, Longfellow declared that the epics that "sang the achievements of Grecian and Roman heroes were rude and unpolished," thereby suggesting why, when he came to write *Hiawatha,* he would choose to prettify potentially heroic Indian legends.[64] In 1839 a critic for the *North American Review* claimed that "The epic, strictly defined, is an obsolete form of poetic art. It would not be acceptable at the present day."[65] Washington Allston was even more blunt: "Epics are out of fashion; even Homer and Virgil would hardly be read in our time, but that people are unwilling to admit their schooling to have been thrown away."[66]

At the height of Manifest Destiny, sustained poetic effort seemed to many – surely to the majority of the citizenry – to be an unconscionable expense of any American's energy. Just as Bryan felt guilty merely to sing of western conquest, and Timothy Flint blamed Dr. Emmons for neglecting medicine, so the achievements of the American economy made heroic poetry seem superfluous. A writer for *Putnam's Magazine* in 1853 noted that, though Ilium had perished by the wooden horse, America's iron horse "shall build an empire and an epic." Three years earlier, *Scientific American* had made an even more revealing claim: "A steamer is a mightier epic than the Iliad, – and Whitney Jacquard and Blanchard might laugh even Virgil, Milton and Tasso to scorn."[67] Americans might not have been able to write their great epic poem, but at least now they could build it!

In the context of these shifts in the climate of literary opinion, Poe's strictures against the epic emerge as only the most intemperate wording of a conventional prejudice. Poe is surely right to argue, rather turgidly, that "The modern epic is, of the suppositious ancient model, but an inconsiderate and blindfold imitation."[68] His sense of literary fashion is also acute: "The epic mania . . . has for some years past, been gradually dying out of the public mind. The day of these artistic anomalies is over" (465). Unfortunately, however, Poe extends his criticism of epic imitations to scorn for their originals. Poe's assertion that *The Iliad* is "based in an imperfect sense of art," is almost as foolish as his conclusion that "the ultimate, aggregate, or absolute effect of even the best epic under the sun, is a nullity" (465). To some degree, Poe is catering to contemporary distaste, but his dismissal of the epic is also prompted by his need for a foil by which to promote his own kind of lyric. Because neither *The Iliad* nor *Paradise Lost* strives for one predetermined effect, for brief intense excitement of soul, or for creation of supernal beauty, they are to be regarded as unpoetic, and ultimately negligible.

Henry Tuckerman's essay "Lyric Poetry" (1850) provides a less self-interested account of the demise of imitative verse epic. Tuckerman argues that the rise of democratic sentiment, international diplomacy, and industrialization all preclude individual displays of heroic valor. A reading public consisting primarily of middle-class women has no interest in martial exploits. Modern readers are impatient with length: "The mere sight of half a dozen cantos of heroics provokes a yawn."[69] Contemporary poetic taste has turned toward an inner landscape where original images can convey the individual soul: "A series of external events, however well described in stately verse, are now deemed less entertaining than a single incident or emotion freshly portrayed from a living mind" (105). Sharing Barlow's hopes for universal republicanism, Tuckerman hopes to bolt the door against Barlow's genre by declaring that the epic poem is now " buried in the grave of nationality" (106). Unless loyalty to nation should resume precedence over regard for humanity, Tuckerman is certain the epic will never be exhumed.

In his own country, Tuckerman's argument has proven correct. Except for one short outbreak at the time of the Columbian exposition,[70] the urge to write imitative and declared verse epics on American subjects remained dormant until Frederic Turner's *The New World* (1985). Even *John Brown's Body* and *Western Star,* which were designed to be recognizably epic narratives, are free of direct borrowings from classical models.

The need for a heroic literature on New World subjects did not die with the imitative epic of ten or forty cantos. While the imitative verse epic was proving unworkable, innovative writers and critics were explicitly arguing that the subjects and even the conventions of epic poetry

should be absorbed into newer literary forms. After Joel Barlow's failure, it was evident to prescient authors that even an extensive modification of traditional epic form simply would not work. They therefore transformed the epic into other genres. Qualities of epic literature were deliberately absorbed into Indian romances by Simms and Cooper, into romantic history by Parkman and Prescott, into that dramatic-epic-poem in prose titled *Moby-Dick,* and into an altogether different kind of heroic poetry by Walt Whitman. The insoluble problem of fashioning American history to make it fit Pope's *Iliad* gradually and thankfully disappeared.

V. AFTERWORD TO PART ONE

Failed writing of the New World's epic poem, we should note in closing, had never been an exclusively American preoccupation. Between 1783 and 1787 André Chénier wrote some 150 separate entries of notes and passages for his masterwork-to-be, an epic poem of 12,000 lines to be titled "L'Amérique." Although Chénier could write verse as powerful and moving as "La Jeune Captive" and *Iambes,* he was no more able to solve the problem of adopting the encylopedic mentality of the Enlightenment to epic narrative than was Joel Barlow. Chénier's fragments are, in fact, the haunting vestige of an era's abiding literary misconception. Chénier was determined to evoke into being, within a literary and geographical entity called L'Amérique, "all the people, the products, the sun, the climate, the religion, the culture, the animals, the natural history, the customs, the habits, the history and the topography of all the countries of the globe."[71] To be worthy of such a poem, Chénier believed he must "learn everything, read everything, see everything, know everything, and express everything" (86). Although he disclaimed all prospect of succeeding, he knew he would have to write as if he were "the divine poet, all spirit, all thought, whose verses reclothed all forms . . . that successively pass before his eyes" (115). America, in Chénier's formulation, has already become the sum of all knowledge and of all values worth preserving, wherever they may be found.

As Chénier's notes proceed, fine lines accumulate as fast as unconnected topics. He mentions, not necessarily in chronological order, sections on the fall of Rome, the Dark Ages, the Wars of the Roses, Gustavus Adolphus, Columbus, Vasco de Gama, Magellan, Henry IV, the St. Bartholomew Massacre, Cortes's conquest of Mexico, Pizarro's conquest of Peru, the creation of the Thirteen United States, and the settlement of Kentucky as described by John Filson. He must "invent something in the style of Achilles' and Aeneas' shields, in order to represent the cardinal moments of world history" (86). He should create a prophetess, someone like Cassandra, who will sing the assassination of tyrants

and the rise of religious tolerance. God and His angels should be made to speak of biblical and modern history without any theological orthodoxy, but with complete scientific knowledge. An invocation to Urania, together with hymns to Morning, Evening, and Marriage, would connect his poem to the one sublime, successful epic of modern times. His controlling purpose must be "to speak prophetically of the Thirteen United States" and to show "how the richness of the political state depends on agriculture" (117). But to do so would require a constant return to ancient models: "Even when we design modern characters and tableaux, it is from Homer Virgil, Plutarch . . . and Aeschylus that we must learn finally to paint them" (89).

Regarded collectively, Chénier's fragments offer no narrative action around which his ever-accumulating subjects could be organized. There is mention of a poet named Alphonse, probably present at the Spanish conquests of the New World, whose mind will have access to all the knowledge that the poem contains. But Chénier was clearly not interested in thinking through the problems of rendering the life and deeds of a hero. To do so would have been, in his view, a demeaning limitation. Chénier's epic had to remain unwritten, not so much because of his involvement in Girondist politics, nor his execution during the Terror, but because the very subject of his poem – everything summoned up by the word "America" – seemed so vast, so important, so wondrous, that it must not be lessened by attending to a particular mortal's deeds.

PART II

TRANSFORMATIONS: THE EPIC IN NEW GENRES

5

RED ACHILLES,
RED SATAN

By 1815 Americans open to new ideas of heroic behavior and epic form confronted perplexing literary crosscurrents offering great opportunity. Clara Reeve, Robert Southey, and Walter Scott had led them to entertain the possibility, heretical to any student of Dryden's *Aeneid* and Pope's *Iliad,* that the medieval romance and the classical *epos* were not only similar, but could be mixed to their mutual benefit. Epic poets might now be conceived, not as moralistic penmen, but as aged wandering minstrels singing heroic lays about a departed civilization. Scott's four narrative poems had provided the model for a new, still unnamed kind of heroic verse – part adventure romance, part heroic lay, part medieval pageantry – written in a short metrical line and free of the conventions associated with blank verse and heroic couplet. Should such a poem be considered an epic? Should one even worry about its classification, as long as it might prove a literary medium more suitable to the New World?

After another decade, two even more heretical possibilities were to emerge. In the face of centuries of authority, America's great heroic work should perhaps be written in the once low but presently popular genre of prose fiction. And perhaps America's heroic subject was not, as Barlow, Bryan, and Paulding had believed, the conquering of the American savage by civilization, but the demise of those noble red peoples who, alone in all of American history, had embodied the qualities of the heroic age.[1]

The change in literary and cultural attitude necessary for the acceptance of these two ideas was, to put it modestly, enormous. Writers and readers had to abandon and then reform the generic categories of their literary education. They had to consider that the heroic essence of American civilization was contained, not in what Europeans brought into this country, but in what they erased from it. As the Republic became increasingly nationalistic in mood, the ghost of Nature's heroic red chieftain reminded Civilization's white readers of all they were still destroy-

ing. Ironically, the search for American heroic values gained lasting literary power only when the rise of Indian romances both subverted the reader's assumptions about the epic genre and challenged expansionist complacence. Whereas Dwight, Barlow, and Paulding could not conceive that a prose romance elegizing Indians might be heroic literature, Cooper and Simms sensed that America's Homeric peoples could best be portrayed in a non-Homeric form. Like Prescott, Melville, and Whitman after them, they captured qualities of epic literature because they were no longer striving to write a literary epic.

I. TRANSITIONS

At first, the breaking down of presumably timeless generic distinctions by English Romantic writers left astute Americans wondering whether there was a recognizable guise in which heroic literature could appear. As early as 1785 Clara Reeve had contended that, because the prose romance told tales of heroic possibilities in heightened language, "a Romance is nothing but an Epic in prose."[2] Southey's long poems may have denigrated epic conventions in the name of originality, but Southey frequently adopted those conventions in altered but recognizable forms. Although Shelley continued to associate "epic" with a poem, he defined "the laws of epic truth" as broadly as "the laws of that principle by which a series of actions of the external universe, and of intelligent and ethical beings, is calculated to excite the sympathy of succeeding generations" – a definition that would embrace "The Rhyme of the Ancient Mariner," "Michael," or "The Revolt of Islam" as epic poems."[3] Byron's well-publicized remark that *Don Juan* "is an epic as much in the spirit of our day as the *Iliad* was in Homer's " could mean almost anything, except that Bryon's contemporaries were living in a heroic age by heroic code for which Homeric conventions were suitable.[4] Readers of Wordsworth's "Prospectus" for *The Excursion* (1814) were asked to consider that the growth of the imagination was the sole remaining possibility for heroic song.

To Americans, however, the crucial figure of literary change was Walter Scott. *The Lay of the Last Minstrel* (1805), which surely gave a title first to Fenimore Cooper (*The Last of the Mohicans,* 1826) and thence to William Gilmore Simms ("The Last of the Yemassee," 1827), combined single combats, international warfare, and escape and pursuit sequences with medieval supernaturalism and pageantry, presenting the whole as the song of an aged singer who resembles no particular figure so much as Wolf's image of Homer, colored somewhat by Gray's "The Bard" and the singers in Macpherson's Selma, Hall of Shells. In an informed essay on Scott, William Hickling Prescott conveyed the impact the poem had upon contemporaries:

He [Scott] took the field as an independent author, in a poem which at once placed him among the great original writers of his country. The "Lay of the Last Minstrel," a complete expansion of the ancient ballad into an epic form, was published in 1805. It was opening a new creation in the realm of fancy. It seemed as if the author had transfused into his page the strong delineations of the Homeric pencil, the rude, but generous gallantry of a primitive period, softened by the more airy and magical inventions of Italian romance, and conveyed in tones of natural melody, such as had not yet been heard since the strains of Burns.[5]

Writing in 1837, Prescott does not hesitate to describe Scott's work as a poem written in "an epic form" rather than "the epic form." By praising *The Lay of the Last Minstrel* as a modern adaptation of epic tradition, Prescott affirms the same change that Scott had advanced tentatively: "As the description of scenery and manners was more the object of the Author than a combined and regular narrative, the plan of the ancient metrical romance was adopted, which allows greater latitude in this respect than would be consistent with the dignity of a regular poem. . . . The machinery, also adopted from popular belief, would have seemed puerile in a Poem which did not partake of the rudeness of the old Ballad, or metrical Romance."[6]

Scott's poem appealed to Americans for reasons beyond its novelty of form. During the 1820's no lines of recent poetry were more prized by Americans than the opening of Scott's sixth canto:

> Breathes there the man with soul so dead
> Who never to himself hath said,
> This is my own, my native land.[7]

Just as these lines provided a justification for a heroic literature that could establish national associations, so Scott's poem as a whole had shown that a new kind of heroic poetry might derive from a nation considered subsidiary to England. When American admirers of Scott began to project a heroic poem about the Indians, the parallels arose almost unconsciously. Proud Scottish chieftains defending their lands against the progressive English became intermingled with dying Indian chiefs defying the march of civilization. What Scotland once had been to England, America quite recently was to Great Britain, and the Indian might long continue to be to the white man.[8]

After the great success of his first three narrative poems, Scott became increasingly explicit about the need for opening up new possibilities for epic verse. In an 1811 review of Southey's *The Curse of Kehama*, Scott noted "how few good epics have appeared" and accounted for the failure of contemporary epics: "It has been laid down as a rule, that a modern should imitate Homer and Virgil in the subject, incident and conduct of the story; instead of requiring him to emulate their spirit, upon a theme

adapted to his own times, studies, and peculiar bent of genius."[9] Scott's well-known "Essay on Romance," written for the 1824 edition of the *Encyclopedia Brittanica,* specifies ways of retaining the Homeric spirit in contemporary literary form. After asserting a distinction between novel and romance, Scott develops the similarities between the metrical romance and the epic poem. Both deal with tales told about founding patriarchs through intervening generations; heroic deeds thereby accrue aspects of "the marvelous or the supernatural . . . embracing the mythological and fabulous history of all nations."[10]

To Scott, there is no essential difference in the matters with which romance and epic are concerned. The distinction depends rather on issues of literary quality and popularity of medium. If a tale of founding is shaped into a unified, credible narrative, it qualifies as epic, but if the same tale is encrusted with supernatural episodes and pictorial detail, it is merely a romance:

> When the art and ornaments of the poet chiefly attract our attention – where each part of the narrative bears a due proportion to the others – . . . the work produced must be termed an epic poem, and the author may claim his seat upon the high and honoured seat occupied by Homer, Virgil and Milton. On the other hand, when a story languishes in tedious and minute details . . . when the supernatural and extraordinary are relied upon exclusively as the supports of the interest, the author . . . is no more than a humble romancer.[11]

No matter how unified a contemporary epic poem might be, however, Scott recognizes that it will never again have a choric function for its people. Thinking perhaps of the Waverley novels, Scott concludes that "Prose romances were written for a more advanced stage of society and by authors whose language was much more copious."[12]

One should not underestimate the degree of exhilarating confusion such statements created. When Scott discusses *Beowulf* and the *Chanson de Roland,* he describes them as romances. Searching for a term by which to classify the poems of Ariosto and Tasso, Prescott settled upon "Epic romance."[13] When George Bancroft described Homer as "wandering from door to door, a vagrant minstrel, paying for hospitality by a song," it is difficult to know whether he is responding to the Homeric poems, to Wolf's theory of them, or to the compelling figure of Scott's last minstrel.[14]

All one can conclude is that a new blending of genres was creating possibilities for two new forms of heroic literature: a narrative verse romance in varying meters and a narrative prose romance appealing to the growing popularity of fiction. Both forms were to deal with heroic acts of national history, but surround them with romance elements: quasi-supernatural occurrences, the testing of a hero through adventures, and

lengthy description of the customs of primitive peoples. For writers willing to concede that these adaptations of tradition might yield convincingly heroic literature in a modern idiom, anxiety over the conventions of epic verse markedly receded.

Americans who first conceived of heroic historical romance, in prose or verse, about the American Indian, may have been ignorant of the facts about the red man, but they were well stocked with conflicting preconceptions. On the one hand, they had read historical sources that, perceiving red men through the lens of heroic poetry, had seen the Indian as a Homeric warrior living on in the American forest. On the other hand, they were equally drawn to the Enlightenment belief that the red man had been Nature's noble savage, Man in all his primordial virtue. The first tradition, which led writers to imagine the Indian as hard, solitary, unyielding, aging, and doomed (Hector, Achilles, Turnus, Satan) would eventually shape characterizations of the Big Serpent, Magua, Mahtoree, Sanutee, and Pontiac. The second tradition, which led writers to imagine the Indian as graceful, generous, pliable, young, and equally doomed (Apollo, Patroklos, Oliver, Chactas) would eventually shape the characterization of Yamoyden, Uncas, Hard Heart, and Occonestoga. Although these two models of Indian heroism were often to appear as separate characters within one work, the way the author shaded them is a crucial measure of his attitude, not only toward the American Indian, but toward the nature of heroism in the New World.

Cadwallader Colden's "Introduction" to *The History of the Five Indian Nations* (1727) is clear testimony to the power of the Homeric lens. Familiar with the red men at treaty signings, but not in the forest, Colden writes of councils of chieftains, feasts, warsongs, rites of hospitality, games, and ceremonial burials. Again and again he likens the Indians' practice of these customs to those of peoples in heroic poetry. The red man's willingness to die for his nation exalts him to heroic stature: "None of the greatest Roman Heroes have discovered a greater Love to their Country or a greater Contempt for Death, than these people called Barbarians have done." Indian ceremonies of convening prompt Colden to assert that "all their extraordinary visits are accompanied with giving and receiving Presents of some Value; as we learn likewise from Homer was the practice in the Old Times." The most telling sign of Colden's recasting Indians as Mycenaean Greeks is his discussion of chieftains' eloquence in war councils. Although Colden admits he was "ignorant of their language," he praises the quality of Indian speech by asserting "the same was practiced by Homer's Heroes."[15]

By the 1780s the notion of noble savagery had blurred Colden's rather one-dimensional view. The five-month journey Chateaubriand made through America in 1791 was motivated, he later insisted, by a desire to

gather materials for his epic on American Indians, *Les Natchez: "J'etois encore tres jeune lorsque je concus l'idée de faire* l'epopée de l'homme de la nature, *ou de peindre les moeurs des sauvages."*[16] The enormously popular prose poems that resulted from this trip, *Atala* (1802) and *Renée* (1803), portray heroic Indians as gentle, followers of Nature's simple ways, melancholy, *philosophes* who almost never seem to have to engage in killing. The American tendency to accept but slightly modify this view of the red man can be inferred from the four-canto poem *Ouabi: or the Virtues of Nature* (1790) by Sarah Wentworth Morton. Mrs. Morton, using the pen name "Philenia, a lady of Boston," imagines intertribal warfare between the Hurons and the Illinois somewhere out on the vast western expanse. Her title hero, Ouabi, Chief of the Illinois, seems at first to be a gentle man of Nature, loving to his wife and protective of his tribe, a figure "form'd by nature's hand divine / Whose naked limbs the sculptor's art defied / Where nervous strength and graceful charms combine." As soon as Ouabi appears on the battlefield, however, his charms must be sacrificed to his attaining Achillean stature in heroic hand-to-hand combat:

> On the far field the adverse heroes join
> No dread artill'ry guards the coward side;
> But dauntless strength, and courage half divine
> Command the war, and form the conq'ror's pride!
>
> Thus before Illion's heav'n-defended towers
> Her godlike Hector rais'd his crimson'd arm;
> Thus great *Atrides* led the Grecian powers,
> And stern Achilles bid the battle storm.[17]

Mrs. Morton, however, is ultimately no more comfortable with bloody Homeric glory than Whittier was to be. She devises a plot in which a disaffected white melancholiac named Celario falls in love with Ouabi's wife and seeks to become a member of the tribe. Ouabi dies in battle, relinquishing his wife to Celario, and thus enabling the gentler red virtues to live on into the future. Like Chingachgook, Sanutee, and Pontiac, Mrs. Morton's stoic warrior-patriarch must die; unlike later male prose writers, Mrs. Morton seeks a racial accommodation that holds forth a future through miscegenation.[18]

Washington Irving, despite his growing need to charm through conventionality, preceded Cooper in making a forceful claim for Indian heroism. His two essays "Traits of Indian Character" and "Philip of Pokanoket" describe New England's oppressed seventeenth-century Indians as "a band of untaught native heroes . . . worthy of an age of poetry;" "No hero of ancient or modern days can surpass the Indian in his lofty contempt of death, and the fortitude with which he sustains all the varied torments with which it is frequently inflicted."[19] When these essays were

assimilated into *The Sketch Book,* their firm accusatory tone, their sense of a lost heroic world, jarred tellingly amid the pretentiously modest genialities of that amateur sketchist, Geoffrey Crayon. And yet, even within the essays themselves, Irving was not fully prepared to embrace the red values he seemed to be exalting. Regretting that the primitive virtues of the Indian are still unsung, Irving seems to call for an American Scott when he observes that "the minstrel has sung of it ['open and desperate courage'] to the loftiest strain of his lyre." Nonetheless, he promptly checks our admiration for Indian heroism by castigating the red hero developing among poets and romancers as a sentimental idealization: "Thus artificially excited, courage has arisen to an extraordinary and factitious degree of heroism."[20]

The more the Indian resembled a Homeric warrior, the more clearly American writers could lay claim to a heroic age. The price of having had a heroic age, however, was accepting the dignity of the Indian's presumably barbarous values. A Christian missionary like John Heckewelder was troubled by the prospect that the Indian code of revenge would arouse clashing responses:

> They [the Indians] have a strong innate sense of justice, which will lead them sometimes to acts which some men will call heroic, others romantic, and not a few, perhaps, will designate by the term barbarous.[21]

Heckewelder could not foresee the literary advantage the next generation was to find in developing these conflicting attitudes. To see Indian war codes as heroic, romantic, and barbarous simultaneously was to induce white readers to wonder whether their world might not be wandering between a lost heroic past and a grand Republic powerless to be born.

Even authors who strove to make a single clear judgment often confronted contradictions of attitude. In 1824 Edward Everett, still committed to a great American literary work, developed "a comparison of the heroic fathers of Greece with the natives of our woods."[22] Intent upon establishing the Homeric stature of the red man, Everett offered the following evidence:

> The ascendency acquired by personal prowess independent of any official rank, the nature of the authority of the chief, the priestly character, the style of hospitality in which the hero slays the animal and cooks the food, the delicacy with which the stranger is feasted before his errand is inquired for, the honor in which thieving is held, and numerous other points will suggest themselves to the curious inquirer, in which the heroic life reappears in our western forests. (398)

The single word "thieving" taints the intended impression of epic heroism with a reminder of savage immorality. Everett can extract himself from the tonal inconsistency of this passage only by claiming that "barbarism, like civilization, has its degrees" (399).

Everett ends his comparison with a sentence that, for a Professor of Greek who revered *The Iliad,* is a bizarre testimony to cultural confusion:

> Nations who must be called barbarous, like the Mexicans, have carried some human improvements to a point unknown in civilized countries; and yet the peasant in civilized countries possesses some points of superiority over any hero of the Iliad, or Inca of Peru. Though we think, therefore, the heroic life of Greece will bear a comparison with the life of our Northern American savages, inasmuch as both fall under the class of *barbarous;* yet the Agamemnons and Hectors are certainly before the Redjackets and Tecumsehs; whether they are before the Logans would bear an argument. (399)

Although Logan might even be as great a hero as Hector, both are somehow inferior to the civilized peasant who, in other equally unspecified ways, lacks the improvements of barbarous cultures!

In spite of his shaky logic, Everett is attempting to resolve the problem of assessing the savage hero by the same device used in imaginative literature – the gradation of barbarous qualities among a range of Indian characters. The Indian conceived as noble savage proved especially needed because he humanized the harshly stoic grandeur of the fighting chieftain. Celario outlives Ouabi, Yamoyden's gentleness balances King Philip's rage, the memory of Uncas seems to outlive the memory of Magua, Matiwan's humanity relieves Sanutee's intransigence, and so forth. Although the chief usually remains the controlling model of the heroic Indian, the doubling of his image with the noble savage both heightens elegiac regret and palliates the reader's fear.

The usefulness of such doubling can readily be seen in the first important work that lacked it, John Augustus Stone's melodrama *Metamora; or the Last of the Wampanoags* (1829). This immensely popular play, with its title reminiscent of Scott, has only one significant male Indian figure. The audience first sees King Philip upstage in a silent, statuesque pose while he is invoked as "the grandest model of a mighty man," "the noble sachem of a valiant race," equipped with "that lofty bearing – that majestic mien – the regal impress sits upon his brow."[23] Honest, kind, hospitable to the Puritans, and the savior of Puritan maidens from forest panthers, Philip appears to be both an epic chieftain and a noble savage. Because of the relentless persecution of a Puritan named Errington, Philip gradually loses all statesmanlike restraint and eventually rouses New England's Indians for genocidal war. In the play's famous last scene, the audience heard the dying Philip, his nobler qualities understandably effaced, proclaiming "The last of the Wampanoags' curses be on you! . . . May your graves and the graves of your children be in the path the red man shall trace! And may the wolf and panther howl o'er your fleshless bones, fit banquets for the destroyers" (40). The power of this closing

scene depended upon the mixture of awe, fear, and guilt with which white audiences contemplated the possibility that the controlling Indian response to dispossession would be the unchecked rage of an Achilles or a Turnus. (This possibility would not be fully and creditably explored until Parkman wrote his single-hero *History of the Conspiracy of Pontiac* [1851].)

The activating call for an American heroic literature about the Indian occurred in consecutive articles in the 1815 issue of the *North American Review*. Under its first editor, William Tudor, the *North American Review* was anything but the stodgily professorial compendium of international learning it would later become. Distressed by American "severity in judging our own productions" and by American "submission to foreign criticism," Tudor set out to promote national letters: "The spirit of the work was national and independent as regarded foreign countries, yet not falling under the dominion of party at home."[24] During the journal's first year, Tudor solicited an essay by Walter Channing with the blunt title "Reflections on the Literary Delinquency of America." *The Columbiad* had evidently convinced Channing that the great American work could not now be written about so recent and so familiar a topic as the Revolution:

> In the most elevated walk of the muses, the Epick, we cannot hope much distinction [*sic*]. . . . We live in the same age; we are too well acquainted with what has been, and is, among us, to trust to the imagination. It would be an 'old story' to our criticks, for the events transpired yesterday, and some of our oldest heroes are not yet dead.[25]

Convinced that heroic literature can concern only the distant past, Channing calls for a complete history of the United States of America, a comprehensive narrative like the later histories of Bancroft, Prescott, and Parkman.

Channing's article suited Tudor's purposes exactly. In his own Phi Beta Kappa address, Tudor had recently reached the same conclusion about the failure of American epic literature, though he had proposed a markedly different solution. Offering his own address as the lead article in the November 1815 issue, Tudor placed Channing's essay after his in a complementary but subordinate position. Like Channing, Tudor begins by attempting to rid readers of the notion that a verse epic on the founding fathers is now possible:

> The American Revolution may some centuries hence become a fit and fruitful subject for an heroick poem; when ages will have consecrated its principles, and all remembrance of party feuds and passions, shall have been obliterated; when the inferiour actors and events will have been levelled by time, and a few memorable actions and immortal names shall remain.[26]

Tudor, however, is not interested either in the gradual winnowing of the true Revolutionary hero, nor in trying to prove that Washington might be reclothed in a Virgilian mold. Preferring a more remote past, Tudor insists that the wars between the Five Nations and the Algonquins, together with the wars between the French and the English, constitute the heroic subject now pertinent and possible for American writers. It is the Indian, not the Revolutionary gentleman, who "possessed so many traits in common with some of the nations of antiquity, that they perhaps exhibit the counterpart of what the Greeks were in the heroick ages" (19).

Tudor draws up a kind of literary prospectus specifying the traits common to Greeks and Indians: martial codes of honor, solitary and exalted heroes, feasts and games, eloquence in tribal council, a pantheon of nature deities, and the virtues of "hospitality, reverence to age, unalterable constancy in friendship" (20). An American writer would be historically accurate if he conceived of Indian eloquence according to the Homeric pattern: "The speeches given by Homer to the Characters in the Iliad and Odyssey form some of the finest passages in those poems. The speeches of the Indians only want similar embellishment, to excite admiration" (26). Without the model of a new heroic subject that Tudor had somewhat ingenuously offered, the historical romances of Cooper and Simms would probably have developed both later and differently.[27]

II. "THE HINT OF AN EPIC"

Scott's change of genre suggests that, before a heroic prose romance about the American Indian could be seriously attempted, a verse romance about the red man might well have to fail. In 1820 Robert Sands and James Eastburn published their collaborative, 250 page, six-canto "poetical romance" titled *Yamoyden,* handsomely printed with engravings by Asher Brown Durand and 80 pages of historical footnotes. Because of Eastburn's untimely death in 1819, the published poem is largely the work of Robert Sands – a friend of Verplanck and Bryant, and later the editor of the *Atlantic* and the *New York Review,* an ambitious lawyer-litterateur for whom, apparently, "the Aeneid was always refreshment when wearied by severer studies."[28] Sands's' invocations mediate between "the Muses of Helicon" and American's "Spirit of Eld"; his metrics mediate between British precedents and Wolf's theory of epic composition. Lays of varying stanza patterns are assembled into "a tale of King Philip's War," beginning *in medias res* with Philip's last convening of the tribes, and ending with the slaughter of Philip's warriors in Mount Hope's "dark, miry bed."[29] Filled with councils, epic similes, natural descriptions, Indian songs, and aged prophets, Sands's poem is, in kind, very like the work William Tudor had anticipated. Not surprisingly, *Yamoyden* received respectful consideration from *Port Folio* and a

twenty-two page assessment by John Gorham Palfrey in the *North American Review,* where it was plausibly described as "a poem between the ballad and the epic."[30]

Yamoyden reverses the judgments passed upon red and white civilizations made by Bryan's *The Mountain Muse* seven years before. Laying claim to the candor of a rude bard, rather than the grandeur of an American Milton, Sands intends his "unpractised minstrel's tributary song" to "rehearse / The closing story of the Sachem's wrong" (4). Sands's Puritans, driven by "soulless bigotry," are persecuted persecutors whose inner emptiness is hidden beneath "avarice" (4); his Indians are "feather-cinctured warriors brave" who die for forest freedom and their "fathers' empire" (4). Sands's attack on Puritanism, remarkably like Williams's *In the American Grain,* is so shrill that Palfrey, a loyal New Englander who was trying to praise Sands's poem, could only complain: "We doubt whether, poetically speaking, and we do *not* doubt whether, historically speaking, it was best to represent the settlers as entirely in the wrong, and the Indians as wholly in the right."[31] Sure that the Puritans were indeed wholly in the wrong, Sands was less confident of the kind of heroism the Indian had embodied. His historical subject suggests that the Indian hero should be King Philip himself – patriot, warrior and wronged chieftain – a man who "Died for his people and his faith / His sceptre, and his liberty" (195). But Sands's title and the fictive plot he adds to history suggest that the truer Indian hero is Yamoyden, a graceful young brave "cast in nature's noblest mold" (125), who has married a white maiden, fathered a Christian child, adopted the agricultural life, and removed himself from racial warfare to an Edenic retreat.

Sands's characterization of Philip is a confusing mixture of the stoic chieftain, Byronic isolate, and savage brute. As a liberty-loving chieftain, "last of all his host," Philip is exalted at his death into "A hero, whose sleepless soul . . . was wise, and bold and true" (195). Yet Philip's appeal derives less from his ability to lead his people in a doomed cause than from his defiant scorn of his inferiors. The reader is meant to sympathize with Philip when he proclaims "Through all the crowds that hemmed me round, / My soul no kindred spirit found" (207). As Philip gathers the tribes for their last battle, he becomes a protoromantic Satan exalted for his crazed, solitary courage: "Brooding mid scenes of perished state, / He mused to madness on his fate" (21). In his most revealing soliloquy, Philip defines his sense of self in the same metaphors Ahab was to employ:

> When, like a blasted trunk, alone,
> Leaf, blossom, bud and scion gone,
> I stand,–the fire, the axe defy,
> And swift consuming bolts on high. (50–1)

Philip's references to his "blasted trunk" and to heaven's "consuming bolts" contain none of Ahab's metaphysical anger; as in Stone's *Metamora,* Philip's stature depends wholly upon his despairing curse against the white man for the undeniable outrages done to the red race.

Sands's shaming of the pretense of white civilization is unequivocal, but his condoning of red rage is carefully circumscribed. The figure of Yamoyden provides him a more comforting, if less credible, model of Indian heroism. At the moment of the Indians' final defeat, Sands contrasts Philip's vengeful defiance with another exemplary deed, Yamoyden's placing his own body in front of a tomahawk thrown at his father-in-law. Whereas Sands's blasted chieftain is a hero because he dies cursing white oppression, Sands's noble savage is a hero because he sacrifices himself for white Christianity. Not surprisingly, the reviewer for *Port Folio* permitted himself an astute sarcasm about Sands's divided notions of Indian virtue:

> Although the name of the poem entitles Yamoyden to be regarded as the hero of the story, it is very questionable whether the merits of this claim might not be fairly asserted in favour of King Philip. Yamoyden, however, was a warrior, a lover, and almost a Christian; and as piety, valour and love are always considered very essential ingredients in the composition of an epic hero, he must be permitted to enjoy this preeminence.[32]

Comparatively colorless and impossibly self-sacrificing though Yamoyden is, he is needed to maintain Sands's wavering allegiances to both red and Christian values.

Unfortunately, Sands discredits Philip by measures even more obviously manipulative. He invents a senseless subplot by which Philip seeks to regain Yamoyden's loyalty by abducting Yamoyden's child, presuming that the blame will fall on the Puritans. Somewhat later, Sands arranges to have Philip preside over a ceremony in which Yamoyden's child is to be burned as a sacrifice to the war god, even though Sands knew that religious infanticide was not an Indian custom. When the Indian crones sing their hateful war songs, Sands has them invoke infernal rather than divine agents:

> Power of darkness! Power of ill!
> Present in the heart and will,
> Plotting, despite of faith and trust,
> Treason, avarice, murder, lust. (172)

Exulting in their evil, the Indians who prepare for defeat little resemble the wronged heroic warriors Sands's first cantos have led the reader to expect. Nor did the Puritans whom Sands detests ever outdo him in assertions of Indian deviltry.

Sands's wildly vacillating responses to the Indian surely explain his

poem's lack of narrative coherence. War songs, council speeches, descriptions of landscape, and Puritan life histories are needlessly protracted; crucial details of character motivation are absent. Sands's excuse, "the fable was defective from our ignorance of the subject" (vi), is belied by his footnotes. Although Palfrey was searching for a heroic regional literature, he could not finally bring himself to praise *Yamoyden* as a poem. Instead, he was content to restate Tudor's prophecy for a great heroic work about the Indian: "Whoever in this country first attains the rank of a first rate writer of fiction, we venture to predict will lay his scene here. The wide field is ripe for the harvest, and scarce a sickle yet has touched it" (484). Whether Palfrey intended the unexpected word "fiction" to connote "narrative prose" or merely "an imagined tale" is impossible to determine.

Sands seems never to have realized that a national heroic romance about the Indian might best be written in prose. After *Yamoyden*, he wrote a long essay on Cortes, but continued to associate New World heroic literature with American Indian warfare. Two years before *The Last of the Mohicans* was published, Sands envisioned a work with "the hint of an epic":

> The creative faculty is wanting; not the materials to be wrought upon. If scenes of unparalleled torture and indefatigable endurance, persevering vengeance and unfailing friendship, hairbreadth escapes, and sudden ambush . . . if faith in wild predictions, and entire submission of the soul to the power of ancient legends and visionary prophecies, are useful to the poet or romancer, here they may be found in abundance and endless variety. The former might even discover the hint of an epic, in some of the traditions belonging to this continent.[33]

What is needed, Sands declares, is "an heroic poem" somehow recounting the wars of the Lenapé through Indian mythology, prophetic machinery, and the Indians' "inexhaustible mine of metaphor and simile" (167). The poem would have to be a romantic lay, somewhat like Scott's but somehow better than *Yamoyden*. In the meantime, Sands could only insist, quite rightly, that the polysyllabic diction of epic poetry was unsuited to the American Indian: "The ornate, overloaded, obviously artificial and often dissolute style of the higher literature of the day, with its endless redundance, useless verbiage, and unmeaning allusions, affords no precedent for our primitial [*sic*] classes" (113).

When Sands died in 1832, he was at work, not on the creation of the new Indian epic, but on an epic parody that would use the meter of *Don Juan*. Preparing to publish the newly discovered manuscript of "Dr. Thorlief Glum Skallagrimston's specimens of the poetical literature of the Esquimaux," Sands finished five stanzas of an epic written, he perhaps needed to insist, "in a strain of levity":

> Of sledge-borne heroes, o'er the cold bright waste,
> Whom mighty dogs, rejoicing, drew to war,
> And of the warrior multitudes who past
> Round where the unfathomed cave extends afar.
> Who heard the ice-bound rock split, unaghast,
> And saw new suns, and many a fiery star,
> I sing in numerous verse–that their renown
> May thus to all posterity go down.[34]

Given Sands's proven inability to work through the problems of a new literary form, it is understandable that this parody, with its sonorous puffery of a nonexistent subject and its deflating final couplet, is perhaps the best of his writing.

III. "FUNERAL FIRES"

The author of *The Last of the Mohicans* was clearly never deterred by the possibility that a heroic romance about the American Indian should be written in verse by any aged minstrel, red or white. In his tetchy review of Lockhart's *Life of Scott*, Cooper was to contend that Scott's great achievement as a writer was that "he raised the novel, as near as might be, to the dignity of the epic."[35] The epic might remain the highest of forms, but the novel was the only genre through which contemporaries could approximate it. Nor was Cooper predisposed to be timid in considering that America's one trace of a heroic culture might have passed away with the last warriors of a red tribe. As early as *The Pioneers* (1823), Cooper's grudging approval of the idea of civilization's march had been qualified by his pictures of the unsightliness and injustice of settlement. In *The Redskins* (1846), Cooper's gentleman narrator, Hugh Littlepage, offers a passing slight upon the pretensions of old Albany's new rival, Troy:

> I wonder the Trojan who first thought of playing this travestie on Homer, did not think of calling the place Troyville or Troyborough! That would have been semi-American, at least, whereas the present appellation is so purely classical! It is impossible to walk through the streets of this neat and flourishing town, which already counts its twenty thousand souls, and not have the images of Achilles and Hector, and Priam, and Hecuba, pressing on the imagination a little uncomfortably. Had the place been called Try, the name might have been a sensible one.[36]

Like Fisher Ames or James Russell Lowell, Cooper was sufficiently appreciative of the inner spirit of *The Iliad* to realize how ill suited it was to a commercial, middle-class democracy. When the children of the Templeton Academy botch their scansion of Virgil, they nicely complement the letter in which Cooper, after jokingly admitting to Benjamin Silliman that he had "never studied but *one* regular [i.e., Greek] lesson in

Homer," promptly added that he had read *The Iliad* in "the latin translation which I read as easily as English."[37]

If American society were as impoverished in ancestral legend and human variety as Cooper claimed in *Notions of the Americans,* then the dying
Indian tribes of the eighteenth century could provide the color and figurative language of poetry. Poetry, in turn, was the sine qua non of
romantic fiction. In his 1831 preface to *The Last of the Mohicans,* Cooper
asserts, "the business of a writer of fiction is to approach, as near as his
powers will allow, to poetry."[38] When Cooper wrote the 1850 preface
to the Leatherstocking series, he ended with a paragraph that suggests
how the conjunction of these two ideas had led him to attempt (with
apologies to Henry Fielding) a tragic-epic-poem in prose:

> It is the privilege of all writers of fiction, more particularly when
> their works aspire to the elevation of romances, to present the beau-
> ideal of their characters to the reader. This it is which constitutes po-
> etry, and to suppose the red man is to be represented only in the squalid
> misery or in the degraded moral state that certainly more or less belongs
> to his condition, is, we apprehend, taking a very narrow view of an
> author's privileges. Such criticism would have deprived the world of
> even Homer.[39]

Throughout the 1850 preface, the phrase "elevation of romance" is linked
with characterizations of the Indians and the heroic Leatherstocking who
so much resembles them. Homer, the only author named in the preface,
provides its closing word.

When Hawkeye first appears in *The Last of the Mohicans,* Cooper endows him with the knowledge that the days of oral transmission of heroic legend are fading fast:

> "I am willing to own that my people have many ways, of which, as an
> honest man, I can't approve. It is one of their customs to write in books
> what they have done and seen, instead of telling them in their villages,
> where the lie can be given to the face of a cowardly boaster, and the
> brave soldier can call on his comrades to witness for the truth of his
> words. In consequence of this bad fashion a man who is too conscien-
> tious to misspend his days among the women, in learning the names of
> black marks, may never hear of the deeds of his fathers, nor feel a pride
> in striving to outdo them.[40]

Cooper's own "black marks" are, of course, the only means by which
Hawkeye's complaint against written language has been preserved.
Everything that troubles Hawkeye about the disappearance of white legends from cultural currency becomes even more troubling when applied
to the tribal histories of the Indians, whose oral legends, even if extant in
1757, let alone 1826, have been distorted in translation. Throughout the
novel, Hawkeye tells us but two oral lays, and they concern the colo-

nists' battle exploits around the Bloody Pond and the blockhouse. From Heckewelder's *Account,* if nowhere else, Cooper had become familiar with the general nature of Indian oral heroic legends, yet he never allows his Indians to tell them. The void in oral epic legend is filled with the matter of medieval romance and American Captivity Narrative. Around the councils, battle scenes and historical "massacre" that comprise the epic substance of *The Last of the Mohicans,* Cooper devises two rescue plots in which the chivalrous protecting of (and deference to) white women defines the heroism of red men as well as white. By thus adapting the Captivity Narrative for purposes of romance,[41] Cooper created a highly popular compromise that avoids patent fakery of Indian legends while praising heroes who protect Civilization's highest flower.

The problems of generic adaptation troubled Cooper less than the dilemma of approving a practicable heroic code. The antebellum American writer who would find an epic in historical Indian conflict was led to ascribe heroic qualities to a race other than his own, to a race then being dispossessed and killed by the very people who would read his book. To depict the Indian as an inhuman savage lusting to scalp white maidens would be historically indefensible and would ultimately diminish the achievement of conquest – as the poems of Bryan and Paulding had sadly shown. To depict the Indian only as an aged stoic hero or a noble savage, however, would deny all sanction to the continuing fact of white conquest. Cooper would pursue the problem as a matter of daily conduct, as well as historical displacement. How far could an enlightened author, bent on the beau ideal of romance, excuse the "virtues" of retaliatory justice (scalping, killing in cold blood) and of stoic endurance (sadomasochistic torture scenes) on the relativistic grounds that these were the norms of courage for a heroic people defending their own lands?

The extraordinarily complex and intricate narrative of *The Last of the Mohicans* rests upon a simple symmetrical arrangement of sections:

1. Exposition (Chapters 1–4)
2. Battle around Glenn's Falls (5–9)
3. Cora and Alice captured by Magua: Captivity Narrative (10–14)
4. Fall of Fort William Henry (15–17). End of Volume I.
5. Cora and Alice recaptured by Magua: Captivity Narrative (18–22)
6. Rescues of Alice, Uncas, and Cora (23–30)
7. Battles between Delawares and Hurons, Uncas and Magua (31–2)
8. Denouement, funeral ceremonies for Uncas (33). End of Volume II.

After the escape and pursuit sequences, the narrative of each volume is resolved in a climactic military action. At the end of the first volume, the fall of Fort William Henry, prefaced with epigraphs from Gray's "The Bard," reveals white principles of military honor through a panoramic

rendering of a historical event. At the end of the second volume, the victory of the Delawares over the Hurons, prefaced with epigraphs from Pope's *Iliad,* demonstrates red war codes as they are practiced in a wholly imagined combat. Only by comparing the two battles do the full complexities of deciding upon a code that is both heroic and morally honorable clearly emerge.

In his first paragraph, Cooper emphasizes that his subject is anything but a celebration of the founding of a western empire. The French and the English, "in quest of an opportunity to exhibit their courage," have learned to make an "inroad" upon any "lovely" and "secret place" in the forest in order to "uphold the cold and selfish policy of the distant monarchs of Europe" (11). Over the entire narrative Cooper casts a perspective of historical futility by remarking that "the incidents we shall attempt to relate occurred, during the third year of the war which England and France last waged, for the possession of a country, that neither was destined to retain" (12). Only within this controlling sense of overall historical doom, so like the *Iliad,* we are allowed to appreciate the momentary heroics of battlefields and forest rescues.

In Cooper's era, the presumably humanitarian, if not Christian, conduct of the white man remained the justification for dispossession of the red.[42] Nostalgia for the demise of Indian virtues could readily be indulged so long as the white man illustrated his ethical superiority. Unfortunately, none of Cooper's European military commanders conducts himself with integrity, loyalty, and success. Webb's refusal to send reinforcements is a self-protective cowardice far worse than the flight from battle of the Huron Reed-That-Bends, who welcomes his own death after being ostracized from his tribe. Duncan Heyward may marry Cooper's fair heroine, but he proves so incompetent in the woods that Hawkeye finally tells him that he could best assist by remaining silent in the rear. Although the most prominent white English officer, Colonel Munro, has the requisite integrity and courage for heroic stature, he proves to be so victimized by chance disadvantages, the disloyalty of Webb, and the treacheries of his environs that he withdraws from the wilderness a beaten, half-senile man. Only white warriors belittle themselves by rescuing others through disguising themselves as bears, jugglers, or doctors. It is Cooper, not a Huron, who states that the Hurons had been "insultingly, shamefully, disgracefully, deceived" by the "whole deception practiced by both Duncan and Hawk-eye" (280).

The hypocrisy of white pretensions to ethical superiority is the controlling theme of Cooper's account of the Fall of Fort William Henry. After introducing the Marquis de Montcalm as the epitome of refined European gentility, Cooper shows him offering Munro honorable and bloodless terms of surrender acceptable by white but not red war codes.

Because Montcalm then stands apathetically by while his 2,000 Huron mercenaries slaughter the retreating English soldiers, their women and their children, Montcalm's deceit seems the most dishonorable of all the barbarities. Intending to qualify the popular memory of Montcalm as a man who "died like a hero on the plains of Abraham," Cooper asserts that Montcalm was "deficient in that moral courage, without which no man can be truly great" (180). By selecting Chapter Seventeen's epigraph from "The Bard," ("Weave we the woof. The thread is spun / The Web is wove. The work is done."), Cooper tacitly likens the fall of the fort to the bloody atrocities through which Christian King Edward I conquered the people of Wales (167).

Indian heroic codes prove to be no more commendable than white. However often Hawkeye may excuse Indian scalping and Indian tortures as red "gifts," Cooper repeatedly describes them with fascinated disgust. The principle of retaliatory justice may motivate Magua, Chingachgook, and Uncas to perform remarkable feats of tracking and endurance, but the principle itself leads only to ever-increasing death. Montcalm's cowardly apathy causes the slaughter at Fort William Henry, but the most graphic brutalities, from the dashing of a baby's head against a rock, to the scalping of the wounded, are committed by red men. Inflamed by the sight of blood, Cooper's Hurons outdo even Achilles in their berserk butchery; Cooper chose to follow Jonathan Carver's *Travels* in picturing victorious Hurons who "kneeled to the earth, and drank freely, exultingly, hellishly, of the crimson tide" (176).

The climactic battle of the second volume proves to be the most hollow of triumphs. Because both the Hurons and the Delawares are being used as pawns in an interimperial struggle, their fighting against one another, as Magua knows, can only hasten their destruction while it underscores their ignorance. Although the Delawares may have routed the Hurons, the fighting in the woods is confused, desultory, historically insignificant, and little like the hand-to-hand confrontations at the end of *The Iliad* and *The Aeneid*. Cora is stabbed, for little apparent purpose, by one of Magua's followers; Magua stabs Uncas in the back out of impulsive frustration over losing his captive; Hawkeye shoots Magua when Magua is immobile and exposed. Like Achilles and Aeneas, Uncas, Magua, and Hawkeye attack their worst enemy to avenge a fallen friend, but Cooper's three men all attack in a way that avoids the risk of equal combat. The irony of the Delawares' triumph is emphasized by the epigraph Cooper chooses from Kalchas's prophecy in book one of *The Iliad*:

> But plague shall spread, and funeral fires increase
> Till the great King, without a ransom paid,
> To her own Chrysa, send the black-eyed maid. (326)

Lest the reader forget the cost of the Delawares' victory, Cooper thus shades their triumph with a reminder of the deaths caused by the demeaning ransoming and abducting of women (Briseis by Agamemnon, Cora by Magua).

The contrast Cooper establishes between his gentle noble savage (Uncas) and his brutal Satanic villain (Magua) proves not to be as clear-cut as it first appears. Isolated from their deserved position as tribal leaders, both Uncas and Magua regain command before the climactic battle. Magua's eloquent accusations of white greed and white deceit merely confirm, in far more inflammatory language, the conclusions reached by Chingachgook, Hawkeye, and Uncas in Chapter Two. Whereas Milton's Satan had sought vengeance against God because of his own limit-defying pride, Cooper's Magua ("Prince of Darkness" [284]) seeks vengeance against the white race because of the tangible injustice done him by Colonel Munro. Uncas and Magua, both wronged and both pursuing vengeance, must be killed together at the tale's conclusion. The red devil who would turn intertribal war into genocidal war cannot remain a continuing forest force. But the noble Apollonian hero whose fine feelings "elevated him far above the intelligence, and advanced him probably centuries before the practices of his nation" (115), cannot be allowed to survive either. Whereas Magua would pose a threat to white conquest through force and cunning, Uncas would pose a challenge to white superiority simply through human example.

The determining differences between Magua and Uncas have little to do with their tribal loyalty, their prowess, or their courage. Unlike Magua, Uncas is given no personal reason for feeling vengeance toward the white man. Uncas's silent acceptance of white authority has its counterpart in his deference to white women.[43] Whereas Uncas sometimes outdoes Duncan Heyward in his chivalrous regard for Alice and Cora, Magua is endowed with the presumably red trait of treating women as serviceable beasts. Hawkeye may believe there is a taboo against miscegenation, but Cooper respects the depth of Uncas's love for Cora. Magua's consummate villainy (a villainy that determines the plot) is his need repeatedly to abduct Cora, not primarily to gain vengeance against Munro, but to satisfy his own tellingly unexplained lust. Ultimately, the protective reverence that some white men and "white" Indians pay to white women may be Cooper's only sure means of maintaining the moral superiority of his own "civilized" and conquering race.

The concluding scene of *The Last of the Mohicans,* surely the finest chapter of fiction any American had yet written, is clearly influenced by the twenty-fourth book of *The Iliad.*[44] The lamentations of Andromache, Hecuba, and Helen over the body of Hector, like the Delaware maidens'

lamentations over the body of Uncas, precede the climactic short laments of the aged father-kings, Chingachgook and Priam, who know that their nation's demise is one with their son's death. The images of fire with which the *Iliad* closes – a fire that envelops Greek and Trojan, Achilles as well as Hector – convey the same foreboding of destruction we find in Tamenund's words: "It is enough. Go, children of the Lenape; the anger of the Manitou is not done" (350). Just as Cooper was the first American to recognize that prose was the better genre for a national heroic literature, so he was the first to recognize that the death of brave men and the end of a heroic age, rather than the panegyric of empire, are the true measure of the epic art.

However similar these endings may be in situation and in spirit, the characters of the mourned heroes differ markedly. Uncas never expresses the epic warrior's quest for glory or renown; instead, Cooper emphasizes Uncas's gentleness and grace. Neither Chingachgook nor Magua can serve as the Indian whose demise can be most mourned. Wholly committed to red values, these older chieftains deeply resent the red man's dispossession. Political enemies though they may be, Magua and the Big Serpent are ultimately alike in their racial ethos. When joined in nightmarish single combat, their bodies become indistinguishably serpentine: "The swift evolutions of the combatants seemed to incorporate their bodies into one" (113). The warrior to be ceremonially elegized must rather be the red man who most closely approximates, and defers to, the white man's moral sensitivity. Through Uncas's death, the best of Indian qualities can be mourned and removed, allowing his less flexible father to remain, a figure of real but lesser challenge to the injustice of dispossession.

Because neither the red man nor the white practices a code both moral and heroic, the closing paragraphs of the novel offer us an alternative that combines yet supercedes them both. The bond between the Big Serpent and Hawkeye, formed over the body of Uncas and beyond the incursions of civilization, is based upon absolute honesty, a mastery of forest skills, and a wordless sense for the divinity of nature. Satanic only in their understanding the twistings of human nature, both men criticize white civilization more persistently than red. And yet neither their heroic deeds nor their apt criticisms can sustain any communal purpose. Reversing the thrust of recent "epic" poems about the West, Cooper portrays the two most admirable men of America's heroic age, not as representative racial figures who justify expansion, but as exceptions who represent a promise never fulfilled. The Big Serpent and Hawkeye, like many a semidivine pair in oral epic poetry (Gilgamesh and Enkidu, Achilles and Patroklos, Beowulf and Wiglaf, Roland and Oliver), seem to have the ability to perform anything except to escape suffering and mortality. Unlike every one of these pairs of heroes, however, Hawkeye and Chin-

gachgook represent no community and have no followers. Embodying the unrealized potential of two passing cultures, they are nothing more, but nothing less, then the last of their several kinds. In the oldest of extant epics, Gilgamesh forms his bond with Enkidu, a dark-skinned hunter from the wilderness, and the two leave civilization to undertake adventurous tasks together.[45] Whereas Gilgamesh finally returns to the city of Uruk to guard the walls he has built, Leatherstocking's heroism has been defined by his departure from the compromised civilization of Templeton.

By the time Cooper had completed all five tales, the importance of the red man's Greek-like heroism had receded, the bond between the Big Serpent and Hawkeye had become increasingly central, and Leatherstocking had finally become the acknowledged "hero" of the entire series.[46] At no time, however, did Cooper suggest that Leatherstocking had solved the problem of how to be a Christian hero in the wilderness. In *The Last of the Mohicans,* Cooper makes two contrasting references to the Roman worship of *Manes* in order to convey the extent of the dilemma. When Magua urges his Hurons to kill Uncas in order to fulfill a tribal custom "to sacrifice a victim to the manes of their countrymen," Cooper admits that Magua is factually correct, but then condemns him for having "lost every vestige of humanity in a wish for revenge" (250). Shortly thereafter, the psalmodist David Gamut, convinced that unresisting death is better than "the damnable principle of revenge," tells Hawkeye "Should I fall, . . . seek no victims to my manes, but rather forgive my destroyers" (274). Caught between Christian principle and forest necessity, Hawkeye replies with the fullest account he ever gives of his forest ethics:

> "There is a principle in that . . . different from the law of the woods! and yet it is fair and noble to reflect upon! . . . It is what I would wish to practyse myself, as one without a cross of blood, though it is not always easy to deal with an Indian, as you would with a fellow Christian. God bless you, friend; I do believe your scent is not greatly wrong, when the matter is duly considered, and keeping eternity before the eyes, though much depends on the natural gifts, and the force of temptation." (293)

Hawkeye's statement begins confidently, but soon breaks down into hesitant qualifications and appeals both to "gifts" and to human weaknesses. Although denouncing revenge and bloodshed, Hawkeye knows that he must always be ready to shoot first in self-protection. The heroism of Cooper's "magnificent moral hermaphrodite"[47] (Balzac's term) clearly depends upon his trying to remain Christian in principle, while surviving by unchristian, if not Indian, displays of deadly prowess.

The few demurrers from the praise with which reviewers greeted *The*

Last of the Mohicans reflect a failure to grant that fiction could incorporate elements of romance and epic. Acute though W. H. Gardiner had been in assessing *The Spy,* he objected to the presumably breathless pace of Cooper's adventure sequences because even a frontier novel should contain "a little quiet domestic life."[48] Lewis Cass's accusation that Cooper's Indians were "of the school of Heckewelder and not of the school of nature"[49] was based upon the constricting premise that no author should imagine red men as they might have been in their irrecoverable forest lives. Two years later, Grenville Mellon heightened Cass's attack into an absurdity:

> The Indian chieftain is the first character upon the canvass or the carpet; in active scene or still one, he is the nucleus of the whole affair; and in almost every case is singularly blessed in some dark-eyed child, whose complexion is made sufficiently white for the lightest hero. This bronze noble of nature, is then made to talk like Ossian for whole pages, and measure out hexameters, as though he had been practicing for a poetic prize.[50]

Mellon's probably deliberate conflation of Homer's metric with Macpherson's prose, like his misleading inferences about Cora and Uncas, are of small importance. His blinding error was his refusal to admit either that Indian life might have shared the spirit of the heroic age or that prose fiction could absorb the spirit of heroic poetry.

IV. "THE VERY PRINCE OF SNAKES"

Only after *The Last of the Mohicans* was published did the likelihood of America's epic appearing in the form of a prose romance about the Indian explicitly emerge. In 1827 the *American Quarterly Review* decided that the only subject of "high romantic fiction" must be the American Indian, because he alone has exhibited "unrestrained passions of the most heroic kind," "high figurative eloquence," and a belief that "supernatural agency directs everything."[51] Two years later, Alexander Hill Everett contended that "a polished and civilized age" could no longer be patient with the "artificial measures, strains and subjects" of heroic poetry. Instead of arguing that the epic was therefore dead, Everett contended for a shift in genre: "Hence a fine history and a fine novel may perhaps be viewed as the greater and lesser epic of a cultivated period, when verse is better reserved for short poems accompanied by music."[52] The boundaries of genre, especially of romance, were becoming so flexible that Homer could even be remade in Sir Walter Scott's image. While calling for an American genius to sing, in prose or verse, the heroic acts of settlement that form "our Iliad and Odyssey," Rufus Choate assured his listeners that "The Iliad and Odyssey of Homer – what are they but great Waverley novels!" National epics like *The Iliad,* Choate was certain, provide us the true history of cultural origins: "The Greek epics

gave us information, for which we are indebted to an old wandering, blind harper – just such another as he who sang the lay of the last minstrel to the ladies of Newark Castle."[53]

To so venturesome a young author and editor as William Gilmore Simms, already the author of "The Last of the Yemassee" (1827), as well as an abandoned heroic poem on Cortes,[54] such ideas held high promise for transferral to South Carolina's past. Maturing in the heyday of Scott and Cooper, Simms was convinced that an American national literature could be woven only from regional legend.[55] Although Simms might not have read Everett's and Choate's calls for a prose epic, he could scarcely have overlooked the following comment on Fénelon's *Telemachus* in the 1831 issue of the *Southern Review,* published in Charleston:

> In a literary point of view, we think the work exercised an influence more extended than has been usually attributed to it. Was it poetry or prose? Was it a novel or an epic poem? These are questions that have often been debated. In fact, it broke down the divisions between the two. It transferred the brilliant descriptions, the lofty characters, the poetical ideas, and even the musical flow of language, which had before been seen only in the *Iliad,* the *Aeneid* or the *Jerusalem Delivered,* into prose literature, and thus led the way in giving novels the constituents of the epic, by which they have, in fact, become the epic poem of the present day.[56]

Although Scott and not Fénelon was provoking the change in conceptions of genre, this review anticipates Simms's well-known declaration in the 1835 "Advertisement" to *The Yemassee: "*The modern Romance is the substitute which the people of the present day offer for the ancient epic."[57] Simms's contribution was not, as has been assumed, to originate this idea, but to be the first to state it concisely, fully, and to a large readership.

Simms's insistence that the romance was the modern form of epic had arisen through his reviewing of contemporary epic poems, as well as his reading of Scott and Cooper. To Simms, Bryan's poem should be compared to Cooper's prose: The "rather limited" materials of *The Mountain Muse* made Bryan's descriptions of forest heroics seem of small import beside Cooper's.[58] But the old epic also remained a needed standard for judging new forms. Simms berates Robert Pollok's verse at length, first by denying that *The Course of Time* "has any claims to the honor of being considered an Epic," and then by demolishing it through an eight-page comparison to *Paradise Lost!*[59] By 1834, when Simms reviewed Robert Montgomery's *Messiah,* he had totally lost patience with the contemporary epic poem:

> Yes, young reader, it is a beautiful marvel resulting from our modern discovery of the lost art of manufacturing epics, to know that the brow of the bard need not be silver'd o'er with age, nor his mind stored with

> knowledge or experience to qualify him for the task. . . . If the tyro only apply himself, assiduously, he can manufacture lines, as the apprentice can pens – by the gross, – furnish cantos, as the merchants can bales – and produce an Epic, "warranted sound," according to order.[60]

The appearance of *The Yemassee* one year after this review is thus the result of a timely conjuncture: Simms's ten-year distance from *The Last of the Mohicans,* his desire to deepen the epic qualities of Indian romance, his disgust for contemporary verse epics, and the currently acute controversy over Indian removal. As *The Yemassee* became available for purchase, both the Seminoles and Creeks were at war against whites; by driving intrusive settlers off their lands, both tribes hoped to resist Jackson's double-edged policy of enforcing either tribal sale of ancestral lands or tribal removal to new ones.[61]

Simms's public avowal of epic romance assumes his generation's belief that epic songs are the main source of historical information about heroic-age peoples. Insisting that he had invented nothing about his Yemassees except their religious mythology, Simms develops epic conventions more elaborately than Cooper. Three extended council scenes (Chapters 10–12, 25, 33–5) lead toward a climactic genocidal battle between red and white. Detailed accounts are given of the speeches, war songs, sacrifices, and prophecies of a heroic-age people devoted to tribal hegemony. When the tribes gather at Pocota-ligo, Simms provides a catalogue of the clans that deserve to be remembered. An authentic Indian language now means eliminating rhymed verse and minimizing poeticized natural imagery. Familiar with Wolf's theory of Homeric verse recitation, Simms devises tribal songs that suggest the *stychic* composition of an oral singer who is repeating formulaic lines:

> Is not this a Yemassee?
> Wherefore is he bound thus–
> Wherefore, with the broad arrow
> On his right arm growing,
> Wherefore is he bound thus–
> Is not this a Yemassee?[62]

Simms adapts these conventions, not because he wishes his romance to *be* an epic (it is explicitly a "substitute"), but because he believes that all precivilized peoples were heroic and instinctual in the same ways. "The elements of all uncultivated peoples are the same," he declares; "The early Greeks, in their stern endurance of torment, in their sports and exercises, were exceedingly like the North American savages" (241). Accordingly, there is no inconsistency in Simms's extending his Indian analogies to another appropriate people: "National pride, or rather the great glory of the clan, was as desperate a passion with the Southern Indians, as with the . . . Highlanders of Scotland" (221). To particularize

the descriptions of one heroic-age people provides the general traits of them all; taken together, they can then have an implied contemporary relevance. Simms's view of history was thus, like Scott's, both dia-chronic and polarized. Although Simms's Yemassee often seem to be Greeks or Highlanders, at other moments they prefigure a proud, intran-sigent South defeated by superior forces of commerce and technology.

Unlike Cooper, Simms directly portrays an interracial rather than in-terimperial war, thereby allowing the Yemassee the dignity of know-ingly fighting their white dispossessors to their own tragic end. The chief of the Yemassee, Sanutee, is an impressive and credible representative of the heroic age. Persuading his less perceptive tribesmen that they must fight for "freedom," Sanutee himself "saw while he deplored the destiny which awaited his people" (20). Like Hector and Turnus before him, Sanutee fights in a doomed cause because his sense of self derives from a recognized heroic code. Skilled, loyal and implacable, Sanutee embraces deceit to gain his ends (Ulysses), sacrifices marital love to presumably higher values (Aeneas), and broods alone upon his inevitable defeat (Sa-tan). Convincingly compared to Cassius, Hector, Satan, and Logan, Sanutee has devised a rebellion "big with the fate of his own and another people" (69). After the defeat and slaughter of his tribe, Sanutee's dying words resonate with a melancholy even more convincing than Tamen-und's, because they are spoken by a hero whose valor, like Hector's, has brought known destruction upon his own people:

> "It is good, Matiwan. The well-beloved has no people. The Yemassee
> has bones in the thick woods, and there are no young braves to sing the
> song of his glory. The Coosah-moray-te [white Governor Gabriel Har-
> rison] is on the bosom of the Yemassee, with the foot of the great bear
> of Apalachia. He makes his bed in the old home of Pocota-ligo, like a
> fox that burrows in the hill-side. We may not drive him away. It is
> good for Sanutee to die with his people. Let the song of his dying be
> sung." (368)

Whereas Cooper fashioned deaths for Uncas and Magua that were sud-den and accidental, Sanutee learns of his imminent death and his tribe's demise through a prophetic dream that "he was not unwilling to be-lieve"(365).

Cooper's disapproval of revenge had been based upon particular battle practices (scalping, torture) and upon their increasingly deadly conse-quence for all. Although he outdoes Cooper in picturing savage atroci-ties, Simms is more concerned with the psychological effect that the code of revenge has upon the individual Indian. The disgracing of Sanutee's lineage through the drunken cowardice of his son Occonestoga compels Sanutee to persuade the Yemassee to strip his son of any place in family and tribe. In the novel's most memorable scene, Sanutee's wife Matiwan

saves their son from complete loss of identity by killing him before the ceremony of tribal rejection can be performed. Such demands of the heroic code – a father's denying his son, a mother's killing him – are clearly presented as acts beyond the white man's capacity to perform. Whether such deeds are a tribute to the heroic will, as well as an offense against human feelings, Simms will not consider. Instead, he emphasizes the ironic outcome of killing a son to save him, and of ostracizing the tribal prince in order to purify the tribal will to war. Distraught with guilt and grief, Matiwan soon mistakes a captive white man for her red son, calls him "Occonestoga," and then frees him from captivity (251–2). The surrogate son whom she thus restores to life, Gabriel Harrison, will prove to be the Governor who will lead Carolina's troops to extinguish the Yemassee.

In these and other ways, *The Yemassee* is less an imitation of *The Last of the Mohicans* than a refashioning of it. Although Simms, like Cooper, insists that his account of Indians "in their undegraded condition" (6) is historically accurate, his rendering of their heroic traits is less varied and considerably harsher. Sanutee resembles Uncas and the Big Serpent because he is a chieftain whose heroic qualities render him "always in advance of the masses clustering around him" (20). Whereas Cooper had pictured three Indians with varying heroic traits (Chingachgook, Uncas, Magua), Simms concentrates red virtues into one man, and then insists upon his superiority to a norm of red barbarity. Cooper's Indians had prayed to a benign Manitou; Simms's Yemassee are Manicheans who more often invoke their dark and bloody war god, Opitchi Maneyto.[63] *The Yemassee* allows no hope for an alternative model of heroism existing apart from both cultures. Neither white scouts who admire Indian ways, nor red chiefs who protect white women, have any place in Simms's novel. Simms's white hero is a governor who, in spite of his friendship with Sanutee, must exterminate the Yemassee. His counterpart in *The Last of the Mohicans,* Duncan Heyward, managed to serve English troops and his Mohican friends simultaneously.[64]

In both romances, the death of the red chieftain's son defines the demise of his heroic race. Occonestoga, last of the Yemassee, is a coward who runs from battle, attempts parricide, and dies in tribal disgrace. The opposite of Uncas in character and deed. Occonestoga serves to remind the reader that the Yemassee, unlike the Mohicans, are partly responsible for their own decline. Many of their chieftains have been more responsive to easy land sales than to their culture's survival. At the end of Simms's novel, we are asked to mourn, not for a noble red youth, but for an aging chief whose virtues have died away even in his own family.

Simms allows the Yemassee the fullest measure of heroic courage in their suicidal battle against the Carolinians: "Their valour was desperate

but cool, and European warfare has never shown a more determined spirit of bravery than was manifested by the wild warriors of Yemassee, striking the last blow for the glory of their once mighty nation" (367). Nonetheless, the reader's admiration for the Yemassee's brave defiance is qualified by the immediate cause of their defeat. Gabriel Harrison's whites defeat Sanutee's Yemassee because the white hero is a smarter military tactician than his red counterpart. Even the Yemassee's courage is ambivalently judged. Simms arranges for Bess Matthews to be transfixed by a rattlesnake's eye both to titillate the reader and to envelop the Indian's virtues in a shadow of red Satanism:

> With them, he [the rattlesnake] is held the gentleman, the nobleman – the very prince of snakes. His attributes are devoutly esteemed among them, and many of their own habits derive their existence from models furnished from his peculiarities. He is brave, will never fly from an enemy, and for this they honour him. If approached, he holds his ground and is never unwilling for the combat. He does not begin the affray, and is content to defend himself against invasion. He will not strike without due warning of his intention, and when he strikes, the blow of his weapon is fatal. (145)

The best qualities of the old heroic code are here rendered serpentine while they are traced back, not to moral absolutes, but to primitive man's observations of animal behavior.

When seen in battle, the snakish Indian often seems much less of a princely gentleman. The novel's one single combat ends when Gabriel Harrison kills the Coosah chieftain Chinnabee, who had coiled his body into a ball to entangle Harrison's legs, had "wriggled like a snake" (337), and who finally dies revealing himself as a "cunning serpent" (338). The Roman Indian Sanutee, who is never allowed to engage in such a demeaning display, is killed by a bullet from an unidentified hand. Heroic in his moment of dying, but not in the method of his death, Simms's noble Indian is brought down by an utterly random act of a technologically superior force.

An enveloping shadow of red Satanism was also useful to Simms because he was advancing contradictory judgments of Indian dispossession. Simms maintains that "our European ancestors were, in many respects, monstrous great rascals" because they dispossessed Indians by phony treaties and sheer force (221). Simms also insists that the Yemassee were "a powerful and gallant race" worthy of comparison to the Romans (10). And yet, Simms was explicitly committed to the belief that whites were "the superior race" (15) who should expel the savage "as the inevitable result of her [Civilization's] . . . progressive march" (69). Rather than confront the issue of why white rascals really were superior to red Romans, the Indians' best qualities could be rendered insidious through dia-

bolic association. By investing the Indian race with the threatening grandeur of Milton's archangel, Simms could exalt and criticize the superseded code of martial heroism through an analogy that was recognizably epic yet conveniently ahistorical.

Reworking the conventions of the epic could also serve, when needed, to taint the justice of the red man's cause. Inventing a religious mythology appropriate for epic-type scenes enabled Simms's class and racial hostilities to dominate his reasoned conclusion that the Indian had been continuously wronged. In order to arouse a war frenzy among the tribes, the Yemassee propitiate Opitchi Maneyto (their "great Moloch") by an elaborate ceremonial sacrifice of a white victim (231). An Irish jobber named Macnamara is slowly tortured with arrows, tomahawks, and torches until his blackened skin runs red with blood and fire. Showing no fear, Macnamara earns the epithet "the heroic Irishman" (262) because he looks and acts like a supremely brave warrior. Heroic according to red values, Macnamara nonetheless taunts his torturers by calling them, seven times, "red-skinned divils" or "red nagers" (234–6). In immediate context, Macnamara's racist labels are clearly meant to elicit the reader's assent. His heroism is a sum of contradictory qualities that reflect divided cultural values. Macnamara imitates Indian bravery under trial, while speaking as if the Indian were a devil-nigger whose composite otherness is wholly repulsive.

The response of Simms's cavalier hero to this prolonged torture scene is even more revealing. Hidden in a thicket, Gabriel Harrison watches Macnamara's heroic defiance of degradation with that sense of helpless awe proper to the epic, "a sentiment of wonder and fascination" (242). Finally escaping from his tormentors, Macnamara suddenly runs directly toward Harrison's thicket, but is beaten by the club of a Seratee chieftan until "the spattering brains were driven wide, and *into* the upturned face of Harrison" (239, italics mine). At this moment, Macnamara has become an indistinguishable mixture of the Irishman, Indian, nigger and devil, together embodying a composite threat to the white cavalier governor's life and supremacy. Simms himself, be it remembered, was the estranged son of an Irish jobber who had fought under Andrew Jackson in the Indian wars.[65] The year after *The Yemassee*'s success, Simms married into the planter class. Psychologically, Macnamara's explosive death thus suggests a son's guilty supplanting of his father. In historical context, however, the scene implies that the dangers of waking up to the reality of the ethnics' revolution may be even worse than the dangers of remaining entranced by it.

Such attitudes remain implicit because the Indian romance ultimately defuses the contemporary issues it uncovers in the past. On one level, to write a romance in 1835 about the dispossession of Southern Indians by

whites was inescapably to involve the reader in the crisis of Indian removal. But by choosing the Yemassee rebellion of 1715, Simms could
safely acknowledge the wrongs of the whites while portraying Southern
Indians as essentially ineducable in the ways of Christian civilization.
Granting Homeric glory to the Yemassee, Simms could exalt red virtues
while wrongly inferring that the Indian cannot adapt to agriculture or
the written word. Readers might indulge in melancholy for an extinct
heroic tribe, yet still believe Simms's uncomplimentary references to the
Creeks and Cherokees (202, 257, 264, 366), two of the tribes who in 1835
were still being "removed."

Park Benjamin's flattering literary comparison, "*The Yemassee* is superior in plot, style and execution to *The Last of the Mohicans*,"[66] no
longer seems defensible. The epic portions of the narrative, compelling
though they are, cannot salvage the whole. In addition to Simms's Indian
chapters, which make up twenty of the book's fifty-two chapters, there
are pages upon pages of predictable rescues, walking stereotypes, forced
humor, insufferable courtships, and adventure episodes that in no way
further the confrontation of the two cultures. The Leatherstocking Tales,
often subjected to similar charges, contain no sections of such sustained
hackwork as Chapters 26–31 or 38–41 of *The Yemassee*.

Simms's failing is not merely one of sloppy writing; it derives from
his conception of the romance epic itself. The original "Advertisment"
to *The Yemassee* associates the epical qualities of prose romance, not so
much with the qualities of the Indians' heroic age, but with the narrative
technique of rendering them:

> The modern romance is a poem in every sense of the word. . . . Its
> standards are precisely those of the epic. It invests individuals with an
> absorbing influence – it hurries them through crowding events in a
> narrow space of time – it requires the same unities of plan, of purpose,
> and harmony of parts, and it seeks for its adventures, among the wild
> and wonderful.[67]

Simms here fastens upon the most trivial aspects of Scott's and Cooper's
aesthetic, and then makes them synonymous with the epic. His many
chapters of filler often cause his heroic prose romance to devolve into
mere adventure, and thereby to sacrifice, not only the narrative thrust
central to epic, but "unities of plan" and "harmony of parts" as well.

By 1853, when Simms reread *The Yemassee* for its second edition, he
perceived that his novel was deeply flawed. Claiming to be "fully conscious of the story's defects and crudities," Simms acknowledged "I see
now a thousand passages through which, had I the leisure, and could I
muster the courage for the effort, I should draw the pen, with the hope
to substitute better thoughts, and improved situations, in a more appropriate and graceful style."[68] This self-criticism was prompted by more

than the convention of modesty. During the intervening decades, Simms
had qualified his insistence that an American epic be written in prose. In
an 1845 review of Schoolcraft's writings, he had even reformed his notion of an American Indian epic:

> The exploits of their warriors, thus chanted in the hearing of the tribe,
> and transmitted through successive generations, would, if caught up,
> and put in the fashion of a living language, be not unanalogous to those
> rude ballads, out of which Homer framed his great poem.[69]

Excited by the possibilities of such a work, Simms exclaims "How such
a history, chanted by a famous chief on his bed of death and glory, could
be made to ring, trumpet like, in a modern ear, by such a lyre as Walter
Scott. We should not need a Milton or a Homer, for the performance"
(146). Once again, Scott's poems seem the proper medium, but Simms
has added a new proviso that the "ballads" must be transcribed versions
of the Indians' own songs, rather than accounts of battles recreated by a
white author.

Although *Hiawatha* was to versify Schoolcraft's Indian legends, Longfellow was not concerned with accurate transcriptions of oral lays into a
heroic song. It is probable that no antebellum white author could have
had the knowledge of Indian oral tradition, the means to record it, and
the poetic ability to translate it.[70] Simms was never to write the poem he
anticipated. Understandably reconciled to the compromised quality of
his hybrid form, Simms would sum up his achievement in a letter to
Evert Duyckinck:

> *The Yemassee* & in fact most of my works are *romances,* not novels. They
> involve sundry of the elements of heroic poetry. They are imaginative,
> passionate, metaphysical; they deal chiefly in trying situation, bold
> characterization and elevating morality. They exhibit *invention* in large
> degree, & their progress is dramatic; the action being bold and salient,
> & with a regularly advancing convergence to the catastrophe.[71]

As a description of *The Yemassee,* Simms's appraisal is largely earned, yet
we may infer from its vague language ("sundry of the elements of heroic
poetry,") Simms's final awareness that a white author's epic romance
about the Indian could convey Satanic heroism only at the expense of
authenticity to oral tradition.

V.   "SATAN OF THIS FOREST PARADISE"

To avoid trivializing adventure sequences, still another shift in
generic thinking would be necessary. The demise of the Indian would
have to be recast as heroic history rather than epic romance. Shortly after
The History of the Conspiracy of Pontiac was completed, Parkman declared
his "special admiration for Cooper's writings," recounted the fictional

absurdities of *The Last of the Mohicans,* and contended that, unlike Cooper's masterful characterization of Leatherstocking, "his Indian characters are . . . for the most part either superficially or falsely drawn."[72] Cooper's portrayal of the struggle of Indian, French, and British forces for possession of North America had suggested to Parkman the subject for his life's work: "I may say without exaggeration that Cooper has had an influence in determining the course of my life and pursuits."[73] And yet, impressed though he was by Cooper's insight that "Civilization has a destructive as well as a creative power,"[74] Parkman nonetheless was sure that the scope of their common subject would now require romantic history, not historical romance, adherence to fact and not loose comparisons of Indians to Greeks.

By shunning the conventions of Indian historical romance, Parkman did away with escape and pursuit sequences, timely rescues, and the need for situating a genteel, marriageable couple in the wilderness. Although Pontiac's besieging of Fort Detroit is as static a situation as Montcalm's besieging of Fort William Henry, Parkman fills his intervening chapters with historical accounts of the clashes between red and white men along the entire line of settlement from Lake George to Southern Virginia. The romancer's unevenness of tone, especially bothersome in *The Yemassee,* is replaced by a sense of one concerted historical action with many local variants. Nonetheless, reduced to its essence, Parkman's *History* closely follows the familiar paradigm of the Indian romance. Through a series of council scenes, a chieftain emerges as a symbolic red hero, only to be ultimately defeated, killed, and mourned as the last representative of his race's barbaric virtues.

In an introductory chapter summarizing the culture of Eastern tribes, Parkman complains that the canting rhapsodies of sentimentalists have made of the Indian "an image bearing no more resemblance to its original, than the monarch of the tragedy and the hero of the epic poem bear to their living prototypes in the palace and the camp."[75] Accordingly, Parkman's Indians are never seen delivering long metaphoric speeches, invoking the Manitou, engaging in single combat, or elegizing their fathers beside a tumulus. And yet, Parkman grants them the virtues of a heroic age: "adherence to ancient usages and customs" (36), "an iron self-control originating in a peculiar form of pride" (62), "love of glory" (62) and "an unquenchable thirst for greatness and renown" (63). Parkman is concerned, however, that his reader never associate these "heroic virtues" (49) with gentleness or sensitivity: "These generous traits are overcast by much that is dark, cold and sinister, by sleepless distrust, and ranking jealousy. Treacherous himself, he is always suspicious of treachery in others" (62). The most contemptible of all literary rhapsodies, to Parkman, is the idea of the noble savage, not only because it is histori-

cally false, but because it deprives the Indian of the unyielding harshness that forms the essence of his heroism.

Precisely because so little was known about the shadowy Pontiac, Parkman could fashion him into the embodiment of his own view, at once dark and exalted, of red heroism. Unlike Tamenund, Chingachgook, or Sanutee, Pontiac is consistently treacherous, untroubled by treaty or promises, and prone to periods of rage and drunkenness. Once disillusioned with the self-serving friendliness of the French, he pursues any plausible means of killing the whites who would have his lands. Pontiac's literary origins are suggested by Parkman's comparison, "Uncas does not at all resemble a genuine Indian. Magua, the villain of the story, is a less untruthful portrait."[76] Unlike Sanutee, whose race hatred is confined by his white friendships and the local bounds of his rebellion, Parkman's Pontiac embodies all the treacherous malignity of Magua released against the national line of settlement. In spite of Parkman's dislike for the false analogies of epic poetry, he calls Pontiac "the Satan of this forest paradise" (175) and twice describes him scheming apart in his hut.

Without slighting Pontiac's lying brutality, Parkman allows Satanic heroism to win our admiration to a degree unacceptable to Cooper or to Simms. The first paragraph of the 1851 "Preface" informs us that Pontiac was "a great and daring champion" (17). Four sentences after identifying Pontiac as the forest Satan, Parkman ascribes to him "the high emotion of the patriot hero, the champion not merely of his nation's rights, but of the very existence of his race" (175). In the absence of any white hero of remotely comparable stature, Pontiac emerges as "the savage hero of this dark forest tragedy" (201). After Pontiac is murdered by a fellow Indian, Parkman cannot resist closing his narrative with one more elevating epic analogy: "Over the grave of Pontiac more blood was poured out in atonement, than flowed from the veins of the slaughtered heroes on the corpse of Patroclus" (478).

Parkman could embrace the romantic Satanism of the Indian more readily than Cooper or Simms because the threat of the Indian to an Eastern audience was more remote in 1851 than in 1826 or 1835. Moreover, Parkman's admiration for defeated men of unconquerable will was by no means confined to whites like La Salle. Within the text of the *History*, however, Pontiac's grandeur is repeatedly linked to the leveling of the American forest. At the end of the first paragraph of the "Preface," Parkman specifies that his *History* "aims to portray the American forest and the American Indian at the period when both received their final doom" (17). The book ends with two sentences that rather than praising civilization's triumph over savagery, emphasize the ironic cost of Pontiac's subjugation:

Neither mound nor tablet marked the burial-place of Pontiac. For a
mausoleum, a city has risen above the forest hero, and the race whom
he hated with such burning rancor trample with unceasing footsteps
over his forgotten grave. (479)

When the forest is replaced by a city that seems no more than a tomb, a
red Satan can finally emerge as the "forest hero" of the age of settlement.

Parkman's closing lament for the loss of red heroic virtue is bitter
rather than nostalgic. As Pontiac and his forest disappear, so do the opportunities to experience God and to prove one's manliness in the wilderness. Throughout his opening chapter, Parkman had condoned the
demise of the Indian by means of a metaphor that allowed readers to
retain their belief in the progress of civilization. "The Indian is a true
child of the forest and the desert" (35), Parkman had begun; "His virtues
. . . would quickly vanish, were he elevated from his savage state" (37).
The Indian thus represents mankind's stage of childish inflexibility, a
stage that the white man, unlike the red, can outgrow:

> He will not learn the arts of civilization, and he and his forest must
> perish together. The stern, unchanging features of his mind excite our
> admiration from their very immutability; and we look with deep inter-
> est on the fate of this irreclaimable son of the wilderness, the child who
> will not be weaned from the breast of his rugged mother.[77]

If the forest life prolongs man's infancy, then the maturity of civilization
must have erased "the germs of heroic virtues" (63). Forest bravery,
Parkman constantly tells us, is a heroic stage we must outgrow. As the
narrative proceeds, however, Parkman's metaphor turns against itself.
Because Pontiac has clearly passed every test of forest manliness, it becomes increasingly difficult to perceive his sixty years of intransigence as
childishness. If the building of an urban "mausoleum" is proof of the
white man's maturity and flexibility, who would prefer that mankind
should have lost true virtue by being "elevated" from the savage state?
Heroism and civilization, Parkman implies, seem to be vexingly incompatible.

In 1849 Caroline Kirkland followed William Tudor, Edward Everett,
and Simms in calling for an American forest epic in prose, a work in
which the aboriginal red Achilles would furnish America an image of
dying heroic valor.[78] Her insistence on a red Achilles misses, perhaps
deliberately, the model crucial to the tradition of American Indian epic.
To see the red man as Satan rather than Achilles allowed for a prototype
who could be both more grand and more dismissable. Dark political
conspiracy, Parkman's Pontiac shows us, was far more readily ascribable
to a Satanic than an Achillean red man. Achilles had earned the enmity
of some gods, but the favor of others; Homer's Greeks had not been

morally superior to his Trojans. A red Satan, however, could display courageous defiance of providential will when challenging the white man, viceroy on earth of the one and only God. A red Satan could be exalted and wrong, courageous and cruel, rebellious and doomed. By fastening upon the Indian as "Satan of this Forest Paradise," white authors could admire red courage, decry colonial racial atrocities, release nostalgia for the heroic age, but still uphold, albeit uneasily, the divine superiority of the progressive white way. The progression from Magua to Sanutee to Pontiac is one in which the rebellious red chieftain becomes ever more dominant, more impressive, but less tractable, as the frontier recedes from Eastern readers.

Ultimately, the subversive impulse of defining America's epic as an embracing of lost red heroism was dissipated by the demand for cultural selfjustification. After *The Columbiad*'s failure, American writers turned back to the Indian, not because they obeyed some *zeitgeist* called "romanticism," but because the culture they saw developing about them, in Troy, Cooperstown, Charleston, or Boston, scarcely seemed to fulfill the heroic vision of a libertarian republic that had seemed plausible to Barlow's generation. Embracing the extinct "epic" Indian, however, proved easier to do in Mrs. Morton's time or in 1826 than after the election of Andrew Jackson. As long as the wrongs done to the Indian seemed remote, a white author could readily afford nostalgia and veneration. When Indian Removal became a national controversy, more circumspection became desirable. Developing the Satanic Indian at the expense of his Apollonian or Achillean counterparts enabled the heroic Indian to assume all the grandeur a prose epic could attain, while displacing the model of red heroism to the ever more remote reaches of the eighteenth century. Although red Satanism led to literary achievement, it thrived upon the unspoken admission that defiant, doomed, heroic Indians needed to be seen as safely past.

VI. A HEROINE ABOVE THE EPIC

Mrs. Kirkland's call for an American Indian Achilles clearly pertains only to a male literary tradition. The recurring clash between male and female perspective upon the question of Indian heroism may be suggested by a final glance at Catharine Sedgwick's historical novel *Hope Leslie* (1827). Primarily concerned with defining the limits of a Puritan daughter's just rebellion against patriarchal control, Sedgwick's novel contains a powerful characterization of a Pequod maiden named Magawisca, who is caught between loyalty to her dying tribal people and loyalty to the charitable Puritan family who have raised her. By allowing Magawisca to recount the Pequod war from the Indian perspective, Sedgwick upends the traditional, New England account of a triumphant

extirpation of red devils and reveals that the Puritans had in fact carried out genocide by the deliberate slaughter of women and children.

After the historical killing, Magawisca's father, a fictional chieftain named Mononotto, becomes in effect the "Last of the Pequods" by determining to take vengeance upon all Puritans, even at the cost of his life. Unlike Magua, Sanutee, or Pontiac, however, Mononotto is never allowed to become a grandly Satanic model of an outmoded heroic code. To Sedgwick, Mononotto's unyielding defiance is both cruel and insanely self-destructive to his own people; in effect, it is nothing more than a repulsive New World variant of Hammurabi's code. Heroism resides, not in the aging red patriarch who dies for tribal honor, but in his spirited daughter, who resolves "that if her father should appear, she might avert his vengeance."[79] And avert it she does. Magawisca places her own body in front of a Pequod who, at Mononotto's command, is about to tomahawk the white woman who has raised her. Later on, when Mononotto resolves to take vengeance through a ceremonial sacrifice of Magawisca's white beloved, Magawisca again places herself beneath a Pequod tomahawk. This time, however the weapon is her father's, and it falls heavily, cutting off his daughter's arm. In both these instances, the higher heroism is the Indian woman's act of offering her self in order to protect the lives of whites who know of a higher morality than retaliatory killing. Sedgwick stages both incidents as melodramatic tableaux in order to identify Magawisca as a new model of "the heroic girl" (63, 93). While remaining an Indian in appearance and daily customs, Magawisca courageously rebels against both white and red fathers in order to follow the new religion of love and mercy. When Mononotto sings the death song of his tribe (a moment of hushed awe in male texts about Indian demise), Magawisca tells him that he could better benefit his people by attending to the ever-renewing song of Nature (84).

When male novelists momentarily considered the possibility that red heroism might have been female, the model they offered was very different. Simms's Matiwan is a mother whose devotion to tribal honor is so great that it enables her to kill her son with her own hands rather than to submit to his loss of tribal identity. Conceiving of the romance as the substitute for the epic, Simms and other male writers had to envisage heroism, male or female, in a context provided by Satan, Turnus, Hector, and Achilles. But when Sedgwick seeks to place Magawisca by literary analogy, she compares her heroic maiden, not to Camilla or Penelope or Andromache, but to "lofty Judith," "gracious Esther" and, especially, to "tender Ruth" (33–4). The alternative red heroism Sedgwick sought through creating Magawisca clearly demanded more than the separation of historical romance from epic; it demanded the abandonment of epic altogether.

6

THE DESTROYING
ANGEL

Since the publication of David Levin's *History As Romantic Art* (1959), the quality and importance of Prescott's *History of the Conquest of Mexico* (1843) have remained almost wholly disregarded. During the last three decades, when American literary studies have been largely concerned with separable national traditions, the very idea of a "Boston Brahmin" devoting his life's work to sixteenth-century Spanish history without visiting either Spain, Mexico, or Peru, has made Prescott's work seem quaint, stuffily traditional, somehow antinational, and finally unimportant. Such assumptions should be challenged. Against the strident nationalism of the post-Jacksonian era, Prescott sought an American heroic literature within the context of the entire New World; from Boston and Pepperell, he promoted an international republic of letters while transforming old themes into new genres. His distant, derisive perspective upon the Republic ("We 'go ahead' like a great lusty brat that will work his way into the full size of a man"[1]) only broadened his consideration of the possible betrayal of republicanism within the entire western hemisphere.

An indefatigable scholar, Prescott believed that the best preparation for writing history was the study of literature, but he did not consider the Spanish Conquest to be merely a matter of antiquarian interest requiring literary color. Of worldwide historical importance, Cortes's conquest was also a prefiguring of contemporary issues. As a Conscience Whig, Prescott believed the annexation of Texas to be a rationalization for extending the territories of slavery. At the same time, his respect for technological advances and for strong leadership persuaded him that nativist sentimentalizing of the common man could be no source of true progress. Such a conflict of attitudes enabled him to describe the confrontation of Spaniard and Aztec in terms applicable to the Spanish New World of 1519, 1836, 1845, and even thereafter. Demanding a consistent moral logic of the historian, Prescott wrote with extreme care, trying to make Cortes's achievements square both with faith in the future of the

158

West and with the words of the historical record. A remarkable synthesis
of historical facts and literary forms, Prescott's *History* is also a compelling narrative of one historian's shifting judgment upon the westward
course of empire, from its origins to its implied present.

In 1839, after completing a detailed outline for a book on the conquest
of Mexico, Prescott perceived that his genre would not be history alone:

> Omit no trait which can display the character of Cortes, the *hero* of
> *the piece,* round whom the interest is to concentrate. The narrative is a
> beautiful epic. It has all the interest which daring, chivalrous enterprise,
> stupendous achievements, worthy of an age of knight-errantry, a mag-
> ical country, the splendors of a rich barbaric court, and extraordinary
> personal qualities in a hero – can give.[2]

Intrigued by the challenge of combining literary forms, Prescott ex-
claimed that he could fashion a historical epic, as well as an epic history,
by investing the conquest with the spirit of chivalric romance and a Greek
sense of fatality:

> In short, the true way of conceiving the subject is, not as a philo-
> sophical theme, but as an *epic in prose,* a romance of chivalry . . . which,
> while it combines all the picturesque features of the romantic school, is
> borne onward on a tide of destiny, like that which broods over the
> fictions of the Grecian poets.[3]

In his published text, Prescott was always to refer to the genre of his
work as a "history." Two years after its publication, however, he expressed his delight with Michel Chevalier's review, which claimed that
"Compared with Prescott's subject, the theme of *The Iliad* seems slight
and empty."[4] After Prescott had absorbed his sources, he became convinced that the Mexican past contained an epic that was more than legend. Accordingly, his *History* must have the grandeur of heroic poetry
without the taint of fiction.

Because of his omnivorous reading in Greek, Roman, Italian, French,
and Spanish literatures, Prescott was prompted, like Joel Barlow before
him, to broaden the concept of an American epic from a national to a
hemispheric context, thereby submerging parochial pride within a New
World perspective. Prescott knew, however, that modern epics like *The
Columbiad* had degraded martial codes of honor at peril of their interest
and credibility. The publication of his *History* in 1843 proved especially
timely for personal, literary, and political reasons. It was written at the
end of fifteen years devoted to the study of epic poems, epic romances,
and Spanish culture; it provided a timely climax to the growing literary
interest, American as well as Spanish, in Cortes's conquest; and it was
published just prior to the onset of the Mexican–American War.[5]

The heart of the subject's appeal rests in the intrinsic fascination of the
conquest itself – the slow, relentless subjugation of millions of warlike,

noticeably "advanced" peoples by a few hundred Spanish soldiers who, at the outset, knew neither where to go, nor whom they might meet. The particulars of the historical situation also seemed to fit conventions of romance, epic, and even the gothic novel: a crusade to convert the infidel, exoticism of landscape, the fidelity of Cortes's Aztec mistress, all the unexpected splendors of Tenochtitlán, the absorbing horror of human sacrifice, and a series of mass battles culminating in a three-month siege. Cortes himself – relentless in pursuit of glory, gold, and God, familiar with his men but proud before his king – seemed the epitome of the complex Spanish character or, in Prescott's words, "not merely the soul, but the body of the enterprise."[6] At various times, the Conquistador had worn the contradictory faces of white settlers; he had been an ingenious brave Christian as well as a cruel and treacherous plunderer. The historical Cortes thus embodied the forces that Spain was thought to bring into the New World. Even twentieth-century historians of New Spain are prone to such summaries as: "The Spaniard appears as a man of epic qualities who descends to the depths of inhumanity. Valiant, cruel, indefatigable, ferocious, courageous and villainous – Spanish character alternates among extremes."[7]

For antebellum Americans, the achievements of Cortes held an added contemporary interest. The conquest, dispossession, and subjugation of the Aztecs was a prior enactment, a kind of historical type, for the conquest, dispossession, and subjugation of the American Indian. When American writers contemplated Cortes's westward march upon Tenochtitlán, when they imagined masses of Aztecs futilely showering arrows upon Spaniards armed with guns, they inevitably saw a more dramatic, intensely concentrated symbol of the conflict between progressive white civilization and Indian barbarism. The fact that Spanish sources often used the term "Indian" to describe any New World native only confirmed an association that would lead Prescott, in his opening book, to compare Mexican tribes to American Indians no less than eight separate times.[8] Although Anglo-American writers saw the conflict as the New World's type for the conquest of savagery by civilization, they were never to be sure whether the total subjugation, indeed enslavement, of the Aztecs should not now serve them as a providential warning rather than a happy prophecy.

During the 1830s and 1840s, the conquest of Mexico became excruciatingly pertinent as the Alamo fell and Texas was settled and annexed, leading Americans into a divisive and controversial war. Having observed Mexico's difficulty in sustaining a republican government, as well as the antic dictatorial posturing of Santa Anna, American writers usually condescended to contemporary Mexico as a poor, decadent, and weak nation. In 1844, Prescott contemptuously referred to "beggarly Mex-

ico."[9] Robert Montgomery Bird opened *Calavar* by describing Mexico as "a distempered republic," so dominated by "the contemptible ambition of its rulers, and the servile supineness of its people" that Mexico City, once the site of Edenic Tenochtitlán, has now become "a sort of Pandemonium."[10] The political and economic fall of modern Mexico could be traced back either to the vicious inhumanity of Cortes or to the volatile laziness of all Southern peoples. Americans of the former persuasion might, like Prescott, be drawn to oppose both the annexation of Texas and the Mexican War. When General Winfield Scott began his march upon Mexico City, however, many believers in ahistorical racial stereotypes were ready to join the expansionist movement of "All Mexico." If "All Mexico" had prevailed as United States foreign policy, it would have reenacted Cortes's annexation of Mexico, justifying the expansion of the American nation under the non–Berkeleyan aegis of military force.[11]

Because so much was at stake in judging the original conquest, it became important to ascertain exactly where along the axis of barbarism and civilization the Aztecs had truly belonged. Like the American Indians or the Greeks, the Aztecs were thought to be a people of the heroic age, living by martial codes of honor and revenge, polytheistic, preliterate, and intensely tribal, who sang of ancestral glories, and who practiced elaborate rituals of worship and hospitality. Montezuma had preceded America's eastern tribes in warily permitting the godlike Europeans to enter Indian lands. His successor Guatemozin, much like Sanutee and Pontiac, had tried to rally all tribes in a heroic, doomed effort to expel the invaders.

To treat Aztecs and North American Indians as if they were interchangeable was to overlook glaring differences. Whereas North American Indian nations were seen as dispersed, nomadic hunting tribes without inherited rulers, the Aztec empire was made up of settled nations whose economy was urban and agricultural, sustained by a network of obligations to an emperor whose title was hereditary. No North American Indian people had built an immense stone city on a lake, nor had they ever constructed aviaries, aqueducts, astronomical calendars, pyramidical temples, or military hospitals. No visitor to North American Indian villages could ever have written, as Cortes and Bernal Díaz did of Tenochtitlán, that the Spaniards were seeing "the most beautiful thing in the world," "like the enchantments they tell of in the legend of Amadis."[12]

Knowing these facts, American writers were nonetheless reluctant to assert the logical conclusion that the Aztecs had been an "advanced" people whose values belonged to the heroic age but whose institutions and artifacts equaled those of Renaissance nation-states. The Aztecs' practices of human sacrifice and cannibalism seemed to relegate them to a stage of

barbarism far more condemnable than that of any North American Indian. In toto, the Aztecs could only be regarded with fascinated perplexity. Although they were thought to represent a state of savagery that must and should have died away in face of white civilization, the Aztecs had also made gold ornaments, quetzal featherwork, and mathematical calculations of an intricacy beyond Spanish imagining. Disgust for Spanish ruthlessness might tempt a writer to assume that the Aztecs had been nature's noblemen exterminated by avaricious civilizers, but this response proved equally inappropriate. Aztec culture not only had lacked primitivist simplicity: The hearts of thousands of battle captives, including at least sixty-two Spaniards, had been cut from their living bodies by Aztec priests who had soaked their uncut hair in the sacrificial blood before a rejoicing populace.

Although Aztec identity was seemingly more complex than Indian, the subjugation of both peoples raised the same issues. When Sands, Bird, and Prescott discuss the Spanish "right of possession" and "right of conquest," the problems of Indian removal and Mexican annexation hover, sometimes explicitly, in the background.[13] Whether doomed resistance might be the highest heroism was a problem that affected the characterization of Guatemozin no less than Sanutee. Whenever American authors try to determine whether Cortes was driven by gold, glory, national mission, or the duty of conversion, they are trying to resolve a question of divided motives that probably absorbs them far more than it did the Conquistador himself. The claim that any means of subduing Aztecs is legitimate led writers back to the conundrum of heroic Indian romances: How can a Christian civilization justify conquering a barbaric people through unchristian means?

Throughout the nineteenth century, Americans who wrote about New World conquests assumed that the Spanish Catholic record had been far more reprehensible than the English Protestant record. Whereas Puritans were seen as exiles of conscience who had bought title to Indian lands, Spaniards were presumed to have come to take rather than to settle. Both nations had proclaimed a mission to convert the heathen, but the Spaniard had allegedly been concerned to extend the power of the Catholic church, not to move the individual soul to grace.[14] Drawn to the Spanish subject as a crucial precursor, American writers were thus prone to distance themselves from the very analogy their words suggest. Whenever the westward course of empire threatens to reveal a skein of white brutality, distinctions between Spanish Catholics and Anglo-American Protestants are likely to be recalled. To be sure, heightening the exoticism of the Spaniard provided the color of romance for epic narrative. Its more important function, however, was to maintain a comforting

ethnic distinction among whites, while still confronting the problematic demise of the New World's heroic-age peoples.

I. SHIFTING ALLEGIANCE

As Prescott attests, the first Spanish writer critical of Cortes had been a priest of New World loyalties, Bartolomé de Las Casas.[15] Early Spanish historians such as Gomora, Díaz, and Solis, whose accounts had long retained a wide readership, portrayed Cortes as a combination of brave warrior, Christian knight, and loyal subject. Antonio de Solis's long credited *History of the Conquest of Mexico,* for example, presents Cortes as "the principal Hero of this History," an explicitly Herculean figure, "amiable, pleasant and discreet in conversation," whose "Judgment, Intrepidity and Constancy . . . are equally to be admired with the indefatigable Perseverance and Valour of the Spaniards."[16] By the late eighteenth century, however, reservations about the Conquistadors common among writers in New Spain had markedly tarnished Cortes's stature. At the outset of the American Revolution, colonials who regarded themselves as natives invaded by British oppressors could even detect a Satanic Cortes hiding behind the uniform of British generals. After denouncing Cortes as a "dying serpent . . . whose faith is murder, whose religion blood," Freneau proclaimed "that Gage and Cortez' errand is the same."[17] At a time when dying chieftains were everywhere acquiring emotional resonance, Guatemozin began to emerge as the Conquest's alternative hero. The beleaguered, landbound peoples of the rebellious American colonies, less worried about dispossessing Indians than about repelling a European army, were especially likely to credit rising suspicion of Cortes. To them, Guatemozin and Cortes became a Januslike composite of heroic man, one face bearing the progress of Christian civilization, the other the valor of the heroic ages.

Information known to American writers about these two symbiotic heroes needs, at this point, a nonjudgmental summary. Hernando Cortes equipped his many-purposed expedition largely at his own expense. His decision to conquer Tenochtitlán may have exceeded Governor Velasquez's instructions, but it was undertaken with the full support of his men, who had reconstituted themselves as a body politic directly responsible to the Spanish King. No one who reads Cortes's *Letters of Relation,* or the accounts of his smashing Aztec idols, can doubt the sincerity of his revulsion at human sacrifice and idolatry. Cortes's men had reason to complain, not that he robbed them of their share of gold, but that there was less gold than he had led them to expect.

Cortes's tactical skills in deploying his few Spanish soldiers, horses, and cannon against vast Mexican armies have never been questioned. His

diplomatic strategies for rekindling his troops' failing courage, for conquering Mexican tribes by dividing them, and for countering Spanish governmental hostility were brilliant and repeatedly successful.[18] Often wounded, Cortes nearly lost his life three times while trying to save his footsoldiers. During the humiliating retreat from Tenochtitlán on the *Noche Triste,* when half his army lay dead and all his guns were abandoned, suffering two head wounds and the loss of two fingers, Cortes resolved to reconquer Tenochtitlán because "Fortune is always on the side of the daring, and . . . we were Christians, confiding in the very great mercy of God, who would never permit us to perish."[19] Throughout the siege he periodically refrained from military actions in order to allow Guatemozin to surrender. His sorrow at Montezuma's death and his regret for the razing of Tenochtitlán are confirmed in many accounts.[20]

Even if Cortes's aheroic hunger for gold is set aside, his courage and determination led to deeds cruel and treacherous by any standard. Suspected spies were usually hung, sometimes mutilated and returned. Aztec women, offered under threat as gifts of good will, were nominally coverted to Christianity in order to be sufficiently pure to serve as concubines. War captives, slaves given as tribute, and some Aztec women were branded on the face with a G (*Guerra*) to mark them as spoils of war. Cortes agreed to a meeting with Cholulan cassiques suspected of treachery, then gave orders that they and all who accompanied them should be shot. At least 3,000 Cholulans, many of them townspeople, were massacred. After repeatedly promising that no harm would befall him, Cortes forced Montezuma to agree to imprisonment, then chained his ankles. Shortly after the Aztecs rose in war, Cortes persuaded Montezuma to try to quiet his people by assuring them that the Spaniards would all leave Mexico. When Montezuma tried to appease his incredulous countrymen, they killed him.

Guatemozin, who had reason for distrusting Cortes, defied the Spaniards until his city and people were annihilated. Cortes rewarded Guatemozin's valor by treating him even less honorably than Montezuma. After Guatemozin surrendered, Cortes told him "Fear not, you shall be treated with all honor. You have defended your capital like a brave warrior."[21] A few days later, Cortes ordered Guatemozin tortured in hopes of extorting hidden gold. After three years of captivity as a prisoner of war, Guatemozin was forced to accompany Cortes's expedition to Honduras; in Aculan, far from Mexico City and Aztec survivors, Cortes ordered Guatemozin to be hung for conspiracy to revolt. No evidence exists to substantiate the charge; Bernal Díaz testified to the response of Cortes's own men: "the execution was most unjust, and was thought wrong by all of us."[22]

Because Gautemozin rose to power during the last stage of the conquest, yet refused to treat with Spaniards, evidence of his character remained as conveniently sketchy as evidence about Pontiac. A devout worshipper of Huitzilopochtlí, the Aztec war god, Guatemozin pleaded unsuccessfully with all Mexican peoples to bury their differences in a common war against Spaniards. His strategies for defending the waterways, streets, and buildings of Tenochtitlán earned the admiration of both Díaz and Cortes. Despite famine, thirst, smallpox, repeated defeat, and the daily destruction of more of his city, neither he nor his people deserted or discussed terms. At the moment of his capture, he asked Cortes to kill him. While under torture, he rebuked the complaint of a fellow victim by exclaiming "And do you think I, then, am taking my pleasure in my bath?"[23] Guatemozin's last words were for Cortes: "I knew what it was to trust to your false promises, Malinche; I knew that you had destined me to this fate, since I did not fall by my own hand when you entered my city of Tenochtitlán. Why do you slay me so unjustly? God will demand it of you."[24]

Although English and American writers grew absorbed in the enigmatic figure of Montezuma, his passivity could not be accommodated to nineteenth-century notions of heroism. Pages are spent trying to resolve the paradoxes of Montezuma's refined manners, aristocratic tastes, priestly barbarities, and cordiality to his Spanish captors.[25] His intelligent wavering seemed to have preluded bravery; his tentative welcoming of the Spaniards as avatars of Quetzalcoatl was regarded as barbaric superstition. Montezuma's famous appeal to Cortes's humanity ("Look at me, and see that I am flesh and bones, the same as you"[26]) seemed a confession of vulnerability, not a plea to preserve the fragility of life. Montezuma's submission to imprisonment and chaining only served to confirm his degradation. Trying to fix Montezuma's character, Prescott finally charges him with "pusillanimity"; "Montezuma might be said . . . to change his sex and become a woman"; much worse, "he had survived his honor."[27] For nineteenth-century writers about the conquest, active resolve remained a precondition of heroic stature. Just as Montezuma's appeasement serves as a foil to Guatemozin's resistance, so Montezuma's sensitive vacillation is a foil to Cortes's implacable will. Not until William Carlos Williams wrote "The Destruction of Tenochtitlán" would Montezuma's refined generosity, and his hope for a prophet's return, be considered as ironic signs of his superiority to Cortes.[28]

Contrary to expectation, the first Anglo-American pre-Revolutionary rendering of the conquest begins by forthrightly attacking Spanish aggression. Zeuma, the Chilean chieftain of James Ralph's blank verse epic, is persuaded to resist "Iberia's cruel sons" after his guardian angel descends from heaven, describes Tenochtitlán's smoking waste, and warns

Zeuma that "fierce Almagro" is but "dread Cortes" under a different name.[29] The proper course for any native American chieftain, the angel insists, is to learn from Montezuma's "abject cowardice and fear" (58) that Spanish technology and Spanish deceit leave heroic death as the only honorable option:

> If war became their choice, superior Force
> Prevail'd; if peace, destructive Fraud entic'd
> Them into Ruin, and ignoble chains
> Oppress'd the mourning Tribes. – Thus timely warn'd,
> O Zeuma! Shun the gilded snare, and trust
> The Sword, and open arms; a soldier ne'er
> Should shrink from Death; and, where the war is just,
> Eternal Honour waits upon his Shade. (64–5)

At the poem's end, Zeuma and his Chilean tribesmen, newly inspired by love of liberty, are brutally slaughtered by Almagro's troops. Benjamin Franklin may have discouraged James Ralph from completing "Zeuma" for reasons other than Franklin's belief that all epic versifying was a waste of time. Ralph's epic was an affront to Franklin's assumption that the civilized man had best displace the irrational barbarian without too much torment of conscience.

Before the publication of Prescott's *History*, American writers obtained their information about the conquest from William Robertson's long, carefully worded account in his *History of America*. Trying to be both impartial and affirmative, Robertson praised Cortes for performing "great things" because of his "indefatigable activity," "calm prudence in concerting his schemes," and "persevering vigour in executing them."[30] As an eighteenth-century Scot, however, Robertson well understood the dignity of a futile resistance to superior power. Guatemozin's endurance shows that he had "the invincible fortitude of an American warrior" (II, 41). On successive pages, Cortes is praised for his "merit and abilities" and Guatemozin for being a "high-spirited prince" (II, 40, 41). Robertson's gathering tale of Spanish expediency and Mexican defeat eventually subverts our expectation of an ennobling subject. Cortes is charged with "barbarous cruelty," "wanton display of power," and "artful policy" (I, 374). His several sins are then cited to deny his nation's achievement: "In almost every district of the Mexican empire, the progress of the Spanish arms is marked with blood, and with deeds so atrocious, as disgrace the enterprising valour that conducted them to success" (II, 49). Cortes's cool acceptance of planned massacres seems finally to have dissuaded Robertson from according epic stature to the conquest as a whole: "No power of words can render the recital of a combat interesting," Robertson remarks, "when there is no equality of danger; and when the narrative closes with an account of thousands slain on the one side, while not

a single person falls on the other, the most labored descriptions . . . command no attention" (I, 357).

For his epic's grand scheme of republican progress from the middle ages to the indeterminate future, Joel Barlow needed a model of Old World villainy from which history could ascend. Although Spanish inquisitors deserved mention, Barlow needed a figure of more direct impact upon the New World. Having read Robertson's *History* closely, Barlow decided to overlook Cortes's valor, Montezuma's weakness, and Aztec sacrifice in order to emphasize broader cultural issues. Tenochtitlán could have remained the center for technological planning in the New World if the butcherous Cortes had not known how to use "blind religion's prostituted name" so effectively.[31] Accordingly, no historical figure, not even Napoleon, roused Barlow to so absolute a denunciation:

> Thine the dread task, O Cortez, here to show
> What unknown crimes can heighten human woe,
> On these fair fields the blood of realms to pour,
> Tread sceptres down and print thy steps in gore,
> With gold and carnage swell thy sateless mind
> And live and die the blackest of mankind. (467–8)

By obliterating nascent republican civilizations in Tenochtitlán and Cuzco, Cortes and Pizarro had retarded New World progress for at least a century.

Robertson's account led Simms to an equally dark but more psychological judgment. Simms's "The Vision of Cortes" (1829) begins by picturing the fearless "lion-heart" conquistador lying wounded on the battlefield but inspiring his discouraged soldiers for the final assault on Tenochtitlán.[32] The Spaniards are collectively described as "base enthusiasts" whose battle standard of the cross (*In Hoc Signo, Vinceremus*) serves only as "a beacon light to death and flame" (8). A summary description of the Aztecs reverses the stereotypes of civilized Spaniard and brutal savage:

> The simple race,
> Who, born not yet to light or grace,
> Ill-fortune render'd to the sway,
> Of savage, less refin'd than they. (32)

Accordingly, the climax of Simms's poem is not the conquest but the black vision that descends upon Cortes shortly after he has, with "demon's fury in his eye," put Guatemozin to the torture (24). Because the Aztec chieftain displays "high magnificence" while denouncing Cortes as a "greedy adventurer," Cortes suddenly doubts the justice of his expedition (25). In Cortes's fevered dream, Guatemozin leads him to a moonlit battlefield and summons up all the corpses, Spanish as well as Aztec, sacrificed for his glory and his gold. Feeling, too late, "the demon

gnawing at the heart," Cortes remains an "impious wretch" whose valor only hides a "warped mind" (31). Like Bird and Prescott, Simms wishes to believe that the relentless killing of Indian/Aztec tribes must have caused momentary guilt, even in Hernando Cortes.

The kind of hero whom distant writers wished Cortes might have been was portrayed in Robert Southey's widely read *Madoc* (1805). Poet laureate of England from 1813 until the year of Prescott's *History* (1843), Southey contended that, although *Madoc* "assumes not the degraded title of Epic," "this would be the greatest poem I should ever produce."[33] His four-hundred-page, blank verse "lay" describes the supposed expedition of a disinherited Welsh prince who sails westward and encounters the Aztecs. According to Southey's invocation, Madoc

> quelled barbarian power, and overthrew
> The bloody altars of idolatry,
> And planted in its fanes triumphantly,
> The cross of Christ.

Only in deeds of religious overthrow is Madoc allowed to resemble Cortes. Indifferent to gold, but filled with missionary zeal, Madoc has come to northern Mexico hoping to settle a community of liberal, tolerant spirits. After cardboard battles, councils, and visions of the afterlife, Madoc succeeds in persuading a minority of Aztecs to follow Christian principles. Seeking "some resting place for peace" (27), Madoc then has warfare thrust upon him by the perfidy of Aztec leaders. At the poem's end, Southey sends the majority of unconverted Mexican tribes on a southern journey toward their encounter with the famous Spaniard:

> So in the land
> Madoc was left sole Lord; and far away
> Yuhidthiton led forth the Aztecas,
> To spread in other lands Mexitli's name,
> And rear a mightier empire, and set up
> Again their foul idolatry; till Heaven
> Making blind Zeal and bloody Avarice
> Its ministers of vengeance, sent among them
> The heroic Spaniard's unrelenting sword.[34]

Southey had clearly trapped himself into elaborating a dim legend that had no historical reach beyond prodding the reader to respect peaceful settlers more than Cortes, while still allowing the Conquistador to remain "the heroic Spaniard." Prescott, who surely saw the absurdity of versifying so empty a myth, nonetheless needed to acknowledge the poet laureate's non-epic epic. In the footnotes to his *History*, Prescott quotes *Madoc* five separate times, without ever remarking upon its merits.[35]

Robert Montgomery Bird's two historical romances, *Calavar* (1834) and its sequel *The Infidel* (1835), comprise a 1,000-page acount of the

conquest from the time Cortes first occupied Tenochtitlán, through the
Noche Triste and the regathering of Spanish forces, to Tenochtitlán's siege
and fall. Bird's judgments upon historical events are decidedly critical of
Spanish conduct and skeptical of the right of conquest. The first sentence
of *Calavar* refers to the conquest as "the havoc which, in the name of
God, a Christian people were working upon the loveliest of his regions."[36] The *Noche Triste,* Bird insists, should be viewed as "the dread-
ful punishment of men who acknowledged no rights but those of power,
and preferred to rob a weak and childish race with insult and murder,
rather than to subdue them, as could have been done, by the arts of
peace."[37]

Whenever Bird makes summary judgments, he adopts a self-
consciously disillusioned and heretically advanced position: because all
gods are imagined, any conquest or defense undertaken in the name of
religion can have no heroic resonance. The conquest of Mexico, viewed
impartially, was caused by a two-sided "moral epidemic." Aztecs super-
stitiously believed that Cortes was Quetzalcoatl; Spaniards supersti-
tiously believed God was on the side of guns and horses. "A moral epidemic nerved the arm of the invaders; another paralyzed the strength of
the invaded. Superstition covered the Spaniard with armor stronger than
his iron mail, and left the Mexican naked and defenseless."[38]

Bird would thus have us believe that the conquest was more akin to
mass pathology than to epic honor. Summing up all the miseries of the
siege, he observes, "To one whose perverted imagination can dwell with
pleasure on 'the pomp and circumstance of glorious war,' no better study
can be recommended than the history of the siege of Mexico."[39] Reluctant to believe his darkening conclusions about both sides, Bird protests
"Can we think that, among the worshippers of the ferocious Mexitli,
and the fierce invaders of his people, there were *none* with natures worthy of a better belief and a nobler cause."[40] By novel's end, the question
proves to have been rhetorical. As famished, diseased Aztec refugees trudge
out of their capital, Bird jeeringly pictures the Spaniards' accomplish-
ment: "A moving mass of widows and orphans, the trophies of a gallant
achievement! The final fruits of the ambition of a single individual!"[41]

Try though he may, Bird cannot make his moral logic square with his
cultural preferences. Although the Spaniards have no right of conquest,
it is good that idolatry and human sacrifice have been erased from the
New World. The conquest serves historical progress, even though all its
deeds seem brutish. Instead of resolving these paradoxes, Bird's characterization of Cortes collapses beneath them. Bird's Cortes is a gallant
among ladies, a soldier among soldiers, a nobleman in court pageantries,
"necessarily crafty" as a tactician, and one of the butchers of history.[42]
Whenever Cortes calls the Mexicans "dogs," "slaves," and "paynim

scum," it is never clear whether the reader is meant to be repulsed by Cortes's bigotry or impressed by the "fiery and fanatical enthusiasm which was the true secret of his greatness."[43] While Bird condemns Cortes for atrocities, he pictures him "mowing right and left with his trusty blade, while his gallant charger pawed down opposition with his hoofs."[44] It is no wonder that Bird's last word on Cortes begs the question of Cortes's stature: "Heaven alone can judge the merit of his acts, for men are yet unwilling to sit in judgment upon the brave."[45]

Guatemozin is rendered from a similarly inconsistent perspective. Bird grants him "a capacity of mind worthy of his unconquerable courage."[46] "Of good and manly stature," Guatemozin accuses Cortes in terse natural metaphors that recall Magua's denunciations of the white race:

> "When Malintzin [Cortes] smiles, the brand hisses on the flesh of the prisoner; when he talks of peace, the great war-horse paws the breast of the dead. . . . His religion is murder, his law robbery; he is strong, yet unjust; he is wise, yet he makes men mad."[47]

At last, however, Guatemozin's intelligence and dignity must be sacrificed to Bird's need to make him fit the title role. When asking Cortes for death, Guatemozin is reduced to "the poor infidel, beseeching, with as much sincerity as simplicity, a death of honour after a life of patriotism."[48] Lest the reader miss the point, the final words of the novel refer to Guatemozin as "a barbarian and *Infidel*."[49] To Bird, Guatemozin's courage derives, not from the beliefs of his barbarous culture, but from some unnamed source beyond it.

The Anglo-American literature of the conquest, from Ralph, Robertson, and Southey, through Simms and Bird, shows how difficult a task Prescott had assumed in proposing to fashion "an epic in prose, a romance of chivalry," with Hernando Cortes serving as "the hero" and "the soul of it." No matter how courageous in battle or persevering in will Cortes may have been, Prescott's contemporaries were predisposed to distrust him, to emphasize his cruelties and deceit at the expense of his questionable achievements. The rising admiration for Guatemozin was an index of the increasingly tarnished stature of Cortes. Prescott's literary problems were no less formidable. As histories, poems, and romances had shown, the subject's size and complexity had tempted many a writer into formless sprawl, episodic adventures, and endless detail. The danger of turning history into romance, Prescott knew, was churning out a "modern antique."[50] Somehow, Prescott's history had to render the romance of chivalry without pseudomedieval fictions; it had to reduce many sources to a shapely narrative without falsifying them; and it had to make a plausible case for Cortes as the hero of an epic in prose.

The same need had been fleetingly perceived by Robert Sands. In his one hundred page "Historical Notice of Hernan Cortes" (1828), Sands

had attempted, without much confidence, to stem the tide of the attack. Cortes's pursuit of gold, Sands points out, "is not inconsistent with the possession of fearless courage . . . or the love of glory."[51] Cortes's sudden insights of strategy show that, like all great men, he had the ability "to design and to execute what seemed to be the result of contingent causes not under his influence" (74).[52] Sands's summary plea in "palliation" of Cortes's brutalities is that "Heroes have all had their foibles and their vices; and so essential does a certain portion of them seem in the composition of their character, that they are gratuitously given to them by all the great epic poets" (99). Setting aside the fact that great epic poets do not parcel out foibles gratuitously, we must still question Sands's assertion. Even at the height of their respective *aristeia,* neither Achilles nor Hector nor Aeneas nor Roland nor Rinaldo ever mutilate spies, torture captives, or massacre women and children. Although the manner in which Ulysses shoots down the suitors resembles Cortes's shooting of the Cholulans, Homer's hero was avenging a proven outrage long inflicted upon his wife and household. Among the dead Cholulans, only a few had even planned to be treacherous to Cortes.

Without denying Guatemozin's bravery, Sands argues that those who have sentimentalized his demise forget that Cortes simply could not permit so able and implacable a foe to live:

> Thus perished the last of the Mexican monarchs. History weeps over his fate. The plea of stern and rigid necessity, cooly considered, will justify Cortes in permitting the sentence passed upon Quauhtemotzin to be carried into execution. (93)

Sands knew, however, that his argument held little appeal for contemporaries. White readers might have been secretly relieved when savages who died for the heroic code had all passed away, but few were prepared to sanction their coldblooded execution. As Sands admitted, "The plea of stern and rigid necessity . . . does not appeal to the heart, at the distance of three centuries; and we should only waste words in attempting to enforce it" (93). Believing that his age would credit no heroic work on the conquest, Sands pursued Cortes no further.

II. "ONE CONCERTED ACTION"

Long before Prescott began writing the *History,* he had been giving thought to the differences between epic and romance. His *Literary Memoranda* and articles in the *North American Review* had discussed issues of the epic genre in the poems of Homer, Virgil, Dante, Ariosto, Tasso, Pulci, Ercilla, and Milton, all of whom he had been rereading along with Spanish historical literature and much else. Unlike Scott, who had conflated epic and romance within the novel, Prescott was frequently at pains to distinguish them, so as to determine which conventions of each might

be appropriate to heroic history. Prescott's claiming his *History* for the epic was no sudden bythought; it was the consequence of fifteen years of literary and historical preparation.

Because romance originates in the Christian middle ages, its notions of honor are different from those of heroic-age bards. The hero of romance, Prescott argues, generally serves "God and the ladies," whereas the Homeric hero fights "in defence of one's country."[53] Romances lessen the dignity of heroic death because they promise justice in the afterlife. In epic poems, the hero prefers his bloody search for glory because the gods show no justice: "The Elysium of Homer can hardly be said to contain one contented inhabitant."[54] Whereas romances ennoble heroes by endowing them with chivalric courtesy, epics concern issues of honor and skill immanent in coarse realities: "The Princess Nausicaa washing her own linen, Ulysses carpentering his own bedstead, Achilles cooking a steak and spreading the table for dinner, are certainly not in the taste of the lordly feudal times, of the Olivers, Rolands, and Percivals, who would sooner have fasted a month, than have condescended to such plebian operations."[55] The thrust of such statements is to associate epic with history rather than legend or eighteenth-century "Invention." Unlike romances, "the poems of Homer were intended as historical compositions."[56] Whenever Prescott writes of epic poems, he treats them as "useful historical documents" that reveal the manners and values of the heroic peoples.[57] In an essay titled "Novel Writing," Prescott even asserts that "the poems of Homer have done more to acquaint us with the domestic constitution of the Greeks, than all their histories put together."[58]

These differences in theme are linked to a crucial change in literary form. Accepting Aristotelian standards, Prescott insists that epic poems achieve unity of action by centering upon one war for tribal or national survival. Medieval romances and Italian romantic epics, by contrast, seem to exist primarily for the literary finish of their episodes:

> The heroic poem required *one concentrated action,* like the Ancient Drama; & every thing which did not promote this one great action was classed among the episodes & of course was to be allowed but seldom. The Romantic, on the other hand, is made up of a great variety of independent individual *actions* (if I may so say) strung together most accidentally & arbitrarily – in short, Episode, which is incidental in the other class, constitutes the soul of the Romantic Epic.[59]

Needing to decide which form is preferable, Prescott argues that the classical epic has more "dignity" and "concentration," but also "less variety & less interest."[60] In order to invest his *History* with needed formal unity, Prescott wrote notes to remind himself, halfway through his writing, that his book, "which is a narrative [*epos*], and nothing else," must above all continue to arouse "interest, interest, interest."[61]

To Prescott, the failure of any imitative epic poem should have been predictable since the sixteenth century, when "the learned Trissino had fashioned a regular heroic poem, with pedantic precision, upon the models of antiquity, so formal and tedious that nobody could read it."[62] Again and again Prescott attacks writers who "have fashioned themselves on a model, and therefore, instead of originals, have produced copies."[63] The classical epic, he concludes, had to evolve (or perhaps devolve) into the romantic epic if the genre were to survive. But romance epics and Christian epics nonetheless became particularly flawed forms. Not only were the poems of Ariosto, Tasso, Spenser, and Milton comparatively diffuse; the end of polytheism meant that "the God of the Christians has no rival or antagonist. Whichever cause He espouses must triumph."[64] Consequently, the great poem of Mr. Milton, despite all its sublimity of subject and purity of thought, does not succeed "as an epic." "The action of his poem & the *interest* it excites are nothing. . . . The Christian Deities constitute so important a portion that there is no scope for action or intrigue & in this it is most opposite to the Epics of Antiquity."[65]

Fortunately, there had been one Christian, romantic epic based upon a human and historical action that could still speak to modern man. Despite the "petty magic" with which Tasso had resolved extraneous incidents, *Jerusalem Delivered* has "a sustained moral dignity superior to any other poem I am acquainted with."[66] The "moral dignity" of Tasso's epic derives from its grand subject, "the religious object proposed by the Crusades." Prescott was particularly moved, however, by Tasso's description of "the approach of Godfrey's army to Jerusalem – the rapturous exclamation of joy, the burst of triumphant songs & immediately after, the humility, the lowly reverence of the penitent Christian."[67]

A worthy modern epic, in sum, must still be, like the classical epic, a useful historical document concerning national warfare. It must have concentrated unity of action; its hero should act for country, rather than God or his lady. It cannot be an imitative poem, nor should it diminish the stature of its heroes by rendering them subservient to the interventions of God or Christ. For a historian deeply engaged in Spanish history, there was one heroic subject upon which such a prose epic clearly could be fashioned. It would be Tasso's mighty theme transferred from the Old World to the New, the moral dignity and the romance of the Spanish crusader, the approach of Cortes's army to the infidel's capital – Tenochtitlán *Delivered*.[68]

Prescott seems never to have considered a national rather than a New World subject. His lengthy review of Bancroft's *History* afforded many an opportunity to reflect upon potentially epic themes, but Prescott resolutely avoided applying heroic vocabulary to the American past. No exception is taken to any of America's grand self-images (the westward

course of empire, God-favored Protestantism, the glorious republican future), but all of these treasured ideals are associated with cultural progress, not epic conflict. America's Indian wars provide no worthy heroic subject. Although northern tribes had been a people of the heroic age, Prescott has no patience with Cooper's or Simms's notions of a red Satan. America's frontier forests may have been a land of "primeval grandeur and beauty" but their only tenants were "the wild animals, or the Indians nearly as wild, scarcely held together by any tie of social polity."[69] Such phrases are quite consonant with Prescott's later comparisons between Indians and Aztecs. In spite of Mexican religious rites, Prescott consistently saw America's red men as less organized, less skilled, less accomplished, and less warlike models of heroic man. The Aztec, not the Indian, was the antagonist worthy of an epic.

The Aztecs, Prescott believed, had been courageous warriors, but not the wronged noble savages to be found in French, American, and even Spanish literature. As early as 1825, Prescott began to study Ercilla's epic poem *La Araucana* (1558) on the Spanish conquest of Chile. Though Prescott felt Voltaire had been unjustly critical of *La Araucana,* he nonetheless complained that Ercilla's narrative was "very clumsily pieced with episodes," filled out with disgressions so awkwardly introduced that they become "an unpardonable excrescence."[70] But Prescott's chief criticism was that a Spanish poet had portrayed honorable Indian barbarians more sympathetically than civilized Christians:

> The author has so managed his story, so as to excite all the interest of the reader in behalf of the barbarians – & a feeling of aversion towards his own countrymen. This has proceeded from his devoting more care to the portraits of the Indians; – to their position in the war, viz. that of an oppressed people struggling to regain their liberty – and lastly, to the revolting cruelty & bigotry which he with too much fidelity imputes to the Spaniards.[71]

Such a statement leaves no doubt where Prescott's predispositions of cultural merit lie. Although Chilean Indians had fought bravely for freedom, Ercilla had reduced them to sentimental victims because of "too much fidelity" to Spanish cruelties. This kind of distortion, common to epic poems, would not, however, be permissible in an epic history. In his own rendering of the conquest, Prescott would thus assume the formidable task of acknowledging Spanish cruelties while upholding Spanish heroism.

III.   "THIS WONDROUS HISTORY"

Prescott's first sentence begins with the customary preposition ("Of all that extensive empire . . .") with which epic poets and their translators have long introduced their subject.[72] His opening paragraph,

an epic "proposition" in prose form, claims that the historically crucial struggle between Aztec and Spaniard transpired in a sublime landscape "grand and picturesque beyond example." The superiority of the Mexican to the American Indian is promptly affirmed by declaring the Aztecs "far surpassing in intelligence [to] that of the other North American races." Challenging comparison with both *Gerusalemme Liberata* and the *Chanson de Roland,* Prescott claims his subject for epic romance by insisting that the Mexican conquest was as "adventurous and romantic as any legend devised by Norman or Italian bard of chivalry." Cortes himself, we must presume, will provide the chivalric romance needed for an epic conflict between peoples of the heroic and Christian ages. But instead of calling Cortes the "hero," as Prescott's outline had specified, the last sentence of the opening paragraph uses an evasive adjective later repeated in two equally crucial passages: "It is the purpose of the narrative to exhibit the history of this Conquest, and that of the remarkable man by whom it was achieved."[73]

Prescott's choice of the seemingly unassuming term "narrative" is both a claim to continue an old genre (*epos*) and the measure of his work's grand achievement. No heroic story, historical or legendary, has ever been shaped and unfolded with greater narrative effect. Of the seven books, the first is a comprehensive survey of Aztec culture, and the last a compressed account of Cortes's life after the conquest. The five middle books follow Cortes from the Discovery of Mexico, through the March to Tenochtitlán, the Spanish Residence in the capital, and the Spaniards' Expulsion, to the final Siege and Surrender. As David Levin has shown, these five books may be analyzed as a heroic play in which, after the nadir of the hero's fortunes at the outset of Book Four, there is a rapid cumulative rise to historical climax and personal triumph.[74]

Prescott's narrative also contains two overlapping but complementary renderings of the withdrawal–devastation–return paradigm. As Joseph Campbell and Vladimir Propp have shown, countless heroic tales (including *The Iliad* and *Beowulf*) picture the devastation of a kingdom wrought by the withdrawal of a hero, whose return is a necessary precondition for renewal or triumph.[75] From the Spanish perspective, Cortes's departure from Tenochtitlán in order to defeat Narvaez leads to the defeat and expulsion of Spanish forces, after which Cortes's return to lead his men and besiege the city ends in Spanish triumph. From the Aztec perspective, the withdrawal first of Quetzalcoatl, and then of Montezuma, causes the increasing devastation wrought by the Spaniards. Expecting Quetzalcoatl to return from the east as a deity with fair skin and flowing beard, their god reappears only in the relentlessly destructive form of Cortes himself.[76]

Whether Prescott's *History* is analyzed in accord with dramatic or epic

patterns, it is a marvel of narrative organization. Whereas the siege provides a grand climax for the whole, individual chapters lead toward summary paragraphs, and individual books end with major historical events. Daily forays and skirmishes are carefully subordinated to the sequence of Cortes's tactical achievements. To sustain the reader's awe and doubt of the outcome, Prescott emphasizes the ever shifting difficulties Cortes faces.[77] Details that might distract attention from the unyielding pursuit of glory, gold, and conquest are removed to footnotes or appendices. Symmetrical without becoming mechanical, Prescott's arrangement of books and chapters enhances the reader's sense of onward movement. Prescott was in fact being unduly modest when he claimed "I may hope that the *unity of interest,* the only unity held of much importance by modern critics, will be found still to be preserved" (6). To anyone familiar with the literary sprawl of previous writings on the subject, Prescott's command of the whole seems more than impressive. It suggests that his skill at narrative is partly attributable to his near blindness. Not unlike a well known ancient bard, Prescott had to retain the shape of a vast heroic subject in his head for many a year.

The steady forward thrust of the narrative deepens the reader's awareness of Cortes's essential trait: "The great feature in his character was constancy of purpose; a constancy not to be daunted by danger, nor baffled by disappointment, nor wearied out by impediments and delays" (681). Cortes's unswervable purpose, in turn, prefigures the relentless march of progressive civilization over all western lands. But the march of the narrative and Cortes's will to conquest were both intended as elements of something still larger – a cosmic sense of heroic inevitability that Prescott associated with the Greeks in general and with Greek epic in particular. Prescott chose Cortes's conquest for the following reason:

> While it [the subject] combines all the picturesque features of the romantic school, it is borne onward on a tide of destiny, like that which broods over the fictions of the Grecian poets; – for surely there is nothing in the compass of Grecian epic or tragic fable, in which the resistless march of *destiny* is more discernible, than in the sad fortune of the dynasty of Montezuma. – It is, without doubt, the most poetic subject ever offered to the pen of the historian.[78]

Cortes's sheer will, the pace of the narrative, and the reader's sense of civilization's march, combine to deepen the sense of relentless fatality. As a consequence, Prescott restricts his epic machinery to a "Providence" which, on the rare occasions it is invoked, decrees the spread of Christian civilization by fair means or foul.[79] By his genius at arranging narrative, Prescott thus attains the fatalistic effect of epic machinery without ever resorting to it.

Uncertain whether Columbus's discovery or Cortes's conquest would

provide the grander theme, Prescott decided that Cortes offered "a far better subject" because "the event is sufficiently grand" and "the catastrophe is deferred – the interest is kept up – through the whole"[80] Columbus's last three voyages detract from the real but fleeting achievement of his first. Although Prescott claims to be unable to rival Irving's *Life of Columbus* ("though armed with the weapons of Achilles, this could give me no hope of success in competition with Achilles himself"[81]), we may wonder whether Prescott's deference was not somewhat disingenuous. Only Cortes, he felt, had possessed the unyielding will needed for a New World history that would convey Achillean implacability.

Prescott was clearly pleased that the history of the conquest could no longer be separated from his legends. Cortes's *Letters of Relation,* he knew, must be regarded as a much-needed effort in heroic self-justification. Bernal Díaz's *History* was an aged soldier's recollection of incidents that "had probably been rehearsed by the veteran again and again to his family and friends, until every passage of the war was as familiar to his mind as the 'tale of Troy' to the Greek rhapsodist" (504). Prescott often cites Cortes's and Diaz's accounts as historical fact, but he recreates battle scenes to accentuate their legendary qualities. He excels in military panoramas that show how a few disciplined Spaniards could have defeated immense masses of vengeful Aztecs. In prose suggestive of oral formulaic composition, alliterative metaphors build upon one another to portray inexorable force. Describing the battle against the Tlascalans, for example, Prescott uses such phrases as: "sharp Toledo steel," "glittering with gold," "clothed in quilted cotton," "drowned by the din of fight," "hissing shower of arrows," "bearing splinters of broken harness," "slowly and steadily the little band of Spaniards," and "the turning tide of battle" (234–40). Judged by the inappropriate standard of originality, such formulaic diction seems trite and repetitive, as does Homer's. In context, however, Prescott's battle sequences serve him well because their diction supports a rhythmic prose appropriate to crucial passages about the stages of a long campaign.

For climactic confrontations, Prescott uses phrases that suggest legendary parallels without specifying them. When Cortes slowly fights his way to the summit of Tenochtitlán's great *teocalli,* he finds himself, very like Achilles and Hector, "face to face on this aërial battlefield, engaged in mortal combat in presence of the whole city" (425). To Prescott, Cortes's greatest exploits are defensive gallantries which, like Roland's braveries at Roncevaux, save his retreating army. When his exhausted soldiers are surrounded at Otumba, Cortes saves them from annihilation by seizing the standard of the Aztec chieftain. A more pointed parallel occurs during the siege, when Cortes rescues his overzealous, ambushed "cavaliers" by guarding their hurried retreat along a narrow causeway. This retreat costs the life of Cortes's "faithful follower, the heroic Olea,"

a solider who, very like Oliver, "fell mortally wounded by the side of his general" (576). At such moments, historical fact neither can nor should be separated from the legendizing of early Spanish sources and from Prescott's cumulative readings in epic poetry.

Prescott hoped to resolve the paradox of Tenochtitlán's high civilization and the Aztecs' barbarism by first insisting on the paradox and then presenting the Spaniard as a higher alternative. Sculpted gold and cannibalism, aqueducts and illiteracy, aviaries and human sacrifice, were contrasting parts of one culture that had combined the brutalities of the heroic age with quasi-Catholic refinement and priestcraft. Prescott called attention to this paradox ("surely, never were refinement and the extreme of barbarism brought so closely in contact with each other" [48]) because the conquistadors, he thought, had combined Christian faith, progressive technology, and love of adventure with the exalted spirit of chivalric romance. As the conquistador merged with the crusader, he acquired an almost protestant concern with faith rather than form, gold rather than tribe, courageous will rather than unthinking duty. Three widely separated sentences convey the strength of Prescott's commitment to the Spaniard's symbolic role: "The cavalier who embarked in them [Cortes's military expeditions] entered fully into chivalrous and devotional feelings" (148); "The life of the adventurer in the New World was romance put into action" (292); "The Spaniard came over to the New World in the true spirit of a knight-errant, courting adventure however perilous, wooing danger, as it would seem, for its own sake" (531).

As his *History* progressed, Prescott developed a personal affinity for the chivalric role designed for Cortes. One of Prescott's secretaries, Edmund B. Otis, recalled the author's own account of the way he planned out the wording of battle sequences:

> Many of his best battle-scenes, he told me, he had composed while on horseback. His vivid imagination carried him back to the sixteenth century, and he almost felt himself a Castilian knight, charging with Cortes, Sandoval and Alvarado on the Aztec foe.[82]

While reenacting the moment of battle, Prescott clearly identified with his romance hero against the heroic ages. Impartial consideration of the motives and consequences of those victorious moments, however, made empathy more difficult to sustain. Epic and romance could be subsumed within history only as long as Cortes's cruelties and avarice could be kept convincingly subordinate to his achievement as a knight-errant.

To render the facts through the lens of medieval romance posed no small problem. Prescott had rightly perceived that Bird's invention of chivalric knights, pure damsels, and lofty dialogue had been all romance and no history, a "modern antique" that amounted only to a "counter-

feit" (431). Cortes's piety, he knew, had been limited to his disgust for Aztec paganism and his unswerving belief that "we fight under the banner of the Cross; God is stronger than Nature" (244). Prescott wisely refrained from claiming that Cortes ever shared the love of Christian virtue that Godfrey and Rinaldo had professed. Unfortunately, however, Cortes's service to his lady had not been reliable either. The devotion of Cortes's Aztec mistress Marina provided an opening for romance that Prescott perpetually declined because he knew that, after the conquest, Cortes had wedded Marina to one of his officers, and then married a Spanish noblewoman himself.

Cortes's semblance to the hero of epic romance had to be confined to his undeniable daring, valor, and inspirational presence. Prescott handles these qualities with convincing care, distinguishing between Cortes's cunning calculations as a strategist and his quick strengths on the battlefield. An imaginative and shrewd tactician, Prescott's Cortes assumes the mantle of a dauntless crusader when in combat. In Prescott's words, "He combined what is more rare, singular coolness and constancy of purpose, with a spirit of enterprise that might be called romantic" (429).

As a hero of romance epic, Cortes thus makes a plausible but thin showing for a writer who aimed at "daring, chivalrous enterprise, stupendous achievements, worthy of an age of knight–errantry."[83] Cortes's stupendous achievements are decidedly there, but any chivalry and devotion he may have possessed are increasingly sullied as Prescott follows him along his bloody course. At every important encounter, the evidence of Cortes's deceit, cruelty, avarice, and bigotry is first acknowledged, and then placed within a mitigating context. Sometimes his harsh acts are justified as strategic necessities even though their severity is deplored. More often, the applicability of terms such as "brutality" or "greed" is denied on the relativistic grounds that Cortes's acts were no worse, indeed often better, than those of European monarchs, other conquistadors, or the leaders of the Inquisition.

Even if such passages contain truth rather than rationalization, Cortes's stature as a hero of epic romance is irreparably damaged. Because Cortes's honor exists only through assertion, the values of the heroic age acquire, almost against Prescott's will, the dignity Cortes gradually loses. As early as the Spaniards' first crucial victory over the Tlascalans, Prescott accords unqualified praise to the Tlascalan general who, believing Cortes to be a treacherous destroyer, urges that the Spaniards must be fought to the death. Xicotencatl should be regarded, not as a "ferocious and sanguinary barbarian," but as a "high and unconquerable spirit, like some proud column, standing alone in its majesty amidst the fragments and ruins around it." The Tlascalan chieftain had the "clear-sighted sagacity" to pierce through Cortes's "thin veil of insidious friendship."

Prescott's reader is surely asked to respect Xicotencatl for having acted upon the "noble patriotism of one who would rescue [his] country at any cost" (243).[84]

At this early point in the narrative, the lesser heroism of Aztec resistance still complements the higher heroism of Christian conquest. But after the mutilation of suspected spies, the massacre at Cholula, and the chaining of Montezuma, Prescott reflects that Cortes's dealings with the Aztec emperor, consider in toto, must be called "a politic proceeding – to which few men could have been equal, who had a touch of humanity in their natures" (350). Such a statement creates an unwelcome need for an alternative hero. In characterizing Guatemozin, Prescott would have to render him admirable only insofar as his determined resistance expressed the reader's growing shock at the extent of Spanish brutalities. If Guatemozin were to become the hero of the siege, however, Prescott's tenuous justification of the march of civilization might collapse.

When Guatemozin first appears, he is compared both to Hannibal for his "religious hatred" of the conquering enemy, and to Joash in Racine's *Athalie* for his willingness to die in defense of his holy city (490). Lacking the rage of such doomed defenders as Hector and Turnus, Guatemozin is portrayed as a temperate leader: "worthy, by his bold and magnanimous nature, to sway the sceptre of his country, in the most flourishing period of her renown; and now, in her distress, devoting himself in the true spirit of a patriot prince to uphold her falling fortunes, or bravely perish with them" (490). Slighting Guatemozin's policy of expanding sacrificial rites, Prescott admires his haughty refusal to treat with Spaniards. At the onset of the siege, Prescott grants that Guatemozin had "a spirit as dauntless as that of Cortes himself" (513). Near the end, Guatemozin seems to be raised above Cortes. His refusal to keep an appointment with the Spanish general is a sign that no word of Cortes could be trusted. When Guatemozin asks Cortes to kill him, he displays "a spirit worthy of an ancient Roman" (607). After Guatemozin is tortured and executed, Prescott describes him, in a phrase leading back through Simms and Cooper to Scott, as "the last of the Aztecs" (648).

Dwelling upon the last days of the siege led Prescott to replace adventure romance with heroic pathos. Strengthened by Guatemozin's spirit, thousands of diseased and starving Aztecs, without arms or one thought of surrender, defiantly endure the daily leveling of their city and the slaughter of their people. Such scenes bear no resemblance to the romance epic Prescott so admired. The delivery of Tenochtitlán has proven to be nothing like the approach of Godfrey's army to Jerusalem. Whereas Tasso had described "the lowly reverence of the penitent Christian," Prescott is compelled to picture the killing of at least 50,000 helpless Aztecs, and the celebration of victory with a banquet.[85] If there is any

"sustained moral dignity" shown during the "deliverance" of Cortes's western Jerusalem, it belongs to the Aztecs, not the Spaniards.[86]

In Book One, Prescott had struggled to keep the Aztecs from seeming too civilized; in Books Four and Five, he had struggled to keep Cortes from seeming too callous; by Book Seven, he is struggling to keep Guatemozin from attaining too much heroic stature. The wording of Prescott's summary characterizations suggests his shifting allegiance. The *History* concludes with six pages of reflections upon Cortes's traits and motives. In these pages, Cortes is praised for his leadership, boldness, military brilliance, unshakeable will, and even his knight-errantry, but the word "hero" is never once applied to him. After the siege, however, Prescott refers to "the dauntless heroism of Guatemozin" (612). Under torture, Guatemozin emerges as "the hero, who had braved death in its most awful forms" (622). In neither passage does Prescott compromise by adding the phrase "hero of the Aztec people;" Guatemozin seems to have become, albeit unintentionally, "the hero."

In the course of writing the *History,* the heroism of dying endurance has grown to transcend, if not replace, the heroism of Christian conquest. Because Prescott's conscious commitment to the superiority of European civilization continues unchanged, he never directly attacks Cortes's stature. The number of paragraphs concerned with Guatemozin are carefully restricted so that Cortes may remain, at the least, "this remarkable man." Nonetheless, the shift in the model of heroic conduct is plainly there. It forms an unsought testament to Prescott's historical honesty and deep respect for men who knowingly die in defense of tribal honor.

In Prescott's view, Cortes's savage deceit in 1520 would not necessarily deny his stature as a force for progress. As long as the right of conquest could be granted, Cortes's military achievements might entitle him to heroic stature in the full sweep of time. Precisely at this point, however, Prescott's progressive assurance falters. When he wrote "the debasing institutions of the Aztecs furnish the best apology for their conquest" (52), he did not forget that the "best" apology is not necessarily an adequate one. After describing the Massacre at Cholula, Prescott admits that "the difficulty that meets us in the outset is, to find a justification of the right of conquest, at all" (275). Pleading historical relativism, or adopting the standards of Cortes's age, might condone the conquest as a historical necessity, but not as a moral type for his own generation.

Four hundred pages later, Prescott still cannot decide whether the superiority of Christian civilization justifies the conquest of a pagan one (613). To deny the right of conquest would halt progress back in the heroic age; to grant the right of conquest would sanction unacceptably cruel means of subjugation. At the conclusion of Prescott's two lengthy

debates upon the issue, he tries to minimize the problem by an identical shift in the grounds of argument: "But whatever may be thought of this transaction [the Massacre of Cholula] in a moral view, as a stroke of policy, it was unquestionable" (278); "Whatever may be thought of the Conquest in a moral view, regarded as a military achievement, it must fill us with astonishment" (614). Such handy shifts ultimately detract from Prescott's epic purpose. Military achievements and political tactics acquire heroic stature, not through historical effect alone, but because of the magnanimity, the greatness of spirit, with which they are undertaken.

Contemporary critical response to Prescott's *History* reveals a longstanding impasse between literary needs and cultural attitudes. Prescott's historical research and literary skills were rightly celebrated, his pictorial tableaux admired, and the interest of his narrative acclaimed. His attempt to justify the conquest by portraying Cortes as a hero of romance aroused responses varying from respectful skepticism to ad hominem denunciation. In part, the attack on Prescott's Cortes was a timely warning against the prospect of another Mexican conquest; some reviewers saw Cortes's admirable traits as Prescott's way of justifying the expansionism to which he was, in fact, opposed. But an even deeper source of indignation may lie in the cumulative literary tradition that had increasingly admired the last of the Aztecs at the expense of the compromised Conquistador.

Prescott's academic associates responded in exact accord with their classical heritage and Prescott's literary purpose. George Ticknor praised Prescott's patience in acquiring "deep foundations for the epic superstructure he contemplated."[87] Edward Everett wrote from London to say that *The Conquest of Mexico* was preferable to *Ferdinand and Isabella* because "the interest is of a more epic kind."[88] Cornelius Conway Felton, whose lifetime preoccupation with *The Iliad* made him skeptical of calling any modern work an epic, found the proper generic term for Prescott's achievement:

> The narrative that follows hurries me forward with more than the interest of romance; while the splendid coloring gives magnificent effect to the descriptions of natural scenery – the appropriate accompaniment of such an heroic history.[89]

None of these academic friends, who were complimenting Prescott personally, chose to divulge his opinion of Prescott's cultural attitudes.

Among the important published reviews, the most affirmative was written by William Gilmore Simms, who described *The Conquest of Mexico* as "this most wondrous history."[90] Reading Prescott's work with the perspective of a Southern Democrat, Simms became far more tolerant of Cortes than he had been fifteen years earlier. He described Cortes as "the greatest of these modern men," a hero through whose brutal excesses

and implacable strength civilized progress was advanced (186–7). Simms, himself of modest origins, came to see Cortes as a self-made man of the people who represented a force of Nature (192). Nonetheless, Simms was anxious to grant Cortes "only that sort of admiration which we yield to military greatness" (186). Cortes's iron bravery was "not at all comparable with that which arises from moral endeavor" (186). Accepting Prescott's notion that Cortes embodied historical destiny, Simms revealed his wary awe by according Cortes "all the inflexibility of the destroying angel" (249).

George Hillard, friend of both Prescott and Hawthorne, rejoiced in the *History* as a masterwork of "our young and glowing literature," a book that is "among the best possessions of a nation, the most enduring monuments of her glory."[91] Hillard could not, however, accept Prescott's promise that his subject was one of heroic grandeur. The very importance of Prescott's book demanded a strong rejoinder:

> There is nothing here that kindles the cheek and suffuses the eye with a proud sense of the divine elements which were mingled with the dust from which man was formed. It is a tale of blood and horror. It is the melancholy record of an exterminating war, waged against an unoffending people, with robber-like rapacity and ruffian cruelty, in which the superior advantages of civilization, science and discipline are found linked with the lowest and basest of passions, and all our sympathies are enlisted in behalf of the heathen and the savage. (159)

Unlike Prescott, Hillard had no admiration for the heroic code. He felt pity for the Aztecs' victimization rather than awe at their resolve. He associated man's "divine element" with "moral grandeur" and "the noblest endowments of mind," not with death-defying bravery (159). Reluctant to criticize Prescott directly, Hillard finally qualified his outrage by accepting Prescott's argument that "We have no right to apply to one age the moral standard of another" (202).

Despite party differences, Prescott might have expected a favorable attitude toward his Cortes from O'Sullivan's *Democratic Review*, a journal then supporting annexation of western lands and about to extend "Manifest Destiny" toward Mexico itself. Instead, the anonymous reviewer called Cortes "a jackal," "a vulture," "a man of whom no good or generous action is anywhere recorded."[92] The disarray of contemporary Mexico was ascribed to the "print of slavery" that Cortes had inflicted upon the land (194). Prescott's apparent willingness to adopt the values of the Conquistador's era was condemned as abandonment of a historian's duty: "History should judge and sentence ages; not copy judgements from them" (195). What most upset the reviewer was that epic literature always had a formative effect on people's thinking and conduct. Apprehensive of another advance upon Mexico, the reviewer

recalled Homer's direct personal influence upon Alexander and Charles the Twelfth, then concluded "Thus men were slaughtered in the eighteenth century for causes directly traceable to the Siege of Troy: and each black drop in the pan of Genius has become a red river flowing on through all that distance" (190).

Such criticisms are temperate by comparison with Theodore Parker's absolutist denunciations. No narrow nationalist, Parker granted Prescott his "great and mighty theme," a subject "more important than the lives of Columbus and his followers."[93] For the first time in a popular history, Parker claimed, convincing epic warfare had involved the clash of two races – red and white. Moreover, Cortes's military achievements surpassed those of any conqueror from the siege of Troy through the crusades (222). But Prescott's attempt to justify the conquest on ethical grounds immired him in degrading falsities no contemporary should believe. Cortes's Spaniards, Parker somehow knew, were "hard, iron men, with rather less than the average intelligence, morality, and piety of their nation" (255). No white man's claim to red men's lands has ever had any substance: "Neither Pope nor Satan could alienate and convey what he did not possess" (246). Cortes was "crafty, insidious and deceitful" (257); "in all but courage and military skill, he appears behind his times" (256).

Unlike other reviewers, Parker condemned the historian as forthrightly as his hero. Throughout the *History,* Prescott showed "little horror" at Cortes's atrocities (259). To believe that the Spaniards cared about converting the infidel was "a poor defence . . . unworthy of an historian like Mr. Prescott" (255). "Mr. Prescott has no sympathy with the Mexicans. . . . In his narrative, he degrades the Mexicans fighting for their homes and the altars of their Gods" (260). By accepting the brutal values of the sixteenth century, Prescott has ironically impeded the true progress of civilization:

> We are sorry to add the name of Mr. Prescott to the long list of writers who have a theory which attempts to justify the crime against mankind, the tyranny of might over right. We are sorry to say of this work in general, and on the whole, that it is not written in the philosophy of this age, and, still worse, not in the Christianity, the wide humanity, which is of mankind. (263)

Above all, Prescott forsook his national duty to embrace the spiritual heroism of every man. "We might naturally look for justice from an American writer, with no national prejudice to blind him," Parker declared, "But no, his sympathy is wholly with the conquerers; the spirit of chivalry is mightier with him than the spirit of humanity" (261).

Most of Parker's onslaught is patently unfair. Prescott had not ignored Spanish cruelties; in fact, reviewers often cited Prescott's own evidence of Spanish atrocities against him. Prescott's sympathies had never been wholly with the conquerors, even at the outset. He had not always adopted

sixteenth-century values, nor sanctioned the right of conquest, nor justified dispossession of tribal lands. Parker's venom, itself a sign of Prescott's success, missed one of the *History*'s greatest merits. Prescott's shifting values, divided judgments, and doubts about the right of conquest
all lend his *History* a poignancy and a power no absolutist position, on
either side, could ever attain. Insofar as Prescott fails, it is because the
seriousness of cultural conflict, precluding any touch of the comic, collapses his historical figures into two-dimensional vehicles for debating
political morality.

Such passionate, distorted attacks on Prescott's *History* suggest that
the troubled hope for an American heroic literature had, in one important way, remained unchanged. The literary finish, masterful structure,
and sheer existence of Prescott's work were cause for celebration, but his
models of heroic behavior remained repellent to many readers. However
valiant the Aztecs' resistance may have been, they were regarded as semi-
civilized pagans who practiced cannibalism and human sacrifice; however
marvelous the Spaniards' military achievement, gold and glory had been
won at the expense of Christian values. Prescott had left his readers no
viable model of contemporary heroism, be it American or universal.
Guatemozin clearly belonged to another historical age; we Americans
now spreading empire's westward course surely could not be thought to
resemble Cortes. Like Joel Barlow, many of Prescott's reviewers wanted
their New World epic without the *mores* of the heroic world, whether
they were Greek, Aztec, Spanish, or Indian. And so, when Prescott gave
them an epic history, they gloried in his literary artifact, shuddered at its
contents, and kept silent about its implications.[94]

Although the reviews of Parker and Hillard must have wounded Prescott deeply, he nonetheless knew what he had accomplished. Writing his
Preface to *The History of the Conquest of Peru* (1847), Prescott looked
backward with pride and regret at the "obvious advantages" of writing
a narrative about the Mexican conquest:

> Few subjects can present a parallel with that, for the purposes either of
> the historian or the poet. The natural development of the story, there,
> is precisely what would be prescribed by the severest rules of art. The
> conquest of the country is the great end always kept in view of the
> reader. From the first landing of the Spaniards on the soil, their subse-
> quent adventures, their battles and negotiations, their ruinous retreat,
> their rally and final siege, all tend to this grand result, till the long series
> is closed by the downfall of the capital. In the march of events, all moves
> steadily forward to this consummation. It is a magnificent epic, in which
> the unity of interest is complete.[95]

The proper generic analogy for his recent History, Prescott now knows,
is the epic, not the drama. Having risked subsuming epic poetry within
prose history, Prescott understandably justifies his success by the "sever-

est" (Aristotelian) rules of unity of interest. His pride is in the literary merit of having sustained narrative intensity for seven hundred pages, rather than in the moral integrity of his historical judgments. Even in this moment of self-justification, however, Prescott's regard for accuracy is remarkable. The words "magnificent epic" refer, not to Prescott's book, which remains a heroic history, but to the historical subject from which his masterwork was wrought.[96]

7

TILL A BETTER EPIC COMES ALONG

It is a mistake, I think, in the criticism of Melville's works, to approach *Moby-Dick* as a novel. On the surface it is a novel; it is a prose narrative of a certain length, dealing with possible men and possible events. But below the surface it is different. The men are possible but they are also fabulous. The prose loosens into extraordinary rhythms. The event is possible, but it is also unique – it is nothing less than the pursuit of "the mightiest animated mass that has survived the flood." What Herman Melville proposes to himself is not the theme for a novel but the theme for an epic.

Padraic Colum, *The Measure* (1922)

Colum's claim that *Moby-Dick* is an epic may be more plausible than the longstanding assumption that *Moby-Dick* is the quintessential American Romance, but both generic claims are far more restrictive than the book Melville actually wrote. For Melville has given us, if we look closely, a Yankee Jonathan's sea initiation, an Anatomy of whaling, several oral tales within one written one, two parodic sermons, occasional poems, a dream vision, many meditations, an etymology, genealogies, a dramatic tragedy, a romance, several hideous and intolerable allegories, and a mock-epic, as well as an epic. The power of Melville's book thus depends on the intellectual energy released by its continuous transformations of genre and of idea. As we read *Moby-Dick,* one genre is forever leading us into another or toward a burlesque of itself; the unverifiable cosmic meanings of the most trivial objects are drawn out until, at chapter's end, they reach self-conscious mockery of their own brilliance. Melville clearly believed that a great literary work could serve as the new American epic only if it were to incorporate and supersede all genres, including previous forms of epic. Recent links between new epic and old history needed refashioning. While deepening Knickerbocker's sense of the comic arti-

fice of words, Melville sought an epic that would be more universal than Irving's, more polytonal than Prescott's, and more contemporary in subject than either had dared to be.

Between 1846 and 1851, while Melville was reading *Paradise Lost,* Dante, Camoens, *Fingal, Télémaque,* Pope's Homer, Irving, and Rabelais (among much else), the attack on the imitative American epic had reached its height. Two anonymous essays, both probably known to Melville, explore the increasingly gloomy prospects for a national epic. An 1848 essay in Duyckinck's *Literary World* contends that railroads, canals, and balloons have rid the world of all gods, that Homeric eloquence has declined into the stump speech, epic games into a circus, "The Tamer of Horses" into a jockey, and Vulcan's forge into a munitions factory. America's one proven epic subject, the Indian, now has no future because "all the savage races will perish." As a consequence "the heroic may altogether disappear in the midst of a torturing, cold-blooded skepticism."[1]

The literary issue of the absent American epic had clearly become a vehicle for denouncing national culture. In 1838 editors of the *Knickerbocker* chose to open a lead essay titled "American Poetry" with a needling observation: " 'Where is the American Epic?' is a question daily asked." The essayist's predictable answer ("The present age is incapable of the epic") is testily substantiated by decrying America's commercial culture, pursuit of wealth at honor's expense, resentment of superior men, and lack of hallowed historical associations.[2] These are, of course, the arguments of Fisher Ames updated in reference, a classicist's jeremiad holding forth no hope for New World regeneration. Like Fisher Ames, the *Knickerbocker* essayist cannot and will not mount any Melvillean revolt against American "literary flunkeyism"[3] because America presumably has no heroic subject. Generations must pass before America might evolve "a lord of the epic"; his emergence seems forever unlikely because the country is "destitute of moral associations, lethargized by utilitarianism and chained by education and influence to British models." Compared to such statements, Melville's mockery of the contemporary imitative epic poem seems revealingly benign. When Melville proposed that "Pop" Emmons's *Fredoniad* should be praised "till a better epic comes along,"[4] he was agreeing with contemporary judgment of Emmons's failure, but also reopening the possibility for an American epic of a completely different kind. If Freedom's spirit could be expressed in free literary form, in varied tones, and in convincing heroic action, perhaps the "better epic" might come along considerably sooner than anyone expected.

Melville's comments on heroic literature show how attempts to evoke unrelieved awe for models of human perfection could only arouse the

modern reader's ridicule. From the outset, Melville mistrusted yet admired the hero who gives his life for honor and glory, be it personal or
national. While reading *Fingal,* Melville underlined, and then scored in
the margin, Macpherson's line "The young warrior did not flee; but met
death as he went forward in his strength."[5] But another of Macpherson's
typically callow sentiments ("He remembers the death of his son, who
fell in the days of his youth") led Melville sarcastically to note "the pathos – none can speak it."[6] When reading Emerson's "Heroism," Melville responded to Emerson's idea of greatness with the same ambiva-
lence shown toward Ahab and Pierre. Beside Emerson's assertion,
"Heroism feels and never reasons, and therefore is always right," Melville wrote "Alas! the fool again."[7] But two paragraphs later, when
Emerson proclaimed, very like Ahab, that "Self trust is the essence of
heroism. . . . Its ultimate objects are the last defiance of falsehood and
wrong, and the power to bear all that can be inflicted by evil agents,"
Melville reversed himself and granted that Emersonian heroism seemed
"noble again."[8]

The chapter of *Mardi* titled "Dreams" tells us the specific sources of
Melville's awakening literary ambition and literary power:

> Like a grand, ground swell, Homer's old organ rolls its vast volumes
> under the light, frothy wave-crests of Anacreon and Hafiz; and high
> over my ocean, sweet Shakespeare soars, like all the larks of the spring.
> Throned on my sea-side, like Canute, bearded Ossian smites his hoar
> harp, wreathed with wild-flowers, in which warble my Wallers; blind
> Milton sings bass to my Petrachs and Priors, and laureats crown me
> with bays.[9]

Like so much else in a book that makes a world of the mind, these sentences are so overwritten that they seem to burlesque the author's claims.
Although Melville attests that Homer, Milton, and Ossian are his literary
ancestors, he simultaneously mocks his own bravado. Good American
writing, after all, never imitates, and the divine William must always
soar unapproachably above!

A later mention of Homer leads Babbalanja to jeering praise of Lombardo's *Kostanza,* a hypothetical work of boundless ambition, as full of
trash as *Mardi,* but also prophetic of some future and greater effort. Babbalanja recalls that the little known Lombardo ("Lumberbard?") had first
procured a ream of vellum as an indispensable preliminary "to the writing of the sublimest epics" (594). Understandably vague about the content and form of the *Kostanza,* Babbalanja huffily defends Lombardo's
work against Aristotelian critics by proclaiming that the world, like the
Kostanza, "lacks cohesion; it is wild, unconnected, all episode" (592).
The *Kostanza* must defy all the unities because "there are things infinite
in the finite; and dualities within unities" (597). Lombardo's sane mad-

ness is clearly Melville's way of introducing a vital literary truth: Any controlled linear narrative of the kind Prescott had written cannot permit the probings of the world's axis that can arise through improving a new genre. Melville's defense of Lombardo's aims (not his words) thus suggests why the many chapters of *Moby-Dick* seem to grow from one to another without planned connections, and why single objects must be seen as multiple symbols, at once comic and serious. To hope to achieve a great work, Lombardo must embrace the ridiculous both in his heroic subjects and in himself.

During the writing of those modest and saleable narratives, *Redburn* and *White-Jacket,* epic literature remained on Melville's mind. Inside his father's guidebook, Redburn discovers nine pages of "a neglected poem by a neglected Liverpool poet," who had written a "noble epic" that no one would willingly read.[10] Judging from the twelve lines Melville supposedly quotes, Redburn has uncovered yet another wretched near-contemporary "epic" written in heroic couplets. Instead of exalting a hero's deeds, the poem merely "sings of Liverpool and the Mersey; its docks, and ships, and warehouses, and bales, and anchors" (147). To Melville, who was always to prefer "stout old Chapman's Homer"[11] to Pope's, the verse form is an anachronism: "This epic, from the specimen before me, is composed in the old stately style, and rolls along commanding as a coach and four" (147). The lines Redburn quotes, in which "the poet breaks forth like all Parnassus," consist merely of a declamatory tribute to Liverpool's maritime enterprise. The Liverpool Bard had clearly attempted to fashion an entire epic poem around a kind of maritime panegyric that Melville would subsume in a single chapter of *Moby-Dick* ("Nantucket"). Simply to celebrate commerce is to embrace a one-dimensional view of life that cannot allow for either the complexity or the comedy of modern epic.

Even though Mickle's translation of *The Lusiads* had been written in heroic couplets and had retained allegorical machinery, as well as cultural panegyric, Melville would continue to praise Camoens's poem without reservation. Of all the characters in Melville's fiction, none is more wholly to be admired than Jack Chase, an egalitarian foretopman who "above all things was an ardent admirer of Camoens."[12] Jack, who quotes Camoens three times, is himself a would-be epic writer who insists " 'I've that here, White Jacket' – touching his forehead – 'which, under happier skies – perhaps in yon solitary star there, peeping down from those clouds – might have made a Homer of me' " (271). Whether the real Jack Chase had suggested to Melville that there could be a Homer of the sea, or whether Melville is ascribing his present epic ambitions back to Jack Chase, is finally neither knowable nor significant. Within the world of *White-Jacket,* Jack Chase lives his epic with a gay abandon. What is crucial is

that Jack Chase, Homer, and Camoens all became mingled in Melville's mind, forming a hypothetical writer of vital and high-spirited sea epic. As Jack exclaims,

> Camoens! White-Jacket, Camoens! Did you ever read him? The Lusiad, I mean? It's the man-of-war epic of the world, my lad. . . . . How many great men have been sailors, White-Jacket! They say Homer himself was once a tar, even as his hero, Ulysses, was both a sailor and a ship-wright. (270)

The mighty book would evidently need more than a mighty theme. It would require a writer whose enthusiasms and experience of the sea would enable him to convey its magnitude directly. Unlike Prescott, Melville could recreate a known heroic life through a flash of memory, thereby releasing laughter at bookish data.

Why, of all the great epic texts, should Mickle's translation of *The Lusiads* have been, next to *Paradise Lost,* the most resonant to Melville's aesthetic sensibility? Both in *White-Jacket* and in *Billy Budd,* Melville refers with special admiration to Camoen's portrayal of the "Spirit of the Cape," a fearsome mythological giant named Adamastor who rises up to confront Vasco de Gama's men as they undergo the great test of rounding the Cape of Good Hope.[13] Unlike Emmons or the Liverpool bard, Camoens had known that a heroic voyage leads toward a menacing monster who is symbolic of life's sudden, deadly hostilities. Camoens's pseudoclassical mythology may be absurd, but Adamastor's place in his heroic narrative had been essential. Melville relocates Camoens's Spirit of the Cape from Good Hope to Cape Horn, then likens the rounding of Cape Horn to the epic hero's descent into hell: "Was the descent of Orpheus, Ulysses, or Dante into Hell, one whit more hardy and sublime than the first navigator's weathering of that terrible cape?" (96). In Melville's own epic, the Spirit of the Cape, Adamastor, was to be greatly expanded and deepened until it merged with the whalemen's legendary Mocha Dick, the sea's ultimate monster, who represents, to Ahab, "all the suble demonisms of life and thought."[14] As "The Try Works" suggests, the *Pequod*'s entire voyage can be viewed as a descent into hell – a descent from which, unlike the underworld "visits" of most epics, Melville's fire-maddened hero never returns.

Melville's enthusiasm for Camoens clearly extends to the entire *Lusiads,* not merely to the account of Adamastor. As the "man-of-war epic of the world," Camoens's poem had acknowledged that the world was a state of unending warfare in which hierarchy, fate's buffetings, and sea cannibalisms abound. In spite of these facts, however, the prevailing spirit of Camoens's work, his "crucibled ore" as Melville later described it,[15] had been celebratory. To Camoens as to Barlow, the voyages of Renaissance explorers had made possible the rise of world commerce. William

Julius Mickle, whom Melville clearly admired, had opened his introduction to *The Lusiads* by declaring "In contradistinction to the Iliad and Aeneid, the Paradise Lost has been called the Epic Poem of Religion. In the same manner may the Lusiad be named the Epic Poem of Commerce."[16] Camoens provided Melville with a precedent for a new narrative epic that might, on one level, celebrate the adventuresome, commercial spirit of which antebellum America was so proud. With the aid of Camoens's example, Nantucketers could be seen as Alexanders confidently parceling out their watery empire. Whaling mates and harpooners could become knights and squires lightheartedly engaged in deadly mock-chivalrous adventure. Melville's narrator could self-consciously don the role of "Advocate" of "this business of whaling," thereby enjoying all the willful exaggerations of his advocacy: "Butchers we are, that is true. But butchers, also, and butchers of the bloodiest badge, have been all Martial Commanders whom the world invariably delights to honor" (108).

Evidence of the way Melville read Homer postdates *Moby-Dick,* but is quite consonant with his differing responses to Ossian and to Camoens. During his trip around Cape Horn in 1860, Melville read Chapman's translation of *The Iliad* and marked those passages in which Hector and Achilles recognize that they must die at the hands of powers beyond them. However, Melville also viewed *The Odyssey* as Homer's comic celebration of a solitary man's ability to confront and surmount the buffetings of the sea gods. Both Odysseus and Telemachus, like Taji and Ishmael, half willingly undergo a fanciful sea voyage into the world of mind.[17] Melville's later reading of Matthew Arnold's essays on Homer prompted similarly divided responses. Melville drew a box around Arnold's insistence on Homer's "noble" manner, but questioned Arnold's conclusion that *Marmion* had been written in "a bastard epic style" suited only to an age of fragmented vision. In the main, however, *The Iliad* seemed to reveal the true Homer. Just as Ahab considered himself doomed in the midst of paradise, so Melville both underscored and marked Goethe's famous comment "From Homer I every day learn more clearly that in our life here above ground we have, properly speaking, to enact Hell."[18]

Melville's responses to epic texts suggest that he associated any new American epic with a willfully improvisational genre allowing for high national feeling, praise for commercial and democratic values, a brooding sense of life's hellish mystery, and a heroic openness to all possible meanings. Not surprisingly, "Hawthorne and His Mosses," taken in its entirety, anticipates just such a work. Our "American genius," our "heroes of the pen," are to combine the power of blackness with a seemingly contradictory belief in "that unshackled, democratic spirit of Christianity in all things."[19] For Melville, however, Hawthorne's "power of black-

ness" – about which we have heard so much – cannot ultimately be severed from Hawthorne's "religion of mirth" (330). To adopt the language of *Moby-Dick,* Melville's hero must sacrifice both life and manly fellowship in order to confront the speechless, placeless powers of evil, but the mighty work as a whole must still find joy in the "Just Spirit of Equality." Exactly how this problem was to be resolved, Melville's review does not attempt to determine. Like *Moby-Dick* itself, "Hawthorne and His Mosses" poses a longstanding problem of literary and cultural values. If heroes are superior men, and heroic literature exalts the honor of heroic death, how can an American epic retain these qualities while still being "bound to carry republican progressiveness into Literature as well as into life?" (335–6).

All evidence suggests that Melville had half completed his comic whaling story before he determined to expand his narrative into the comic-tragic-epic-poem-in-prose we now read.[20] At the time Melville made his decision (the fall of 1850), he exulted in having no clear idea of the form that national literature should assume. Dwight and Barlow had fretted over the problem; Prescott had worked out every detail of a solution. "Hawthorne and His Mosses," however, smilingly belittles *The Fredoniad,* proclaims "we want no American Miltons," and insists "it is better to fail in originality than to succeed in imitation."[21] All Melville will conclude is that our national genius, our literary messiah, will arrive speaking words that seem crabbed and ugly according to traditional standards. He will arrive, not in the expected Roman chariot, but laughing astride an ass, so that you may not know Him. While reading *Mosses from an Old Manse* in July of 1850, Melville came upon Hawthorne's mocking evocation of America's "Master Genius," the author who would write "our first great original work, whether moulded in the form of an epic poem, or assuming a guise altogether new." In the margin, Melville scored this passage four separate times, but left no further comment.[22]

For Prescott, the outlines of an epic conflict and the qualities of its hero had been there in the historical record. It had been his task, and his great achievement, to perceive within that immense body of historical data an epic narrative of the most shapely kind. His problems had been those of selection, of imaginative recreation, and of providing a moral defense for the conquest. Melville's problems were of a decidedly different nature. He had to exalt a confessedly "shabby" (7), ill-paid occupation into a deathly conflict worthy of epic and tragedy as well as comedy. His whaling officers and sailors would have to speak a language both recognizably heroic and convincingly American. But his hero, like Irving's Stuyvesant, would have to be wholly invented from literary precedents: Achilles, Prometheus, Faustus, Lear, Satan, Frithiof, Carlyle's Cromwell, with more than a touch of Quixotic Idealism and Stuy-

vesant's bearish intransigence. A sea-antagonist worthy of his fire-seeking hero would have to be found among the legends of American whaling lore. The hero would thus become a summation of epic literary tradition, but the narrator would express a Yankee Jonathan's democratic attitudes toward him. Half-reverential and half-mocking, predisposed to distrust, Ishmael must forever suspect his own irrepressible awe at Ahab's grandeur.

Melville's success in *inventing* a convincing heroic legend against these obstacles is surely one of the miracles of literary history. Given Melville's love of polytonal improvising, we should not be surprised that Melville's invocation is to be found in chapter twenty-six, that his whalemen often use comically inappropriate Miltonic and Shakespearean diction, that his fourteen epic similes[23] often seem defiantly obtrusive, or that his narrative ends, as self-consciously as possible, with a protracted three-chapter, three-day battle. These are the parodic exercises in originality that must have been welcome to any author who, in 1850, sought to transform Old World poetic epic into new seriocomic prose form. Who can be sure whether Ishmael's epic similes likening Ahab to prairie wolves and grizzly bears are meant to aggrandize a hero, satirize a hero, or satirize the epic? Does "The Try Works" provide a modern visit to hell that expresses the Truth of truths? Is it the dreaming of a green loner who nearly capsizes the ship? Or might it be Ishmael's own game with his reader, his attempt to "try out" a bit of literary blubber to see if it "works?"

I. "THE RELIGION OF MIRTH"

Like Knickerbocker, Ishmael is hardly averse to playful mockery of the artifices of Dan Homer, Dan Virgil, and the tradition that follows them. The "boggy, soggy, squitchy" oil painting in the Spouter Inn, Ishmael slyly and misleadingly tells us, prophecies that an exasperated whale will impale himself upon the three mastheads (12). Weighty lists of absurd tribes ("Tongatabooans, Erromanggoans, Pannangians, and Brighggians") and of the whaleman's royal genealogy ("Perseus, St. George, Hercules, Jonah and Vishnoo! There's a member-roll for you!") are offered up for readers who still long to hear the catalogues of superior men (31, 363). Elijiah is at once the most crazed of biblical prophets and the most scrofulous of epic sibyls. Father Mapple heaps up five consecutive epic similes, all of them grotesquely overwritten, in order to convince his congregation of the immensity of Jonah's guilt (45). The cetology section, which earnest Melvilleans have long regarded as a compendium of truth and fact, ends with a chapter appropriately named "The Tail." Unable to see within the head of the "faceless" sperm whale, Ishmael resorts to careful examination of "his back parts," knowing that his futile efforts at an anatomy have earned him a concluding mock-epic

Proposition: "Other poets have warbled the praises of the soft eye of the antelope, and the lovely plumage of the bird that never alights; less celestial, I celebrate a tail" (375).[24] Even the Invocation to Man's "august dignity" (117), serious though it surely is, ends by singling out Cervantes and Bunyan, not Homer and Milton, as its literary exemplars. For Melville, "august dignity" is clearly to be found in the comic and the common, as well as in a figure as awesome and kingly as Captain Ahab.

Melville's parodies of epic type scenes repeatedly imply the absurdity of contemporary clichés about the Satanic savage. Queequeg seems less a Polynesian than a wry variant of the epic Indians who had stalked through the pages of American poetry and fiction for forty years. Equipped with tattoo warpaint and tomahawk pipe, Queequeg worships his God by whittling away its nose, performs his shaving ablutions with a harpoon razor, achieves comic feats of prowess for others' benefit (striking the tar spot), and cheerfully indulges in his Ramadan because he shares Ishmael's un-Miltonic belief that "hell is an idea first born of an undigested apple-dumpling" (85). A savage who is as Christian as this world permits, Queequeg's character suggests that the white man's ascribing of savagery solely to other races should become more extinct than the *Pequod*. Because all the world is a whaler, sharkishness and cannibalism abound everywhere, in ourselves as in our occupations.

Melville's mockery of the conventions of red Satanism does not cease when Ahab emerges from his cabin to redirect the *Pequod*'s quest. The red man's presumably implacable need to avenge a personal wrong resurfaces as Ahab's essential trait, whereas Queequeg and Tashtego, though they never defy their captain, remain indifferent to Ahab's rage. When Queequeg "delivers" Tashtego from the sweet oblivion of drowning in spermaceti, the presumed inhumanity of two nonwhite races is tacitly challenged. Shortly after Ahab boasts at length of his assault upon the gods' consuming fire ("The Candles"), Melville provides Tashtego a four-line chapter in which the Indian laughs at the storm while calling aloud for the rum needed to make it bearable. Similarly, Ahab's grand verbal preparations for death contrast with Queequeg's silent readying of the coffin that will become Ishmael's only means to life. Even Tashtego's nailing the flag to the sinking mast may be less an act of animal vengeance than a jaunty tribute to all that is being lost. Throughout *Moby-Dick,* Queequeg and Tashtego superficially look and act like stereotypical red heroes, but their motives and inner character are laughably unlike the familiar image of awesome red ferocity. Melville first elicits all those apprehensions that Cooper, Simms, and Parkman had aroused in white readers, then dissipates them by showing us that everyman has both his insular Tahiti and his howling Infinite, however he may define them.

Although Ishmael's role as writer leads him to conceive of Ahab as

both a tragic and an epic hero, Ishmael's own attitudes as a common sailor are usually skeptical of human grandeur, if not overtly mock-heroic. Ishmael knows that whaling has bred in him a "genial, desperado philosophy," moods of the hyena, "certain queer times and occasions in this strange, mixed affair we call life when a man takes this whole universe for a vast practical joke" (226). The ever new and ever bizarre mixings of life repeatedly prevent him from accepting the gravity of any single truth. Accordingly, Ishmael often seems, like Knickerbocker, bent upon emphasizing the artifice of all he creates. To Ahab, Perth's harpoon is the epic weapon, but to Ishmael, the perceptual relativism reflected from the doubloon provides the truer weapon of understanding. Fedallah is so absurdly Mephistophelian, so mechanical in denying Ahab's claims for self-determination, that we half suspect Ishmael of inventing Fedallah as a literary joke.[25] Ishmael's dire warning against the narcissistic end of masthead standers like himself should not be taken too seriously; it is preceded by mockery of other "modern standers-of-mast-heads" – like George Washington, Napoleon, and Nelson – all of whom now exist only as "a lifeless set" of heroic statues (155).

Laughter at life's vast joke is directed at the crux of the *Pequod*'s quest in a late chapter titled "A Bower in the Arsacides." Because epic journeys must probe the world's penetralia, Ishmael recounts his own quest for the whale's innermost secret. Thanks to "my late royal friend Tranquo, king of Tranque," Ishmael was once allowed to explore the church/skeleton of the great sperm whale. Trailing his Thesean ball of twine, Ishmael discovers that, at the inmost center of all meaning, "naught was there but bones" (450). Ahab's white whale, Ishmael well knows, is the only 'machinery' still available for the writing of his epic tale. His intervening deity may never divulge a truth because it has neither meaning nor divinity. Should this surmise be valid, Ishmael's *Moby-Dick* would become as much of a "distended bladder" as Knickerbocker's *History*.[26]

In Bakhtin's view, the "novelization" of the epic did away with the unchanging, closed, elevated style of the heroic poem. Heroic verse was replaced by a multilayered mode of prose discourse, variously called polyglossia or heteroglossia, that could speak to the contrarities of the modern temperament.[27] William Cullen Bryant's complaint about the monotony of Dwight's and Barlow's couplets ("an artificial elevation of style, from which it is impossible to rise and descend, and which allows just as much play and freedom to the faculties of the writer as a pair of stilts allows the body"[28]) could be extended, in kind though not in degree, to the prose styles of historical romancers and romantic historians in the next generation. Ishmael's narrative voice is the first to break apart the sustained elevation of divisible heroic *or* mock-heroic modes, achieving a style that alternates quickly between latinate abstractions and

American slang, periodic sentence and abrupt exclamation, a style that leaves the reader on the edge between epic and mock-epic.

Two examples, from the book's beginning and end, may suffice to suggest the pertinence of Bakhtin's idea to Melville's prose:

> What of it, if some old hunks of a sea-captain orders me to get a broom and sweep down the decks? What does that indignity amount to, weighed, I mean in the scales of the New Testament? Do you think the archangel Gabriel thinks anything the less of me, because I promptly and respectfully obey that old hunks in that particular instance? Who ain't a slave? Tell me that. Well, then, however the old sea-captains may order me about – however they may thump and punch me about, – I have the satisfaction of knowing that it is all right; that everybody else is one way or another served in much the same way – either in a physical or metaphysical point of view, that is; and so the universal thump is passed round, and all hands should rub each other's shoulder-blades, and be content. (6)

Ishmael ranges easily here between "old hunks" and "the universal thump," between "Who ain't a slave?" and "a physical or metaphysical point of view." Long rhetorical sentences alternate with short exclamations; appositives rub up against colloquialisms like "I mean," "well, then," and "that is." No level of discourse is satirized at the expense of any other, but no language or style is allowed to be the vehicle of Truth either. Ishmael will often return to the controversy about cosmic fatality and individual free will, using other metaphors and other rhetorical strategies in meditations like "The Mat-Maker" or "The Castaway." But no reader should conclude that Ishmael's equable tone, achieved here by his mixing of linguistic levels, shows that he is indifferent to the issue involved. Polyglossia is Ishmael's means of protecting himself against the spiritual despair (he calls it "my hypos") that results from worry over the universe's insoluble riddles.

The advantage of mixed tonalities is especially apparent whenever Ishmael chooses self-consciously to transform epic conventions. After hundreds of pages of speculation about the white whale, the reader is finally allowed to see him:

> A gentle joyousness – a mighty mildness of repose in swiftness, invested the gliding whale. Not the white bull Jupiter swimming away with ravished Europa clinging to his graceful horns; his lovely, leering eyes sideways intent upon the maid; with smooth bewitching fleetness, rippling straight for the nuptial bower in Crete; not Jove, not that great majesty Supreme! did surpass the glorified White Whale as he so divinely swam. (548)

This crucial moment is rendered in a manner designed to frustrate every possible conclusion. The long-imagined great white whale, supposed sum

of the world's malignity, at last materializes in all his gentle joy, only to
swim silently away from the observor's eye. His rippling, gliding motion is conveyed with satiric inappropriateness by comparing his motions
to those of a bull. Moby-Dick is presumably "glorified" by being likened to a God who casts "lovely, leering eyes" upon a maid.

The passage tempts us to assert that Ahab is correct in assuming the
whale to be not merely the agent but the principal of the Deity. And yet,
the unlike likeness between them is asserted, not through factual statement, but through the enjoyed elaboration of one form of the epic simile
(the "not" . . . "not" . . . "did surpass" formula). Diedrich Knickerbocker, who had visualized Stuyvesant as a painting, would have relished the irony of Ishmael's reifying the whale by parodying a convention of epic literature. Whether the whale is here glorified or mocked,
whether he is revealed as a benevolent or a ravishing God, whether he is
an observed animal or a literary invention, remains impossible to determine.

Through many such passages, the balking of all hope for resolution
comically proceeds. Either Ishmael leads his search for meaning to a
question, or he contradicts himself in one paragraph, or he contradicts
himself in some succeeding passage. His constantly inventive shifts of
genre only make the reader ever more aware of the artifices of them all.
Bakhtin's description of how the novelization of the epic functions in
Tom Jones and *Don Juan* applies as readily to Ishmael's shifting discourses:

> They [novelized genres] become more free and flexible, their language
> renews itself, by incorporating extra-literary heteroglossia and the
> "novelistic" layers of literary language, they become dialogized, per-
> meated with laughter, irony, humor, elements of self-parody and fi-
> nally – this is the most important thing – the novel inserts into these
> other genres an indeterminacy, a certain semantic openendedness, a liv-
> ing contact with unfinished, still evolving, contemporary reality.[29]

For Bakhtin, however, the process of novelization means the utter death
of the old "closed" form: "laughter destroys the epic, and in general destroys any hierarchical distance" (23). But it is precisely here that Bakhtin's
claim seems less applicable to older genres novelized in nineteenth-
century American texts. In them, the epic remains together with the
laughter. Stuyvesant is Irving's truculent hero as well as history's fool;
Thoreau in his beanfield is both less and more than Achilles; Whitman's
self is comic procreator and heroic democrat together. And so it is in
Ishmael's grand *Kostanza*. While Ishmael struggles to retain his spirit of
equable raillery, Ahab's monoglossic voice gains increasing power. Ahab
may be a monomaniac and fool, but Ishmael also describes him as if he
illustrated C. M. Bowra's summary of the vital code of oral epic: "the

secret of this poetry is that it sees in heroic death the fitting fulfillment of a heroic life."[30]

II. "TOPMOST GREATNESS, TOPMOST GRIEF"

If Melville were to persuade his reader of "The Honor and Glory of Whaling" (361), he would need to provide far more than one chapter's facetious genealogy enlisting Perseus, St. George, Herakles, Jonah, and Vishnoo, along with the knights and squares of the *Pequod,* as courageous whalemen. By comparing whalehunters to savage Iroquois, and by allowing Tashtego to nail the flag to the sinking mainmast, Melville endows all of the *Pequod*'s multiracial crew with the physical prowess and courage of America's one heroic-age people. The ever-widening enterprise of Nantucketers enables them to be seen as modern Alexanders. Father Mapple's ostentatious pieties aside, any puritan spirituality the American whaleman might have had has been supplanted by commercial values that can nonetheless be heroic. When the *Pequod*'s whalemen break the Sabbath in order to "cut in" their dead whales, "you would have thought we were offering up ten thousand red oxen to the sea gods" (303). During the whalehunter's times of leisure, he carves scrimshaw of such intricacy that it possesses as much "maziness of design, as the Greek savage, Achilles' shield" (270).

These kinds of magnifying heroic comparisons, no matter how skillful, are bound to collapse into mere rhetoric unless the heroic quality of the whaleman's daily pursuit can be directly conveyed. It is precisely at this level of narrative that Melville is almost unfailingly successful. Knowing that the essence of the heroic life is the readiness to die, Melville asserts "Yes, there is death in this business of whaling – a speechlessly quick chaotic bundling of a man into Eternity" (37). So vivid and accurate a metaphor might seem convincing enough by itself, but Melville confirms his assertion by narrative prose as compelling as the following paragraph from "The First Lowering":

> It was a sight full of quick wonder and awe! The vast swells of the omnipotent sea; the surging, hollow roar they made, as they rolled along the eight gunwales, like gigantic bowls in a boundless bowling-green; the brief suspended agony of the boat, as it would tip for an instant on the knife-like edge of the sharper waves, that almost seemed threatening to cut it in two; the sudden profound dip into the watery glens and hollows; the keen spurrings and goadings to gain the top of the opposite hill; the headlong, sled-like slide down its other side; all these, with the cries of the headsmen and harpooners, and the shuddering gasps of the oarsmen, with the wondrous sight of the ivory Pequod bearing down upon her boats with outstretched sails, like a wild hen after her screaming brood; – all this was thrilling. Not the raw recruit, marching from

> the bosom of his wife into the fever heat of his first battle; not the dead
> man's ghost encountering the first unknown phantom in the other world;
> – neither of these can feel stranger and stronger emotions than that man
> does, who for the first time finds himself pulling into the charmed,
> churned circle of the hunted sperm whale. (223–4)

No mockery here. Beginning with a risky claim upon the emotions of epic sublimity ("wonder and awe"), Melville earns these terms by eight superbly descriptive phrase units, separated by semicolons, which together convey the sequence of sensory experiences during a lowering. The ever-shifting alliterative patterns suggest the ever-changing rapidity of the experiences themselves. In order to render the imminent danger of a lowering, Melville emphasizes the momentary balance of the whale boat on the very edge of the wave; he then deepens our sense of calm before peril by means of the longest, most rhythmically suspended, phrase unit of the paragraph.

The cumulative sequence of images is designed to lead, of course, to the two comparisons at the paragraph's end. These similes, though not in the conventional form of the epic simile (the extended "as . . . so" comparison), nonetheless suggest it in both structure and content. By comparing the whaling tyro to the raw recruit and to the dead man's ghost, Melville links whaling both with the traditional subject of epic (battle) and with perhaps its most familiar convention (the visit to the underworld). Confronting the whale thus becomes, in Goethe's phrase, an enacting of hell upon earth, a pursuit that encourages mortal indomitableness in acute forms.

When Ishmael uses the epic simile seriously, he is likely to exalt the power of individual resistance to external forces. In the two following similes, Melville and Virgil liken Ahab and Aeneas to massive ancient trees that stand firm against the storms of divine enmity and Dido's wrath. Printing Melville's prose as blank verse will render Melville's transformation of epic convention even more clear:

> As in the hurricane that sweeps the plain,
> Men fly the neighborhood of some lone,
> Gigantic elm, whose very height and strength
> But render it so much the more unsafe,
> Because so much the more a mark for thunderbolts;
> So at these last words of Ahab's
> Many of the mariners did run from him
> In a terror of dismay.
>
> > (*Moby-Dick,* conclusion of "The Candles," p. 508)[31]

> Ac, velut annoso validam cum robore quercum
> Alpini Boreae nunc flatibus illinc
> Eruere inter se certant; it stridor, et altae

Consternunt terram concusso stipite frondes;
Ipsa haeret scopulis, et, quantum vertice ad auras
Aetherias, tantum radice in Tartara tendit:
Haud secus adsiduis hinc atque hinc vocibus heros
Tunditur, et magno persentit pectore curas;
Mens immota manet; lacrimae volvuntur inanes.

(*The Aeneid*, IV, 11. 441–9)[32]

The hurricane and thunderbolts sent upon Ahab by nameless powers cause the lone, gigantic elm neither to bend nor to weaken. To Melville, the destroying power of the hurricane only renders Ahab all the more grand because the tree is the special and conspicuous mark of hostile forces. Virgil's interest had been in tenuous endurance, the process by which the stout oak can remain firm even though its high branches fall and it groans under the blast. Whereas Melville contrasts Ahab's self-destructive defiance to the fears of lesser men, Virgil insists that Aeneas' greatness lies in his remaining resolute for Italy even though Dido's words and Dido's grief pierce his heart ("magno persentit pectore curas"). Virgil's simile stresses the agony of quelling human feeling in pursuit of a grander cultural purpose; Melville's simile exalts intransigent defiance, while implying its suicidal end.

At its irreducible narrative core, Melville's romance succeeds as epic because it illustrates the paradigm of the heroic folk tale. In his authoritative study of comparative heroic mythology, Joseph Campbell provides a model of the heroic quest that illuminates Melville's narrative in suggestive ways. Ahab, like Campbell's archetypal hero, attains heroic stature by assuming the duty of slaying the tyrant monster that has terrorized his people. Lured by repellent heralds and forewarned by omens, Ahab persists in venturing into the "fateful region" where his heroic test awaits him. Be it a forest, the sea, or an alien land, the fateful region, Campbell asserts, is a "free field for the projection of unconscious content."[33] In Melville's novel, the sea is repeatedly described as a narcissistic mirror into which each whale-hunter projects his deepest fears and desires. Ahab projects upon the whale all the "intangible malignity" of life (246), an intangible malignity that may be in nature, but that unquestionably lives in Ahab as the source of both his earthly insanity and his otherworldly perception.

Before Campbell's hero can confront the tyrant monster, he passes through three particularly important stages of initiation. He penetrates to a source of unknown, primordial knowledge that Campbell both literally and metaphorically describes as "the belly of the whale" (90). He meets with a goddess or dark queen who provides him fuller knowledge of the monster's identity (109). He seeks atonement with his father, or a father figure, from whom his quest has estranged him (126). Because

Melville combines the separate enounters of the heroic quest into Ahab's monomaniacal search for vengeance, these three initiatory meetings must be subsumed within one. To Ahab, and often to Ishmael, the white whale becomes the symbol of all hidden, primordial Truth; to be wedded to Moby-Dick (as Ahab finally is) is to penetrate to the source of life's mystery, to the navel of the world.[34] When Ahab looks at the dying whale, he ascribes his own fire worship to him and then addresses an unknown infidel queen, a "dark Hindoo half of nature" (497), which he clearly wishes both to love and to destroy. At the end of "The Candles," Ahab finally finds his "sire" by "reading" him into the corpusants' flames. By grasping the "foundling fire" of knowledge, Ahab knowingly seeks to become one with his "fiery father," even though he knows that such defiant worship can end only in the most self-consumptive of atonements (508). Repelled by the dark goals of Ahab's quest, Ishmael cannot withhold his awed fascination for the man who has sought them.

Moby-Dick's departures from the paradigm of Campbell's "monomyth" are no less important. Ahab does not attack the tyrant monster in order to save his people and their civilization. Instead, he pressures reluctant crewmen to bind themselves to his quest, and then sacrifices them, albeit willingly, to his own notions of a grand, heroic death. In the heroic mythologies Campbell examines, the monsters figure primarily as real and imminent destroyers much like Grendel and the dragon in *Beowulf*. Although the climactic event of Melville's epic remains a physical confrontation with the monster, the import of that confrontation has become primarily metaphysical rather than communal. Viewed in an American context, Ahab's desire to rid the world of malign inscrutability mirrors the Transcendentalists' ideal of American individualism. By reading "all nature's sweet or savage impressions . . . untraditionally and independently" (73), Ahab willfully separates himself from wife, child, and his own crew, thereby embodying a liberty of spirit in extremis. But viewed more broadly, Ahab's willingness to grant physical objects an unknowable but primary spiritual identity changes traditional epic narrative into an international, Faustian, and modern mode. With no thought of Melville as an example, Lukacs grasped the inmost significance of *Moby-Dick*'s generic transformation. Those novels that search after the ungraspable phantoms of life have become modern man's form of epic:

> The novel is the epic of a world that has been abandoned by God. The novel hero's psychology is demonic; the objectivity of the novel is the mature man's knowledge that meaning can never quite penetrate reality, but that, without meaning, reality would disintegrate into the nothingness of inessentiality.[35]

It is precisely this sense of a world where meaning derives from searching after ever-receding meaning that informs Melville's epic novel from beginning to end.

Melville's crucial divergence from the monomyth of heroic mythology is that the last of Campbell's three stages (Departure, Initiation, Return) has no counterpart. After the traditional hero has penetrated to the source of knowledge and slain the monster, he brings back the runes of wisdom, the elixir, the whale's secret, or the golden fleece in order to restore communal order and renew his people. In those rare instances when the hero does not wish to return, a representative of his community is dispatched to summon him. The survival of Ishmael, which is needed to tell the narrative, is the only trace of a return Melville will allow. It is a crucial component of Melvillean heroism that Ahab does not wish to return. His willingness to die in the crazed hope that he might know, or possibly destroy, the agent of malign inscrutability, remains the essence of his nobility, a nobility even Starbuck finally grants him. Whatever community may exist in Nantucket seems, however, to have retained little or no interest in Ahab's demise. Ishmael retells the *Pequod*'s story without suggesting that it has had any resonance for other whalemen or even for Peleg and Bildad. By comparison with the paradigm of heroic myth, *Moby-Dick* is a heroic tale whose cultural significance can only be written down for future readers. Although four generations of twentieth century readers have found varying kinds of an essential American identity in Ahab, the form of *Moby-Dick* shows that Ahab was a hero who was invented from non-American literary traditions, not transcribed from native oral legend.

Among the literary analogues that contributed to the creation of Melville's overreaching hero, we probably now know enough of Aeschylus's and Shelley's Prometheus, of Byron's Manfred, of Shakespeare's Lear, and of Marlowe's Faustus. Measuring Ahab's stature in the context of Melville's familiarity with epic literature is just as revealing as comparisons to dramatic tragedy. Ulysses's wily control of his crew, Hector's doomed boasting, Achilles's monomaniacal rage to avenge Patroclus's death – these are all of obvious pertinence to the genesis of Melville's hero. How much does Melville's account of the Straits of Sundra owe to Scylla and Charybdis? Would Ahab's moment of quiet intimacy with Starbuck ("The Symphony") have been conceivable without the magnificent meetings of Hector with Andromache?

To these familiar influences, we should add Scandinavian epic and saga. In four different passages, Melville links Ahab's quest to the journey of a "Scandinavian sea-king" (73). The import of these general comparisons can be suggested by considering the one Scandinavian epic we know Melville read before writing *Moby-Dick* – Esaias Tegnér's *Frithiof's Saga*. A hero after Campbell's model, Frithiof defends his people against usurpers, embarks on a long journey, and returns to reorder his kingdom after being atoned with his family. Before his return, however, Frithiof burns down the holy temple of Balder, thereby exiling himself to the life

of a pirate, whalehunter, and heretical freebooter. In Canto Ten, Tegnér describes Frithiof confronting a whale ridden by two demons, one of whom, like Mocha Dick and Moby-Dick, "bears the rude shape of a monstrous ice bear."[36] When Tegnér's hero proclaims himself "an outlawed, homeless man," and embraces the sea as "my bride," his defiant self-assertion is expressed in political terms very like Ahab's:

> And Thou, thou broad unfettered sea!
> What are these other kings to Thee,
> Who with their lordly airs would awe
> And make their despot glances law?
> The only sovereign is he,
> The most undaunted of the free,
> Who sees Thee in thy wrath, nor quails;
> Unmoved, when Thy worst mood prevails. (147)

Despite the unfortunate jingle of the translator's tetrameter couplets, the passage ascribes the highest heroic sovereignty to those sea voyagers who refuse to quail before the wrath of the sea gods. When Ahab, proclaiming his own sovereignty in himself, gazes out over the sea and hoots at the "great gods" as mere cricket-players and pugilists, he extends Frithiof's spirit of defiance beyond the limit that allows for reclamation.

Among the epic figures similar to Ahab, Milton's Satan is by far the most important and the most problematical. When reading Shelley's *A Defence of Poetry*, Melville was to double score Shelley's claim, "Milton's Devil as a moral being is as far superior to his God, as one who perseveres in some purpose which he has conceived to be excellent in spite of adversity and torture, is to one who in the cold security of undoubted triumph inflicts the most horrible revenge upon his enemy."[37] Quite clearly, Shelley presumed that Satan was convinced of the heroic good of his actions; he also believed Satan's supposed perseverance to be a higher heroism than Christ's riskless victory in Milton's sixth book. But if Melville accepted romantic Satanism in so unqualified a form, we should find both a close correlation between Ahab's motives and Satan's, and an unequivocal celebration of Ahab's pursuit of the devil's purposes. A closer study of Melville's text suggests that he was too accurate a reader of Milton ever to engage in either of these simplistic readings.

The similarities between the physical descriptions of Satan and Ahab show Melville's desire to place Ahab within the *developing* tradition of epic martial heroism. Awesome in his "high broad form," scorched face, livid scar, and "regal, overbearing dignity," Ahab first appears standing silently, pondering his revenge upon the whale (123–4). In similar fashion, the rebellious angels observe their "dread commander" standing before them like a tower:

> Dark'n'd so, yet shone
> Above them all th'Arch Angel: but his face

Deep scars of Thunder had intrencht, and care
Sat on his faded cheek, but under Brows
Of dauntless courage, and considerate Pride
Waiting Revenge.[38]

As so often in great epic literature, imitation serves to transform tradition. Ahab's scarred strength and "firmest fortitude" are from the outset granted a self-sacrificial moral integrity Milton never allows Satan. With no apparent irony, Ishmael tells us that Ahab "looked like a man cut away from the stake" (123); he stands before his men, as Satan never can, "with a crucifixion in his face" (124).

Ahab is most dignified at those moments when his inner likeness to Satan seems least apparent. Satan's confession while gazing at Paradise ("the more I see / Pleasures about me, so much more I feel / Torment within me" [275]) is clearly the literary source of Ahab's line "damned, most subtly and most malignantly! damned in the midst of Paradise" (167). Ahab, however, plausibly believes himself to be damned by whatever power supercedes his own; he demonstrates, as well as claims, that he is "gifted with the high perception" (167). Satan is tormented, not only because he cannot participate in Paradise, but because, unlike Ahab, he has set out to destroy it.

Similarly, Ahab's soliloquy expressing defiant worship of the corpusants' fire is Melville's counterpart to Satan's famous address to the sun. Satan's soliloquy, to be sure, is no less defiantly worshipful than Ahab's, but Satan ends by bidding farewell to all Hope, all Fear, all Remorse and all Good (113). Instead of trying to unite himself with the burning fire beyond, Satan turns away from the sun, thereby limiting his emotions to "pale, ire, envy and despair."[39] Ahab, by contrast, stands erect before the trinity of flames, declares with pride that "the queenly personality lives in me" (507), and concludes with the energizing affirmation "Leap up! Leap up, and lick the sky! I leap with thee; I burn with thee; would fain be welded with thee" (508).

Such passages are not subversive, romantic affirmations of Milton's Satan. Ahab's resemblance to Satan suggests continuity in genre but a change in heroic definition. In their emotional responses both of these grand, ungodly godlike figures may be driven by pride, revenge, and hatred of the powers above, but the goals they seek, and the means they employ, could hardly be more different. Milton's Satan seeks to exact revenge against a God he knows to be good by means he knows to be evil ("Evil be thou my Good" [313]). Half-persuaded that the universe is Manichean, Ahab seeks to strike through the mask, to know whether the inscrutable is malicious, and then, if it be evil, to destroy it. Shunning the risks of challenging God directly, Satan pursues the devious, unheroic course of revenging himself upon God by spitefully corrupting man. Whereas Satan avoids conflict with God so that he can more readily do

evil, Ahab lives only to confront the principal or agent of evil, and then to wreak his hatred upon it. Even if Ahab's view of the whale is insane, his motives are ennobling. His desire to rid the world of evil attests to a greatness of spirit that Satan, who at his best is motivated by "Honour and Empire with revenge enlarg'd" (125), can never possess.

These vast differences in motive and method cause Satan progressively to degenerate, while Ahab's grandeur only increases along with his destructive monomania. At the outset of their revenge, Satan and Ahab share a similarity of spirit as well as physical appearance. Both are willing, in Satan's words, to lose the field in order to maintain "the unconquerable Will, / And study of revenge, immortal hate, / And courage never to submit or yield" (12). Satan, however, as C. S. Lewis long ago demonstrated, thereafter descends "from hero to general, from general to politician, from politician to secret service agent, and thence to a thing that peers in at bedroom or bathroom windows, and thence to a toad, and finally to a snake."[40] As soon as Satan begins to promote Belial's venal, insidious plan of using man to revenge himself against God, his seeming intransigence begins to falter. In Satan's later soliloquys, his unconquerable will disintegrates into vacillation and self-doubt, which in turn end in despair. His need to adopt ever more demeaning disguises reinforces his growing inability to use words for any purpose other than deception. Instead of maintaining the courage never to submit or yield, Satan allows Belial to be his spokesman, flees before Abdiel's courage, and eventually subdues Adam and Eve, not by example of defiant bravery, but by flattery and lies.

Ahab's great victory is his ability, in the face of sure and total defeat, to remain unswervable in his Will, Hate, and Courage. Dismembered for no known cause, Ahab has no need to confuse revenge with spite, as Satan does. Consequently, Ahab's sense of self grows ever deeper, whereas Satan's is dissipated in lies and masks. The proximity of Moby-Dick enables Ahab rightly to proclaim "In the midst of the personified impersonal, a personality stands here" (507). When Satan returns to Pandemonium to receive plaudits for his victory, Milton turns his planned triumph into a "dismal universal hiss" and then reduces all the fallen archangelic host to serpents.[41] Ahab's last speech, by contrast, is arguably his greatest moment:

> Oh, now I feel my topmost greatness lies
> In my topmost grief. Ho, ho! From all
> Your farthest bounds, pour ye now in,
> Ye bold billows of my whole foregone life,
> And top this one piled comber of my death!
> Towards thee I roll, thou all-destroying but
> Unconquering whale; to the last I grapple with thee;

> From hell's heart I stab at thee; for hate's sake
> I spit my last breath at thee. (571–2).

Differing levels of language ("ye bold billows" and "ho, ho"; "my top-most greatness" and "I spit at thee") here combine, as in Shakespearean soliloquy, into one statement that dignifies rather than belittles the speaker. Unlike Ishmael, Ahab evidently still believes that word conforms to thing. Because Ishmael's polyglossic language serves ambiguity, not resolution, Ishmael must recount Ahab's speeches for us with sparse comment, allowing Ahab's voice a resonance equal to his own.

The stature Ahab gains through the power of his believed and courageous words is itself a measure of Melville's desire to transform Miltonic tradition. Satan grandly dominates Books One and Two, lies eloquently to initiate the actions in Books Four and Six, lurks in honey-tongued disguises in Book Nine, is humiliated in Book Ten, and then disappears. Ahab is not even referred to until Chapter Sixteen, does not appear until Chapter Twenty-eight, recedes through the cetology chapters (55–90), and then reemerges to dominate the reader's attention from Chapter Ninety-nine to the Epilogue. To account for Ahab's growing prominence by asserting that Melville was revising his largely completed whaling story is not an adequate explanation. Melville chose to revise in such a way that the figure of Ahab, introduced after the narrative was well begun, would grow upon his reader until, in Ishmael's words, the entire *Pequod* "seemed the material counterpart of her monomaniac commander's soul" (423).

The Satan who clearly engaged Melville's imagination was the heroic rebel who might have existed before the action of *Paradise Lost* began on Hell's burning lake. If we can imagine a Satan truly driven by Will, Courage, Hate, and Revenge, who dared to attack God directly in order to discover forbidden knowledge, we would possess the outline of a Satan similar to Ahab. In the epic poem Milton wrote, however, the grand defiant quest for forbidden knowledge is merely an eloquent lie Satan employs in order to deceive Eve. Extratextual evidence also suggests that Melville was captivated by the promise rather than the reality of Satan. On a dining room wall at Arrowhead, Melville hung John Martin's drawing of Satan titled "Satan Exalted Sat."[42] Martin's interest, like Melville's, was in the grand, diabolic figure who, at the beginning of Milton's second book, seems to dominate the world.

In the manuscript of "Hawthorne and His Mosses," Melville's attack on American literary flunkeyism had originally contained these sentences:

> We want no American Goldsmiths; nay, we want no American Miltons. It were the vilest thing you could say of a true American author,

that he were an American Milton. Call him an American and have done, for you cannot say a nobler thing of him.[43]

Before publication of the essay, Melville agreed, probably at Duyck-inck's suggestion, to change "an American Milton" to "an American Tompkins."[44] Melville's original intent in dismissing "vile" American Miltons was obviously not to denigrate the author of *Paradise Lost*. Surely he sought to distinguish his already planned recasting of Milton's rebellious archangel from the many wretched American imitations of Milton's epic.

Iconoclasm, defiance, and belief in one's own words were qualities Satan had displayed only intermittently. For Carlyle, those qualities had constituted the true inner force of history. To Melville, who read *On Heroes, Hero Worship and the Heroic in History* in 1850, Carlyle must have suggested ways in which Satan's claims of grandeur had been realized in historical heroes of far higher purpose. Carlyle's superior and rebellious loner is intended to retain a melancholy authority far beyond the attitudinal posing of the Byronic hero. "A deep, great genuine sincerity," Carlyle declares, "is the first characteristic of all men in any way heroic."[45] Freeing the word "hero" from its associations with epic poetry and dramatic tragedy, Carlyle invokes one embattled, worldwide heroic temperament that appears in the vocation appropriate to a particular culture. Again and again Carlyle associates his fire-driven heroes with a Scandinavian rather than a Grecian temper; the Norse spirit, Carlyle contends, has "the genuine Thought of deep, rude, earnest minds, fairly opened to the things about them; a face-to-face and heart-to-heart inspection of all things" (19).

The pertinence of Carlylean heroism to the characterization of Ahab is especially evident in Carlyle's portrayal of England's arch-Protestant hero, Oliver Cromwell. Calvinist, tyrannous commander, and hater of evil, Carlyle's Cromwell remains unswervably committed to the Puritan cause. His heroic stature exacts the very same price as Ahab's pursuit of the whale:

> Consider him. An outer hull of chaotic confusion, visions of the Devil, nervous dreams, almost semi-madness; and yet such a clear, determinate man's-energy working in the heart of that. A kind of chaotic man. The ray as of pure starlight and fire, working in such an element of boundless hypochondria, *un*formed black of darkness! And yet withal this hypochondria, what was it but the very greatness of the man? (217)

Here, if anywhere, is the contemporary source for Ishmael's double-edged insistence that "all mortal greatness is but disease" (74). For Melville as for Carlyle, we worldlings have become so fearfully suspicious of heroism that we try to convince ourselves that monomania can only be man's insanity, not heaven's sense.

Nonetheless, Melville complicates Carlyle's rather preachy hero-worship of grandly aggrieved prophets. The examples Carlyle selects to affirm his heroic model (Odin, Mahomet, Dante, Luther, Knox, Cromwell, Rousseau, Burns, Napoleon) are all men who embodied emerging
historical and/or religious forces. All were in possession of certain fiery
truths that lesser later men needed to accept. However heroic Ahab may
be in temper and in motive, he is seeking a fiery knowledge whose very
existence is never certain. Ahab's quarrel cannot be with anything so
simple, so merely national, as the Calvinists's God.[46] Because Ahab in-
habits our modern world of unknowable truths and masked enemies, his
heroic valor, wholly admirable in the context of traditional epic, becomes questionable by contemporary standards that are no less important. Carlyle has no need to be concerned for the thousands slaughtered
in the name of a Cromwell or a Bonaparte; he is sure both these heroes
were bearers of a higher, historical good. Because Ishmael can pass no
final judgment on Ahab's purpose, he must uneasily exalt Ahab's courage, while deploring its human and communal consequences.

III.   EQUALITY AND SUPERIORITY?

Concern over Ishmael's vanishing presence as narrator might re-
cede if we stopped applying post-Jamesian standards of fictional craft and
began regarding *Moby-Dick* as a prose epic. Primary epics, of course,
have no known author; they are inherited, communal legends retold in
formulaic language by an anonymous bard whose purpose is to sing the
traditional song as best he can. The singer's function is choric rather than
active; he celebrates a heroism he does not personify. By deciding to have
the *Pequod*'s story told by an anonymous green Jonathan named Ishmael,
Melville has selected a narrator, representative of New England folk culture, who can lend comedy and cultural authenticity to his highly literary
epic. The implications of the name "Ishmael" suggest, however, that
there is ultimately no community to which the tale may be recounted.
"The Town-Ho's Story" can be preserved for us in the form of an oral
tale Ishmael presumably told – in circumstances very like those specified
in the "Preface" to *Don Juan* – at the Golden Inn Tavern in Lima. But
Moby-Dick can only be published as a secondary literary epic that pre-
serves, for unknown readers, the illusion of an anonymous tale teller.

The narrative voice of any epic, primary or secondary, must reaffirm
the values of people for whom the heroic legend is retold. Ishmael's "genial, desperado philosophy" (226), so integral to American epic, must
not overpower all possibility of his advancing new heroic values. "Hawthorne and His Mosses" anticipates that great American writers shall speak
for "the unshackled, democratic spirit of Christianity in all things" (339)
as well as "republican progressiveness" (335). It is only fitting, therefore,

that Ishmael's invocation be an uncompromising affirmation of the divine spirit of equality and democracy:

> This august dignity I treat of, is not the dignity of kings and robes, but that abounding dignity which has no robed investiture. Thou shalt see it shining in the arm that wields a pick or drives a spike; that democratic dignity which, on all hands, radiates without end from God; Himself! The great God absolute! The centre and circumference of all democracy! His omnipresence, our divine equality!
>
> If, then, to meanest mariners, and renegades and castaways, I shall hereafter ascribe high qualities, though dark; weave round them tragic graces; if even the most mournful, perchance the most abased, among them all, shall at times lift himself to the exalted mounts; if I shall touch that workman's arm with some ethereal light; if I shall spread a rainbow over his disastrous set of sun; then against all mortal critics bear me out in it, thou just Spirit of Equality, which hast spread one royal mantle of humanity over all my kind! Bear me out in it, thou great democratic God! (117).

Such an invocation embraces values of deeper spiritual reach than Jacksonian political democracy. Ishmael assumes that the inner divinity of the common man has become the heroic essence of a new people. The "just Spirit of Equality" that will serve as Ishmael's epic muse is to lead him to celebrate the ineradicable divinity visible in meanest mariners. For Melville, this transcendent divinity was man's birthright regained by two recent revolutions and nourished by the openness of the New World. The equality of all human souls was the essence of "republican progressiveness" – protected by political constitutions, empowered by nature's force, and evident in the manly good fellowship sea and forest frontiers made possible.[47]

In shaping his epic, Melville thus faced the complex problem of making his Muse ("the just Spirit of Equality") consistent both with his proposition ("The Honor and Glory of Whaling") and his heroic narrative (Ahab's self-destructive assault on evil). But his metaphors from medieval romance, which effectively satirize the *Pequod*'s hierarchy ("Lord," "knights," "squires," "serfs"), were so applicable in daily fact that they leave scant room for the "just Spirit of Equality" in the new commercial world. Neither Flask, nor the carpenter, nor the blacksmith, nor the carousing sailors of the *Walpurgisnacht* revel ever seem to have any divine spirit within them. These contrarieties, important though they are, pale beside the problem of portraying Ahab as the hero of an avowedly democratic and egalitarian epic. Not only does Ahab, like the Carlylean hero, scorn his men as mere cogs in his machine, as "unrecking and unworshipping things" (164) who may be sacrificed to his higher cause. Ahab's admirable heroic purpose, to rid the world of its ruling evil deity,

is based upon metaphysical premises totally at variance with Ishmael's invocation.

Ishmael may wish to dismiss insoluble problems by laughing at them, but his need to judge Ahab repeatedly compels him to weigh the effect the "just Spirit of Equality" might have upon the power of blackness. At the outset, Ishmael wishes to believe that Ahab is God's selectest champion culled from "the kingly commons" (117). As Ahab's tyrannous domination of his crew becomes increasingly apparent, Ishmael's images for kingship darken from "that certain sultanism of his [Ahab's] brain" (147) to "fiery eyes of scorn and triumph" that prove Ahab's "fatal pride" (519). In "The Lee Shore" and "The Whiteness of the Whale," however, it is Ishmael, not Ahab, who seeks to persuade us that it is better to be drowned in the howling infinite than to survive by turning aside from life's invisible spheres. Nonetheless, Ishmael is no less eloquent than Starbuck in emphasizing the price Ahab makes others pay for his valor. At times, Ishmael believes Ahab's monomania to be a sign of his insanity; at other times, it is a sign of divinest sense. When Ishmael theoretically likens the *Pequod*'s journey to "an Anacharsis Cloots deputation" (121), he smiles at the futile gestures of any revolutionary who, in the name of Man's divinity, seeks to lay the whole world's grievances before the bar. But when Ahab proclaims and carries out his assault on evil, as in "The Quarter Deck," his power is so transcendent that Ishmael admits "Ahab's quenchless feud seemed mine" (179).

To argue that Ishmael's darkening view of Ahab shows his prevailing commitment to the "just Spirit of Equality" is a misleading temptation. In spite of "The Try Works," Ahab is never grander or more human than in his last moments. When Ahab shares his grief with Starbuck, Ishmael pays him highest tribute: "From beneath his slouched hat Ahab dropped a tear into the sea; nor did all the Pacific contain such wealth as that one wee drop" (543). Before the crew sets out on the second day of the chase, Ishmael proudly accepts the compact that has bound all individual liberty beneath Ahab's will: "They were one man, not thirty. . . . All the individualities of the crew, this man's valor, that man's fear; guilt and guiltlessness, all varieties were welded into oneness, and were all directed to that fatal goal which Ahab their one lord and keel did point to" (557). When Ahab sets out on the third day, Starbuck calls him "noble heart" (566) rather than blasphemer. As Ahab rows out to his death, Ishmael abandons his longstanding suspicion that Ahab must be possessed by the devil's despair. When the whale surfaces for the last time, Ishmael redirects his Satanic metaphor: "maddened by yesterday's fresh irons that corroded in him, Moby Dick seemed combinedly possessed by all the angels that fell from heaven" (567).

The "just Spirit of Equality" is a muse Ishmael would like to affirm, but cannot demonstrate. Throughout the epic, it remains a standard by which Ahab is often criticized, but its absence as a fact renders it increasingly inappropriate to the heroic actions we witness. As the narrative proceeds, the pertinence of the democratic invocation wanes, and the stature of Ahab grows ever more central. As soon as Ishmael condemns Ahab by democratic or Christian standards, his admiration for Ahab's heroic courage is sure to resurface.

Ishmael senses the difficulty of bringing his invocation and his heroic narrative to ethical resolution. While squeezing lumps of whale sperm, Ishmael laughs at his own ecstatic visions of human brotherhood and domestic felicity. A scant ten pages later, he celebrates – equally self-consciously – the "Catskill eagle in some souls" that, however low into the gorge it may fly, "is still higher than other birds upon the plain" (425). Such shifts are signs of intellectual honesty rather than confusion. Ahab's evident superiority could never be compatible either with the "just Spirit of Equality" or with the American relish for deflating heroic pretension. The new epic literature, Melville knew, must both honor and question the stature of heroes seemingly superior in deed as well as attitude. Not all men are heroes, but one man might nonetheless represent the promise of New World culture. If the ship of state might be coming to an unexpectedly apocalyptic end, Ahab's countrymen would at least be reminded that epic grandeur and defeat had long been indivisible.

Throughout *Moby-Dick* all these ideas have to remain possibilities to be vividly exemplified at appropriate moments. To protest their inconsistency is an idle folly. As literature, their intermixture only enriches the book's significance without detracting from its firm, narrative center. Literary nationalists could protest that some variant of the "just Spirit of Equality" had been deemed essential to the American epic ever since the era of Tucker, Dwight, and Barlow. Traditionalists could reply that Ahab's readiness to die in honorable combat reaches far further backward – through Indian and Aztec literature, Scandinavian saga, Ossian, Camoens, *The Song of Roland, Beowulf,* and Virgil to Homer and Gilgamesh. Accompanying them both was a spirit of raillery against all pretense, Old World or New, a spirit that Irving had momentarily sounded in a Byronic mode, but that Melville was democratizing. However unlikely the assimilation of these three elements might be, all were needed for America's new unclassifiable heroic work. Somehow, Melville had managed to laugh at life's impermanence and literature's artifice, to glorify a spiritual autocrat, and yet to make the hope for divine equality seem admirable, even if unobtainable.

IV. ANOTHER ORPHAN

After the aged Ahab has drawn the *Pequod* into the Descartesian vortex, the world is quite literally left to lesser and younger Ishmaels. In Ahab's death, the epitome of the old heroic code, given a new metaphysical cast, seems to have passed away, perhaps forever. Ishmael addresses us from some less important society in which he clearly occupies no important place and from which he anticipates no important actions. His book, however, not only marks an end to an older kind of heroic literature; it predicts and exemplifies the new. Ishmael may remain marginal as a man, but he increasingly claims centrality as an author. In the act of writing *Moby-Dick*, Ishmael moves from being society's lonely outcast to being the world's expansive recreator. Exhilarated by the significance of his writing, he also laughs at himself for assuming that the world will care.

The energizing prospect of the writer becoming the comic hero of his own modern epic leads Ishmael to typically contradictory responses. At first he is gravely ceremonial about his possible achievement: "All the honor and glory" for having written a precious manuscript is to be ascribed to a whale ship that "was my Yale College and my Harvard" (112). But the absurdities of any system of classifying the whale soon leads Ishmael to self-puffery of a sexual and architectural sort: "For small erections may be finished by their first architects; grand ones, true ones, ever leave the copestone to posterity" (145). Sometimes Ishmael the writer, rather than Ahab the captain, becomes the true diver after metaphysics: "Oh Ahab! what shall be grand in thee, it must needs be plucked at from the skies, and dived for in the deep, and featured in the unbodied air" (148). At other times, the act of writing becomes a comic version of Ahab's Prometheanism: "With a frigate's anchors for my bridle-bitts and fasces of harpoons for spurs, would I could mount that whale and leap the topmost skies, to see whether the fabled heavens with all their countless tents really lie encamped beyond my mortal sight" (271).

As his book nears its end, however, Ishmael's once tentative assertions of the pen's power ("I am in earnest; and I will try" [136]; "This whole book is but a draught" [145]; "I try all things; I achieve what I can" [345]) are given total comic release:

> One often hears of writers that rise and swell with their subject, though it may seem but an ordinary one. How, then, with me, writing of this Leviathan? Unconsciously my chirography expands into placard capitals. Give me a condor's quill! Give me Vesuvius' crater for an inkstand! Friends, hold my arms! For in the mere act of penning my thoughts of this Leviathan, they weary me, and make me faint with their outreaching comprehensiveness of sweep, as if to include the whole circle

of the sciences, and all the generations of whales, and men, and masto-
dons, past, present, and to come, with all the revolving panoramas of
empire on earth, and throughout the whole universe, not excluding its
suburbs. Such, and so magnifying, is the virtue of a large and liberal
theme! We expand to its bulk. To produce a mighty book, you must
choose a mighty theme. No great and enduring volume can ever be
written on the flea, though many there be who have tried it. (456)

Crockett's brag about the powers of the body here becomes Crockettlike
brag about the powers of the word. The laughter of mock-epics that treat
minutiae like the flea is now to be applied to the largest of animals. By
writing his book, Ishmael can lay his own claim upon the bulk of the
whale, thereby superseding the intransigent Ahab, whom Moby Dick
can and will defeat. Ishmael's heroic subject is both "an ordinary one"
and yet "a mighty theme" because it includes the present as well as the
past – "the whole universe," not just its American suburb.

The tone of Ishmael's self-tribute remains grotesquely comic in its
assertion of the value of sheer size. Armed with his condor quill pen and
his crater inkstand, Ishmael has come "magnifying" himself to the verge
of a mock-epic apotheosis. Walt Whitman, blowing his self up into a
"kosmos," with his palms covering continents, could readily have heard
his own barbaric yawp sounding in Ishmael's voice. In Ishmael's self
description, the generic worries of Barlow, the careful restraints of Prescott are implicitly dismissed in the face of the New World's joyful ex-
pandabilities.

Shortly after *Moby-Dick* was published, Horace Greeley ventured to
describe Melville's book as "a 'Whaliad,' or the Epic of that venerable
old leviathan who esteemeth iron as straw."[48] Perplexed by the book's
genre, Duyckinck's friend William Allen Butler wrote: "We do not know
how we can better express our conception of [Melville's] general drift
and style in the work under consideration than by entitling it a prose
Epic on Whaling."[49] Aside from these two fleeting comments, however,
there seems to have been no attempt to locate Melville's work within the
traditions of epic or heroic romance. Among the considerable number of
reviews, there is a telling reluctance to discuss the issue of the genre of
national or New World literature – an issue Melville's text suggests on
every page. Part of the silence is due, of course, to the already established
cliché that Melville was a writer of entertaining, exotic narratives who
failed when he ventured into romance or metaphysics. Added to this
suspicion, however, was the prevalent wearied disbelief in the very idea
of the American epic. In 1843, the epic dimensions of Prescott's *History*
had been acknowledged, and Prescott's attempt to render Cortes as a
hero had been sharply attacked. Nine years later, after the drubbings that
the American epic had received from Poe, Longfellow, Lowell, Haw-

thorne, and Tuckerman, the prospect of further discussion must have aroused only a yawn, or the condescension of kindly silence.

By the mid-nineteenth century, American literary nationalists finally had been given two masterful prose works whose international subjects clearly belonged within the widening generic parameters of the epic tradition. For differing reasons, both works proved to be unacceptable either as American or New World epics. Without ever condoning annexation, Prescott had resisted the antiexpansionists' belief that New World heroism must be universally tolerant, pacifistic, and egalitarian. Although Melville shared the progressive values of literary nationalists, he knew too much about the tragic power of heroic poetry ever to endorse them wholeheartedly. Whereas Prescott had chosen the most timely of historical subjects, but applied predemocratic values to them, Melville wrote his "Whaliad" at a time when the disgraced genre of epic was still thought to preclude the comedy needed to revivify it.

Moby-Dick was to be, as Melville suspected, the "inmost leaf" of his achievement, after which "the flower must fall to the mould."[50] To regard Melville's writings from *Pierre* through *Billy Budd* as signs of fading powers is, of course, a critical luxury that only the existence of a *Moby-Dick* can justify. Nonetheless, Melville's failure to achieve recognition as a transformer of epic tradition seems to have remained among the many ironic perceptions of his later days. At some time after 1860, Melville wrote a diptychlike pair of poems that linked his own literary fortunes with those of his admired predecessor in modern sea epic. "Camoens Before" summons back Lombardo's and Ishmael's hopes that they might "flame to the height of ancient song" by gazing long into purgative fires, thereby separating Truth from "flying herds of themes" and from "new worlds of dreams." "Camoens After" measures the gains Melville feels his epic effort has won:

> What now avails the pageant verse,
> Trophies and arms with music borne?
> Base is the world; and some rehearse
> How noblest meet ignoble scorn.
> Vain now the ardor, vain thy fire,
> Delirium mere, unsound desire:
> Fate's knife hath ripped the chorded lyre.
> Exhausted by the exacting lay,
> Thou dost but fall a surer prey
> To wile and guile ill understood;
> While they who work them, fair in face,
> Still keep their strength in prudent place,
> And claim they worthier run life's race,
> Serving high God with useful good.

>   "Camoens (After)"[51]

Ishmael's joy in the absurd magnifications of writing the new epic has vanished. Defiant accusations against "Fate's knife" and scorn for the common herd, attitudes reminiscent of Ahab, have proven to be the last cindered apple of Melville's endeavor.

8

"AN EPIC OF DEMOCRACY?"

"The Care & Feeding of Long Poems" was Henry's title
for his next essay, which will come out when
he wants it to.
A Kennedy-sponsored bill for the protection
of poets from long poems will benefit the culture
and do no harm to that kind Lady, Mrs. Johnson.

John Berryman, *Dream Songs*, #354 (1966)

I.

Berryman's defensive mockery of his own poem expresses joy
in his determined pursuit of an admittedly problematic tradition. The
legacy of Whitman's personal epic, it seems, is forever to question its
own brashest claims. Works like *Leaves of Grass* seem the essence of
modernist poetic ambition, yet their authors worry whether such poems,
taken as a whole, are more than endlessly protracted, self-indulgent dream
songs. To assess Whitman's claims upon modern epic demands flexibility without abandoning all terms of definition. As Melville's *Mardi* reminds us, to ask the question properly may be more important than any
answer we might provide.

Durable and persuasive epics may appear in prose rather than verse,
may invent legends rather than transmit them, may glorify national destiny or ignore it, may end in heroic death or heroic conquest. Epics may
be written or sung, may concern a past history or a present fiction. They
may certainly slight the many conventions (Proposition, Invocation, catalogues, similes, type scenes, etc.) that for centuries were considered essential to the epic genre. Whether any epic can abandon continuous narrative, however, is deeply problematic, for the very word *epos* connotes
the telling of sequential deeds, whether they have begun *in medias res* or

not. Aristotle may have demanded an absolute shapeliness of narrative that many a great epic lacks, but his insistence that epics must be stories told about human actions has not yet been effectively overturned.[1] Far more is at stake here than the generic question of whether celebrative, nonnarrative poetry strains the definition of *epos* into a meaningless catchall. The crucial issue is whether any extended work of heroic literature can abandon narrative tale-telling and yet remain readable and memorable to the people who must, finally, determine its epic stature. Whether or not *Leaves of Grass* is considered an American epic by the academy, Walt Whitman foresaw its ultimate test: "The proof of a poet is that his country absorbs him as affectionately as he has absorbed it."[2]

The 1855 Preface, Whitman's public letter to Emerson, *An American Primer*, and "Song of Myself" all would have us believe that *Leaves of Grass* is a self-generated, "autocthonous" song that "tallies" with its country's spirit because it defies all literary precedents, especially old bards who glorified battle (Homer) or feudalism (Shakespeare). This stance, crucial to establishing the independence of New World song, only confirms Whitman's sensitivity to notions of the heroic current among recent men of letters. Whitman's controlling motive, he repeatedly said, was to "faithfully express, in literary or poetic form, and uncompromisingly, my own physical, emotional, moral, intellectual, and aesthetic Personality."[3] Whitman's conviction that the self's visionary power has replaced battle bravery as the essence of modern heroism aligns *Leaves of Grass* both with *The Excursion* and *The Prelude*. "To put a *Person*, a human being (myself, in the latter half of the Nineteenth Century, in America,) freely, fully and truly on record"[4] is a democratic recasting of the "heroic argument" Wordsworth had advanced in book three of *The Prelude*:

> Of Genius, Power,
> Creation and Divinity itself
> I have been speaking, for my theme has been
> What pass'd within me. Not of outward things
> Done visibly for other minds, words, signs,
> Symbols or actions; but of my own heart
> Have I been speaking, and my youthful mind.[5]

For Whitman, as for Wordsworth, internal battle has replaced external battle, and heroism is revealed in perceptions rather than actions. Unlike Wordsworth, however, Whitman insists on extending his experiences and his heroic perceptions to all men, not merely to Americans, because New World culture has made universal heroism possible. Wordsworth established the idea of a personal epic, but retained chronological narrative while tracing the growth of the poet's mind. Developing Wordsworth's personalism, Whitman democratizes heroic perception, but

abandons even a personal narrative in order to celebrate the heroic potential of all men.

Tocqueville was to offer perhaps the shrewdest model for the new heroic poetry of the self. Although he does not use the word "epic," Tocqueville's model American poet has known the disillusionments of recent epic attempts. The American poet, Tocqueville concludes, believes himself deprived of all intervening deities, all myths, all class differences, all superior heroes, all reverence for the past. In their place, the democratic poet possesses two related subjects: Man and his march across the Western continent. On the one hand, the American poet must find the heroic model of all democratic individuals in himself: "I need not traverse earth and sky to discover a wondrous object, woven of contrasts, of infinite greatness and littleness, of intense gloom and amazing brightness, capable at once of exciting pity, admiration, terror, contempt. I have only to look at myself."[6] On the other hand, the American poet will be drawn toward submerging his self within the "magnificent image" of men en masse devoting their energies to the westward march of democracy.[7] Here Tocqueville exactly predicts the two reflexive processes upon which "Song of Myself" would be built: taking All into the Self, then projecting the Self into All; inspiration and then respiration; loafing on the grass, and traveling the open road.

After the publication of Democracy in America, similar notions of America's heroic self-image could be found in calls for contemporary heroic poems. In 1845, Duyckinck lamented "We have no great poem of action or invention at all approaching an Epic character," but he was also certain that "a quick-witted, inventive people . . . who have subdued mountains and thickets and whirlpools" would soon have their "laughingly effortless energy" properly commemorated.[8] Edwin P. Whipple, whom Whitman much admired, wrote an essay titled "Heroic Character" in which he contended that, for sensitive moderns, "Heroism is no sparkling epigram of action, but a luminous epic of character."[9] To Whipple, the highest hero could never again be the soldier, the patriot, nor the reformer, but would be a prophet possessing "ecstatic spiritual vision" and "unwearied spiritual energy" (102). Emerson's call for an American Homer, which Whitman clearly had read, summoned a Genius with tyrannous eye who would perceive "the value of our incomparable materials," a value evident even "in the barbarism and materialism of the times."[10] What is remarkable in all these claims is that none of them worry about the old need to specify a hero, narrative, or deed. Unlike both Melville and Prescott, Duyckinck, Whipple, and Emerson believe that the substance of New World epic literature must reside in the heroic potential that has been gathering energy in each of our selves.

The problems and the promise of this new personal epic are thought-

fully explored in Jones Very's forty-page essay titled "Epic Poetry" (1839).[11] In a colossal but handy misreading of the epic's origin, Very concludes that the Homeric world was mankind's childhood, a simple era when physical problems were resolved in physical ways.[12] Once Christian civilization began, human dilemmas became spiritual and psychological, leading poets like Dante and Milton to embody interior conflicts in physical confrontations. Now, however, the Progress of the Mind has "unfolded a new form of the heroic character, one which finds no paradise, nay, no heaven for itself in the creations of Milton, and for whom the frowns of Dante's hell have no terror" (3). As modern man perceives the world, action has become primarily mental and power primarily verbal: "The wonder and interest of the world is now transferred to the mind, whose thought is action, and whose word is power" (15).

Very's belief that these Transcendentalist notions of change are true leads him to conclude that any new epic poem that represents greatness in deeds will be a dead relic:

> It is in the greatness of the epic action that the poets succeeding Homer, if we except Milton, have failed; and the causes which have operated against them, will always operate with increasing force against every attempt to represent the present or future developments of the heroic character in action. (14–15)

"Action" in the Aristotelian sense is thereby barred from future heroic verse; astute contemporaries know that any individual's deed is merely particular, whereas the spirit is universal. In a twice repeated comment prophetic of "Song of Myself," Very concludes that the taking of Troy was only of interest because "Man viewed himself with reference to the world; not, as in the present day, the world in reference to himself" (12, 31, 34). Because modern man divides his universe into the Me and the Not Me, no past action of any other man will ever again have the heroic resonance necessary for epic.

Although the entire tradition from Homer through Milton's imitators thus emerges as a historical curiosity, Very is nonetheless reluctant to conclude that epic poetry is therefore dead: "Could intellectual power be represented with the same objectiveness as physical power, there might be as many epics now as there are great minds" (36). The difficulty now, Very concludes, is to find adequate poetic means of picturing spiritual conflict. "What can *now* alone make any subject for epic interest great, is the action made *visible* of a superior intellect on an inferior" (36). Searching for modern heroic works that have reified the new spiritual heroism, Very offers The Prelude, Sartor Resartus, and the Meditations and Harmonies of Lamartine. But Very does not call any of these works epics, nor does he suggest how the spiritual conflicts within them possess a convincing heroic quality. At the essay's end, Very virtually retracts his hope

for a new kind of heroic poetry. Wordsworth, Carlyle, and Lamartine seem to have been groping toward a dead end: "We have thus endeavored to show the inability of the human mind, at the present day, to represent objectively its own action on another mind, and that the power to do this could alone enable the poet to embody in his hero the present development of the heroic character, and give to his poem a universal interest" (37).

"Epic Poetry" stops at the threshold of the questions that were to bedevil writers of personal or visionary epic from Walt Whitman through Charles Olson: How does one sustain a long, heroic poem without narrative? Can the poet's imaginative powers convincingly replace bravery as the essence of heroism? How does one represent inner spiritual conflict in visual images? Can the link between the poet's voice and his culture's vitality be maintained without absurd self-aggrandizement? How much self-mockery is permissible if the visionary writer is still to be the hero? Finally, are such poems the modern development of the epic tradition, or only the ironic evidence of its irrelevance and impossibility?

With the advantage of twentieth-century hindsight, Lukacs succinctly defined the problems Very could only suggest:

> The aesthetic problem, the transformation of mood and reflexion, of lyricism and psychology, into genuinely epic means of expression, is therefore centered on the fundamental ethical problem – the question of necessary and possible action. The human type of the central character in works of this kind is in essence a contemplative rather than an active one, and so the epic representation of such a type is faced with the problem of how his rhapsodically retiring or hesitant behaviour can be translated into action.[13]

Apart from the pushing and hauling, projecting his world from one leaf of grass, the poet of "Song of Myself" is a contemplative, solitary, and rhapsodic protagonist if ever there were one. By simply proclaiming the superiority of vision over analysis, Whitman craftily sidestepped the problematic issues Very had raised about new heroic verse. Worry not, the 1855 Preface assures us. Embodying New World spiritual heroism in visual images is to become the new form of action; greatness is the poet in each of us.

II. INVENTING THE SELF

At the time Whitman wrote the first edition of *Leaves of Grass*, he was certain of one genre to which his poems did *not* belong:

> The expression of the American poet is to be transcendent and new. It is to be indirect and not direct or descriptive or epic. Its quality goes through these to much more. Let the age and wars of other nations be chanted and their eras and characters be illustrated and that finish the

verse. Not so the great psalm of the republic. Here the theme is creative and has vista.[14]

This crucial quotation, habitually overlooked by those who would associate Whitman's great early verse with the epic, severs New World heroic poetry from Old World epic tradition. For Whitman, "epic" clearly refers to finished, descriptive poems that deal with the past wars of European nations. His own New World heroic poetry, by contrast, shall be an ever-changing "psalm" that shall invoke, through indirect suggestion, the grand future of these states and every self within them. The term "psalm" suggests that *Leaves of Grass* is to be regarded as America's prophetic scripture, a new form of verse more closely aligned to the Bible or the Upanishads than to Homer. The word also suggests, however, that Whitman has found a solution to Very's problem of visualizing the psychological impress of a great spirit upon lesser ones. All New World democrats become the psalmist's imagined audience. The poet appears in two sometimes indistinguishable guises: an oral bard lifting republican spirits, and a soapbox orator relishing his own brag. True poetry is not the verse on the page, but its effect upon every contemporary it can reach.

Prophetic psalmody, not epic narration. This distinction is quite consistent with other testimony about Whitman's initial literary purpose. The Carlyle he greatly admired was a visionary who "shakes our comfortable reading circles with a touch of the old Hebraic anger and prophecy."[15] True prophecy, Whitman then explains, is not mere prediction, but projection: "It means one whose mind bubbles up and pours forth as a fountain, from inner divine spontaneities revealing God" (250). Whitman may also have known Carlyle's charge that Virgil and Milton had sacrificed their poetic powers to "that fatal consciousness, that knowledge that they are writing an epic – the plot, the style, all is vitiated by that one fault."[16] When explaining "the preparation of my poetic field" in "A Backward Glance," Whitman claims to have been convinced by Poe's argument "that there can be no such thing as a long poem" (569). If Whitman had read "The Poetic Principle" shortly after its publication in 1849 he would have encountered Poe's claim that "the ultimate, aggregate or absolute effect of even the best epic under the sun, is a nullity."[17] Although Whitman insisted he had believed the long poem to be outdated before reading Poe, he also acknowledged that "Poe's argument, though short, work'd the sum out and proved it to me."[18]

Statements of the 1850s attest that Whitman knew *Leaves of Grass* must be free of the "fatal consciousness" of his attempting any kind of epic: "Take no illustrations from the ancients or classics"; "Don't fall into the Ossianic, by any chance"; "Old forms, old poems, majestic and proper in their own lands, here in this land are exiles"; "What is to be done is to

withdraw from precedents"; "Not the first recognition of gods or god-desses, or Greece or Rome"; *Paradise Lost* is "offensive to modern science and intelligence."[19] Perhaps the clearest statement of Whitman's disruptive antitraditionalism is to be found in *An American Primer*:

> I say we have here, now, a greater age to celebrate, greater ideas to embody, than anything ever in Greece or Rome – or in the names of Jupiters, Jehovahs, Apollos and their myths. . . . What is America for? – to commemorate the old myths and the Gods? To repeat the Mediterranean here? – No: – (Na-o-o) but to destroy all these from the purposes of the earth, and to erect a new earth in their place.[20]

For the early Whitman, the supposed greatness of epic tradition – with all its superior heroes, hoary conventions, outmoded Gods, and tragic overtones – was perhaps the literary "myth" most in need of destruction. "To destroy" the old conventions would not transform the epic, but end it.

Although the epic needed to be discarded, heroism had to be redefined so that the psalmist's audience would risk creating their "new earth." Throughout the 1855 preface, Whitman links the word "heroism" with androgynous traits that neither Achilles, Ulysses, Aeneas, Cortes, nor Ahab had valued or exemplified. "Liberty takes the adherence of heroes wherever men and women exist"; "Here is the hospitality which forever indicates heroes"; "A heroic person walks at his ease through and out of that custom or precedent or authority that suits him not."[21] Protean flexibility, rebelliousness, liberty, hospitality, openness to all people – these are the qualities of an ideal democratic Self whose timelessness is proclaimed with blithe disregard for the entire literary past. Such rebelliousness against heroic literary traditions, far beyond anything imagined by Prescott or Melville, proved to be one of the great liberating forces in the history of poetry. Without Whitman's willingness to defy Old World tradition simply because it was Old World tradition, his discovery of organic free verse might not have been possible.[22] Those who would see Whitman within a tradition of epic literature should recognize that the energy sustaining his early verse came not from his adaptation of traditions (as for Prescott and Melville) but from his defiant rejection of them.

To write a heroic poem that would not be regarded as "direct or descriptive or epic" drew Whitman toward new techniques that would better fit democratic prophecy. Instead of the highly finished verse forms and sublime diction of Pope and Milton, Whitman would incorporate slang, colloquialisms, and foreign words into a fully polyglossic American idiom that could convey all truth precisely because it was "barbaric yawp" (89). A nonnarrative structure for his own "long poem" could be achieved by replacing a single hero's deeds with everyman's heroic vision. At the outset the reader was to be confronted with a photograph of

a cocky, shirtsleeved American Genius with whose namelessness everyone could identify. Instead of an elaborate Proposition repeating the conventional phrase "Of ———— I sing," America's heroic poem would begin with a brash seriocomic self-assertion, immediately democratized:

> I celebrate myself
> And what I assume you shall assume
> For every atom belonging to me as good belongs to you. [23]

If each celebrated Self contains everyone (Christ, beggar, mountain man,
and whore), the Muse and any divine machinery must emanate entirely
from within the poet. The Self's ecstatic vision accordingly begins, not
when an external muse inspires the singer, but when the Self's body and
soul are sexually joined into one. Toward the end of his "kosmic" vision,
the poet can brag that he has first outbid, then purchased, and finally set
aside such "old cautious hucksters" as Jehovah, Zeus, Hercules, Brahma,
Manito, (Carlyle's) Odin, and (Prescott's) "hideous-faced Mexitli" (71–
2). After "accepting the rough, deific sketches to fill out better in myself" (72), Whitman resolves all worry about the deity by the seemingly
offhand remark, "In the faces of men and women I see God, and in my
own face in the glass" (83).

The jaunty tone of "Song of Myself" enables Whitman to tread the
margin between heroic and mock-heroic. We laugh at the Self's giantism
because we recognize that to be "kosmos" is to be an artifice always in
process, a quantity of energy forever being created and transformed by
the poet's own words:

> This hour I tell things in confidence,
> I might not tell everybody but I will tell you.
>
> Who goes there! hankering, gross, mystical, nude?
> How is it I extract strength from the beef I eat?
>
> What is a man anyhow? What am I? and what are you? (43)

The hidden origin of these lines is the epic type scene of a God's arrival,
that marvelous moment when an Athena, Venus, or Raphael assumes
visual shape and provides direction to a hero's life. Here, however, the
God who arrives is the poet's own Self, invoked by four of his own
exclamatory adjectives as if He were a separate being. Those four adjectives ("hankering, gross, mystical, nude"), which are contradictory in
content and many-layered in language, point toward a Self whose divinity exists in a comic "hankering" after the undefinable. The Self who
"goes there" in fact yields up no revelation at all. Whitman slyly begins
by promising to tell any and every reader "things in confidence," but he
ends by asking five questions to which there are no answers. His tone
can be both heroic and comic because the unanswerability of all five

questions proves to be of no moment beside the sheer energy of the mystical human animal.

Only the less important epic conventions were transformed rather than tacitly upended. Whitman's catalogues (Sections 15 and 33) have to be longer than Homer's because they are declared to be potentially limitless. When Homer named the ships and warriors that came to Troy, he was singling out special men and special peoples to be communally remembered for their special undertaking. Whitman's catalogues make boastful show of a world where every individual and every occupation have equal, divine stature. In similar fashion, Whitman jokingly transforms the long prophecy spoken atop a high hill. Irrelevant now is the tradition that reserved glorious visions only for single heroes, but then made the unknowable future wearisomely available to all. In the forty-sixth section of "Song of Myself," the poet leads "each man and each woman of you . . . upon a knoll" and then points down "the public road" every democratic hero is to tread (80). Instead of recounting the future in historical detail, as Anchises, Virgil, Michael, and Hesper had done, Whitman abruptly counsels:

> Not I, not any on else can travel that road for you,
> You must travel it for yourself.
> ....
> You are also asking me questions and I hear you
> I answer that I cannot answer, you must find out for yourself. (80)

In order to deflate this stale epic convention, Whitman makes good use of American slang ("Shoulder your duds, dear son") while modifying the oldest of metaphors for the moment of sudden insight ("Now I wash the gum from your eyes"[24]). Unlike Melville, Whitman thus mixes levels of language in order brashly to assure us that Truth exists in every rank and order. But because there is now no single truth for all people, the divine herald must be the outsized poet himself, whose ultimate heroic act (vaunted "procreations" notwithstanding) is to release the visionary imagination of the listener. The new epic journey is to loaf on the grass.

Despite such transformations of tradition, there are compelling intrinsic reasons for agreeing with Whitman's judgment that the 1855 *Leaves of Grass* should not be regarded as any new kind of epic. The most obvious argument, that everyone cannot be a hero without heroism losing all meaning, is probably the least important. Like Barlow, Whitman is intent upon suggesting mankind's potential rather than stating a fact; surely Achilles, Odysseus, Aeneas, and Beowulf had been held forth as models whom the poems' audiences might in some way imitate. The clearly traceable development of the visionary experience provides a

structure that sustains a poem of the moderate length of "Song of My-self."[25] It is rather Whitman's attitudes toward death and war that force us to separate his poem from epic literature. As soon as any poet con-tends that "the smallest sprout shows there is really no death" (30), he has denied his hero the renown of sacrificing his life for honor or com-munity. It is never "lucky to die" (30) in epic literature, nor can Hector or Roland, Guatemozin or Ahab, ever grow from under the reader's bootsoles.

Because mortality has no meaning, Whitman can readily celebrate both the victories and the defeats of war, but he cannot exalt heroic death. To show how "agonies are one of my changes of garments" (62), Whitman devotes sequential sections of "Song of Myself" to the deaths of a fire-man and an old artillerist, to the murder of 412 Texas Rangers, and to the *Bon Homme Richard*'s victory over the *Serapis*. In none of these ac-counts does an individual emerge who knowingly seeks death for the sake of honor; in all of them, Whitman's emphasis is on the sudden, unexpected suffering, the "agonies" of wartime. The purpose of being the man who suffered and was there is clearly not to glorify heroic death but to prepare the reader to recognize, two sections later, that the Self's truest identity is Christ. As soon as "the corpses rise . . . the gashes heal . . . the fastenings roll away" (69), everyman's transfiguration into im-mortal life renders the tragedy of sacrificial death quite superfluous. Within the poet's visionary experiences, the sequence from travel to war to death to resurrection to prophecy lends to sections 30–48 a coherent, nonnar-rative "action," but it is a structure that works against the epic tradition, rather than within it.

"Song of Myself" is thus a work that enables us to differentiate clearly between heroic literature and epic, not so much in form as in attitude toward the conduct of life. Admittedly, no long poem has better illus-trated that all heroic literature involves some kind of quest after life-enhancing knowledge. It was, after all, Joseph Campbell and not Walt Whitman who observed that "Any blade of grass may assume, in myth, the figure of the savior and conduct the questing wanderer into the sanc-torum of his own heart."[26] But because Whitman renders heroic death irrelevant, his poem willfully defies the sense of tragic dignity common to epic literature from *Gilgamesh* through Melville. To proclaim the Self divine is to replace mortal courage with visionary daring. In 1855 Whit-man celebrates that change, insisting that the power of his new verse is not traceable to any epic precedent.

III. SINGING THE NATION

The 1867 and 1871 editions of *Leaves of Grass* were assembled by a poet who has greatly qualified, if not reversed, his insistence that his

New World poetry is not of the epic kind. The 1867 edition is the first to begin with "One's Self I Sing," a poem which, in form and content, is clearly a Proposition for an epic. To the 1871 edition, Whitman added two new poems, "As I Ponder'd in Silence" and "Song of the Exposition," which describe a "Phantom" muse of war poetry and the Berkeleyan migration of the epic muse from Greece to America. Lest readers miss his new generic intent, Whitman added the phrase "and sing myself" to the first line of his longest poem. The Divine Literatus invoked in *Democratic Vistas* no longer defies Old World bards; instead, he seeks to combine the fire of the Jewish prophet, "the epic talent of Homer," and the manly pride of Shakespearean heroes with the new truths of democracy and science.[27] By the time Whitman wrote his 1872 preface titled "As a Strong Bird on Pinions Free," he was prepared to describe *Leaves of Grass* as an "attempt at utterance, of New World songs, and an epic of Democracy" (739). The clearest sign of his altered intent occurred during his preparation of the fourth edition of 1867. In his notebooks Whitman added up the number of words in *Leaves of Grass* and compared his total with those of five other texts: The Bible, *The Iliad, The Aeneid, The Divine Comedy,* and *Paradise Lost.*[28]

Although Whitman never specified why *Leaves of Grass* always had been (or had recently become) an "epic of Democracy," we can recover some of the reasons for his change of intent. In the 1860 edition of *Leaves of Grass* Whitman's attitude toward death had darkened remarkably. "As I Ebb'd with the Ocean of Life" describes death as the end of life's tidal wreckage. The carols sung to death in "Out of the Cradle, Endlessly Rocking" and "When Lilacs Last in the Dooryard Bloom'd" welcome Death as a soothing release from the pain of living, rather than a lucky moment of reassimilation. Whitman happened to arrive at this grim consolation shortly before the onset of the Civil War, which he, like many others, welcomed as a tragic test through which republican greatness was to be triumphantly reaffirmed. The poet who had once scorned war as a subject for New World heroic poetry soon incorporated *Drum-Taps* into *Leaves of Grass* and came to regard it as essential to his newly epic endeavor.

In addition to these causes, we may advance a more conjectural motive. After four editions of *Leaves of Grass* had been published to no widespread acclaim, Whitman had begun to recognize that his country had not absorbed him with the same fervor that he had absorbed his country. To align his book within the epic tradition, to regard the *Leaves* as a New World development of Homer and Milton, was to claim for his book the stature he understandably felt it had long deserved.

The Civil War made later editions of *Leaves of Grass* more national and patriotic, less a heroic poem for the entire New World. The reunion

of North and South became the necessary political premise of Whitman's restored faith in the individual. Because death was final after all, a young man's uncomplaining endurance of death now proved the valor of the reconstructed American Self. Anxious comparisons to epic tradition, very like chaplain Brackenridge's claims for the Revolution, now surface in the letters Whitman wrote about the dying wounded he saw in hospitals of the Union army:

> To these, what are your dramas and poems, even the oldest and tear-fullest? Not the old Greek mighty ones, where man contends with fate (and always yields) – not Virgil showing Dante on and on among the agonized & damned approach what here I see and take a part in.[29]

As the war receded, its importance as a validation of American heroism grew ever stronger, both as a historical fact and as the central event of *Leaves of Grass*. In "Memoranda During the War" (1875), Whitman asserts that the Civil War was "the Vertebrer of Poetry and Art, (of personal character too,) for all future America (far more grand, in my opinion, to the hands capable of it, than Homer's siege of Troy)."[30] By 1881 Whitman was contending that the War of the Secession would prove to be for American poetry exactly "what the ancient siege of Illium and the puissance of Hector's and Agamemnon's warriors proved to Hellenic art and literature, and *all* art and literature since" (italics mine).[31] When Whitman wrote "A Backward Glance" (1888), the import of America's Trojan War had so grown upon him that it led him into a revealing falsity: "I know very well that my 'Leaves' could not possibly have emerged or been fashion'd or completed, from any other era than the latter half of the Nineteenth Century, nor any other land than democratic America, and from the absolute triumph of the National Union arms" (566). To ignore the fact that three editions of *Leaves of Grass* had been fashioned and completed before the war shows the fading of Whitman's belief that the Self's heroism could be convincingly portrayed in a universal vision rather than in historic national warfare.

The two poems that open the 1891 edition reveal Whitman's new desire to connect his book directly with epic tradition. "One's Self I Sing" (1867) fits a version of his former heresies into the conventional form of an epic Proposition:

> One's-Self I sing, a simple separate person,
> Yet utter the word Democratic, the word En-Masse.
>
> Of physiology from top to toe I sing,
> Not physiognomy alone nor brain alone is worthy for the Muse,
>   I say the Form complete is worthier far,
> The Female equally with the Male I sing.

Of life immense in passion, pulse, and power,
Cheerful, for freest action form'd under the laws divine,
The Modern Man I sing. (1)

Here the cocky personal self who had greeted us in the 1855 volume has
receded into an earnest Modern Man. "The Muse" is invoked in the
traditional form as an inspirational force outside of the speaker. Whitman's stress is on modernity rather than universality, on evocations of
abstract forces that had once been concretely embodied. The poet's direct
claim upon his reader ("What I shall assume, you shall assume") has been
replaced by a Tocquevillean conundrum of republican theory: How can
men who are purportedly equal and alike still exemplify American individuality? To celebrate the equality of the Modern without proposing
any narrative is exactly suited to the postwar bard who has begun to
think of his book as an epic of democracy.

"As I Ponder'd in Silence" (1871) announces Whitman's new epic purpose with an evasive ambiguity needed for a poet who knows that both
"Song of Myself" and "Drum-Taps" are to follow. While pondering his
growing book of poems, Whitman is astonished when a terrible "Phantom," identified as "The genius of poets of old lands," suddenly rises to
admonish him:

"What singest thou?" it said,
"Know'st thou not there is but one theme for ever-enduring bards?
And that is the theme of War, the fortune of battles,
The making of perfect soldiers."

Whitman's reply to the Old World muse is to agree with its conclusion,
but redefine its demand:

"Be it so," then I answer'd,
"I too haughty Shade also sing war, and a longer and greater one than
any,
Waged in my book with varying fortune, with flight,
advance and retreat, victory deferr'd and wavering,
(Yet methinks certain, or as good as certain, at the last,) the field, the
world,
For life and death, for the Body and for the eternal Soul,
Lo, I too am come, chanting the chant of battles,
I above all promote brave soldiers!" (2)

Whitman's reply clearly asserts that, for New World bards, the warfare
of life has supplanted martial conflict; an inner spiritual conflict, as Jones
Very had believed, has become the true heroic argument for modern
man. And yet these lines do not wholly exclude battle heroism. The war
greater than any, waged with advance, retreat, and deferred victory, certainly might include the great War of Secession. Just as life is often seen

as inner war in "Song of Myself," so the Civil War would become a
metaphor of inner conflict in "Drum-Taps."

Whitman's comparisons of the Trojan War with the Civil War all assert that, for some unspecified reason, the Civil War demonstrated the
higher heroism. The "Drum-Taps" section of *Leaves of Grass* enables us
to infer Whitman's reasoning. The finality of death lends a tragic heroism
to today's young soldiers as well as to Hector or Turnus, but modern
battle-deaths are of a different kind. The young men of "Vigil Strange I
Kept on the Field One Night," "A Sight in Camp in the Daybreak Gray
and Dim," or "The Wound Dresser" are not heroic because they knowingly died for honor. They are heroic because they nobly suffered an
unjust, unexpected death for the sake of the nation's restoration. The
differing fates of the vanquished point towards a similarly progressive
historicism. The future faced by Hector's Trojans, Turnus's Italians,
Sanutee's Yemassee, or Guatemozin's Aztecs hardly provided comforting assurance of the world's moral justice. To Whitman, however,
America's heroic tragedy has had a purgative outcome confirmed but not
created by the will of the individual. "Reconciliation" suggests that the
face of the Southern enemy has been washed white by the poet's kiss.
The irrevocable deadness of the Southerner reminds us, however, that
the poet's love is, in practical effect, little more than a gesture. Consequently, poems like "Over the Carnage Rose Prophetic a Voice" subordinate the individual to political abstractions:

> The dependence of Liberty shall be lovers,
> The continuancy of Equality shall be comrades.
>
> These shall tie you and band you stronger than hoops of iron,
> I, ecstatic, O partners! O lands! With the love of lovers tie you.
>
> (Were you looking to be held together by lawyers?
> Or by an agreement on a paper? or by arms?
> Nay, nor the world, nor any living thing, will so cohere) (316)

Timeless extrahuman forces of Liberty and Equality now tie former enemies together in love. To be the nation's wound-dresser is to offer one's
individuality to the greater service of a political reconciliation that is itself
providential. As "Passage to India" was to show ("O Thou transcendent
. . . Swiftly I shrivel at the thought of God" [419]), Whitman's representative self, no longer seeing God's face in the glass, quietly abandons the
comic vaunt of self-sufficiency.

Whitman's longer postwar poems show how his new hopes for a
democratic national epic drew him away from celebrating the life force
in all things and back to panegyric based on cultural symbols. "Song of
the Exposition" (1871) returns to the continuities of Berkeley's *Translatio*

Studii. No matter how new in manner Whitman's lines may be, they are a century old in matter:

> Come Muse Migrate from Greece and Ionia
> Cross out please those immensely overpaid accounts,
> That matter of Troy and Achilles' wrath, and Aeneas', Odysseus' wan-
> derings,
> Placard "Removed" and "To Let" on the rocks of your snowy Parnas-
> sus,
> Repeat at Jerusalem, place the notice high on Jaffa's gate,
> and on Mount Moriah,
> The same on the walls of your German, French and Spanish castles,
> and Italian collections,
> For know a better, fresher, busier sphere, a wide untried domain
> awaits, demands you. (196)

Wretched imitative poems may have vastly overpaid the American debt to Old World epics, but Whitman nonetheless urges the old Muse to emigrate to America. Instead of maintaining his defiance of epic tradition, Whitman is now intent upon adapting it to a "wide, untried domain" – much like Barlow or Paulding three generations before him.

Once his invocation has been completed, Whitman can find no narrative, no deed, no person, and no event that might convey his sense of American heroism. He begins with the half-serious notion that, amid rapidly industrializing America, the Muse must find heroism in democracy's products:

> By thud of machinery and shrill steam-whistle undismay'd,
> Bluff'd not a bit by drain-pipe, gasometers, artificial fertilizers,
> Smiling and pleas'd with palpable intent to stay,
> She's here, install'd amid the kitchen ware! (198)

Now apologizing for his rudeness of manner, Whitman proceeds to substitute an imagined symbol as evidence of America's heroic culture.

> We plan even now to raise, beyond them all,
> Thy great cathedral sacred industry. (199)

Throughout six remaining pages, Whitman invokes his industrial cathedral, sometimes likening it to New York's Crystal Palace,[32] sometimes to the Union, sometimes to any American museum or hall of science, and finally to the flag itself. If the "Song of the Exposition" could convince us that the old Muse can still make poetry of her new scientific and democratic habitat, Whitman's verse might, sad to say, have been more imitative but considerably better. The "Song of the Exposition" has, of course, nothing to do with epic discourse at all. It is patriotic rhetoric in praise of material things, none of which Whitman invests with significance for the human spirit. As literature, such verse is no more persua-

sive than Barlow's couplets; as cultural prophecy, it is hollow beyond
Barlow's imagining.

In the final edition of *Leaves of Grass,* the long poem entitled "By Blue
Ontario's Shore" was placed immediately after "Memories of President
Lincoln" and "Drum-Taps," almost precisely halfway through the volume. Containing some 300 lines from the 1855 Preface, to which in 1867
Whitman added five new sections, "By Blue Ontario's Shore" was clearly
intended to provide a reinvocation of the muse suitable for a newly reunited nation. In place and in kind, it recalls Milton's reinvocation at the
beginning of Book Seven of *Paradise Lost* when his Argument turned
from heavenly warfare to creation and the Fall. Whitman begins his poem
with new lines in which the epic muse, still "A phantom, gigantic su-
perb," reaccosts him, demanding that Whitman "Chant me the carol of
victory," "strike up the marches of Libertad," and sing "the song of the
throes of Democracy" (340). In Section Seven "Libertad" makes her
promised appearance, looking perilously like an eighteenth-century Columbia who has been to Appomatox:

> Lo, high toward heaven, this day,
> Libertad, from the conqueress' field return'd,
> I mark the new aureola around your head,
> No more of soft astral, but dazzling and fierce,
> With war's flames and the lambent lightnings playing,
> And your port immovable where you stand. (346)

Humorless republican iconography had evidently not expired with *The
Fredoniad.* Before statuesque Libertad departs, she divulges that "the mission of poets" is not to sing the deeds of heroes but to praise the "warlike
flag of the great Idea" (348). Never exactly defined, "the great Idea"
presumably links both Democracy and Progress with the power, growth,
and prosperity of these newly reunited states.

To wrap heroism in the flag does not accord well with old lines from
the 1855 Preface praising a poet who is "no arguer" but judges "as the
sun falling around a helpless thing" (347). The bard of "By Blue Ontario's Shore" is so intent on his "great Idea" that he neglects both the Self
and the concretely realized objects that the Self had once absorbed. The
similar placement of Whitman's and Milton's reinvocations, whether intended by Whitman or not, is sadly to his disadvantage. In 1867 Whitman had as good reason as Milton to acknowledge that he had "fall'n on
evil days" and therefore must "fit audience find, though few."[33] Whitman, however, will not allow his own troubles (dismissal, lack of recognition, sexual uncertainties, doubts of democracy) to enter into a volume supposedly designed to "put a Person, a human being (myself, in
the latter half of the Nineteenth Century, in America,) freely, fully and

truly on record" (573–4). At the outset of "By Blue Ontario's Shore," the Phantom of epic poetry charged Whitman to deliver "the song of the throes of Democracy." Anyone who seeks the "throes of Democracy" will find them neither in "By Blue Ontario's Shore," nor in *Leaves of Grass;* they will be found only in the prose of *Democratic Vistas,* where their frank acknowledgment would not threaten the impact of his epic's "great Idea."

"Passage to India" is the most ambitious long poem Whitman wrote after he became intent upon making his book an epic of democracy. Although the poem is blessedly free of the absurd machinery of "Song of the Exposition," it too is declamation rather than narrative, panegyric and not epic. The westward course of empire may now have enabled the muse to pass forward (or back) to India, but the source of greatness still lies in cultural promise rather than in a person's deeds. Heroism is no longer released through the boastful energies of the Self; it originates in three technological advances (the Suez canal, the transcontinental railroad, the Pacific cable) that will release the energies of entire cultures. A poet whose vision of a heroic, exploratory future is based squarely upon technology can no longer be sure that size is only development, or that a mouse is miracle enough to stagger sextillions of infidels. The very ordering of sections in "Passage to India" argues that the soul is finally more than the body. At the poem's end we are asked to stop "eating and drinking like mere brutes" and to cast off upon journeys beyond even India:

> Sail forth – steer for the deep waters only.
> Reckless, O Soul, exploring, I with thee, and thou with me,
> For we are bound where mariner has not yet dared to go,
> And we will risk the ship, ourselves and all.
>
> O my brave soul!
> O farther, farther sail!
> O daring joy, but safe! are they not all the seas of God?
> O farther, farther, farther sail! (421)

Although the "passages" invoked throughout the poem have scarcely mentioned death, Whitman implies the possibility of death in the line "And we will risk the ship, ourselves and all." His poem's end, however, reassures the reader that the soul's new seas are all "safe" because they are "the seas of God." To urge readers toward so grand a future of metaphysical voyaging partakes of a spirit more akin to Tennyson's Ulysses than to Homer's Odysseus, whose goal, after all, was Ithaka, and who was anything but "reckless."

The accommodation Whitman wished to make with epic tradition becomes fully explicit in a poem of "Good-bye My Fancy" titled "Old

Chants" (1891). The poet who had once written "What is to be done is to withdraw from precedents" sought, at the last, to tie his song *to* precedents:

> An ancient song, reciting, ending,
> Once gazing toward thee, Mother of All,
> Musing, seeking themes fitted for thee,
> Accept for me, thou saidst, the older ballads,
> And name for me before thou goest each ancient poet.
>
> (Of many debts incalculable
> Haply our New World's chiefest debt is to old poems.) (547)

The accusatory Phantom of Old World epic has here been supplanted by a kindly, maternal muse who speaks "with courteous hand and word" (547). Walt Whitman has become merely her amanuensis; instead of celebrating himself, he gazes about "seeking themes fitted for thee."

Among the "old chants" whose titles the maternal muse specifies there are precious few "ballads." The New World's "chiefest debt" is clearly to another tradition:

> The Hindu epics, the Grecian, Chinese, Persian,
> The Biblic books and prophets, and deep idyls of the Nazarene,
> The Iliad, Odyssey, plots, doings, wanderings of Eneas,
> Hesiod, Eschylus, Sophocles, Merlin, Arthur,
> The Cid, Roland at Roncesvalles, the Niebelungen,
> The troubadors, minstrels, minnesingers, skalds,
> Chaucer, Dante, flocks of singing birds,
> The Border Minstrelsy, the bye-gone ballads, feudal tales,
>   essays, plays,
> Shakspere, Schiller, Walter Scott, Tennyson. (547)

With few exceptions, Whitman's newly proclaimed debts compromise a catalogue of epic and romance. His poem ends, not by contrasting Old and New World song, but by assimilating them. As the "Mother of All" crosses the threshold into *Leaves of Grass,* she looks back upon all the old chants, "Well pleased, accepting all, curiously prepared for by them, / Thou enterest at thy entrance porch" (547). No mention is here made of sudden changes beyond the threshold.

If one were to accept "Old Chants" as a confession of the true origin of *Leaves of Grass* (1855), "Song of Myself" could not have been written. A muse so welcoming of the old chants, so "well pleased" with all epics and romances from Homer to Scott, would have felt little need to pit democracy against feudalism, to subvert all notions of a superior hero, or to evolve a new verse form. In spite of its list of heroic texts, "Old Chants" does not define the genre to which *Leaves of Grass* belongs; it merely indicates the genre to which the aged Whitman wished it might have belonged. The poet who in 1855 had dismissed *Paradise Lost* as "of-

fensive to modern science and intelligence" concludes "A Backward Glance" by defining his "purpose enclosing all" as an American's attempt "to justify the ways of God to man," in the words of John Milton's "well-known and ambitious phrase" (572). If Whitman were now serving as the American Milton, why not also lay retrospective claim upon the fathers of all invention? In *Specimen Days* (1882), Whitman began to insist that in his youth he had liked to "race up and down the hard sand, and declaim Homer or Shakespeare to the surf and sea-gulls by the hour."[34] This claim may be Whitman's most durable fraud. In 1855 Whitman seems to have known enough Homer, Shakespeare, and Milton to be sure that their poetry was quite unlike the comic heroic verse he then thought appropriate for democratic man.

IV. LEAVINGS

For fifteen years after the 1855 Preface had become "By Blue Ontario's Shore" (1856), Whitman worked on drafts for a second prose preface, which was probably to be titled "Inscription at the Entrance of Leaves of Grass." Among nine drafts for this second preface, all of which were misplaced when Whitman moved from Washington to Camden in 1873, is a long paragraph beside which Whitman added the self-reminding phrase "some good points":

> Not Prometheus is here, nor Agememnon, nor Aeneas, nor Hamlet, nor Iago, nor Antony, nor any of Dante's scenes of persons, nor ballad of lord or lady, nor Lucretian philosophy, nor any special system of philosophy, nor striking lyric achievement, nor Childe Harold, nor any epic tale with beginning, climax and termination, yet something of perhaps similar purpose, very definite, compact.[35]

Of all the aging Whitman's self-delusions, the last word of this passage may be the saddest. Among the world's great books of verse, surely *Leaves of Grass,* even in the 1860 edition, is one of the least compact. To place it within the tradition of the epic, where beginning, climax, and termination have long been a correctly felt need, is to do his own early verse a great disservice. Although in 1891 Whitman was still trying to convince himself that "The cumulus character of the book is a great factor,"[36] the last edition of *Leaves of Grass* can be read consecutively only through the most dogged determination. The "epic of Democracy" was in fact a self-deluding rubric under which Whitman would collect the lyrics of a lifetime and combine them with longer poems of grand cultural prophecy.[37] To follow the epic intentions of Cooper, Prescott, and Melville leads us directly to their strengths. To pursue Whitman's gropings after a democratic epic immerses us in "Song of the Exposition" rather than "Song of Myself," in "Over the Carnage Rose Prophetic a Voice" rather than "When Lilacs Last in the Dooryard Bloom'd."

Whitman's draft for his second preface proceeds with still another argument for his subsuming the epic:

> In the poems taken as a whole unquestionably appears a great Person, entirely modern, at least as great as anything in the Homeric or Shakespearian characters, a person with the free courage of Achilles, the craft of Ulysses, the attributes even of the Greek deities. Majesty, passion, temper, amativeness, Romeo, Lear, Antony, immense self-esteem, but after democratic forms, measureless love, the old eternal elements of first-class humanity. Yet worked over, cast in a new mould, and here chanted of.[38]

The simple, separate person, Walt Whitman, a kosmos, of Manhattan the son, has here been utterly lost in a literary grab bag of Old World traits occasioned by Whitman's need to feel that his book is the equal of *The Iliad* and *King Lear*. Neither here nor in *Leaves of Grass* are we ever made aware that these particular virtues of Old World heroes have been "cast in a new mould" and assimilated within an "entirely modern" American Self. Only in Whitman's late assertions of purpose do the lines of epic continuity even appear to remain unbroken. Surely this paragraph, considered in toto, is not among Whitman's "good points"; one wishes it had been cancelled rather than lost.

At the end of his life Whitman knew that *Leaves of Grass,* judged as a single, coherent work of national literature, had immense failings. He wrote Richard Maurice Bucke that, despite thirty-three years of "hackling" at his book, he could still see "its numerous deficiencies and faults."[39] In the prefatory note to "Good-bye My Fancy," he admitted "I have probably not been enough afraid of careless touches, from the first – and am not now – nor of parrot-like repetitions – nor platitudes and the commonplace" (537). In spite of his English reputation and his band of American disciples, Whitman knew that *Leaves of Grass* had been widely accepted neither as a New World prophecy, nor as New World epic. His last word on the subject of a national literature declares that "Homer has held the ages, and holds [them] to-day," whereas in America there is only "a yet to be National Literature."[40]

I recognize the probable futility of heeding Whitman's original declaration that *Leaves of Grass* is not epic poetry. For most readers, the word "epic" remains indissolubly connected with the word "poem." Whitman is, by anyone's reckoning, among the world's great poets. He wrote poems affirming America's heroic greatness and combined them into a massive book. He himself described his life's work as "an epic of democracy." Against so formidable a combination of facts, mere reason and a regard for chronology seem but the minor weapons of those who write scholarly monographs.

My self-defense is that a futile argument may nonetheless be of im-

portance. The many twentieth-century poets who have made their several "pacts" with Walt Whitman have followed him in the creation of long poems that ascribe heroic value to the poetic imagination. Pound, Crane, Williams, Berryman, and Olson seek to combine lyric, comic, and prophetic poems into a cumulative volume that will bear an unmistakeable if slippery connection to the epic tradition. *The Cantos* begin with a translation from *The Odyssey;* Crane sought a comparison between *The Aeneid* and *The Bridge; Paterson* was to be "a reply to Greek and Latin with the bare hands"; *77 Dream Songs* was a "pseudo-poem or epic . . . found in an abandoned keyhole and transmitted to me by enemies"; Charles Olson assumes the voice of Maximus, a godlike spirit of all time in one place.[41] Whether one calls these works "personal epics," "poetical autobiographies," "tales of the tribe" or "self-generated myths," they will always remain long, loosely unified works, without narrative, without a culturally accepted hero, and written in a literary form valued by a miniscule fraction of the reading public. The troubles that all six poets experienced in concluding their magnum opus attest that the genre extends organicism toward shapelessness. The personal epic seems to end only with the death of the poet whose imaginative powers comprise its heroism. In all these respects, the writing of a personal epic is at variance with the basic connotations of the term *epos.*[42]

If my argument is correct, it is thus likely to be ignored. As long as Homer and Milton, Whitman and Williams, continue to be read and admired, as long as Americans wish to believe their culture possesses some special significance, there will be reviewers, readers, and poets who will regard long poems as some kind of American epic. The emergence of a durable heroic literature, however, requires the power of the proper medium, as well as the Arnoldian powers of the man and the moment. Unfortunately, the aging Whitman forgot his youthful recognition that "the expression of the American poet" could be neither "descriptive nor epic." His late claim upon the epic should no longer obscure the timely acuity of his earlier rejection of the term. In 1855 the best works of Cooper, Simms, Parkman, Prescott, and Melville had all shown that the epic could be far more readily transformed into narrative prose than visionary verse. Although heroic literature has clearly survived, *the* American epic poem, in any form, died at the moment Whitman began to claim he had written it. However heroic and indigenous "Song of Myself" may be, *Leaves of Grass* is not the centerpiece of American epic verse, but the massive cause of its continuing impossibility.

PROSPECT

Halfway through Tom Wolfe's *The Bonfire of the Vanities* (1987), beleaguered bond king Sherman McCoy listens absentmindedly to an after-dinner speech at a desperately fashionable Fifth Avenue dinner party. The speaker and guest of honor, a haggard British poet named Lord Aubrey Buffing, who is reputed to have been on the short list for the Nobel Prize, tries to strike a tone of light-hearted confession:

> The United States deserve an epic poem. At various times in my career I considered writing an epic, but I didn't do that either. Poets are also not supposed to write epics any longer, despite the fact that the only poets who have endured and will endure are poets who have written epics. . . . No, we poets no longer even have the courage to make rhymes, and the American epic should have rhymes, rhyme on top of rhyme in a shameless cascade, rhymes of the sort that Edgar Allan Poe gave us.[1]

Wolfe's mockery of a rhymed epic for contemporary America is inseparable from his recognition that the demand for one has somehow, ludicrously, lingered on. Lord Buffing's mention of Poe, however, suddenly turns his speech in a quite different direction. Buffing speaks of "The Masque of the Red Death" as a prophetic allegory of the contemporary pleasure whirl, which is likely to end in the death of Prospero and his self-immured seekers of oblivion. After acknowledging "I cannot be the epic poet you deserve. I am too old and far too tired, too weary of the fever called 'living' " (356). Lord Buffing sits down, leaving the room to an intruder named Silence who prevails because the guests are momentarily anxious that they might not have understood something possibly profound.

On one level, Lord Aubrey Buffing serves as the barely standing proof that Poe's strictures against the contemporary epic were entirely correct. An epic poem on America means nothing to any guest present, none of whom could be imagined to exist in such a poem. Consequently, Aubrey

Buffing becomes the stand-in for another Poe, an intrusive foreign presence ("the spectral Englishman," Wolfe calls him) who grimly shows
the bizarre significance of a "crazy" allegory about a medieval plague.
Poe's gothic tale replaces America's epic poem, but only because the tale's
pertinence has been measured by the epic's failure. When Sherman McCoy
returns home, he finds himself troubled by Buffing's speech, and not
only because Buffing is dying of Aids: "That mannered, ghostly English
voice had been the voice of an oracle. Aubrey Buffing had been speaking
straight to him, as if he were a medium dispatched by God himself. . . .
The meaningless whirl, the unbridled flesh, the obliteration of home and
hearth! – and, waiting in the last room, the Red Death" (357–8). Manhattan's bonfire of the vanities, it seems, has become Poe/Buffing's ultimate triumph.

Nonetheless, an American verse epic against the Poundian tradition of
the long "personal" epic has recently been attempted. Frederick Turner
intends his *The New World: An Epic Poem* (1985) "to serve as an opening
to a postmodern creative era."[2] Reacting against the "self-concern of
Wordsworth's *Prelude* and Eliot's shattered mini-epic *The Waste Land*"
(viii), Turner seeks to revive narrative epic by taking "a step beyond the
short free verse existentialist imagist lyric poem which has dominated
the modernist period" (vii). Clearly repulsed by the personalism and
fragmentation of poems such as *The Cantos, Paterson,* or Berryman's *Dream
Songs,* Turner would restore the possibilities of narrative epic by bringing back both an "outward glance at the world" and a heroism based
upon the "sacrifice" of the individual to the greater welfare of the community (viii, ix). The announced theme of *The New World* is "the discovery of a third mode of knowledge, belief, and commitment that tran-
scends the contemporary dilemma of fanatical blind faith and affectless
hedonistic relativism" (ix). For Turner, this third mode entails a healthy
acceptance of caste, an end to the cash nexus, a rebonding of the family,
fighting absolute evil in the name of known good, and surrendering self
to the general welfare. Turner's problem is to give narrative substance to
his proscripts for change. To convey these values in action, Turner sets
his epic in the Ohio countryside in 2376 A.D., and then pictures heroes
and villains fighting on horseback for strategic strongholds, equipped
with resinite armor and laser swords. Experiencing such a poem becomes something like reading versified *Ivanhoe* while watching *Star Wars*.

For Turner to have regarded his poem as rebellious prophecy accords
with America's oldest epic tradition. Relentless futurism in a genre once
defined by its concern with the distant past has been a distinguishing trait
of American epic since Barlow's *Columbiad*. Like Barlow, Turner writes
epic because of his belief that a better future can be created only if we can
imagine it (vii). Projecting his sense of the present onto the twenty-fourth

century, Turner pictures the New World as an anarchic dystopia. The religious right ("The Mads") and the urban druggies ("The Riots") are the Scylla and Charybdis between which an enlightened remnant of cultured intellects must steer in order to recreate the freedom of one for all. After centuries of pogroms against the middle class, a post-holocaustal America evolves in which self-contained farms, supported by new technology, provide an alternative to gutted cities. From such farming communities, the chivalrous and educated "Frees" will convince cowering suburbanites ("The Burbs") that the mind can transcend materialism. Our post-Marxian labor theory of value (denigrating labor by regarding it as pain and money) will give way to an "obligation theory of value" enabling labor to become a happy privilege (44). The three gods whom the "Frees" worship are known to be personifications of human qualities; the central icon in their cathedral is a sculpted statue of noble falling Man ever suspended over the pit. The hero's climactic deed is to kill the black Christ of fundamentalism with his laser sword Adamant. In order to do so, he must first give up his conception of merely personal honor; his reward is to give his dying body to the community so that it metamorphoses into the icon of Man.

Unlike Barlow's truly futuristic prophecies, Turner's science fiction is curiously restorative. The good life he imagines in twenty-fourth-century Ohio resembles nothing quite so much as Crèvecoeur's model of an American farmer, now technologically advanced, yet still devoted to family, neighbor, and seasonal rhythms. Turner's red-haired, widely educated heroine, Ruth Jefferson McCloud, shows her wisdom only by marrying the hero, who is named James George Quincy, daughter of Mary Madison and George Quincy. James George Quincy has his epic weapon prepared by goldsmith Matthew Revere; he is advised in council by General Jack Sherman and rhetorician Samuel Adams; he worships in Mount Verdant Cathedral, is taught independence of spirit by Shaker McCloud, and lives in Mohican County, where the two political parties are the Whigs and the Tories. Joel Barlow's epic had opened outward toward one new world, but Turner's *The New World* narrows into parochial nostalgia.

To Fredric Jameson, the distinguishing trait of the postmodernist sensibility is a self-conscious borrowing or quoting of previous artifacts based upon assumptions that new styles are exhausted, and our shared experiences are mostly aesthetic.[3] Turner's need to invent a hero and create a fable propel his poem toward postmodernism as Jameson defines it. Consider Turner's view of epic tradition:

> For every hero has spent something left over
> by a predecessor, whether by theft or parody, lies
> or calculated humility; Achilles more tragic

than Gilgamesh mourning his friend, and more hysterical;
Odysseus making a virtue of second best,
always the family man; Parsifal owing
it all to the Grail, with his Christ-face covering
over all the contingencies; all human vanities;
and the anti-heroes, making a vice of necessity (75).

Turner's belief that epic has become an exhausted genre through feeding upon its own heroes forces him into the position of rebuilding a hero from the ashes of twentieth-century "antiheroes." James George Quincy is created wholly through borrowing. The titles and incidents of many sections ("Journey out of Exile," "The Three Tests," "The Frost Bride," "The Death of the Father," "Adventures," "The Fall of the King") read as if Turner were versifying the consecutive stages of heroism in Joseph Campbell's *Hero with a Thousand Faces*. In his preface, Turner states "The plot of the poem is related to several great stories," and then lists Odysseus, Burnt Njal, Parsifal, Snow White, Krishna and Arjuna, the American Civil War, "American Frontier stories of testing," and the tradition of chivalric romance (viii). To be sure, the epic has always transformed itself through literary imitation, but the premise of the great epics has always been that the fable once was real. At best, Turner's willful artifice leads to a well-made pastiche in which the reader enjoys the allusions. Such enjoyment should not, however, preclude our remembering Lukacs's warning against would-be epics that transcend known, sensual reality.

At worst, such a postmodernist collage leads Turner to risk borrowings that contradict his values. A protagonist with a name like James George Quincy must be a kind of national apprentice hero who gains heroism through trials, but his rugged, blond-haired, blue-eyed physique, combined with his agile innocence, suggest the vacuous, all-white virtues of Luke Skywalker. The fundamentalist villain, black-suited Simon Raven, looks, fights, and abducts women very much as Darth Vader does. Turner will grant his heroine wisdom as long as she stands in for Thomas Jefferson. The New World's oracular prophet is a sybiline black man named Kingfish, but the dialect Kingfish is made to speak recalls the Amos 'n Andy Show rather than Eliot's Fisher King. Such characterizations may be high camp, but they make low epic and restore little Enlightenment.

In two different ways, *The New World* demonstrates that the twentieth-century long poem is no vessel for the epic. It would be foolish to deny that the poems of Pound, Crane, Williams, Olson, and Berryman were all intended as a twentieth-century form of epic. Not only are they an outgrowth of the epic as Wordsworth and Whitman had redefined it; they often create in us the awe, literary as well as thematic, associated

with the genre. But Turner is right to suggest that long imagistic poems without narrative cannot appeal to a wide readership. Sometimes the major modernist poets have claimed to represent or embrace their culture, but more often they have archly opposed it. Consequently, none of their long poems has attained a choric function for their people beyond the claims still advanced for them by the academy. Turner's poem, on the other hand, contains all the narrative epic conventions Le Bossu had demanded, yet ultimately debases the epic because its experimental basis is wholly speculative and parasitical. Great claims have not been made for Turner's work, not only because of its internal failings, but also because the subtitle "an epic poem" arouses small popular interest in the 1980s.

After 1865 the important continuation of the epic impulse in American literature lay not in the followers of Whitman, but in various prose genres: Parkman's *History,* Norris's trilogy of romances; Sandburg's *Lincoln;* Dos Passos's *USA;* perhaps Hemingway's *For Whom the Bell Tolls* and Mailer's *The Naked and the Dead.* These works, like the long poems that followed *Leaves of Grass,* were intended to incorporate and supplant elements of epic tradition. One advantage of prose, however, was the simple and crucial fact that, between 1865 and 1950, the American people still eagerly read prose, even if it was lengthy. An equal advantage was that prose had retained *epos* (narrative), whereas Whitman was leading heroic poetry toward an amassing of visionary lyrics. The one long twentieth-century heroic poem the American people once actually read was Stephen Vincent Benét's *John Brown's Body* (1928), a poem now ignored by scholars but possessed of a strong narrative line. By mentioning names as unfashionable as Sandburg and Benét, I mean to suggest that we scholars, continuing to associate literary quality with irony, intellectual complexity, and imagistic concision, may not have been in the best position to view our century's transformations of epic. Whether after midcentury the word "epic" should properly be applied only to the dominant media of film and television is a wry possibility far beyond my ken.

NOTES

INTRODUCTION

1 Imitative verse epics written by Americans between 1770 and 1860 include the following:

Completed and published: Timothy Dwight, *The Conquest of Canaan* (1785); Richard Snowden, *The Columbiad* (1795); Thomas Brockway, *The Gospel Tragedy: An Epic Poem* (1795); John Blair Linn, *The Death of Washington: A Poem in Imitation of the Manner of Ossian* (1800); Elhanahan Winchester, *The Process and Empire of Christ* (1805); Joel Barlow, *The Columbiad* (1807); Daniel Bryan, *The Mountain Muse* (1813); Anonymous, *An Epick Poem* (post-1815); Alexis Eustaphieve, *Demetrius: The Hero of the Don, an Epic Poem* (1818); Richard Emmons, *The Fredoniad* (1827); Jacob Dixon, *Divination Overruled: An Epic Poem in Four Parts* (1833); Thomas Hedges Genin, *The Napolead* (1833); R. F. Astrop, "The Washingtonian, an Epic Poem" (1835); Walter Marshall McGill, *The Western World* (1837); Johnson Pierson, *The Judiad* (1844); Phineas Robinson, *Immortality: A Poem in Ten Cantos* (1846); Thomas L. Harris, *An Epic of the Starry Heaven* (1855); Alfred Mitchell, *The Coloniad* (1858).

Published incomplete: Anonymous, *The Columbiad* (1795); Anthony Hunn, *Sin and Redemption* (1812); Alexis Umphraville, *The Siege of Baltimore* (1817); Hiram Haines, "The Virginiad" (1825); James McConochie, *The Henriade* (1846).

Planned or partly written, then abandoned: Nathaniel Tucker, "America Delivered: An Heroic Poem" (1783); Philip Freneau and Washington Irving, untitled epics on Columbus; Richard Alsop, "The Conquest of Scandanavia"; Robert Sands, "The Settlement of Greenland."

This list is surely incomplete.

2 Charles Olson, "Projective Verse," in *The New American Poetry*, ed. Donald M. Allen (New York: Grove, 1960), pp. 386–90.

3 John Milton, *Paradise Lost*, ed. M. Y. Hughes (New York: Odyssey, 1935), p. 270.

4 Timothy Dwight, "The Friend," #4, in *American Museum*, 5 (1789), 565–7.

5 Robert Lowell, "Epics" (begun in the late 1960s, first published in 1980), in *Robert Lowell: Collected Prose*, ed. Robert Giroux (New York: Farrar, Straus, & Giroux, 1987), p. 221.

243

6 Georg Lukacs, *The Theory of the Novel* (1914), translated by Anna Bostock (Cambridge, Mass.: MIT Press, 1971), pp. 129, 146. Paul de Man evidently distrusted the ways in which Lukacs's *The Theory of The Novel* implies a linear conception of time: "Hence the necessity of narrating the development of the novel as a continuous event, as the fallen form of the archetypal Greek epic, which is treated as an ideal concept but given actual historical existence" (de Man, *Blindness and Insight* [Minneapolis: University of Minnesota Press, 1983], pp. 58–9). De Man's rather condescending sentence exactly describes why Lukacs's plausible model has proven so useful for my purposes. Lukacs saw the issue of the transformation of epic into novel in the same terms as early-nineteenth-century Euro-American critics. Continuity of development, de Man often forgot, is not necessarily a chimera, either for the history of literature, or for a particular literary history. "Temporality" is not always "rhetoric."

7 Mikhail Bakhtin, "Epic and Novel" (1941), in *The Dialogic Imagination,* ed. Michael Holquist, translated by Caryl Emerson and Michael Holquist (Austin: University of Texas Press, 1981), p. 39. Katerina Clark and Michael Holquist have shown that in 1924 Bakhtin began to translate Lukacs's *The Theory of the Novel.* By 1940, when Bakhtin wrote "Epic and Novel," he was increasingly dissatisfied with Lukacs's viewpoint. Clark and Holquist conclude: "Whereas Lukacs mourns the death of the epic and the rise of the novel, Bakhtin, who sees epic tendencies as still living in nonnovelistic genres, takes delight in their erosion in the novel" (see Clark's and Holquist's *Mikhail Bakhtin* [Cambridge, Mass.: Harvard University Press, 1984], pp. 91, 288). I interpret the disagreements between Lukacs's and Bakhtin's texts slightly differently.

8 Jane Tompkins, *Sensational Designs: The Cultural Work of American Fiction 1790–1860* (New York: Oxford University Press, 1985), p. 38.

9 Bakhtin, "Epic and Novel," *The Dialogic Imagination,* p. 35.

10 Thoreau, *Walden; or Life in the Woods,* ed. J. L. Shanley (Princeton: Princeton University Press, 1971), pp. 228–32.

11 Thoreau, entry of January 21, 1852, in *Journal,* ed. B. Torrey and F. H. Allen (New York: Dover, 1962), I, 209–11. Thoreau's first attempt to render the battle of the ants had been written ten years earlier in two stanzas of "My Books I'd Fain Cast Off, I Cannot Read" (1842):

> Here while I lie beneath this walnut bough,
> What care I for the Greeks or for Troy town,
> If juster battles are enacted now
> Between the ants upon this hummock's crown?
>
> Bid Homer wait till I the issue learn,
> If red or black the gods will favor most,
> Or yonder Ajax will the phalanx turn
> Struggling to heave some rock against the host.

In this humorless and abstract first version, Homer's book must simply be cast off as an unreadable burden; a more real and more just battle transpires around us in nature. The *Journal* entry of 1852 is surely not an observation of that January day, but a winter's literary exercise in which an old memory is turned into plain, concrete narrative. In its final version in *Walden,* the ant

battle reacquires a Homeric reference that is suffused with ambiguity and humor. ("My Books I'd Fain Cast Off, I Cannot Read" in *Collected Poems of Henry Thoreau*, ed. Carl Bode [Baltimore: Johns Hopkins University Press, 1964], p. 76).

12 According to this sentence, the battle would have taken place in September of 1845, while Thoreau was living in the cabin at Walden. As demonstrated earlier, however, the battle must have taken place before Thoreau published "My Books I'd Fain Cast Off" in 1842. Both the *Journal* and *Walden* versions show Thoreau's remarkable ability to make an old memory both concrete and complex. Is it possible, given the vagueness of Thoreau's first poetic rendering, that he never witnessed the ant battle at all? Could he rather be inventing and elaborating problems of natural behavior that point backward to Homer and forward to Darwin?

13 *Walden*, p. 230. Compare Thoreau's prose to the following couplets from the climactic battle of "The Rape of the Lock" (*Poetry and Prose of Alexander Pope*, ed. Aubrey Williams [Boston: Houghton Mifflin, 1969], p. 98):

> Triumphant *Umbriel* on a Sconce's Height
> Clapt his glad Wings, and sate to view the Fight:
> Propt on their Bodkin spears, the Sprights survey
> The growing Combat, or assist the Fray. (V, ll.53–6)

14 See Stuart Curran's chapter, titled "The Epic," in *Poetic Form and British Romanticism* (New York: Oxford University Press, 1986), pp. 151–67.

15 In spite of the absence of publishers' sales figures, there can be no disagreeing with Nina Baym's conclusion about women's domestic fiction: "these novels were read in unprecedented numbers" (Nina Baym, *Woman's Fiction* [Ithaca, N.Y.: Cornell University Press, 1978], p. 21). Baym's subsequent book, *Novels, Readers and Reviewers* (Ithaca, N.Y.: Cornell University Press, 1984) provides conclusive evidence that American reviewers of the 1840s and 1850s were certain that the novel had become the nation's dominant literary genre.

CHAPTER 1

1 "A Poem on the Rising Glory of America" (1772 version), in *The Poems of Philip Freneau*, ed. F. L. Pattee (Princeton, N.J.: Princeton University Press, 1963), p. 78. J. F. S. Smeall's study of the poem's revisions suggests that these four lines were written by Brackenridge for delivery at the 1771 Princeton commencement exercises. See J. F. S. Smeall, "The Respective Roles of Hugh Brackenridge and Philip Freneau in Composing 'The Rising Glory of America,' " *Publications of the Bibliographic Society of America*, 67 (1973), 263–81.

2 John Adams, letter to John Trumbull, April 28, 1785, The Adams Papers, The Massachusetts Historical Society, 1953, microfilm reel 107. On April 4, 1786, Adams wrote from Grosvenor Square to both Timothy Dwight and Joel Barlow to commend them for having written *The Conquest of Canaan* and *The Vision of Columbus* (Adams Papers, reel 113). Assuring both young poets that their poems were superior to those of any English contemporary, Adams consoled them against the probability that their republican attitudes would give their poems sparse sales in England. Considered together, these three letters show us how insistent John Adams was in promoting heroic

poetry that "does honour to America" (letter to Timothy Dwight, April 4, 1786). For the benefit of the Republic, Adams sought to persuade all three poets to consider artistry as the servant of political persuasion.

3 R. W. Emerson, "The Poet," in *Selections from Ralph Waldo Emerson*, ed. S. E. Whicher (Cambridge, Mass.: Houghton Mifflin, 1957), p. 238.

4 Robert Frost, "Maturity No Object," Introduction to *New Poets of England and America* (New York: Meridian, 1957), p. 11.

5 See Joseph J. Ellis, *After the Revolution: Profiles of Early American Culture* (New York: Norton, 1979), Chapter One.

6 Samuel Low, "Peace" (1784), in *Poems* (New York: T. & J. Swords, 1800), II, 135.

7 Untitled poem of St. John Honeywood, *Massachusetts Spy*, January 14, 1779, p. 4.

8 *Columbian Magazine*, (1786), 85.

9 John Blair Linn, *The Powers of Genius* (Philadelphia: Ashbury Dickins, 1802), p. 50.

10 Linn, "Ode," *Literary Magazine and American Register*, 4 (1805), 157.

11 Warren Dutton, "The Present State of Literature" (Hartford, Conn.: Hudson & Goodwin, 1800), p. 15.

12 David Humphreys, "Poem on the Happiness of America," *American Museum*, 1 (1787), 252.

13 Noah Webster, "To the Author of the *Conquest of Canaan*," *American Magazine*, 1 (1788), 265–6.

14 Phillis Wheatley, "To Maecenas," *Poems on Various Subjects Religious and Moral* (London: A. Bell, 1773), p. 2.

15 Jane Turell, "On the Poems of Sir Richard Blackmore," in Samuel Kettell, *Specimens of American Poetry* (Boston: Benjamin Blom, 1829), p. 65.

16 Benjamin Franklin, *Autobiography and Selected Writings*, ed. Larzer Ziff (New York: Rinehart, 1956), p. 41. A portion of Ralph's poem was printed in Samuel Kettell's *Specimens of American Poetry* under the title "Zeuma or the Love of Liberty."

17 Cotton Mather, *Magnalia Christi Americana* (Cambridge, Mass.: Harvard University Press, 1967), p. 25.

18 Edward Everett, "Oration on the Peculiar Motives to Intellectual Exertion in America," in *The American Literary Revolution: 1783–1837*, ed. R. E. Spiller (New York: Doubleday, 1967), p. 296.

19 Everett, "Oration," p. 316.

20 Agnes Marie Sibley, *Alexander Pope's Prestige in America: 1725–1835* (New York: King's Crown Press, 1949), p. 8.

21 Thomas Jefferson, "Thoughts on English Prosody," in *The Writings of Thomas Jefferson*, ed. A. A. Lipscomb (Washington: Jefferson Memorial Association, 1903), XVIII, 448.

22 Sibley, *Alexander Pope's Prestige in America*, pp. 71–2; D. M. Foerster, *The Fortunes of Epic Poetry* (New York: Catholic University Press, 1962), p. 101.

23 Leon Howard, *The Connecticut Wits* (Chicago: University of Chicago Press, 1943), pp. 6, 18.

24 "Trumbull's Rank Epic Poets" appears in *Extracts from the Itineraries and Other Miscellanies of Ezra Stiles,* ed. F. B. Dexter (New Haven, Conn.: Yale University Press, 1916), p. 407. At least twenty, usually pseudonymous, short mock epics were published in America between 1790 and 1820 under such titles as *The Paxtoniade, The Spunkiad, The Lousiad, The Brandiad, The Festivaliad,* and so forth. The genre seems to have risen and fallen with Federalist sentiment: J. S. J. Gardiner, Lemuel Hopkins, Brockholst Livingston, and T. G. Fessenden all used the genre for antidemocratic satire.

25 R. W. Emerson, Journal, August 17, 1834, in *Emerson in His Journals,* ed. Joel Porte (Cambridge, Mass.: Harvard University Press, 1982), p. 127.

26 The four poems are published in *The Connecticut Gazette,* February 24, 1775; *The Connecticut Courant,* August 18, 1778; *The Massachusetts Spy,* January 7, 1779; and *The Pennsylvania Journal,* May 10, 1780.

27 H. H. Brackenridge, "Fragment of a Sermon" (1776) in *Gazette Publications* (Carlisle, Pa.: Alexander & Phillips, 1806), p. 265. Unless otherwise stated, all italics in quoted passages appear in the original text.

28 *Works of Fisher Ames* (Boston: T. B. Wait & Co., 1809), pp. 115–33.

29 Robert T. Paine, *Works in Prose and Verse* (Boston: J. Belcher, 1812), pp. 329–42.

30 "On the Connection of Literature with Political Business." *Boston Magazine,* 3 (1785), 246–7. In 1800 Tunis Wortman illustrated the difference between political *judgment* (available to any republican citizen) and artistic *genius* (inherent in a select natural aristocracy) by the following distinction: "To imitate the epic strains of the Iliad, the Aenead, or Paradise Lost, presupposes the possession of an extraordinary faculty, in addition to judgment, usually expressed by the appellation genius" (*A Treatise Concerning Political Enquiry* [New York: Da Capo Press, 1970], p. 64). It is telling that Wortman believed *imitation* of Homer or Milton could be an example of Genius; Wortman says nothing about the need for Genius to transform epic models.

31 John Quincy Adams, *Lectures on Rhetoric and Oratory* (Cambridge, Mass.: Hilliard & Metcalf, 1810), I, 73–80.

32 "On Homer," *Port Folio,* 8 (1822), 388–91.

33 George Bancroft, "Order of Greek Studies," *North American Review,* 18 (1824), 104.

34 Charles Brockden Brown, review of Southey's *Joan of Arc, The Monthly Magazine and American Review,* 1 (1799), 225–6.

35 Quoted in David Lee Clark, *Charles Brockden Brown* (New York: Duke University Press, 1966), p. 70.

36 Brown, *The Literary Magazine and American Register,* 7 (1807), 92.

37 Brown, ibid., 4 (1805), 343.

38 Benjamin Rush, *Essays, Literary, Moral and Philosophical* (Philadelphia: Thomas & William Bradford, 1806), p. 24.

39 *The Works of Joel Barlow,* ed. W. K. Bottorff and A. L. Ford (Gainesville, Fla.: Scholars' Facsimiles & Reprints, 1970), I, 847.

40 Ibid., I, 848. A ninety-five page poem in heroic couplets celebrating the American navy and merchant marine was soon to be published, complete

with an invocation to Zephyr and accounts of Jason, Ulysses, Aeneas, Columbus, Vasco de Gama, and Magellan (Archibald Johnston, *The Mariner* [Philadelphia: Edward Earle, 1811]).

41 John Quincy Adams, *Lectures on Rhetoric and Oratory*, I, 245.

42 John Greenleaf Whittier, *Literary Recreations and Miscellanies* (Boston: Ticknor & Fields, 1854), p. 428. Sometimes, however, American outrage at the heroic world dissolves in the face of the need for an American epic. Mrs. Sarah Wentworth Morton's "Beacon Hill" (1797) begins by denouncing the epic because Homeric Invention has always falsified "blushing Truth," leaving behind only a "crown of fame, / Where all was action, save an empty name." Because Clio will be the American's Muse, "No more the *fabled action* claims our care, / The tales of Ilion, and the Latian war." By poem's end, however, the achievements of Revolutionary heroes lead Mrs. Morton to reverse herself. Although her *Beacon Hill* is merely "a local poem," she asks that "Some bard more blest may the high strain prolong, / Till free Columbia feel the sway of song, / Till, as the streams of epic music roll, / Past scenes of glory fill the patriot's soul" (Morton, *Beacon Hill* [Boston: Manning & Loring, 1797], pp. 13, 50).

43 William Cullen Bryant, "Preface" to *The Iliad* (Boston: Houghton Mifflin, 1870), pp. xi, xii; letter to John Bryant quoted in Charles H. Brown, *William Cullen Bryant* (New York: Scribner, 1971), p. 484.

44 Similar statements occur in the *North American Review*, 6 (1818), and in *Port Folio*, 1 (1801), 23. Contrast the judgmental fervor of the American authors to the impartial tone of David Hume: "The ideas of manners are so much changed since the age of Homer, that although *The Iliad* was always among the ancients conceived to be a panegyric on the Greeks, yet the reader is now almost always on the side of the Trojans, and is much more interested for the humane and soft manners of Priam, Hector, Andromache, Sarpedon, Aeneas, Glaucus, nay, even of Paris and Helen, than for the severe and cruel bravery of Achilles, Agememnon, and the other Grecian heroes" (letter of 1759 defending Wilkie's *Epigoniad*, printed in *The Works of the English Poets*, ed. A. Chalmers [London: J. Sharpe, 1810], XVI, 112-21).

45 See George F. Sensabaugh, *Milton in Early America* (Princeton: Princeton University Press, 1964), pp. 4, 166-83).

46 John Trumbull, "Prospect of the Future Glory of America" in *Poetical Works* (Hartford: Samuel G. Goodrich, 1820), p. 159. Trumbull's confidence in an American Milton is a striking change from the worshipful humility of Mather Byles's "Written in Milton's Paradise Lost" (1727) and Samuel Low's "On Milton's Paradise Lost" (ca. 1770). To Byles and Low, Milton is so obviously unsurpassable that Americans can only admiringly paraphrase his achievement.

47 Charles Brockden Brown, *Literary Magazine and American Register*, 7 (1807), 92.

48 *Port Folio*, 4 (1807), 358.

49 *Literary Magazine and American Register*, 7 (1803), 15.

50 *The Major Poems of Timothy Dwight*, ed. W. J. McTaggart and W. K. Bottorff (Gainesville: Scholars' Facsimiles & Reprints, 1969), pp. 545-6.

51 Some of these poems surely maintain a dialogue with British biblical epics of the same era. Stuart Curran cites Richard Cumberland's *Cavalry* (1792), Cumberland's *The Exodiad* (1807), Charles Hoyle's *Exodus* (1807), and Joseph Cottle's *The Messiah* (1815) (Curran, *Poetic Form and British Romanticism* [Oxford: Oxford University Press], pp. 161–7).

52 Job Durfee, *Whatcheer* (1832), in *Complete Works,* ed. Thomas Durfee (Providence: Gladding & Proud, 1849), p. 5.

53 Brackenridge and Freneau, "The Rising Glory of America" (1786 version) in *Poems of Freneau,* ed. H. H. Clark (New York: Hafner, 1960), pp. 9, 4, 16.

54 C. J. Ingersoll, *Inchiquin, The Jesuit's Letters* (New York: I. Riley, 1810), p. 83.

55 S. L. Knapp, *Lectures on American Literature* (1829) (Gainesville, Fla.: Scholars' Facsimiles & Reprints, 1961), p. 188.

56 *Monthly Anthology and Boston Review,* 6 (1809), 242.

57 *The Columbian Magazine,* 1 (1786), 67–8.

58 H. H. Brackenridge, "An Eulogium of the Brave Men Who Have Fallen In The Contest With Great Britain," *United States Magazine,* 1 (1779), 346.

59 *The Massachusetts Magazine,* 1 (1789), 117–18.

60 The poem to which Freneau refers is a blank verse epic called *The Columbiad,* of which, in its unpublished state, Freneau prints a selection. This apparently lost poem is not to be confused with *The Columbiad* (1807) by Barlow, *The Columbiad* (1795) by Richard Snowden, or *The Columbiad* (1893) by Franklyn Quinby.

61 Freneau, *The Time-Piece,* 2, October 9, 1797.

62 H. T. Swedenberg, *The Theory of the Epic in England: 1650–1800* (Berkeley: University of California Press, 1944), p. 156.

63 *Essays of John Dryden,* ed. W. P. Ker (Oxford: Clarendon, 1900), II, 154.

64 Alexander Pope, *The Iliad of Homer,* in The Twickenham Edition of the *Poems of Alexander Pope,* ed. M. Mack, N. Callan, R. Fagles, W. Frost, and D. M. Knight (New Haven, Conn.: Yale University Press, 1967), VII, 94.

65 Joseph Addison, *The Spectator,* ed. D. E. Bond (Oxford: Clarendon, 1965), III, 10–11.

66. Andrew Ramsay, "A Discourse on Epic Poetry" (1717), prefatory essay to Francois Fénelon's *Les Aventures de Télémaque* (Paris: A. Delain, 1830), p. 19.

67 Voltaire, *An Essay on Epick Poetry* (1727) (Gainesville, Fla.: Scholars' Facsimiles & Reprints, 1970), pp. 41, 48.

68 Henry Home, Lord Kames, *Elements of Criticism* (Edinburgh: A. Millar, 1762), III, 36.

69 Hugh Blair, *Lectures on Rhetoric and Belles Lettres* (Edinburgh: W. Cruch, 1813), III, 215.

70 Charles Brockden Brown, *Monthly Magazine and American Review,* 1 (1799), 225.

71 E. M. W. Tillyard, *The English Epic and its Background* (New York: Oxford University Press, 1966), pp. 498–509; Douglas Knight, *Pope and the Heroic Tradition* (New Haven, Conn.: Yale University Press, 1951), pp. 76, 102–6.

72 Voltaire, *An Essay on Epick Poetry,* p. 63.

73 Ibid., p. 129.

74 "Classical Learning," in *Writings of Hugh Swinton Legaré* (Charleston, S. C.: Burges & James, 1845), II, 37–8.

75 *Literary Magazine and American Register,* 3 (1805), 14.

76 Letter of Nathaniel Tucker to his sister Elizabeth Tucker, undated, but written in 1783. Nathaniel Tucker's papers, including the manuscript of "America Delivered" and correspondence concerning it, are in the Tucker–Coleman Collection at the Swem Library of the College of William and Mary.

77 Nathaniel Tucker, "America Delivered: An Heroic Poem in Three Parts," Tucker–Coleman Collection.

78 Letter of Nathaniel Tucker to Elizabeth Tucker, 1783.

79 Letters of Nathaniel Tucker: to Elizabeth Tucker, 1783; to Elizabeth Tucker July 12, 1783; to St. George Tucker August 6, 1784.

80 *North American Review,* 18 (1824), 401.

81 *Columbian Magazine,* 1 (1786), 83. The quotation of *The Aeneid* is from book one, lines 204–5.

82 "The Bunker Hill Monument," in *Works of Daniel Webster* (Boston: Little, Brown, 1851), I, 68. The quotation of *The Aeneid* is from book six, lines 726–7.

83 David Humphreys, "Poem On the Happiness of America," in *The Miscellaneous Works of David Humphreys* (1804), ed. W. K. Bottorff (Gainesville, Fla.: Scholars' Facsimiles & Reprints, 1968), p. 29.

84 Edward Everett, *Orations and Speeches on Various Occasions* (Boston: Little, Brown, 1850), p. 77.

85 Byron, *Don Juan,* ed. Leslie A. Marchand (Cambridge, Mass.: Houghton Mifflin, 1958), p. 247.

86 Richard Snowden, *The Columbiad: Or, A Poem on the American War, in Thirteen Cantos* (Philadelphia: Jacob Johnson, 1795), pp. 26, 9. The poem was reprinted in Baltimore in 1802.

87 Joseph Dennie, *The Spirit of the Farmer's Museum* (Walpole, N.H.: Thomas & Thomas, 1801), p. 214.

88 Marcus Cunliffe, "Introduction" to M. L. Weems, *The Life of Washington* (Cambridge, Mass.: Harvard University Press, 1962), pp. xiii–xxiii; James D. Hart, *The Popular Book in America* (Berkeley: University of California Press, 1961), pp. 47–50. Quotations of Weems are from Cunliffe's edition of the 1809 text.

89 Jay Fliegelman, *Prodigals and Pilgrims: The American Revolution Against Patriarchal Authority* (Cambridge, Eng.: Cambridge University Press, 1982), pp. 199–202, 224–5.

90 John Blair Linn, "The Early Poetry of Greece," in *The Poetical Wanderer* (New York: Thomas Greenleaf, 1796), p. 7.

91 Linn, *The Death of Washington: A Poem in Imitation of the Manner of Ossian* (Philadelphia: John Ormrod, 1800), pp. 9, 25.

92 The last alternative seems the most likely. In a letter to his employer and prospective publisher Matthew Carey, Weems wrote, "I've something to whisper in your lug. Washington, you know, is gone! Millions are gaping to read something about him. I am very nearly primed and cocked for 'em" (E. E. F. Skeel, ed., *Mason Locke Weems: His Works and Ways* [Norwood,

Mass.: Plympton Press, 1929], I, 8). See Lewis Leary's account of the motives for, and changes in, Weems's various versions of the *Life of Washington* (Leary, *The Book-Peddling Parson* [Chapel Hill: Algonquin Books, 1984], pp. 81–101).

CHAPTER 2

1 John Milton, "The Reason of Church Government" (1641) in *Milton's Prose Writings* (London: J. M. Dent & Sons, 1927), p. 353.

2 William Cowper, review of *The Conquest of Canaan, Analytical Review,* 3 (1789), 531.

3 Leon Howard, *The Connecticut Wits* (Chicago: University of Chicago Press, 1943), p. 90.

4 Timothy Dwight, letter to Noah Webster, June 6, 1788, published in T. A. Zunder, "Noah Webster and *The Conquest of Canaan,*" *American Literature,* 1 (1929), 201–2.

5 Kenneth Silverman, *Timothy Dwight* (New York: Twayne Publishers, 1969), pp. 30–41. See also Silverman's *A Cultural History of the American Revolution* (New York: T. Y. Crowell, 1976), 500–3.

6 Lawrence Buell, *New England Literary Culture* (Cambridge, Eng.: Cambridge University Press, 1986), p. 170.

7 Dwight, "Letter to Noah Webster," pp. 201–2.

8 Ibid., p. 201.

9 W. J. McTaggart and W. K. Bottorff, eds., *The Major Poems of Timothy Dwight* (Gainesville, Fla.: Scholars' Facsimiles & Reprints, 1969), p. 558.

10 *The Conquest of Canaan,* in Taggart and Bottorff, *The Major Poems of Timothy Dwight,* pp. 273–6.

11 Kames, *Elements of Criticism* (Edinburgh: A. Miller, 1762), III, 235–6.

12 Milton, *Paradise Lost,* ed. M. Y. Hughes (New York: Odyssey, 1935), p. 236.

13 *The Conquest of Canaan,* p. 58.

14 Alexander Pope, *The Iliad of Homer* (New Haven, Conn.: Yale University Press, 1967), book xvi, 11. 444–5; book xxiii, 146–9.

15 Sacvan Bercovitch, *The American Jeremiad* (Madison: University of Wisconsin Press, 1978), p. 130. As Emory Eliott has shown, Dwight's unchanged insistence that America was the sure means to the Millennium created, in 1785, an additional complex of problems: "But a millennial expectation of ultimate national salvation in some future epoch would not inspire farmers and laborers to sacrifice their energies for the good of all, nor would it help to suppress the problems of corruption, slavery, and economic inequality that were already present among the chosen" (Emory Elliott, *Revolutionary Writers: Literature and Authority In The Early Republic* [New York: Oxford University Press, 1982], p. 61).

16 Noah Webster, "The London Reviewers Reviewed," *American Magazine,* 1 (1788), 565. Although Lemuel Hopkins also sought to approve Dwight's poem ("it contains so many more moral sentiments then The Iliad"), Hopkins had to admit that his associate's epic was no match for Homer or Milton. Hopkins then showed both his own satirical temperament and his prophetic good taste in closing his review with the remark that Trumbull's *M'Fingal* was "a mas-

terpiece of its kind" (Hopkins, "Miscellaneous Thoughts on the Poems of Messrs. Dwight and Barlow," *The American Mercury*, August 25, 1788).

17 Joseph Dennie, *The Spirit of the Farmer's Museum* (Walpole, N.H.: Thomas & Thomas, 1801), p. 142.

18 *Analectic Magazine*, 7 (1816), 272.

19 Samuel Knapp, *Lectures on American Literature* (1829) (Gainesville, Fla.: Scholars' Facsimiles & Reprints, 1961), p. 165.

20 Bryant, "Essay on American Poetry," *North American Review*, 7 (1818), 202.

21 Ezra Stiles, *Literary Diary* (New York: Scribner, 1901), II, 531; III, 175.

22 Ezra Stiles, *Extracts From the Itineraries and Other Miscellanies of Ezra Stiles*, ed. F. B. Dexter (New Haven, Conn.: Yale University Press, 1916), p. 407.

23 Dwight, "The Friend," *American Museum*, 5 (1789), 567.

24 Dwight, *The Conquest of Canaan, The Major Poems of Timothy Dwight*, p. 13.

25 Freneau, "On Epic Poetry," in *The Prose of Philip Freneau*, ed. P. M. Marsh (New Brunswick, N.J.: Scarecrow Press, 1955), pp. 264–5.

26 Freneau, "The Rising Empire" (1795), in *The Poems of Philip Freneau*, ed. F. L. Pattee (Princeton, N.J.: Princeton University Press, 1902), II, 9.

27 Philip Freneau (Robert Slender), "Advice to Authors" (1788), in *The Prose of Philip Freneau*, p. 91.

28 Freneau, *The Time-Piece*, 2, October 8, 1797.

29 Leon Howard, *The Connecticut Wits*, p. 139.

30 T. A. Zunder, *The Early Days of Joel Barlow* (New Haven, Conn.: Yale University Press, 1934), p. 77.

31 James Woodress, *A Yankee's Odyssey: The Life of Joel Barlow* (Philadelphia: Lippincott, 1958), p. 51.

32 Howard, *The Connecticut Wits*, p. 140.

33 Barlow's note to book two of *The Columbiad*, in *The Words of Joel Barlow*, ed. W. K. Bottorff and A. L. Ford (Gainesville, Fla.: Scholars' Facsimiles & Reprints, 1970), II, 802. Subsequent references refer only to the page number of the second volume of this edition. Bottorff and Ford reprinted the 1825 edition of *The Columbiad*, which incorporates Barlow's final revisions. The note from which this quotation is drawn had been printed as "A Dissertation on the Genius and Institutions of Manco Capac" following book two of *The Vision of Columbus*. Barlow was thus implying, only two years after *The Conquest of Canaan* had been published, that Dwight had erred in his choice of epic subject.

34 Lewis Leary, "Joel Barlow and William Hayley: A Correspondence," *American Literature*, 12 (1945), 325–34.

35 William Hayley, *An Essay On Epic Poetry* (1782), ed. Donald Reiman (New York: Garland Publishing, 1979), pp. 86, 111, 5. In asserting Hayley's probable influence on Barlow, I am following a suggestion of Stuart Curran (*Poetic Form and British Romanticism* [Oxford: Oxford University Press, 1986], p. 247, n. 23).

36 Barlow, *The Columbiad*, Book Ten, 11, 255–62, in *The Works of Joel Barlow* II, 763.

37 On the need of Revolutionary writers to view literature as a secular ministry, see Emory Elliott, *Revolutionary Writers*, pp. 11, 17, 18. Assessing Barlow's

importance to British contemporaries, Stuart Curran concludes "Barlow, however, is important not just as an index to his culture or as an influence in its impact on French thinking, but also in the way he promotes a generic shift in the Romantic epic" (*Poetic Form and British Romanticism,* p. 171).

38 Reviewers and readers of *The Columbiad* have long made fun of the extended battle that occurs between Flood and Frost while Washington is crossing the Delaware. Cecilia Tichi has argued that such Machinery is Barlow's way of emphasizing that the greatest forces are both environmental and political: "The battle for liberty is thus connected with the battle to reform the environment. . . . Barlow asserts in it a relationship between the Revolution and the freeing of vast continental acreage to man's reforming hand" (Cecilia Tichi, *New World, New Earth* [New Haven, Conn.: Yale University Press, 1979], p. 145).

39 "[Columbus] is, in fact, the ideal type of reader of the American epic as it was to develop. He looks on and, comprehending the history he envisions, is somehow changed; or at least his exacerbations are assuaged. The vision is meant to do its work on him" (Roy Harvey Pearce, *The Continuity of American Poetry* [Princeton, N.J.: Princeton University Press, 1961], p. 64.

40 Hesperia was the western land where Aeneas was told by Apollo to found the second Troy. See *The Aeneid,* III, ll. 147–71. As a son of sun, Barlow's Hesper is no longer a place but a spirit that could animate all readers.

41 Georg Lukacs, *The Theory of the Novel,* trans. Anna Bostock (Cambridge, Mass.: MIT Press 1971), p. 46.

42 *The Columbiad,* p. 620. Samuel Eliot Morison noted that Horatio Gates was the least inspiring of American generals: "His brother officers never liked him, and soldiers observed that, unlike Washington, he never exposed his person to bullets" (*The Oxford History of the American People* [New York: Oxford University Press, 1965], p. 247).

43 *Monthly Anthology and Boston Review,* 7 (1809), 294–5.

44 Woodress, *A Yankee's Odyssey,* pp. 248–9.

45 Francis Jeffrey, *Edinburgh Review,* 15 (1809), 24–40; *Boston Review and Monthly Anthology,* 7 (1809), 114–30; *Port Folio,* 1 (1809), 59–68; C. J. Ingersoll, *Inchiquin, the Jesuit's Letters* (New York, 1810), pp. 81–92; *American Review of History and Politics,* 4 (1812), 245–6; *The Analectic,* IV (1814), 158; William Cullen Bryant, *North American Review,* 7 (1818), 198–211; Edward Everett, *North American Review,* 14 (1822), 7; *Port Folio,* 8 (1812), 257; Samuel Kettell, *Specimens of American Poetry* (1829), II, 11; James R. Lowell, *North American Review,* 69 (1849), 203.

46 *Edinburgh Review,* 15 (1809), 39.

47 *Port Folio* opened its review with the following sardonic paragraph: "A quarto epic poem – polished by twenty years labour – issuing in all the pomp of typographical elegance from an American press – the author an American – the theme, the history of our country! What an era in our literature! What an epoch in the history of our arts! What a subject for the reviewer!"

48 *North American Review,* 69 (1849), 203.

49 "American Literature," in *Works of Fisher Ames* (Boston: T. B. Wait, 1809), p. 464. How remarkably similar Ames's sentence is, in thought and syntax, to C. S. Lewis's familiar summation of the life described in "primary" epic

poetry: "Today we kill and feast, tomorrow we are killed, and our women led away as slaves" (*A Preface to Paradise Lost* [New York: Oxford University Press, 1961], p. 30).

50 *North American Review,* 2 (1815), 40.

51 James A. Hillhouse, *Dramas, Discourses and Other Pieces* (Boston: Little, Brown, 1839), II, 94, 96. The essay was first delivered as an 1826 Phi Beta Kappa oration at Yale.

52 Thomas Hedges Genin did, however, carry out Hillhouse's plea that an American epic be written on a European subject. In 1833 Genin published *The Napolead,* twelve books of blank verse recounting the Napoleonic wars from the Battle of Borodino to the escape from Elba. Genin's preface and his poem are defiantly traditional. He prides himself on the magnitude and unity of his action, the credibility of his machinery (allegorical personages such as Shame, Deceit, and Reason), and his Miltonic councils. When Genin circulated proposals for his completed epic in 1815, Theodore Dwight mocked the very idea of the poem: "In old times it used to be a serious job to make a poem. We mean when such men as Milton and Dryden and Pope wrote." A New Yorker who had known De Witt Clinton, Genin moved to St. Clairsville, Ohio, in 1817 with his poem unpublished. A lawyer, journalist, and abolitionist, Genin never abandoned his epic ambitions. When *The Napolead* finally was published, the editor of Genin's works admits, "No bookseller was interested in it." Despite Genin's detailed knowledge of Napoleon's military strategy, his epic shows no sense of purpose beyond its own completion. (Biographical facts and quotations taken from the introduction to *Selections From the Writings of the Late Thomas Hedges Genin* [New York: Edward O. Jenkins, 1869]).

CHAPTER 3

1 For the background of eighteenth-century attitudes toward burlesque, satire, and mock epic see the following: Richmond P. Bond, *English Burlesque Poetry 1700-1750* (Cambridge: Harvard University Press, 1932); A. F. B. Clark, *Boileau and the French Classical Critics in England: 1660-1830* (New York: Burt Franklin, 1970; originally published 1925); Margaret Anne Doody, *The Daring Muse: Augustan Poetry Reconsidered* (Cambridge, Eng.: Cambridge University Press, 1985); Ian Jack, *Augustan Satire: Intention and Idiom in English Poetry 1660-1750* (Oxford: Clarendon, 1952); John Jump, *Burlesque* (London: Methuen, 1972); Stuart Tave, *The Amiable Humorist* (Chicago: University of Chicago Press, 1960). Bond's study has been especially useful in clarifying conceptions of the genre. My phrase "trivial causes" borrows from the Proposition of "The Rape of the Lock": "What dire Offence from am'rous Causes springs, / What mighty Contests rise from trivial things / I sing. . . ."

2 Dryden's remarks upon his abandoned epic poem are to be found in his "Discourse Concerning the Origins and Progress of Satire" (1693), in *The Works of John Dryden, Poems 1693-1696,* Vol. IV, ed. A. B. Chambers and William Frost (Berkeley: University of California Press, 1974). The fullest discussion of Pope's "Brutus" is in Miriam Lerenbaum's *Alexander Pope's Opus Magnum, 1729-1744* (Oxford: Clarendon, 1977). Johnson's remarks on Pope's *Iliad* are

in his "Life of Pope," in *Lives of the English Poets,* ed. G. B. Hill (Oxford: Clarendon, 1922), II, 397.

3 Throughout this chapter, the word "parody" is used in its eighteenth-century sense: an imitative variation meant to be recognized. Johnson's *Dictionary,* for example, defined "parody" as "a kind of writing, in which the words of an author or his thoughts are taken, and by a slight change adapted to some new purpose" (*A Dictionary of the English Language* [1775], London: Times Books, 1979, n.p.).

4 Joseph Addison, *The Spectator* #249, December 15, 1711, in *The Spectator,* ed. Donald F. Bond (Oxford: Clarendon, 1965), II, 467–8. John Dryden, "Discourse of Satire," p. 83; John Ozell, Dedication to *Boileau's Lutrin: A Mock Heroic Poem* (1708), quoted in Bond, *English Burlesque Poetry,* p. 37.

5 Joseph Wharton, *The Adventurer,* February 12, 1754; James Beattie, *Essay on Laughter and Ludicrous Composition* (1778). Both quoted in Bond, *English Burlesque Poetry,* pp. 56, 61.

6 Dryden, "Discourse of Satire," p. 13; Alexander Pope, "Postscript" to *The Odyssey* (1726), in *The Collected Poetical Works of Alexander Pope,* ed. H. W. Boyton (Boston: Houghton Mifflin, 1903), p. 638. Nicholas Boileau, *L'Art Poétique* (1674), ed. René D'Hermies (Paris: Librairie Larousse, n.d.), pp. 91, 94; Richard Cambridge, preface to *The Scribleriad* (1751), quoted in Bond, *English Burlesque Poetry,* p. 52.

7 The comic writing of the American Revolutionary era has usually been viewed as general satire and considered apart from its origins in the English debate between burlesque and mock-epic. Important studies include: Peter M. Briggs, "English Satire and Connecticut Wit," *American Quarterly,* 37 (1985), 12–29; Bruce Granger, *Political Satire in the American Revolution* (Ithaca, N.Y.: Cornell University Press, 1960); George L. Roth, "New England Satire on Religion," *New England Quarterly,* 28 (1955), 246–54; Roth, "American Theory of Satire: 1790–1820," *American Literature,* 29 (1958), 399–407; Roth, "Verse Satire on Faction: 1790–1815," *William and Mary Quarterly,* 17 (1960), 473–85; Lewis P. Simpson, "The Satiric Mode: The Early National Wits," in *The Comic Imagination in American Literature,* ed. Louis D. Rubin, Jr. (New Brunswick, N. J.: Rutgers University Press, 1973), pp. 49–61. George L. Roth has traced some 150 short political mock epics between 1780 and 1815, mostly of Federalist persuasion. Using the mock epic form as a way of guarding the Republic against demagoguery seems to have been an almost inexhaustible impulse. Titles in addition to *M'Fingal* and the collaborative *Anarchiad* include Matthew Carey, *The Porcupiniad* (Philadelphia, 1790); J. S. J. Gardiner, *Remarks on the Jacobiniad* (Boston, 1798); T. G. Fessenden, *French Politics Ingrafted on Hopkintonian Superstition* (Boston, 1799); Lemuel Hopkins, *The Democratiad* (Philadelphia, 1795); Brockholst Livingston, *Democracy: An Epic Poem* (New York, 1794); J. G. Percival, *The Commerciad* (Boston, 1809). These are, of course, only titles by names still recognized; many of the poems were anonymous or pseudonymous.

8 Alexander Cowie mentioned Trumbull's youthful plans for an epic (Cowie, *John Trumbull, Connecticut Wit* [Chapel Hill: University of North Carolina Press, 1936], pp. 18–19). Trumbull's response to *The Conquest of Canaan* is

discussed by Victor F. Gimmestad, *John Trumbull* (New York: Twayne Publishers, 1974), pp. 142–3. Trumbull mocked MacPherson in a footnote to the opening of *M'Fingal* (*The Satiric Poems of John Trumbull*, ed. Edwin T. Bowden [Austin: University of Texas Press, 1962], p. 104). Trumbull's comment on his position as America's first satirist is quoted by Robert A. Ferguson (*Law and Letters in American Culture* [Cambridge, Mass.: Harvard University Press, 1984], p. 101). Trumbull stated his preference for Swiftian Hudibrastics in his unpublished "Critical Reflections" dated 1778. The title "M'Fingal" plays upon the popularity of MacPherson's pseudoepic by suggesting that Trumbull's Tory antihero is another false-dealing Scot; the name's sound also echoes Dryden's "MacFlecknoe."

9 Letter of Trumbull to Silas Deane, May 27, 1775, quoted in Gimmestad, *John Trumbull*, pp. 81–2.

10 Letter of Trumbull to John Adams, November 14, 1775, quoted in Gimmestad, *John Trumbull*, p. 88.

11 Letter from Trumbull to the Marquis de Chastellux, dated May 20, 1785. The letter was partially reprinted by Trumbull in *The Poetical Works of John Trumbull LLD* (Hartford: Samuel G. Goodrich, 1820), II, 230–2.

12 Trumbull, letter to Marquis de Chastellux, *Poetical Works*, II, 232.

13 *The Satiric Poems of John Trumbull*, p. 101. "Beauty is the task, so that meaning may flow free of verbiage that wearies the ear."

14 Trumbull, letter to Marquis de Chastellux, p. 232.

15 See Alexander Cowie's account of the ways *M'Fingal* was used for political purposes (*John Trumbull, Connecticut Wit*, pp. 183ff.). Samuel Kettell, *Specimens of American Poetry with Critical and Biographical Notices* (Boston: Benjamin Blom, 1829), I, 179.

16 Milton, *Paradise Lost*, ed. Merritt Y. Hughes (New York: Odyssey Press, 1935), pp. 367, 370.

17 *The Anarchiad: A New England Poem*, ed. Luther G. Riggs (New Haven, Conn.: Thomas A. Pease, 1861), pp. 4–6.

18 *Poetry and Prose of Alexander Pope*, ed. Aubrey Williams (Boston: Houghton Mifflin, 1969), p. 378.

19 Ibid., p. 61.

20 Barlow, "The Hasty-Pudding," in *The Works of Joel Barlow*, ed. W. K. Bottorff and A. L. Ford (Gainesville, Fla.: Scholars' Facsimiles & Reprints, 1970), II, 87. Barlow did not designate a genre; "The Hasty-Pudding" has the subtitle "A Poem in Three Cantos."

21 Letter from Joel to Ruth Barlow, November 1812, quoted in James Woodress, *A Yankee's Odyssey* (Philadelphia: Lippincott, 1958), p. 304.

22 Barlow, "Advice To A Raven In Russia" in Woodress, *A Yankee's Odyssey*, pp. 338–9.

23 See Daniel Marder, "Introduction" to *A Hugh Henry Brackenridge Reader* (Pittsburgh: University of Pittsburgh Press, 1970), and Daniel Marder, *Hugh Henry Brackenridge* (New York: Twayne Publishers, 1967), pp. 54–60.

24 Ferguson, *Law and Letters in American Culture*, pp. 120–4. Brackenridge's "The Modern Chevalier" may be found in his *Gazette Publications* (Carlisle, Pa:

Alexander & Phillips, 1806) and then in the appendix to the 1815 edition of *Modern Chivalry*. Brackenridge's account of changing from Hudibrastic verse to Cervantic prose is quoted in Claude M. Newlin's "Introduction" to *Modern Chivalry* (New York: American Book, 1937), p. xxiii.

25 At some time after 1853 Melville reread the Knickerbocker *History*. Of the six passages that Melville scored in the margin, four pertain to Peter Stuyvesant, including one passage in which Irving refers to "the brimstone-coloured breeches and splendid silver leg of Peter Stuyvesant, glaring in the sunbeams" (Walker Cowan, *Melville's Marginalia* [Harvard University Dissertation, 1965], VI, 340–51). Here and in later chapter I develop long-slighted connections between Irving and later writers that have been briefly suggested by William Hedges and Martin Roth. See William L. Hedges, *Washington Irving: An American Study, 1802–1832* (Baltimore, Md.: Johns Hopkins University Press, 1965), pp. 87–8. Martin Roth has used the term "burlesque comedy" to describe a mode of narration, at once whimsical and ebullient, common to Irving, Melville, and Whitman (*Comedy and America: The Lost World of Washington Irving* [New York: Kennikat, 1976], pp. 3–13).

26 Washington Irving, *A History of New York from the Beginning of the World to the End of the Dutch Dynasty*, in *Washington Irving: History, Tales and Sketches*, ed. James Tuttleton (New York: The Library of America, 1983), p. 406. The Library of America reprints the first, more abrasive edition of 1809, which I have followed throughout. Filiopietistic expectations toward historical writing during the early national period have been studied by Jay Fliegelman, *Prodigals and Pilgrims: The American Revolution Against Patriarchal Authority* (Cambridge, Eng.: Cambridge University Press, 1982), Chapters 7–8; Michael Kammen, *A Season of Youth* (New York: Knopf, 1978); John McWilliams, *Hawthorne, Melville and the American Character* (Cambridge, Eng.: Cambridge University Press, 1984), pp. 26–36. The judgment of Irving's *History* is from Robert Ferguson's *Law and Letters In American Culture*, p. 158.

27 Michael Kammen, *Colonial New York: A History* (New York: Scribner, 1975), pp. 48–72.

28 In this respect, Knickerbocker's attitudes are remarkably like William Hedges's summary of Irving's: "There is much in him which suggests a sense of the world as ungraspable. . . . He cannot be sure that he has any identity beyond that of being one in a scrambling democratic throng. . . . His sense of inevitable decay was to be his substitute for a theory of history" (*Washington Irving, An American Study*, pp. 3, 4, 42).

29 Byron often expressed his delight in the Knickerbocker *History* to American visitors. See Leslie A. Marchand, *Byron: A Portrait* (Chicago: University of Chicago Press, 1970), pp. 344, 376.

30 Bryant, "A Discourse on the Life, Character and Genius of Washington Irving" (New York: Putnam, 1860), p. 18. British readers of the era were perhaps more ready to accept literature that conveyed relentless skepticism. The *Edinburgh Magazine*, for example, had judged the Knickerbocker *History* to be worth "a whole Congress of Joel Barlows" (*Edinburgh Magazine and Literary Miscellany*, 7 [1810], 544).

31 Noah Webster, *An American Dictionary of the English Language* (New York: S. Converse, 1828; New York & London: Johnson Reprint Corp., 1970). Samuel Kettell, *Specimens of American Poetry* (1829), I, 179, 182, 182.

CHAPTER 4

1 Dixon Wecter, *The Hero in America* (1941), republished with a preface by Robert Penn Warren (New York: Scribner, 1972), p. 182.
2 Constance Rourke, *American Humor* (New York: Doubleday, 1953), p. 60.
3 Edward Pollock, "Thoughts Toward a New Epic," *The Pioneer or California Monthly Magazine,* II (1854), 65–78.
4 Bret Harte, quoted in Benjamin T. Spencer, *The Quest for Nationality* (Syracuse, N.Y.: Syracuse University Press, 1957), p. 282.
5 Frank Norris, letter to W. D. Howells, March 1899, quoted in Franklin Walker, *Frank Norris: A Biography* (New York: Russell, 1963), p. 239.
6 *Responsibilities of the Novelist, Complete Works of Frank Norris* (Port Washington, N.Y.: Kennikat Press, 1967), VII, 48, 49.
7 "The Epic of the West: Its Hero," pamphlet essay in the Widener Library, Cambridge, Mass., no author, no date, p. 1.
8 *Analectic Magazine,* 12 (1818), 240.
9 "Early American Poetry," *American Quarterly Review,* 2 (1827), 509. See also Solyman Brown, *An Essay on American Poetry* (New Haven, Conn.: Hezekiah Howe, 1818), p. 47.
10 Orestes Brownson, "Address to the United Brothers Society of Brown University" (1839), in *Brownson's Works* (Detroit: T. Nourse, 1885), XIX, 23.
11 *North American Review,* 30 (1830), 279.
12 *North American Review,* 33 (1831), 302; *American Quarterly Review,* 20 (1836), 504–5.
13 Thomas Peirce, *The Muse of Hesperia* (Cincinnati: Philomathic Society, 1823), pp. 14, 30.
14 Timothy Flint, *Recollections of the Last Ten Years* (1826) (New York: Knopf, 1932), p. 67.
15 Henry Nash Smith, *Virgin Land* (Cambridge, Mass.: Harvard University Press, 1950), pp. 54–63.
16 See Richard Slotkin, *Regeneration Through Violence* (Middletown, Conn.: Wesleyan University Press, 1973), pp. 268–312. While exploring the Ohio River Valley, Filson has Boone declare: "No populous city, with all its varieties of commerce and stately structures, could afford so much pleasure to my mind, as the beauties of nature I found here." Boone later reverses himself: "Many dark and sleepless nights have I been a companion for owls, separated from the chearful [sic] society of men, scorched by the Summer's sun, and pinched by the Winter's cold, an instrument ordained to settle the wilderness. But now, the scene is changed. Peace crowns the sylvan shade . . . and plenty, in league with commerce, scatters blessings from her copious hand" (John Filson, *The Discovery, Settlement and Present State of Kentucke* [New York: Corinth, 1962], pp. 56, 80–1).
17 Daniel Bryan, *The Mountain Muse: Comprising the Adventures of Daniel Boone*

and the Power of Virtuous and Refined Beauty (Harrisonburg, Va.: Davidson & Bourne, 1813), pp. 27–9.

18 Compare Bryan's description of Boone: "Generous, guileless, kind / The gripe of sneaking Avarice ne'er compress'd / His princely heart" (46).

19 John Bakeless, *Daniel Boone; Master of the Wilderness* (New York: Stackpole & Co., 1939), p. 336.

20 Daniel Bryan was the son of Boone's sister and Boone's brother-in-law, William Bryan. When members of the Bryan and Boone families migrated to St. Charles, Missouri, in 1799, Daniel Bryan remained behind and settled in Virginia. Bryan continued to publish volumes of verse, all in praise of civilized and Christian virtues. In the preface to *The Appeal for Suffering Genius* (1826), Bryan calls *The Mountain Muse* "the wild offspring of a rude undisciplined fancy" (v). Bryan's *Thoughts on Education* (1830) begins with the lines "Not mine the power to sweep with magic skill / The golden chords of the celestial lyre / O'er which Urania sheds her beams divine."

21 Bakeless, *Daniel Boone*, p. 394.

22 *Analectic Magazine*, 6 (1815), 170.

23 William Gilmore Simms, *Southern Literary Gazette*, 1 (1828), 312–13.

24 James Kirke Paulding, "National Literature" (1820), in *The American Literary Revolution*, ed. R. E. Spiller (New York: Doubleday, 1967), pp. 384, 385, 383.

25 Paulding, *The Backwoodsman* (Philadelphia: M. Thomas, 1818), pp. 144–6.

26 William Carlos Williams, *Paterson* (New York: New Directions, 1958), n.p.

27 Both comments are quoted in W. I. Paulding, *Literary Life of James K. Paulding* (New York: Scribner, 1867), p. 96.

28 *Port Folio*, 7 (1819), 26–39.

29 *American Monthly Magazine and Critical Review*, 4 (1819), 161–76.

30 *The Letters of James Kirke Paulding*, ed. R. M. Aderman (Madison: University of Wisconsin Press, 1962), p. 60.

31 Walter Marshall McGill, "Preface" to *The Western World* (Maryville, Tenn.: F. A. Parham, 1837), p. 5.

32 McGill, *The Western World*, pp. 116, 212, 247.

33 John William Ward, *Andrew Jackson: Symbol for an Age* (New York: Oxford University Press, 1962). Ward does not mention McGill's poem, but notes the frequency with which Jacksonians described their hero as a "second Washington" (pp. 42, 189, et passim).

34 Ward, *Andrew Jackson*, pp. 13–29. Ward mentions that shortly after the Battle of New Orleans, Representative Troup of Georgia declared to the House "Language cannot do justice to the merits of General Jackson and the troops under his command. . . . It is a fit subject for the genius of Homer" (7). Within a few years, an anonymous bard penned *An Epick Poem* to celebrate Jackson's victory in thirty pages of heroic couplets.

35 Richard Emmons, *The Fredoniad; or, Independence Preserved: An Epic Poem on the Late War of 1812* (Boston: William Emmons, 1827), I, 76.

36 Timothy Flint, *Western Review*, 2 (1828), 176–81.

37 Frances Trollope, *Domestic Manners of the Americans* (London: Dodd, Mead, 1927), p. 271.

38 "The Literary Life of Thing-um Bob, Esq.," in *Collected Works of Edgar Allan Poe,* ed. T. O. Mabbott (Cambridge, Mass.: Harvard University Press, 1978), III, 1126.

39 Melville, "Hawthorne and His Mosses" (1850), in *The Literature of the United States,* ed. W. Blair, T. Hornberger, R. Steward, and J. Miller (New York: Scott Foresman, 1969), II, 38.

40 Melville, "Hawthorne and His Mosses," p. 38.

41 Rourke, *American Humor,* p. 60. See also Rourke's *Davy Crockett* (New York: Harcourt Brace, 1934).

42 *Davy Crockett: American Comic Legend,* ed. R. M. Dorson, Introduction by H. M. Jones (New York: Rockland Editions, 1939). Dorson and Jones reassert Rourke's claim that the Crockett almanac stories are "America's own crude and grotesque epic" (xxvi).

43 Melville, *Moby-Dick,* ed. H. Hayford, H. Parker, and T. Tanselle (Evanston and London: Northwestern–Newberry, 1978), p. 363.

44 Hawthorne, "A Select Party" in *Mosses from an Old Manse,* Vol. X of the Centenary edition (Columbus: Ohio State University Press, 1974), p. 72.

45 Hawthorne, "P's Correspondence," in *Mosses from an Old Manse,* p. 300.

46 Hawthorne, *The Bilthedale Romance,* Vol. III of the Centenary edition (Columbus: Ohio State University Press, 1964), p. 129.

47 Lowell, *A Fable for Critics, The Writings of James Russell Lowell* (Boston: Houghton Mifflin, 1890), III, 87.

48 Longfellow, *Kavanaugh, a Tale* (Boston: Ticknor & Fields, 1859), p. 113. Longfellow's novel was first published in 1849.

49 Letter from Irving to Henry Tuckerman, January 8, 1856, in Pierre Irving, *Life and Letters of Washington Irving* (New York: Putnam, 1864), IV, 207.

50 Irving, "Edwin C. Holland" (1814) in *Reviews and Miscellanies, Irving's Works,* ed. Pierre Irving (Philadelphia: Lippincott, 1873), p. 332.

51 Thomas Lake Harris, *An Epic of the Starry Heaven* (New York: Partridge & Brittan, 1855), p. 182.

52 "James Gates Percival," *The Writings of James Russell Lowell* (Boston: Houghton Mifflin, 1890), II, 153.

53 Ibid., p. 151.

54 Ibid., p. 149.

55 Ibid., pp. 151–2.

56 Lowell, "Longfellow's *Kavanagh*: Nationality in Literature," *North American Review,* 69 (1849), 203.

57 Lowell, "James Gates Percival," pp. 152–3.

58 Lowell, "Longfellow's *Kavanagh*: Nationality in Literature," p. 210.

59 C. C. Felton, "Preliminary Remarks" to *The Iliad* (Boston: J. Munroe & Co., 1847), p. 409.

60 Joel Barlow, *The Columbiad, The Works of Joel Barlow,* ed. W. K. Bottorff and A. L. Ford (Gainesville, Fla.: Scholars' Facsimiles & Reprints, 1970), II, 689.

61 Robert Southey, "Preface" to *Madoc* (Boston: Munroe & Francis, 1805), p. vii.

62 "Observations on Poetry," *Port Folio,* 8 (1812), 256–7.

63 John Neal, *Blackwoods Magazine* (1824), reprinted in *American Writers,* ed.
F. L. Pattee (Durham, N.C.: Duke University Press, 1937), p. 77.

64 Longfellow, "The Defence of Poetry," *North American Review,* 34 (1832), 67.

65 *North American Review,* 48 (1839), 367.

66 Washington Allston, *Lectures on Art and Poems,* ed. R. M. Dana, Jr. (New
York: Baker & Scribner, 1850), p. 123.

67 The quotations from *Putnam's Magazine* and *Scientific American* are cited by
Leo Marx in *The Machine in the Garden* (New York: Oxford University Press,
1964), pp. 202–3.

68 Poe, "The Poetic Principle" (1849), in *Selected Writings of Edgar Allan Poe,* ed.
E. H. Davidson (Boston: Houghton Mifflin, 1956), p. 465.

69 Henry Tuckerman, *The Optimist* (New York: Putnam, 1850), p. 104.

70 John Campbell, *Republica* (1891); Henry Iliowizi, *Quest of Columbus* (1892);
Samuel Jefferson, *Columbus: An Epic Poem* (1892); John Howell, *Columbus*
(1893); Franklyn Quinby, *The Columbiad* (1893).

71 André Chénier, "L'Amérique" in *Oeuvres Poétiques de André Chénier* (Paris:
Librairie Garnier Frères, 1924), II, 86. Translations by J. M.

CHAPTER 5

1 I am especially indebted to the following studies of white attitudes toward
the Indian during the nineteenth century: Louise K. Barnett, *The Ignoble Savage: American Literary Racism 1790–1890* (Westport, Conn.: Greenwood, 1975);
Robert F. Berkhofer, Jr., *The White Man's Indian* (New York: Knopf, 1978),
Part III, pp. 72–111; Richard Drinnon, *Facing West: The Metaphysics of Indian-
Hating and Empire Building* (Minneapolis: University of Minnesota Press, 1980),
Part III, pp. 117–215; Roy Harvey Pearce, *Savagism and Civilization* (Baltimore, Md.: Johns Hopkins University Press, 1965); Michael Paul Rogin, *Fa-
thers and Children: Andrew Jackson and the Subjugation of the American Indian*
(New York: Random House, 1975). These works trace a unanimity of cultural attitudes that Berkhofer has succinctly summarized: "The quest for
American cultural identity, the role of the United States in history, faith in
the future greatness of the nation, and the fate of the Indian and the frontier
in general were all seen as connected by the White Americans of the period.
What reconciled the ambivalent images of nature, the Indian, and the frontier
was an ideology of social progress that postulated the inevitable evolution of
the frontier from savagery to civilization" (*The White Man's Indian,* p. 92). I
hope to prove that the tradition of epic was a far more important lens for
viewing the Indian than has yet been realized. Viewing American Indians as
the last mutants of Homeric Greeks prompted many writers to rebel, albeit
unwillingly, against the prevailing ideology of progress.

2 Clara Reeve, *The Progress of Romance* (New York: Facsimile Text Society,
1930), I, 51.

3 Percy Bysshe Shelley, "A Defence of Poetry" (1821), in *Shelley: Selected Poems
Essays and Letters,* ed. E. Barnard (New York: Odyssey, 1944), p. 555.

4 Byron, as quoted in Thomas Medwin, *Journal of the Conversations of Lord
Byron* (New York: Wilder & Campbell, 1824), p. 112. Such statements illus-

trate John Jump's summary of Romantic aesthetics: "The Romantics rejected the doctrine of kinds and the rules associated with it. They held that each true poem evolves in accord with organic laws, into its own unique final form. Instead of poems that belong to kinds, they created individual poems" (John Jump, *Burlesque* [London: Methuen, 1972], p. 51). The great difficulty – as these same statements also show – was that these new "individual" poems were usually evoked or described through the old terminology.

5 W. H. Prescott, "Sir Walter Scott" (1837), in *Biographical and Critical Miscellanies* (Boston: Phillips, Sampson, & Co., 1857), p. 191.

6 Scott, "Advertisement" to *The Lay of the Last Minstrel,* in *The Poetical Works of Sir Walter Scott.* (New York: Appleton, 1870), pp. 22.

7 Scott, *The Lay of the Last Minstrel,* p. 99.

8 The same contrast would later be used for regional self-justification. Many Southerners saw themselves as Cavaliers opposing Roundheads or as heroic Highlanders defending themselves against the commercial progressive North. See William R. Taylor, *Cavalier and Yankee* (New York: Braziller, 1961), 211–25 et passim.

9 Walter Scott, review of Southey's *The Curse of Kehama* (1811), in *Miscellaneous Prose Works* (Paris: Baudry's European Library, 1838), III, 166.

10 Walter Scott, "Essay on Romance" (1824), in *Essays on Chivalry, Romance and the Drama* (London: Frederick Warne, 1887), p. 68.

11 Scott, "Essay on Romance," p. 69. In his commanding study of the American historical romance, George Dekker interprets the significance of these distinctions differently than I shall. Pursuing the implications of Scott's definition, Dekker shows that American historical romances were often tales of patriarchal foundings and their dissolutions, of communities and *patriae,* of one subject matter that subsumed the epic within romantic fiction. This perspective enables Dekker to view *The Wept of Wish-ton-Wish, The Scarlet Letter, Israel Potter, My Antonia, The Age of Innocence, The Great Meadow, The Fathers,* and *Absalom, Absalom!* as one coherent tradition that essentially replaces the epic.

I regard the rise of the *Waverley* tradition as only one generic shift, albeit a crucial one, within a continuing problem of redefining epic as heroic literature in many new guises. The calamitous failure of the eighteenth-century epic poem, apparent exactly at the time of Scott's essay, made the survival of epic through its transformation all the more desirable. Once Indians and Aztecs could be perceived as the New World counterparts of Homeric Greeks, both the subjects and type scenes of epic could be made new within metrical lays and heroic histories, as well as in fictional romances. Scott's insistence on tying historical romance to times of patriarchal foundings leads Dekker to place works like *The Last of the Mohicans* and *Moby-Dick* in a less than central place within American heroic fiction. However peripheral one may judge these romances to be, it is hard to deny their self-consciously historical, heroic, and epic qualities. See George Dekker, *The American Historical Romance* (Cambridge, Eng.: Cambridge University Press, 1987), especially p. 61.

12 Scott, "Essay on Romance," p. 92. Nina Baym has shown that by 1840 the terms "novel" and "romance" had become virtually indistinguishable among

American reviewers (Baym. *Novels, Readers and Reviewers* [Ithaca, N.Y.: Cornell University Press, 1984], pp. 224–48). Cooper, Simms, and Parkman, however, all use the term "romance" in conjunction with Indian fiction, and are all, in varying ways, indebted to Scott. In this particular context, then, "romance" may continue to be a useful generic category.

13 W. H. Prescott, "Italian Narrative Poetry," *North American Review*, 19 (1824), 340.

14 George Bancroft, "The Office of the People in Art, Government and Religion" (1835), *Literary and Historical Miscellanies* (New York: Harper, 1855), p. 419.

15 Cadwallader Colden, *The History of the Five Indian Nations* (New York: Allerton, 1922), Vol. I, pp. xxii, x, xxxii, xxiv, xxviii.

16 Francois René de Chateaubriand, "Preface" to *Atala, Poesies Par Chateaubriand* (Paris: Garnier, 1881), p. 1. Not until 1826 was Chateaubriand finally to publish the full text of *Natchez*. In his preface, he carefully assures his reader that all the conventions of epic poetry can and have been transferred to a French prose work on the American Indian: *"Ainsi donc, dans le premier volume des* Natchez *on trouvera le merveilleux, et le merveilleux de toutes les espèces: le merveilleux chretien, le merveilleux mythologique, le merveilleux indien; on rencontera des muses, des anges, des demons, des genies, des combats, des personnages allegoriques: La Renomeé, Le Temps, La Nuit, La Mort, L'Amitié. Ce volume offre des invocations, des sacrifices, des prodiges, des comparaisons multipleé, les unes courtes, les autres longues, longues à la facon d'Homere, et formant de petits tableaux"* (*Poésies par Chateaubriand*, pp. 184–5). So self-conscious an appropriation of epic was little noticed in America, and only in part because *The Last of the Mohicans* was published in the same year. Alexander Hill Everett remarked that, though Chateaubriand had intended "an epic poem in prose, . . . we are rather surprised that his mature judgment should not have induced him to suppress it entirely" (*North American Review*, 27 [1828], 229). Anxiety to imitate the epic was clearly becoming dated.

17 Sarah Wentworth Morton, *Ouabi: Or, The Virtues of Nature* (Boston: I. Thomas & E. T. Andrews, 1790), pp. 14, 19.

18 The resolution of Mrs. Morton's *Ouabi* forms a revealing contrast to Dwight's *Greenfield Hill* (1794), published only four years later. After berating the Pequods as Satanic barbarians through most of the fourth book, Dwight asks his countrymen to indulge a tear for the benighted folk whom the heroic Stoughton has slain: "And, O ye Chiefs! in yonder stray home, / Accept the humble tribute of this rhyme, / Your gallant deeds, in Greece, or haughty Rome, / By Maro sung, or Homer's harp sublime, / Had charm'd the world's wide round, and triumph'd over time" (Dwight, *Greenfield Hill: A Poem in Seven Parts* [New York: Childs & Swaine, 1794], p. 105). Unlike Mrs. Morton, Dwight can afford a final Homeric tribute because the seventeenth-century perspective of the poem makes the Indian problem seem wholly past.

19 Washington Irving, "Philip of Pokanoket," *The Analectic Magazine*, III (1814), 509; "Traits of Indian Character," *The Analectic Magazine*, 3 (1814), 151–2.

20 Irving, "Traits of Indian Character," p. 151.

21 John Heckewelder, *An Account of the History, Manners and Customs of the Indian*

Nations (Philadelphia: Transactions of the American Philosophical Society, 1819), p. 89.

22 Edward Everett, "Politics of Ancient Greece," *North American Review,* 18 (1824), 398. Almost every phrase of Everett's long comparison exactly illustrates the stadialist model of progress that George Dekker discusses in chapter three of *The American Historical Romance,* pp. 73–84.

23 John Augustus Stone, *Metamora; or The Last of the Wampanoags,* in *Metamora and Other Plays,* ed. E. R. Page (Princeton, N. J.: Princeton University Press, 1941), pp. 10, 11, 12.

24 William Tudor, "The North American Review," *Miscellanies* (Boston: Wells & Lilly, 1821), p. 58.

25 Walter Channing, "Reflections on the Literary Delinquency of America," *North American Review,* 2 (1815), 39.

26 William Tudor, "An Address to the Phi Beta Kappa Society," *North American Review,* 2 (1815), 14.

27 Later calls for epic literature about America's Greeklike Indians include John Dunne's "Notes Relative to Some of the Native Tribes of North America," *Port Folio,* 30 (1818), 231; William Tudor, *Letters on the Eastern States* (New York: Kirk & Mercein, 1820), 247–51; William Gilmore Simms, "Literature and Art Among the American Aborigines" in *Views and Reviews in American Literature* (1845) (Cambridge, Mass.: Harvard University Press, 1962), pp. 130–45; Mrs. C. M. Kirkland, "Preface" to Mrs. Mary Eastman's *Dacotah* (New York, 1849), pp. 9–11.

28 Gulian Verplanck, "Introduction" to *The Writings of Robert C. Sands* (New York: Harper, 1834), I, 4. New York's literary community was then small and closely connected. Parke Godwin mentions a dinner party in 1824 at which Bryant, Catharine Sedgwick, Halleck, Cooper, and Sands were all present (*Biography of William Cullen Bryant* [New York: Appleton, 1883], I, 189).

29 Robert Sands and James Eastburn, *Yamoyden: A Tale of the Wars of King Philip* (New York: Clayton & Kingsland, 1820), pp. xii, 4, 247.

30 John Gorham Palfrey, review of *Yamoyden, North American Review,* 12 (1821), 466.

31 Palfrey, review of *Yamoyden,* p. 484.

32 Anonymous review of *Yamoyden, Port Folio,* 35 (1820), 464.

33 Robert Sands, "Domestic Literature," first published in the *Atlantic* (1824), later collected in *The Writings of Robert Sands,* ed. G. Verplanck (New York: Harper, 1834), I, 107.

34 Both the poem and Sands's headnote were published in "Memoir of Robert C. Sands," *The Knickerbocker,* 1 (1833), 58.

35 James Fenimore Cooper, "Review of Lockhart's Life of Scott," *The Knickerbocker,* 12 (1838), 363–4.

36 Cooper, *The Redskins, The Novels of James Fenimore Cooper* (New York: W. A. Townsend, 1859), p. 96.

37 James F. Beard, ed., *The Letters and Journals of James Fenimore Cooper* (Cambridge, Mass.: Harvard University Press, 1960), II, 99.

38 Cooper, 1831 Introduction to *The Last of the Mohicans,* ed. J. A. Sappenfield

and E. N. Feltskog (Albany: State University of New York Press, 1983), p. 7.

39 Cooper, "Preface to the Leather-Stocking Tales" (1850), in *The Last of the Mohicans,* ed. W. Charvat (Boston: Houghton Mifflin, 1958), p. 14.

40 Cooper, *The Last of the Mohicans,* p. 31.

41 See Richard Slotkin, *Regeneration through Violence: The Mythology of the American Frontier* (Middletown, Conn.: Wesleyan University Press, 1973), p. 485; and Michael D. Butler, "Narrative Structure and Historical Process in *The Last of the Mohicans,*" *American Literature,* 68 (1976), 117–39.

42 See Roy Harvey Pearce, "A Melancholy Fact," Chapter Two of *The Savages of America* (Baltimore Md.: Johns Hopkins University Press, 1965), pp. 53–7; and Robert F. Sayre, "Savagism," Chapter One of *Thoreau and the American Indians* (Princeton, N.J.: Princeton University Press, 1977), pp. 3–27.

43 Characterizing the "good Indian" in American frontier romances, Louise Barnett has observed, "Although he moves among Indians, some contact with whites has elevated him to a superior position from which he may deplore certain savage usages of his fellows. It is important to note that this figure is not simply a noble savage, but a noble savage upon whom certain aspects of white civilization have been engrafted. Whatever the circumstances, the good Indian has become good primarily through intercourse with whites, and his goodness is expressed chiefly by his services to them" (Louise K. Barnett, *The Ignoble Savage* [Westport, Conn.: Greenwood, 1975], p. 91). Uncas looks and acts like this stereotypical "good" Indian, but he neither rejects Delaware culture nor embraces Christian civilization.

44 See Joel Porte, *The Romance in America* (Middletown, Conn.: Wesleyan University Press, 1965), p. 40.

45 Alexander Heidel, *The Gilgamesh Epic and Old Testament Parallels* (Chicago: University of Chicago Press, 1970), p. 19.

46 Cooper, "Preface to the Leather-Stocking Tales," pp. 11, 12.

47 Honoré de Balzac, review of *The Pathfinder* (1840), in *Fenimore Cooper: The Critical Heritage,* ed. G. Dekker & J. McWilliams (London: Routledge & Kegan Paul, 1973), p. 196. On Leatherstocking as a noble savage, see Barrie Hayne, "Ossian, Scott and Cooper's Indians," *Journal of American Studies,* 3 (1969), 75.

48 W. H,. Gardiner, review of *The Last of the Mohicans, North American Review,* 23 (1826), 191.

49 Lewis Cass, "Indians of North America," *North American Review,* 22 (1826), 67.

50 Grenville Mellon, review of *The Red Rover, North American Review,* 27 (1828), 140.

51 Anonymous review of *York Town: A Historical Romance, American Quarterly Review,* 2 (1827), 45.

52 Alexander Hill Everett, review of Irving's *Life of Columbus, North American Review,* 28 (1829), 130.

53 Rufus Choate, "The Importance of Illustrating New-England History by a Series of Romances Like the Waverly Novels," an address delivered at Salem, 1833, in *The Works of Rufus Choate* (Boston: Little, Brown, 1862), I, 326, 327.

54 Simms's forty-five page poem "The Vision of Cortes" was, he wrote, "originally introduced in one of larger dimensions on the subject of the Incas,
which I was wise enough to destroy" (Simms, *The Vision of Cortes, Cain, and
Other Poems* [Charleston, S.C.: James S. Burges, 1829], p. 7).

55 In the "Preface" to a reissue of *The Wigwam and the Cabin,* Simms insisted
"To be national in literature, one must needs be sectional" ([New York:
A. C. Armstrong, 1856], p. 4).

56 "French Novels," *Southern Review,* 7 (1831), 344. It is possible that Simms
wrote this review.

57 Simms, "Advertisement" to *The Yemassee: A Romance of Carolina* (New York:
Harper, 1835), I, vi.

58 Simms, review of the works of Daniel Bryan, *Southern Literary Gazette,* 2
(1829), 312.

59 Simms, review of Robert Pollok's *The Course of Time, Southern Literary Gazette,* 1 (1828), p. 237.

60 Simms, "John Milton vs. Robert Montgomery," *The Knickerbocker,* 3 (1834),
120. The reviews of Pollok and Montgomery were ascribed to Simms by Edd
Winfield Parks, *William Gilmore Simms as Literary Critic* (Athens: University
of Georgia Press, 1961), p. 55.

61 See Michael Paul Rogin, *Fathers and Children: Andrew Jackson and the Subjugation of the American Indian* (New York: Random House, 1975), pp. 220–40.

62 Simms, *The Yemassee,* ed. C. Hugh Holman (Boston: Houghton Mifflin, 1961),
p. 173.

63 After claiming in the first edition that his account of the Yemassee was historically accurate, Simms acknowledged in the preface of 1853 that his rendering of Yemassee "mythology" had been "a pure invention" (4).

64 Jane Tompkins has suggested a plausible reason for the allegiance between
Cooper's "good Indians" and good colonials: "Cooper's good Indians often
embody 'lost' virtues associated with the heroes of epic, romance, and the
Old Testament, while the tribal life they lead incorporates values associated
with pre-Revolutionary stability and cohesiveness" (Jane Tompkins, *Sensational Designs* [New York: Oxford University Press, 1985], p. 111).

65 Richard Drinnon, *Facing West* (Minneapolis, 1980), p. 143; Joseph Ridgely,
William Gilmore Simms (New Haven, Conn.: Twayne Publishers, 1962), pp.
19–20. For Simms, the Indian romance could express attitudes that had troublesome implications for public policy. Simms's view of the Yemassee war
in his *History of South Carolina* (1840), by contrast, grants no justice to the
Indian cause. The Yemassee are portrayed as "stealthy enemies" who "plun-
dering and murdering without mercy . . . threatened the very existence of
the colony" (Simms, *The History of South Carolina* [Charleston, S.C.: S. Bab-
cock, 1840], pp. 65, 97). Similarly, Simms's 1831 newspaper description of
Creek chieftain William McIntosh had concluded "There is less of dignity
than low cunning in his features – he was, I believe, a kind of Indian Van
Buren, and was more of the intriguing and wily politician, than the free,
frank and generous warrior" (*The Letters of William Gilmore Simms,* ed.
M. C. S. Oliphant, A. T. Odell, T. C. D. Eaves [Columbia: South Carolina
University Press, 1952–6], I, 26).

66 Park Benjamin, review of *The Yemassee, New-England Magazine,* 8 (1835), 489.

67 Simms, "Advertisement" to *The Yemassee* (New York: Harper, 1835), I, vi.

68 Simms, Preface of 1853 to *The Yemassee,* pp. 4–5.

69 Simms, "Literature and Art Among the American Aborigines," in *Views and Reviews in American Literature* (1845), ed. C. H. Holman (Cambridge, Mass.: Harvard University Press, 1962), p. 145.

70 During the 1830s a Delaware heroic poem titled *Walam Olum* ("painted record") was transcribed from oral delivery and then translated into disconnected English prose. The poem describes the creation of the world by Manito, the struggle against Manito led by the evil snake god, the subsequent coming of sickness, death, and anger into Delaware life, and the eventual saving of the tribe from a flood by the heroic warrior Nanabush. Whether the obvious resemblance of this poem to *Genesis* and to *Paradise Lost* is due to archetypal parallels, to the education of the translator, or to forgery will probably never be known. See Daniel G. Brinton, *The Lenapé and their Legends* (Philadelphia: D. C. Brinton, 1885), pp. 148–59, and Alan R. Velie, *American Indian Literature* (Norman: University of Oklahoma Press, 1979), pp. 93–135. Two versions of the Iroquois epic "Dekanawida" were written down at the beginning of the twentieth century. See Kristin Herzog, *Women, Ethnics and Exotics* (Knoxville: University of Tennessee Press, 1983), Chapter 6, pp. 167–78.

71 Simms, Letter to Evert Duyckinck, 1855, in *Letters of William Gilmore Simms,* III, 388–9.

72 Francis Parkman, letter to the Cooper Memorial Committee, *Fenimore Cooper: The Critical Heritage,* p. 248; "The Works of James Fenimore Cooper" (*North American Review,* 1852), in *Fenimore Cooper: The Critical Heritage,* p. 252.

73 Parkman, letter to the Cooper Memorial Committee, p. 248.

74 Parkman, "The Works of James Fenimore Cooper," p. 256.

75 Parkman, *The Conspiracy of Pontiac,* sixth edition, introduction by Samuel Eliot Morrison (New York: Collier–Macmillan, 1962), p. 61.

76 Parkman, "The Works of James Fenimore Cooper," p. 255.

77 Parkman, *The Conspiracy of Pontiac,* p. 63. Michael Rogin has shown how antebellum Americans made political use of this metaphor. See Chapter Four, "Children of Nature," in *Fathers and Children: Andrew Jackson and the Subjugation of the American Indian* (New York: Random House, 1975), pp. 113–25.

78 Caroline Kirkland, "Preface" to Mrs. Mary Eastman's *Dacotah* (New York: Wiley, 1849). Concluding that the Indian "has as many qualifiactions for the heroic character as Ajax, or even Achilles," Mrs. Kirkland urges "Nothing is wanting but a Homer to build our Iliad material into lofty rhyme, or a Scott to weave it into border romance" (ix). Until the American Homer–Scott should appear, the most that could be done was to encourage ethnologists "to be recording fleeting traditions and describing peculiar customs" (ix).

79 Catharine Maria Sedgwick, *Hope Leslie,* ed. M. Kelley (New Brunswick and London: Rutgers University Press, 1987), p. 56.

CHAPTER 6

1 Letter of 1847 in *The Correspondence of William Hickling Prescott: 1833–1847*, ed. R. Wolcott (Cambridge: Massachusetts Historical Society, 1925), p. 629.

2 Entry written in 1839, *The Literary Memoranda of William Hickling Prescott*, ed. C. Harvey Gardiner (Norman: University of Oklahoma Press, 1961), II, 29.

3 Prescott, *Literary Memoranda*, II, 32.

4 Prescott, letter to Count Adolphe de Circourt, 1845, in George Ticknor, *The Life of William Hickling Prescott* (Philadelphia: Lippincott, 1882), p. 27. Chevalier's ninety-page review assesses the epic qualities of Prescott's *History* at length: *"Auprès d'un tel sujet le thème de l'Iliade paraît exigu et pâle. Qu'est-ce en effect sinon la brouille et la racommodement d'Achille et d'Agamemnon avec une action qu'on ne peut qualifier de finale, car elle ne termine rien, dans laquelle le principal des défenseurs de Trois est vaincu et tué par le plus vaillant des Grecs? L'Enéide n'est pas sur de plus larges proportions. . . . On croirait avoir pris lecture d'un poème épique ou d'un roman de chevalerie, tant les évènements et les simples incidents y sont sur des proportions grandioses"* (Michel Chevalier, "La Conquête du Mexique," *Revue des Deux Mondes*, XI [1845], 226–7).

5 A brief overview of this literature may prove helpful. There are only three extant primary sources about the conquest: Hernando Cortes, *The Five Letters of Relation* (1520); Bernal Díaz, *True History of the Conquest of New Spain* (1560s), and a collection of Aztec poems and recollections, edited by Miguel Leon-Portilla, called *The Broken Spears* (1962). The important early Spanish histories of the conquest are by Antonio Gomora, *Chronicles of New Spain* (1553), and Antonio Solis, *History of the Conquest of Mexico* (1684).

The first epic poem written by an American, James Ralph's *Zeuma; or the Love of Liberty* (1729), likens Aztec resistance to the defiance of Spanish conquest by Zeuma, chief of a Chilean tribe. Ralph's poem was followed by Edward Jerningham's *The Fall of Mexico* (London, 1775), a sixty-page recasting of Solis's prose into heroic couplets in which Guatemozin, not Cortes, serves as the hero. Before the publication of Prescott's *History* (1843), Americans obtained their knowledge of Cortes through William Robertson's one-hundred-page account of the conquest in his *History of America* (1777). In 1828 Robert Sands wrote a one-hundred-page "Historical Notice" of Cortes. William Gilmore Simms's "The Vision of Cortes" (1829) was probably part of an epic poem in manuscript. Robert Montgomery Bird wrote two lengthy heroic romances, *Calavar* (1834) and *The Infidel* (1835), concerning the conquest. Simms, Sands, and Bird were all familiar with Robert Southey's quasi-epic poem *Madoc* (1805), in which a Welsh prince sails to the New World and reluctantly conquers Aztec tribes. Prescott cites Aztec as well as Spanish sources; he read Robertson, Southey, Sands, and Bird with care.

6 Prescott, *History of the Conquest of Mexico and History of the Conquest of Peru* (New York: Random House, Modern Library, n.d.), p. 681.

7 Charles Gibson, *Spain in America* (New York: Harper & Row, 1966), p. 36.

8 Prescott, *History of the Conquest of Mexico*, pp. 9, 32, 33, 34, 47, 54, 77, 91.

9 Wolcott, ed., *The Correspondence of William Hickling Prescott*, p. 250.

10 Robert Montgomery Bird, *Calavar; or The Knight of the Conquest. A Romance of Mexico* (Philadelphia: Carey, Lea, & Blanchard, 1834), pp. xii, xiii.

11 See Frederick Merk, "All Mexico," in *Manifest Destiny and Mission in American History: A Reinterpretation* (New York: Knopf, 1963), pp. 107–44.

12 Cortes, *The Five Letters of Relation,* ed. Francis A. MacNutt (New York: Putnam, 1908), II, 107; Bernal Díaz del Castillo, *The True History of the Conquest of New Spain* (1632), trans. A. P. Maudsley (New York: Farrar, Straus, & Cudahy, 1956), p. 109.

13 Robert Sands, "Historical Notice of Hernan Cortes," *The Writings of Robert C. Sands* (New York: Harper, 1835), pp. 62–5; Robert Montgomery Bird, *The Infidel; or The Fall of Mexico. A Romance* (Philadelphia: Carey, Lea, & Blanchard, 1835), I, 72–3; II, 177; Prescott, *History of the Conquest of Mexico,* pp. 52, 191, 275–8, 613.

14 See Prescott, *History of the Conquest of Mexico,* p. 276, fn. 11; Sands, "Historical Notice of Hernan Cortes," pp. 23, 68; Bird, *The Infidel,* I, 73.

15 Bartolomé de las Casas, *History of the Indies* (1558). See Prescott, *History of the Conquest of Mexico,* pp. 203–9.

16 Don Antonio de Solis, *The History of the Conquest of Mexico,* trans. Thomas Townsend (London: H. Lintot, 1753), pp. 7, 37, 58, 385.

17 Philip Freneau, "A Trip To Boston" (1775), in *Poems of Philip Freneau,* ed. F. L. Pattee (Princeton, N.J.: Princeton University Press, 1902), I, 165–6.

18 Tzvetan Todorov provides compelling evidence of Cortes's skill at improvising linguistic and visual signs in order to vanquish Montezuma. See Todorov's *The Conquest of America: The Question of the Other,* trans. Richard Howard (New York: Harper & Row, 1985), pp. 98–123.

19 Cortes, *The Five Letters of Relation,* I, 305.

20 Cortes, *The Five Letters of Relation,* I, 252; II, 107, 124; Díaz, *The True History of the Conquest of New Spain,* p. 310.

21 Prescott, *History of the Conquest of Mexico,* p. 607.

22 Diaz, *The True History of the Conquest of New Spain,* p. 387 (quoted by Prescott, p. 649).

23 Prescott, *History of the Conquest of Mexico,* p. 622. In Diaz's and Solis's accounts, Guatemozin says "Am I lying on a bed of flowers?"

24 Prescott, *History of the Conquest of Mexico,* p. 647. Malinche ("The Mountain") was the Aztecs' epithet for Cortes.

25 In explaining Montezuma's behavior, the moral polarity of savagery and civilization served nineteenth-century historians poorly. Todorov argues that the Aztecs' limited pictography, belief in cyclical time, and insistence on foreomened events rendered them long unable to adapt to the unique threat posed by the Spaniards: "Masters in the art of ritual discourse, the Indians are inadequate in a situation requiring improvisation. . . . Everything happens as if, for the Aztecs, signs automatically and necessarily proceed from the world they designate, rather than being a weapon intended to manipulate the Other" (Todorov, *The Conquest of America,* pp. 87, 89–90).

26 Cortes, *The Five Letters of Relation,* p. 235.

27 Prescott, *History of the Conquest of Mexico,* pp. 438, 422.

28 Williams, "The Destruction of Tenochtitlán," *In the American Grain* (1925)

(New York: New Directions, 1963), pp. 27–38. Williams grants Montezuma "aristocratic reserve," "tact, self-control, and a remarkable grasp of the situation." His supposed weakness was only forbearance: "Montezuma has left no trace of cowardice upon the records" (34).

29 James Ralph, *Zeuma: Or The Love of Liberty. A Poem in Three Books* (London: C. Ackers, 1729), pp. 1, 57. Prescott knew that Charles Brockden Brown's first planned work had been an epic poem on the conquest of Mexico. Prescott treats such an endeavor as juvenalia (Prescott, "Memoir of Charles Brockden Brown," *Biographical and Critical Miscellanies* [New York: Harper, 1945], p. 5).

30 William Robertson, *The History of America* (Albany: E. & E. Hosford, 1822), I, 332.

31 Joel Barlow, *The Columbiad,* in *The Works of Joel Barlow,* ed. W. K. Bottorff and A. L. Ford (Gainesville, Fla.: Scholars' Facsimiles & Reprints, 1970), p. 468.

32 Simms, "The Vision of Cortes," in *The Vision of Cortes, Cain and Other Poems* (Charleston, S.C.: James Burges, 1829), p. 8.

33 Robert Southey, 1805 Preface to *Madoc, The Poetical Works of Robert Southey,* Vol. V (London: Longman, Orme, 1838), pp. xxi, xi.

34 Southey, *Madoc,* p. 395. Mexitli is another name for Huitzilopochtli, the Aztec war god.

35 Prescott, *History of the Conquest of Mexico,* pp. 31, 73, 235, 294, 557. Elsewhere, Prescott confirmed or illustrated historical fact by citing passages from Milton, Homer, Lucan, Virgil, Dante, Ariosto, *El Cid, La Araucana,* and Scott's *Marmion.* In Prescott's view, epic poetry provided evidence at least as reliable as memoirs or post factum histories.

36 Bird, *Calavar,* I, 3.

37 Ibid., II, 240.

38 Ibid., I, 206–7.

39 Bird, *The Infidel,* II, 91.

40 Ibid., I, 73.

41 Ibid., II, 227.

42 Bird, *Calavar,* II, 18.

43 Ibid., I, 182.

44 Bird, *The Infidel,* II, 164.

45 Ibid., II, 228.

46 Ibid., II, 96.

47 Ibid., I, 164. "Malintzin" is another form of "Malinche."

48 Ibid., II, 223.

49 Ibid., II, 228.

50 Prescott, *History of the Conquest of Mexico,* p. 431.

51 Robert Sands, "Historical Notice of Hernan Cortes," in *The Writings of Robert Sands* (New York: Harper, 1835), I, 19.

52 Robert Sands here anticipates Todorov's argument for Cortes's astonishing success: "For Cortes, as we have seen, speech is more a means of manipulating the Other than it is a faithful reflection of the world. . . . By his mastery

of signs Cortes ensures his control over the ancient Mexican empire" (Todorov, *The Conquest of America*, pp. 118–19).

53 Prescott, "Romance in the Heroic and Middle Ages," *United States Literary Gazette*, 2 (1825), 387.

54 Prescott, "Romance in the Heroic and Middle Ages," p. 388.

55 Ibid., p. 386.

56 Prescott, "Poetry and Romance of the Italians," *North American Review*, 33 (1831), 47.

57 Prescott, "Romance in the Heroic and Middle Ages," p. 343.

58 Prescott, "Novel Writing," *North American Review*, 25 (1827), 195.

59 Prescott, *Literary Memoranda*, I, 23–4.

60 Ibid., I, 24.

61 Ibid., II, 69.

62 Prescott, "Italian Narrative Poetry," *North American Review*, 19 (1824), 373. Prescott is referring to Trissino's *Italia Liberata* (1557).

63 Prescott, "Kenyon's Poems," *North American Review*, 48 (1839), 402.

64 Prescott, *Literary Memoranda*, I, 20–1.

65 Ibid., I, 21.

66 Ibid., I, 22.

67 Ibid., I, 22.

68 Prescott shared Barlow's wide New World perspective, but his concept of a new epic was exactly opposite to Barlow's. Whereas Barlow believed in modifying the old poetic form to make it suit futuristic purposes, Prescott subsumed the epic within a prose history, then demanded classical standards of unity. When asked to write a history of the contemporary Mexican War, Prescott firmly declined, noting, "I had rather not meddle with heroes who have not been under ground two centuries at least" (H. T. Peck, *William Hickling Prescott* [London: Macmillan, 1905], p. 90). No remark could be further removed from Barlow's literary procedure.

69 Prescott, review of Bancroft's *History of the United States, North American Review*, 52 (1841), 78.

70 Prescott, *Literary Memoranda*, I, 56.

71 Ibid., I, 56.

72 Prescott, *History of the Conquest of Mexico*, p. 9. Even in American verse, the convention was to last as late as the 1930s:

> Of that world's conquest, and the fortunate wars:
> Of the great report and expectation of honor:
> How in their youth they stretched sail.
>> (Archibald MacLeish, *Conquistador* [Boston: Houghton Mifflin, 1932], p. 25).

73 Prescott, *History of the Conquest of Mexico*, pp. 9, 143, 685.

74 David Levin, *History as Romantic Art* (Stanford, Cal.: Stanford University Press, 1959), p. 163. See also Donald Ringe, "The Artistry of Prescott's *History of the Conquest of Mexico*," *New England Quarterly*, 26 (1953), 455–77; Ringe, "The Function of Landscape in Prescott's *The Conquest of Mexico*," *New England Quarterly*, 56 (1983), 569–77.

75 See Joseph Campbell, *Hero with a Thousand Faces* (Cleveland: World Publishing Co., 1970), pp. 245–56; Vladimir Propp, *Morphology of the Folk Tale* (Austin: University of Texas Press, 1968), p. 50. The "functions" Propp finds in folktale structure correspond rather closely to Campbell's "monomyth," although the terms used to describe them differ widely.

76 In his *Letters of Relation,* Cortes acknowledged that he had encouraged the Aztecs to believe that he was Charles V and/or Quetzalcoatl. Todorov argues that Cortes himself "provided the missing link" between the Conquistador and the Aztec deity (Todorov, *The Conquest of America,* p. 117).

77 "Prescott keeps his hero walking always on the edge of ruin; and the succession of dilemmas makes forward movement seem imperative" (David Levin, *History as Romantic Art,* p. 171).

78 Prescott, *Literary Memoranda,* II, 32.

79 See Prescott, *History of the Conquest of Mexico,* pp. 51, 143, 212, 465.

80 Prescott, *Literary Memoranda,* II, 68.

81 Prescott, *History of the Conquest of Mexico,* p. 7.

82 George Ticknor, *Life of William Hickling Prescott* (Philadelphia: Lippincott, 1882), p. 434.

83 Prescott, *Literary Memoranda,* II, 29.

84 The hostilities between the highly developed, quasi-republican state of Tlascala and the feudal, agricultural state of Cholula (Book III, Chapter II) seem to prefigure the American conflict between North and South. As in Simms's *The Yemassee,* the national dimension of the conflict is never allowed to be explicit. Prescott was suspicious of allegorical readings of epic texts that allowed the poet to become the prophet. In his essay on *Don Quixote,* his example of "overrefined criticism" was "the efforts of some commentators to allegorize the great epics of Homer and Virgil, throwing a disagreeable mistiness over the story, by converting mere shadows into substances, and substances into shadows" *North American Review,* 45 [1837], 22).

85 Prescott, *Literary Memoranda,* I, 22.

86 Prescott, *Literary Memoranda,* I, 27. Prescott notes that Father Olmedo had to intervene and rebuke the "excess" of the victory banquet (611). Contrast the Spaniards' exultation to the humility of Tasso's crusaders as described in the stanza that had so moved Prescott:

> To that delight which their first sight did breed,
>   That pleased so the secret of their thought,
> A deep repentance did forthwith succeed,
>   That rev'rend fear and trembling with it brought.
> Scantly they durst their feeble eyes dispread,
>   Upon the town, where Christ was sold and bought,
> Where for our sins he, faultless, suffered pain,
> There, where he died, and where he lived again.
>
> (Tasso, Jerusalem Delivered, trans. Edward Fairfax [London:
J. Porser, 1749] Canto III, Stanza 3, p. 50.)

87 Ticknor, *Life of William Hickling Prescott,* p. 183.

88 Edward Everett, letter to Prescott, 1843, quoted in Ticknor, *Life of William Hickling Prescott,* p. 198.

89 Cornelius Conway Felton, letter to Prescott, 1843, in *The Correspondence of*

William Hickling Prescott: 1833–1847, ed. Roger Wolcott (Cambridge: Massachusetts Historical Society, 1925), p. 415. E. P. Whipple also argued that Prescott had achieved a Homeric poem within a prose history: "The result of all his [Prescott's] labors, research, thought and composition, was a history possessing the unity, variety, and interest, of a magnificent poem. It deals with a series of facts, and exhibits a variety of characters which, to have invented, would place its creator by the side of Homer" (Whipple, "Prescott's *Histories*" [1848], in *Essays and Reviews* [New York: D. Appleton, 1849], II, 219).

90 William Gilmore Simms, "Cortes and the Conquest of Mexico," originally published in *Southern Quarterly Review,* 6 (1844), 163–227; reprinted in *Views and Reviews in American Literature* (Cambridge, Mass: Harvard University Press, 1962), p. 189.

91 George Hillard, "Prescott's *History of the Conquest of Mexico,*" *North American Review,* 58 (1844), 179.

92 Anonymous, "Prescott's *Conquest of Mexico,*" *United States Magazine and Democratic Review,* 14 (1844), 191, 193, 194.

93 Theodore Parker, "Prescott's *Conquest of Mexico,*" *Massachusetts Quarterly Review* (1849); reprinted in *The American Scholar,* ed. G. W. Cooke (Boston: American Unitarian Association, 1907), p. 223.

94 The *Edinburgh Review* shared none of the American reviewers' suspicions that, in seeking to make a hero of Cortes, Prescott had whitewashed a brute. Instead, the Aztecs were dismissed as "ignorant savages" and Prescott was mildly chided for being too critical of Cortes: "With the single exception of the death of Guatemozin, we are unable to recall any important act of [Cortes's] public life which we think would deserve strong reprehension" (*Edinburgh Review,* 81 [1845], 472). During Prescott's 1850 trip to England, he probably received more acclaim than had yet been accorded any American author. Prescott dined with Palmerston, Peel, Thackeray, Macauley, Lockhart, Rogers, Bentley, Dickens, and John Murray; he was received by Queen Victoria and was granted an Oxford DCL (Harvey Gardiner, *William Hickling Prescott* [Austin: University of Texas Press, 1969], pp. 301–15).

95 Prescott, "Preface" to *History of the Conquest of Peru* (New York: Random House, n.d.), p. 727.

96 Literary renderings of the conquest of Mexico did not die out between Prescott's *History* and Williams's *In the American Grain.* Two historical romancers immediately tried to capitalize on Prescott's success: J. H. Ingraham, *Montezuma, the Serf* (1845), and Edward Maturin, *Montezuma, the Last of the Aztecs* (1845). In the 1850s, Augustin Louis Taveau of Charleston began an epic poem titled *Montezuma,* of which five cantos in heroic couplets were completed. "La Noche Triste" (1890) was Robert Frost's first published poem. Lew Wallace's popular romance, *The Fair God* (1873), considered in the context of these other works, suggests that the interest of later generations shifted steadily away from Guatemozin toward Montezuma, from the Mexican analogy toward the process of cultural misunderstanding. The resonance of "the last of the Aztecs" accordingly drops away. Neither William Carlos Williams nor Tzvetan Todorov, for example, has any interest in Guatemozin.

CHAPTER 7

1 Anonymous review of a prose translation of *The Iliad, Literary World*, 2 (1848), 431–2.

2 Anonymous, "American Poetry," *The Knickerbocker*, 12 (1838), 383–8.

3 Melville, "Hawthorne and His Mosses," in *Herman Melville: Representative Selections*, ed. Willard Thorp (New York: American Book Co., 1938), p. 338. In the manuscript Melville had written "this Bostonian leaven of literary flunkeyism towards England." Melville may have been thinking of Longfellow's recently published *Kavanagh* (1849), Lowell's review of it (*North American Review*, 1849), or Henry Tuckerman's *The Optimist* (1850). All three Bostonians had recently displayed no small deference to British literary tradition, along with scorn for the American epic.

4 "Hawthorne and His Mosses," p. 337.

5 Walker Cowan, *Melville's Marginalia*, Ph.D. Dissertation, Harvard University, 1965, VII, 247. Like all who write about Melville, I am deeply indebted to Merton M. Sealts, *Melville's Reading* (Madison: University of Wisconsin Press, 1966), which has recently been revised and enlarged (Columbia: University of South Carolina Press, 1988).

6 Cowan, *Melville's Marginalia*, VII, 242.

7 Ibid., V, 18.

8 Ibid., V, 18.

9 Melville, *Mardi* (Chicago: Northwestern–Newberry, 1970), p. 367.

10 Melville, *Redburn* (Chicago: Northwestern–Newberry, 1969), p. 147. Redburn's mockery of dull heroic verse provides an additional reason for believing that Melville wrote the review of Southey's *Commonplace Book* that appeared in the 1849 *Literary World*. One of the review's few critical remarks is its slighting reference to *Madoc* and *Joan of Arc* as "long narrative poems, at least of epic labor and research if not always of epic force" (*Literary World*, 4 [1849], 87). See Richard S. Moore, "A New Review by Melville," *American Literature*, 47 (1975), 265–70.

11 Melville, *White-Jacket* (Chicago: Northwestern–Newberry, 1970), p. 318. See Melville's 1858 letter to George Duyckinck in which Pope's Homer is described as one of Milton's "bankrupt deities" by comparison with Chapman's (*The Letters of Herman Melville*, ed. M. Davis and W. Gilman [New Haven Conn.: Yale University Press, 1960], p. 191). There can be no question that Melville promptly read the edition of Pope's Homer he bought in 1849. In *White-Jacket*, Jack Chase quotes Pope's *Iliad* to Captain Claret, who is not impressed (214).

12 Melville, *White-Jacket*, p. 14.

13 See Brian F. Head, "Camoens and Melville," *Revista Camoniana*, 1 (1964), 36–75.

14 Melville, *Moby-Dick*, ed. H. Hayford, H. Parker, and G. T. Tanselle (Evanston and Chicago: Northwestern–Newberry, 1988), p. 198. All subsequent references to *Moby-Dick* are to this edition.

15 "Camoens (Before)," in *Collected Poems of Herman Melville*, ed. H. P. Vincent (Chicago: Hendricks House, 1947), p. 380.

16 Camoens, *The Lusiad; or The Discovery of India, an Epic Poem*, trans. William Julius Mickle (Oxford: Jackson & Lister, 1776), p. i. Later on in his introduction, Mickle repeats his point: "It is the Epic Poem of the Birth of Commerce" (xlvii). To Mickle, as to Melville, modern epic poems after Milton had all proven "miserably uninteresting" (cxxxvii).

17 See Cowan, *Melville's Marginalia*, VI, and R. W. B. Lewis, "Melville on Homer," *American Literature*, 22 (1950), 166–76. Although it is risky to reconstruct an interpretation from marginal notations, it seems undeniable that Melville habitually marked important passages of which he approved, but annotated passages with which he quarrelled.

18 Cowan, *Melville's Marginalia*, I, 183, 190, 171.

19 "Hawthorne and His Mosses," p. 339.

20 See James Barbour, "The Composition of *Moby-Dick*," *American Literature*, 47 (1975), 343–60.

21 "Hawthorne and Mis Mosses," p. 338.

22 Cowan, *Melville's Marginalia*, V, 339.

23 *Moby-Dick*, pp. 45, 123, 125, 153, 165, 205, 272, 354, 357, 383, 412, 508, 548, 557.

24 The pun on the word "tail" situates Ishmael as a writer of mock-epic in a second sense. The pun also likens Ishmael/Melville to "the bird that never alights."

25 With his one white tooth protruding from his steely lips, Fedallah is the stagiest of snakes, "such a creature as civilized, domestic people in the temperate zone only see in their dreams, and that but dimly" (231).

26 Irving, *A History of New York*, p. 720. Irving's *History* and Melville's novel both belong to the tradition explored in Robert Alter's *Partial Magic*. Alter observes "One of the characteristic reflexes of the self-conscious novel is to flaunt "naive" narrative devices, rescuing their usability by exposing their contrivance, working them into a highly patterned narration which remainds us that all representations of reality are, necessarily, stylizations" (Alter, *Partial Magic: The Novel as a Self-Conscious Genre* [Berkeley: University of California Press, 1965], p. 30).

27 M. M. Bakhtin, *The Dialogic Imagination* (Austin: University of Texas Press, 1981), pp. 7, 12, 271–5.

28 William Cullen Bryant, "Essay on American Poetry" (1818), in *Prose Writings of W. C. Bryant*, ed. P. Godwin (New York: Russell & Russell, 1964), I, 52.

29 Bakhtin, *The Dialogic Imagination*, p. 7.

30 C. M. Bowra, *Heroic Poetry* (London: Macmillan, 1952), p. 77.

31 The blank verse of this prose paragraph could be made virtually regular simply by placing the world "Many" in line seven at the end of the preceding line. As this example suggests, Melville's pentameters are endstopped no less frequently than Milton's.

32 Allen Mandelbaum has translated Virgil's simile as follows:

> As when, among the Alps, north winds
> will strain against each other to root out
> with blasts – now on this side, now that – a stout
> oak tree whose wood is full of years; the roar

> is shattering, the trunk is shaken, and
> high branches scatter on the ground; but it
> still grips the rocks; as steeply as it thrusts
> its crown into the upper air, so deep
> the roots it reaches down to Tartarus:
> no less than this, the hero; he is battered
> on this side and on that by assiduous words;
> he feels care in his mighty chest, and yet
> his mind cannot be moved; the tears fall, useless.

(*The Aeneid of Virgil* [New York: Bantam, 1971], p. 96).

33 Joseph Campbell, *Hero with a Thousand Faces* (Cleveland: The World Publishing Co., 1970), pp. 58, 79.

34 In Pip's crazed, clairvoyant view, the doubloon is "the ship's navel," which, if ever unscrewed, must lead both to knowledge and to death (435). Similarly, Campbell's hero must penetrate to "the umbilical point through which energies of eternity break into time" (41). "Thus the World Navel is the symbol of continuous creation: the mystery of the maintenance of the world through that continuous miracle of vivification which wells within all things" (41).

35 Georg Lukacs, *The Theory of the Novel*, trans. Anna Bostock (Cambridge, Mass.: MIT Press, 1971), p. 88.

36 Esaias Tegnér, *Frithiof's Saga*, trans. W. E. F. and H. G. (London: A. H. Baily & Co., 1835). Duyckinck had a copy of this translation in his library, together with an 1838 translation by R. G. Latham. It is not known which translation Melville borrowed. By 1850, Tegnér's poem had been translated five times into English, eight times into German, and into at least eight other European languages.

37 Cowan, *Melville's Marginalia*, V, 113.

38 Milton, *Paradise Lost*, ed. M. Y. Hughes (New York: Odyssey, 1935), p. 31.

39 These are the words Melville was to apply, not to Ahab, but to John Claggart. See *Billy Budd, Sailor (An Inside Narrative)*, ed. H. Hayford and M. Sealts (Chicago: University of Chicago Press, 1962), p. 165, fn. 137.

40 C. S. Lewis, *A Preface to Paradise Lost* (New York: Oxford University Press, 1961), p. 99.

41 *Paradise Lost*, Book X, pp. 331–2. The most tactile humiliation of Milton's triumphant fallen angels occurs shortly hereafter, when they reach for the Fruit and chew "bitter ashes" . . . "thir jaws / With soot and cinders fill'd" (334). In "The Symphony" Melville transforms Milton's passage, dignifying Ahab when he acknowledges the price of his sacrificing his love for wife and child: "Like a blighted fruit tree he shook, and cast his last, cindered apple to the soil" (545).

42 Henry F. Pommer, *Milton and Melville* (Pittsburgh: University of Pittsburgh Press, 1950), p. 10. It is probable that Melville owned Martin's drawing in 1848 and hung it at Arrowhead when he moved there in 1850.

43 See Willard Thorp, ed., *Herman Melville: Representative Selections*, p. 424.

44 "Tompkins" is probably a mistaken spelling of Thomas Tomkins (1743–1816), author of *Rays of Genius* (1806) and *Poems on Various Subjects* (1807).

Isaac Disraeli had ridiculed him in his well known *Curiosities of Literature* (1841). Melville annotated Disraeli's book, but not until 1859.

45 Thomas Carlyle, *On Heroes, Hero-Worship and the Heroic in History*, ed. C. Niemeyer (Lincoln: University of Nebraska Press, 1966), p. 45.

46 Ahab refers to "the gods" on pp. 168, 464, 471, 522, 527, 553. The sperm whale is compared to Jove on pp. 346, 347, 548, 549. It is a tribute to Melville's artistry that the many passages in which nineteenth-century Quaker whalemen are made to refer to Jove and the gods have not seemed ridiculous anachronisms. Ahab's belief in a strife-torn universe makes his polytheistic references seem appropriate.

47 Melville's most expansive statements of this heady national faith may be found in *Redburn*, p. 169, and in *White-Jacket*, p. 151.

48 Horace Greeley, review of *Moby-Dick*, *New York Daily Tribune*, November 22, 1851, in *Melville: The Critical Heritage*, ed. W. G. Branch (London: Routledge & Kegan Paul, 1974), p. 273.

49 William Allen Butler, review of *Moby-Dick*, *Washington National Intelligencer*, December 16, 1851, in *Melville: The Critical Heritage*, p. 283.

50 Melville, letter to Hawthorne, June 1851, in *The Letters of Herman Melville*, p. 130.

51 "Camoens (Before)" and "Camoens (After)," in *Collected Poems of Herman Melville*, ed. H. P. Vincent (New York: Hendricks House, 1947), pp. 380–1. On the degree of Melville's identification with Camoens in the 1860s, see George Monteiro, "Poetry and Madness: Melville's Rediscovery of Camoens in 1867," *New England Quarterly*, 51 (1978), 561–5. Melville's pleasure in criticizing contemporary life against the heroic standard of epic poetry became apparent as early as 1859. After spending a morning at Arrowhead, a Williams College undergraduate named John Thomas Gulick remarked that "the ancient dignity of Homeric times afforded the only state of humanity, individual or social, to which he could turn with any complacency" (Jay Leyda, *The Melville Log* [New York: Harcourt Brace, 1951], II, 605). Gulick's statement should not be taken at face value. He was clearly anxious to display a student's wearied disgust with the stature of Homer; Melville had long delighted in guying sophomoric gestures, including his own.

CHAPTER 8

1 "In the Epic poem, as in Tragedy, the story . . . should turn about a single action, one that is a whole, and is organically perfect – having a beginning, and a middle, and an end" (Aristotle, *On the Art of Poetry*, ed. L. Cooper [Ithaca, N.Y.: Cornell University Press, 1947], p. 75).

2 Whitman, Preface to *Leaves of Grass* (1855), in *Walt Whitman, Leaves of Grass: Comprehensive Reader's Edition*, ed. H. W. Blodgett and S. Bradley (New York: Norton, 1968), p. 729. Unless otherwise noted, all references to Whitman's writings are to this text.

3 Whitman, "A Backward Glance O'er Travel'd Roads" (1889), p. 563.

4 Whitman, "A Backward Glance," pp. 573–4.

5 William Wordsworth, *The Prelude or Growth of a Poet's Mind*, Book III, ed. E. De Selincourt (Oxford: Clarendon, 1959), p. 80, ll. 171–7.

6 Alexis de Tocqueville, *Democracy in America,* the Reve-Bradley edition (New York: Random House, 1945), II, 76.

7 Tocqueville, *Democracy in America,* II, 138.

8 Evert Duyckinck, "Literary Prospects of 1845," *American Whig Review,* 1 (1845), 146–51.

9 Edwin P. Whipple, "Heroic Character" (1857), in *Character and Characteristic Men* (Boston: Houghton Mifflin, 1893), 101.

10 Emerson, "The Poet," in *Essays: Second Series* (Cambridge, Mass.: Riverside Press, 1883), p. 40. In March of 1842 Whitman heard Emerson's lecture on "The Poet"; he called the lecture "one of the richest and most beautiful compositions, both for its matter and style, we have heard anywhere, at any time" (Justin Kaplan, *Walt Whitman: A Life* [New York: Simon & Schuster, 1980], p. 101).

11 Jones Very, "Epic Poetry," in *Essays and Poems* (Boston: Little, Brown, 1839), pp. 1–37.

12 To someone of Very's persuasion, it would be futile to note that *The Iliad* is not about the taking of Troy but the anger of Achilles.

13 Georg Lukacs, *The Theory of the Novel,* trans. Anna Bostock (Cambridge, Mass.: MIT Press, 1971), p. 116.

14 Whitman, Preface to *Leaves of Grass* (1855), p. 712. Whitman was to repeat the first two sentences of this passage in his anonymous review of *Leaves of Grass* in the *United States Review.* See Milton Hindus, *Walt Whitman: The Critical Heritage* (London: Routledge & Kegan Paul, 1971), p. 36.

15 Whitman, *Specimen Days,* in *Prose Works: 1892,* ed. F. Stovall (New York: New York University Press, 1963), I, 250. During 1846 and 1847 Whitman wrote notices of *Sartor Resartus* and *On Heroes, Hero Worship and the Heroic in History* for the Brooklyn *Daily Eagle.*

16 Thomas Carlyle, *Lectures on the History of Literature, Delivered April to July 1838* (New York: Scribner, 1892), p. 52.

17 Poe, "The Poetic Principle," in *Literary Criticism of Edgar Allan Poe,* ed. R. L. Hough (Lincoln: University of Nebraska Press, 1965), p. 34.

18 Whitman, "A Backward Glance," p. 569.

19 Justin Kaplan, *Walt Whitman,* p. 169; Whitman's public letter, "Whitman to Emerson, 1856" in *Leaves of Grass,* p. 733; Whitman's review of *Leaves of Grass* in Hindus, *Walt Whitman: The Critical Heritage,* p. 36.

20 Whitman, *An American Primer,* ed. Horace Traubel (Boston: Small, Maynard & Co., 1904), pp. 32–3.

21 Whitman, Preface to *Leaves of Grass* (1855), pp. 720, 709, 717.

22 Milton's headnote on the verse form of *Paradise Lost* provides a precedent for the opposite argument. To Milton, an epic written in blank verse constitutes "ancient liberty recover'd to Heroic Poem from the troublesome and modern bondage of Riming" (6). One could contend that Whitman's "free verse" extends Milton's rebellion by proclaiming his democratic poetic liberty from the Old World's heroic couplet. To Whitman, however, American Liberty was a new spirit, not an ancient spirit now recovered. In 1855 Whitman, like Melville, was opposed to any "American Milton."

23 Walt Whitman, *Leaves of Grass* (1855), ed. Malcolm Cowley (New York:

Viking, 1959), p. 25. For convenience of reference, I retain the title and section numbers Whitman added to the 1881 edition of "Song of Myself," but I
quote the lines of the 1855 edition from Cowley's text. Richard Chase's insistence that "Song of Myself" is "on the whole comic in tone" always bears
remembering (Chase, *Walt Whitman Reconsidered* [New York: William Sloane
Associates, 1955], p. 59).

24   but to nobler sights
Michael from Adam's eyes the Film remov'd
Which that false Fruit that promis'd clearer sight
Had bred

(Paradise Lost, XI, ll. 411–13).

25 The many attempts to trace a structure in "Song of Myself" differ more in
details and in terminology than in the basic progression traced throughout
the sections. See the following: Malcolm Cowley, "Introduction" to *Leaves
of Grass* (1855), pp. xiv–xx; James E. Miller, Jr., *A Critical Guide to Leaves of
Grass* (Chicago: University of Chicago Press, 1966), pp. 6–35; E. F. Carlisle,
The Uncertain Self: Whitman's Drama of Identity (Lansing: Michigan State University Press, 1973), pp. 177–204; Ivan Marki, *The Trial of the Poet* (New
York: Columbia University Press, 1976), pp. 150–205.

26 Joseph Campbell, *Hero with a Thousand Faces* (Cleveland: World Publishing
Co., 1970), p. 44.

27 Whitman, *Democratic Vistas*, in *Prose Works: 1892,* II, 421.

28 See Kaplan, *Walt Whitman,* p. 318. For information about editions of *Leaves
of Grass* I am indebted to the Blodgett-Bradley edition and to Thomas Edward Crawley, *The Structure of Leaves of Grass* (Austin: University of Texas
Press, 1970), Chapter Five.

29 Whitman, letter to Nathaniel Bloom and John F. S. Gray, March 19, 1863,
in *Walt Whitman: The Correspondence,* ed. E. H. Miller (New York: New
York University Press, 1961), I, 82.

30 Whitman, "Memoranda During the War" (1975), in *Walt Whitman: Prose Works
1892,* I, 321.

31 Whitman, "Poetry To-Day in America," In *Walt Whitman: Prose Works 1892,*
II, 483–4.

32 For information about New York's Crystal Palace exhibition of 1853 see Paul
Zweig, *Walt Whitman: The Making of the Poet* (New York: Basic Books, 1984),
pp. 209–11.

33 Milton, *Paradise Lost,* ed. M. Y. Hughes (New York: Odyssey, 1935), p. 218.

34 Whitman, *Specimen Days,* in *Prose Works: 1892,* I, 12. Whitman claimed to
have continued his Homeric recitations as late as 1881: "I had a leisurely bath
and naked ramble as of old, on the warm-gray shore-sands, my companions
off in a boat in deeper water – (I shouting to them Jupiter's menaces against
the gods, from Pope's Homer)" *Prose Works: 1892,* I, 273.

35 Draft for preface to *Leaves of Grass,* in *Walt Whitman's Workshop,* ed. C. J.
Furness (New York: Russell & Russell, 1964), p. 136.

36 Whitman, letter to Richard Maurice Bucke, December 6, 1891, in *Walt Whitman: The Correspondence,* V, 270.

37 David Daiches noted that Whitman "does not write epics; but he cultivates an epic pose in order to write lyrics" ("Walt Whitman: Impressionist Prophet," in *Leaves of Grass One Hundred Years Later,* ed. M. Hindus [Stanford, Cal.: Stanford University Press, 1955], p. 110).

38 C. J. Furness, ed., *Walt Whitman's Workshop,* p. 136.

39 Whitman, letter to Richard Maurice Bucke, December 6, 1891, in *Walt Whitman: The Correspondence,* V, 270.

40 Whitman, "American National Literature" (*North American Review,* 1891), in *Prose Works: 1892,* II, 664.

41 Hart Crane, letter to Otto Kahn, September 12, 1927, in *The Letters of Hart Crane,* ed. B. Weber (New York: Hermitage House, 1952), p. 309; William Carlos Williams, *Paterson* (New York: New Directions, 1958), n.p.; John Haffenden, *John Berryman: A Critical Commentary* (New York: New York University Press, 1980), p. 59.

42 During a 1962 *Paris Review* interview, Ezra Pound told Donald Hall that "An Epic is a poem containing history. The modern mind contains heteroclite elements. The past epos has succeeded when all or a great many of the answers were assumed, at least between author and audience, or a great mass of audience." When asked specifically about the origin and structure of *The Cantos,* Pound said "The problem was to get a form – something elastic enough to take the necessary material. It had to be a form that wouldn't exclude something merely because it didn't fit" (*Paris Review Interviews,* Second Series [New York: Viking, 1965], pp. 38, 57). Pound's definition of epic would admit Lucretius, "Absalom and Achitophel," and *The Ring and the Book,* to say nothing of *John Brown's Body* or *Brother to Dragons.* His standard of "form" for *The Cantos* seems no less inclusive. If material that does not fit is not to be excluded, what should or could be set aside?

PROSPECT

1 Tom Wolfe, *The Bonfire of the Vanities* (New York: Farrar, Straus, & Giroux, 1987), pp. 354–5. Quoted by permission of publisher.

2 Frederick Turner, *The New World: An Epic Poem* (Princeton, N.J.: Princeton University Press, 1985), vii.

3 Fredric Jameson, "Postmodernism and Consumer Society," in *The Anti-Aesthetic: Essays on Postmodern Culture,* ed. H. Foster (Port Townsend, Wash.: Bay Press, 1983), pp. 111–25.

INDEX

Page numbers for an extended discussion of an author are italicized.

1-31-91

DEMCO